Administration for Development in Nigeria

Introduction and Readings

Edited by Paul Collins

AEP

African Education Press
8 Denton Street, Abute Metta, Lagos, Nigeria
9 University Road, Yaba, Lagos, Nigeria

Administration for Development in Nigeria
was first published by African Education
Press, 8 Denton Street, Abute Metta, Lagos,
Nigeria in August 1980.

ISBN 978 2308 00 5

Copy-edited by Lorne Larson
Designed by Mayblin/Shaw
Typeset by Sapphire Set
Cover design by Jacque Solomons
Printed by Redwood Burn Limited
Trowbridge and Esher

Grateful acknowledgement is made to the editors of *The African Review, Nigerian Journal of Economic and Social Studies, Proceedings of the Nigerian Economic Society, Journal of Commonwealth and Comparative Politics, Quarterly Journal of Administration* and *Odu* for permission to reproduce amended versions of articles originally published in their journals. Acknowledgement is also made to Ibadan University Press for permission to reproduce an excerpt from Christopher Beer's *The Politics of Peasant Groups in Western Nigeria* (1976).

Contents

Contributors

Paul Collins is Senior Lecturer in Public Administration at the School of Administration, University of Ghana. He has held teaching and research positions at the University of Dar es Salaam, the University of Sussex, and Sao Paulo University (Brazil). He has also taught in Nigeria at Ahmadu Bello University and the University of Ife. He is the author of *Decentralization and Local Administration for Development in Tanzania.*

Ojetunji Aboyade is Professor of Economics at the University of Ibadan. He is author of *Foundations of an African Economy* and *Issues in the Development of an African Economy.*

Adebayo Adedeji is Executive Secretary of the Economic Commission for Africa. He was formerly Professor of Public Administration and Director of the Institute of Administration at the University of Ife. He is the author of many books and articles on African administration. He served as Federal Commissioner for Economic Planning and Reconstruction during the preparation of the Third Nigerian National Development Plan.

Adefolu Akinbode is Lecturer in Extension Administration and Supervision in the Department of Extension Education and Rural Sociology at the University of Ife. He is the author of various articles on agricultural development administration in Western Nigeria.

Stanley Barrett is Assistant Professor in the Department of Anthropology at the University of Guelph in Canada. He carried out fieldwork in Western Nigeria between 1969 and 1974. He is the author of *Two Villages on Stilts.*

Christopher Beer works for the International University Exchange Fund. He is the author of *The Politics of Peasant Groups in Western Nigeria.*

Belle Harris is Senior Lecturer at the North East London Polytechnic. She spent several years teaching and conducting research into local administration in Tanzania. She was also formerly Lecturer in the Department of Local Government at the Institute of Administration, Ahmadu Bello University.

Gordon Idang is the Head of the Political Science Department at the University of Nigeria, Nsukka. He is the author of *Nigerian Internal Politics and Foreign Policy.*

E.O. Idusogie is the Regional Food Policy and Nutrition Officer for the FAO Africa Region. He has written widely on agriculture, food, and nutrition in Africa.

Nelson Kasfir is Associate Professor in Government at Dartmouth College, U.S.A. He is the author of *Participation in Africa's Shrinking Political Arena* and several articles on African development administration.

Roger King is currently at the Agricultural Extension and Rural Development Centre, University of Reading. He was formerly Research Fellow at the Institute for Agricultural Research, Ahmadu Bello University.

James O'Connell is Professor of Peace Studies at Bradford University. He was formerly Professor of Government at Ahmadu Bello University.

S.O. Olayide is Professor of Agricultural Economics at the University of Ibadan.

Dupe Olatunbosun is Professor at the Nigerian Institute of Social and Economic Research, University of Ibadan. He is the author of *Nigeria's Neglected Rural Majority.*

Michael Olisa is Senior Lecturer in Political Science at the University of Nigeria, Nsukka. He has been involved in the work of the Rural Development Administration Research Unit at the university.

Terisa Turner works at the United Nations Centre on Transnational Corporations. She has carried out field research into the political economy of the oil industry in Nigeria.

Peter Waterman is Co-ordinator of the Industrial Relations Programme of the Institute of Social Studies at The Hague. He has carried out research and written various articles on labour in Nigeria.

Introduction
Paul Collins

The first decades of independence in Africa have witnessed an increasing concern with developing public services capable of operating as more effective agents of change in executing the policies of government.[1] At the central civil service level, initial crash localization programmes had to be undertaken everywhere, and in countries where political experimentation took place – such as the establishment of one-party systems or military regimes – the working out of relations between public servants and the new politicians presented new challenges. More recently a number of countries have set up public or civil service commissions to make recommendations for the improvement of internal civil service management, reflecting the feelings in many cases that the inherited systems were in some respects ill-suited to the post-independence situation. Another factor promoting the increasing search for alternative policies and techniques for public service management is the changing role of the public sector itself and the increasing intervention of government in economic development.

Academic writing about these events has not always been either unified or relevant.[2] However, despite the current academic debate about the concept and concerns of 'development administration', the public services of the 'new' states continue to cope with a range of problems involved in promoting economic development and raising the levels of living of the broad masses of the citizenry. Stated at its simplest, the subject matter of development administration is the emergent development policies, programmes and projects of any country embarking upon the various paths of social and economic change; the primary instrument for effecting change is public administration.[3] The study of 'development' administration may be said to differ from that of 'public' administration in that the former is concerned with the operation of government institutions *under certain conditions* – where there are wide and new demands, but where there is at the same time low administrative capacity and severe obstacles facing implementation. In short, development administration is concerned with the achievement of change under conditions where change is difficult. Put more concretely, its focus is on a range of instrumentalities employed to achieve the ends of national social and economic development – the machinery of planning, the role of government administration in promoting industrial and agricultural development, the public corporations, marketing boards and co-operatives, government-organized community development projects, and – of course – administrative reform at all levels of the public service.

The concern with administrative reform marks a further qualitative difference between 'development' administration and 'public' administration. Early studies of public administration in the 'new' states were rather narrowly concerned with improving administrative performance – particularly in view of the post-independence efforts at national planning, the crash training programmes for civil service localization, the proliferation of public corporations, and the expansion of 'nation building' or community development projects. Feedback from these efforts has suggested to many – both practitioners and analysts – that effective development administration requires a high level of creative assessment and innovation on the part of planners that envisages not simply the improvement of administrative performance but a restructuring of existing government machinery and administrative behaviour to make it more suited to sustain planned economic, social and cultural change.[4]

The purpose of this Reader is to explore some of these broad concerns in the Nigerian context by bringing together a series of case studies and analyses of public sector agencies in operation in the various areas of national and local development.

Nigeria is one of the largest countries, and certainly the most populous and wealthy nation, in independent sub-Saharan Africa. As a Federation she supports some 20 civil services – an expanding Federal administration, 19 recently-created State administrations,[5] and numerous subordinate local authorities. An initial period of political instability, followed by one of military rule, has inevitably conferred enormous responsibilities on the Nigerian civil services, particularly at the Federal level.[6] In addition, the increase in oil production since the end of the Civil War in 1970 has generated vast revenues, largely to be managed by top Federal civil servants.

Like other Anglophone African countries, Nigeria inherited a civil service modelled on the British during the later colonial period. And like many of these countries – Tanzania, Kenya, Zambia, Ghana, for example[7] – Nigeria has under military rule carried out two major public service reviews. The most recent of these is the 1975 Public Service Review Commission.[8] In essence the Report of the latest Commission is a dramatic re-affirmation of the centrality of public administration to Nigeria's national development effort, providing in its recommendations a package of recipes for enhanced administrative performance and productivity in the future, as well as rewards for service already done. Paradoxically, the Review, or at least the way in which its salary increase proposals were implemented, was one of the major factors behind the July 1975 coup which replaced General Gowon and many of the top military officers and civil servants in his government. The incoming regime of the late General Murtala Mohammed not only sacked many of the former civil servants but also set in train a series of *ad hoc* but potentially far-reaching administrative reforms. The course and nature of administrative reform under military rule in Nigeria is the subject of the concluding chapter of this Reader.

In Nigeria, as in most other ex-colonial and less industrialized countries, it is important to bear in mind the social and economic context and role of public administration.

First, public administration in the less industrialized countries is intrinsically bound up with politics, particularly in one-party or non-party (military) regimes where traditional models of civil service political neutrality seem less appropriate. Second, the social and economic environment of public administration in Africa is also more important because of the 'corrupting' pressures that may arise therefrom. These may take various forms, structural and cultural. On the one hand, the 'impartiality' of civil servants may be affected by 'extended family' and ethnic ties. On the other hand, a civil servant's integrity may be tested in an economic environment dominated by private vested interests in competition for state patronage. A central fact of life in most less developed countries is that the state, in the absence of a well-developed indigenous private sector, has hitherto been the main agent of national developments – a role which has been complicated in various ways, not the least in Nigeria, by the dominance of foreign companies in key sectors of the economy.

These companies, often the subsidiaries of large multinational corporations, tend to set the pace in offering high levels of remuneration to their rapidly indigenizing managerial cadres. In Nigeria this in recent years has attracted high-level manpower away from the public to the private sector, particularly to the oil companies and conglomerates like the United Africa Company. Alternatively, income-maximizing public servants have been vulnerable to more informal pressures from the private sector, particularly those involved in the administration of government contracts.

At the same time, the civil war import bans and the post-war oil boom and increase in public expenditure in Nigeria has led to the emergence of an indigenous entrepreneurial elite, particularly in the transport, construction and commercial sectors. This expanding group has mounted a lobby for increased opportunities *vis-a-vis* foreign companies and has even contested the legitimacy of state sector expansion. Thus the role of public administration is an ambiguous one at Nigeria's present transitional stage of economic development, particularly when thus faced with the conflicting demands of national interest, foreign and domestic private capital. This is reflected for example in recent experiences with central planning and public enterprise in Nigeria where certain state initiatives have been frustrated by a lack of any general commitment to a clear national strategy as well as by organizational weaknesses on the part of government agencies themselves.[9] This problem is placed in theoretical perspective in the first chapter. There, Nelson Kasfir argues that much of the existing literature on African administration has been concerned with or influenced by inappropriate models and that relatively less attention has been paid to the operating characteristics of African bureaucracies themselves.

An exception to this general trend towards abstraction and imbalance is a growing body of literature based on studies within and without Africa, 'middle-range' in theoretical scope but focussed firmly on administrative behaviour. Kasfir suggests that the latter may be grouped into two theoretical approaches: the 'decision-making' and 'productivity' approaches. A combination of the two approaches, it is argued, will yield the most useful total understanding of administrative behaviour. The productivity and decision-making approaches each asks a different question about administrative activity. The productivity approach focuses on the *consequences* of administrative behaviour, whilst the decision-making approach is about *internal* dynamics of administration. The decision-making approach is concerned with the particular factors which influence an administrator when he makes decisions, and these include the premises and assumptions – conscious and unconscious – on which the administrator's decision is based. The productivity approach on the other hand focuses on inputs and outputs: it asks what inputs are necessary (training, administrative reforms, manpower planning, etc.) to improve the capacity of the administration to achieve national development goals. These themes are taken up again in the concluding chapter where the current issues of administrative reform in Nigeria are reviewed.

Central Planning

It will be recalled that one of the prime causes of the growth of interest in 'development administration' during Africa's first decade of political independence has been the changing role of the public sector itself and the increasing intervention of government in the promotion of planned social and economic change. Early efforts in this direction took the form of the establishment of central planning agencies as part of the expanding machinery of government.

As Gordon Idang points out in his chapter, central planning as it emerged after 1945 was inevitably concerned with the setting up of targets for export growth, together with establishing shopping lists required for the construction of infrastructure appropriate to the export-oriented economy. The role of government was essentially limited to the servicing of the import-export trading and extractive activities of foreign, monopolistic private enterprise dominating the economy. The major instrument of colonial planning was the annual accounting and budgetary process. Since Independence most African states have formulated some kind of plan for social and economic development. Plans have featured a common commitment to the promotion of economic growth and higher standards of living *per capita*. Plans have differed, however, as regards the institutions for implementation and the role of the state.

In these respects, two major modes of planning are distinguished as theoretical possibilities: 'capitalist' and 'socialist'. Capitalist planning operates simply by setting targets for economic growth, leaving basic decisions concerning fulfilment of these targets to private enterprise. The assumption is that leaving this to the private sector will lead to the most efficient allocation of resources. Socialist planning on the other hand operates by first formulating targets for the whole economy to ensure overall growth, and in particular the achievement of higher standards of living for the masses of working people. Second, socialist planning seeks to ensure the implementation of the targets set by the establishment of consciously planned institutions within the framework of socialized ownership of the means of production. This, of course, rests upon a socialist view of the state which assumes the ownership of the bulk of the means of production and distribution, either directly or indirectly, through co-operatives and institutions of worker participation. Thus the socialist approach to planning rejects the capitalist argument that resource allocation should be left to the unplanned interaction of market forces. The socialists argue that this would only lead to private accumulation of profits and possibly to exploitation. Also, the socialists argue, private firms left unchecked invest only in trade or even in the production of luxury goods, rather than in vital economic development projects such as fertilizer or farm equipment factories.

At the level of plan formulation the actual political and administrative process by which socialist and capitalist plans are formulated do not differ that much, except for the scope and content of plan goals and the institutions for implementation. Under socialist planning the state plays a major directive role in implementation, whilst under capitalist planning this is left to market forces in the dominant private sector.

In practice the role of government in the 'mixed' and 'dependent' economies of Africa is a complex one. At Independence the state sector extended itself in some countries only to the public corporations, which functioned to assist industrial and agricultural development projects sponsored by the private sector. Further development of the state sector has depended upon a number of factors including the ideological orientation and effectiveness of national policy-makers, the extent of foreign private investment, as well as the strength of indigenous capitalist groups.

Nigeria's Second National Development Plan (1970–74), analysed by James O'Connell in his chapter, marks a turning point in the development of the state sector in Nigeria, committing the government, at least in principle, to increased participation in the national economy.

Public Enterprise

The section on public enterprise is introduced with an essay by Otejuni Aboyade which reflects upon the performance of the Nigerian public enterprise system. The initial popularity of the public corporation to manage new areas on behalf of the state lay in an (imported) belief that certain activities within an expanding state sector were better devolved to semi-autonomous public corporations where the rigidities of inherited public administration methods and procedures did not impede efficient and flexible decision-making.[10] An adequate case literature has now accumulated on the organizational problems and operational performance of bodies like the Western Nigerian Development Corporation,[11] and the overall picture which emerges is somewhat depressing. Something of an impasse seems to have been reached suggesting the need for a new level of analysis. Aboyade attempts in his chapter to put the problems of public enterprise in fresh perspectives. He argues that the historical forces that have shaped the Nigerian public enterprises have resulted in a policy confusion, reflecting the transitional state of Nigerian society with its mixed economy and limited public sector. The basic organizational dilemma of the Nigerian public enterprise system can only be resolved when the basic philosophy is accepted that the public sector is at once an instrument for planning the production of goods, and the opportunity for re-allocating economic power relations in any society that claims to be progressive.

Some of these underlying dilemmas and ambiguities are seen at play in Turner's case study of Nigerian National Oil Corporation. Despite the various policy commitments since the Civil War to expand direct state sector participation in, and control over, the oil industry, the Corporation under the Gowon regime was kept weak and selected foreign interests served. Turner examines the way in which collaborationist elements in the responsible Ministry prevented the necessary shift in power from that Ministry to the Oil Corporation. In doing so she focuses on one of the critical aspects of what should have been part of the Corporation's role: auction and crude sales, and shows the way in which the Ministry proscribed any direct participation by the Corporation. The frustration of the Oil Corporation also amounted to the suppression of a new young breed of technocrats which the industry had itself called into being. It was also a factor underlying the July 1975 coup.

The increasing importance of this technocrary had been hinted as earlier by the Udoji Public Service Review Commission with its emphasis on technical efficiency. What the 1975 coup may hint at is the growing ascendancy within the civil service of elements favouring a public sector capable of playing a more effective role *vis-a-vis* foreign capitalist and local vested interests. The mass dismissals after the coup of corrupt and collaborationalist civil servants paved the way for the consolidation of a more technocratic state as the organizational basis of a successful national capitalism. The emergency of the 'technocrats' is also commented on by James O'Connell in the context of the Second Plan.

Government and Private Sector

The final section of Part II focuses on government and the private sector, on the ways in which the state seeks to control and guide (for national development purposes) private enterprise and its employees.

There are, of course, good reasons why governments in the ' new ' states should wish to control these two elements of the private sector. First, many of the enterprises active in key areas of the economy are foreign-owned and do not always and voluntarily operate within the framework of the national interest. Second, workers in large (and usually foreign-owned) private companies (as well as some of the public utilities like the ports, railways, electricity and water supply) have from the early colonial period in some cases been able to take effective (and sometimes class-based) mass action against their employees and even the government in power. The first case study in this section examines the working of the Nigerial Enterprises Promotion Decree, a by-product of the increasingly interventionist stance adopted by the Second National Development Plan.

The programme of indignization launched by the 1972 and 1977 Nigerian Enterprises Promotion Decree marks a limited but significant participation of government in industrial development. In pursuit of the Decree's objective to expand Nigeria's indigenous private sector by excluding non-citizens from a number of categories of commercial service and small-scale industrial activity, the machinery of government at Federal and State levels were assigned various roles in facilitating the transfer of ownership and control of affected enterprises. In addition, supporting public sector institutions like the Nigerian Bank for Commerce and Industry and the Industrial Training Fund were set up.

Whilst the Decrees are an important, if modest, instrument of national economic control *vis-a-vis* foreign investors, the indigenization policies recently implemented evidence continued ambiguities over the role of the state and the issues of allocating sectors to public and private enterprise; this reflects the heavy legacy of economic institutions inherited from Nigeria's colonial and neo-colonial periods. Thus the organizational approach adopted by the NEPD was essentially one of *ad hoc* interventionism in support of private enterprise. The option to boost the indigenous private sector rather than expand the public sector may be related to poor experiences with public enterprise in Nigeria since Independence as well as the relative strengths of foreign and indigenous capitalist groups.

A central argument of the case study is that continued ambiguities over the role of the state, combined with certain other factors, have given rise to the articulation of conflicts of interest within Nigerian society. These conflicts, be they geographically, sectionally or class-based, are to some extent inevitable in a society characterised by uneven development and a sharply skewed pattern of income distribution, and where the state takes the initiative to adjust the relations between indigenous and foreign private capitalist interests. Whilst there may be some initial political costs, they are part of the challenge of economic independence and decolonization.

Whilst the state has, so far, been less than effective in managing relations between foreign and domestic private enterprise, it has been markedly more successful in controlling the labour 'front'. In the second reading of the section, Peter Waterman, through a case study of the Lagos Port cargo-handling industry, examines the relation between the state and organized labour in Nigeria. After tracing the trend towards 'corporativism' in the government's handling of the unions, Waterman concludes that in Lagos Port at least the broad responses of labour has been to accept the government ideology of 'industrial peace'. This has been the case with the Nigerian Ports Authority employees whose organizations have, with a few exceptions been co-opted. This contrasts with the sector of the industry operated by private dock labour contractors. There, union militancy has been more persistent. In the latter case, however, labour has been keen to get inside the charmed circle of government employment (the Nigerian Ports Authority) where relatively good conditions, security, possibilities of promotion and civilized supervision are enjoyed.

These divergent patterns of co-operation and antagonism in the Lagos Port case are paralleled by the varying response of labour to the organization and structure of other areas of the economy. For example, as the case study of the Nigerian Enterprise Promotion Decree shows, relatively privileged labour in some of the large expatriate companies campaigned against the complete indigenisation of their industries, claiming they faced either redundancy or lower wages and security under private Nigerian ownership. In contrast, as the Nigerian National Oil Corporation case study shows, workers in that industry pressed for more Nigerianization.

Taken together, the events and analyses presented by the contributions to this section of the Reader are highly suggestive in determining the nature of the Nigerian state and its relationships with the major economic categories – foreign and indigenous private enterprise and organized labour in the various sectors. Presently, neither category appears to be in a relationship of direct or permanent antagonism. Worker strategy and tactics are shaped by present ambiguities and conflicts within the ruling group – between those favouring expanded state sector employment (*vis-a-vis* private enterprise) and those favouring the continued dominance of foreign interests in the high profit, oligopolistic sector. Likewise, the relationship of indigenous enterprise to the state has been varied. In some ways this has been rooted in the continued dominance of foreign companies in key sectors and the limits it has placed on opportunities. Sometimes indigenous entrepreneurs have supported the state as the provider of opportunities, for example, by way of contracts. On other occasions, they have been in conflict with the state – either over the expansion of the state sector itself or the continued support of the state for foreign private investment – both of which limit opportunities for the indigenous private sector.

Meanwhile, ambiguities over the role of the state, as described by Aboyade, remain and are at the very basis of political stability itself. As the essays on the Nigerian Enterprises Promotion Decrees and administrative reform suggest, the July 1975 coup has underlined dramatically the continuing need to consolidate a stable alliance of classes and an effective power base for the state. The latter remains a major source of the private accumulation of capital and an arena in which people compete for resources. Since the state lacks a class base, it will continue to support the local bourgeoisie, although in ways which will not affect in any fundamental sense the dominant position of foreign capital. But since these in themselves are insufficient to provide a power base, the state must necessarily expand its own already overdeveloped bureaucratic apparatus. The Udoji Public Service Commission Review, analysed in the concluding chapter, is a case in point here.

Local Administration for Development

Turning to local administration for development , we find a range of public and quasi-public agencies – some quite specialized – involved in the various aspects of rural administration and development. They include Community Development Departments, agricultural extension services, marketing co-operatives, and to a lesser extent – local government institutions.

The view taken here of local administration is, therefore, a broad one. Local government, in the sense of democratically-elected local bodies employing a staff and having powers of taxation and expenditure is only one aspect. By and large, given the dwindling manpower and other resources of local government in Africa, coupled with the centralizing tendencies of central policy-makers, local authorities have been increasingly limited to the provision of services to the local taxpayer and have been less involved in agricultural and infrastructural development projects. Harris examines the paradoxical situation where the successful demand for the creation of new states in Nigeria has resulted in the reduction of resources and areas of jurisdiction available to local government authorities. Bureaucratic institutions have been strengthened at the expense of participatory ones. Where government development agencies have been seen to be incompetent – or irrelevant – 'self-help' associations have arisen to fill the gap. The chapters by Olisa and Barrett respectively examine case studies of this trend. In theory, agricultural co-operatives also ought to be a form of self-help initiative generated voluntarily by farmers. In African practice, this has usually not been the case. King (on Northern Nigeria) and Beer (on Western Nigeria) examine the often ambivalent relationship between government and co-operatives; they also analyze the role of literacy and leadership in the successful functioning of co-operatives.

Historically and organizationally, local development administration comprises a very loosely integrated and co-ordinated proliferation of bureaucratic and technical agencies variously concerned with rural development and administration.[12] Thus local levels have, in many countries, been where some of the most dramatic changes in the inherited machinery of government have taken place, particularly in the rural sector. Elements of the inherited administrative machinery have been restructured and new patterns of relations with the 'centre' created. Most of these have involved various forms of centralization and decentralization (depending on the circumstances) aimed at improving the effectiveness and capacity of local administration through the redistribution of powers and resources between levels of government. The justification of changes of these kinds has been an increasing policy commitment to 'rural development' or 'bringing government closer to the people', requiring an improvement in patterns of provision and access to government-controlled goods and services for hitherto neglected groups.

Tanzania, for example, has taken steps to reduce urban bias and to establish the administrative and organizational framework for the redistribution of benefits in favour of the rural areas, particularly their less developed parts. Nigeria has also been attempting to ensure a more even pattern in the provision of economic opportunities – in her case, by creating smaller administrative units. This has been done by splitting up the former Regions and, more recently, the new States themselves in order to reduce the possibilities of discrimination in the allocation of public offices and resources against minority groups.[13]

Complex a field though it is, two key issues may be pinpointed for the student of development administration at local levels.

The first is that of co-ordination: the challenges posed by weak integration of administrative structures for any area-based planning. The second is that of participation: the need for improved relations between local staff (as planners, decision-makers, tax collectors, community development and agricultural extension workers) and the public (as communities, producers, taxpayers, consumers and beneficiaries of government policies, services and projects).

A number of solutions have been attempted in countries facing the two-fold challenge of co-ordination and participation. Some countries have set about improving institutional relations between development-oriented agencies of government by setting up committees as co-ordinative and participatory devices. For example, Tanzanian Regional and District Development Committees bring together representatives of government administrative and technical departments as well as party and local government office-holders. Other countries such as Kenya have created special integrated rural development agencies – multifunctional organizations which bring together a range of technical and administrative staff for some specific development task such as the implementation of village settlement schemes. Institutional proliferation has also been reduced to some extent by some local government reforms whereby local authorities have been subordinated to, or fused with, the field administration of central government.

In all cases a certain dilemma exists under the prevailing manpower conditions between maximizing values of co-ordination on the one hand and the values of participation and equity of access on the other. For example, the virtual abolition of semi-autonomous local authorities might have benefits by way of creating a more integrated administrative system, but may also entail political costs where local government institutions provided some of the few channels of local popular participation. Also, special rural development agencies may have certain advantages in that they concentrate their operations at a level uniquely 'close to the people'. On the other hand, given the scarce manpower resources often available, it is unlikely that sufficient agencies of this kind can be created to service all rural areas equally.

The Changing Pattern of Central-Local Relations

Since Independence in Nigeria, the objectives and forms of centralization and decentralization have largely been determined by the peculiar needs of the political system. Thus, because of the complexities of the federal system and the uneven development amongst its parts, much of the emphasis in local administrative reform has been upon the attempt to achieve acceptable spatial patterns in the provision of economic opportunities and amenities.[14] This has taken the form of creating small sub-federal political and administrative units. First, there was the creation of Mid-West State out of the Western Region in 1964,[15] followed by the creation of 12 States out of the former 4 Regions in 1966.[16] The reluctance of the dominant ethnic group of the Eastern Region, the Ibos, to accept splitting of 'their' Region into three was one of the causes of the Civil War. More recently, in 1976, a further 7 states were created out of the 12. In all cases the rationale has been the perceived need to reduce the power of subnational units *vis-a-vis* the centre (particularly in 1966), and to reduce the possibilities of discrimination in the allocation of public offices and resources against minority groups within the subnational units themselves.[17]

In terms of the needs of rural development and administration, the demands of political stability have been contradictory in a number of ways. The creation of States has tended to over-emphasize vertical relations at the expense of horizontal ones making difficult the establishment of area-based planning, for example. Moreover, it has based the new subnational units of government on existing patterns of social and political behaviour, diverting considerable resources in the process. Thus, as one analyst has observed,[18] Nigeria, because of the coincidence of a military regime and oil revenues, has been able to buy political stability, although it should be added that this has been at the expense of directly productive (possibly rural) investment.

From below, the creation of States has usually been seen as a question of access to power and benefits by certain groups. As another analyst has observed: 'The short-term interests of the educated elite would always be served by the creation of as many states as possible; each would possess its battery of Commissioners . . . its Permanent Secretaries, its Civil Service Commission and judiciary and the rest.'[19] In this way, and in several others, the creation of States may be a regressive step in terms of providing a framework for rural development – despite the slogan 'bringing government closer to the people'.

First, the States have been established politically in response to demands for the localized supply of functions, goods and services rather than rational planning criteria. Adoption of the latter might have lead to the selection of ecological zones for regional or area-based planning. The consequences of this are now becoming apparent in the current *Third National Development Plan* which has had no choice but to adopt the existing States as the basis for regional planning and development.[20]

Second, where new state capitals were and are again being created, the costs of establishing and maintaining new ministries diverts resources away from development expenditure. This is particularly unfortunate since, apart from large inter-state projects of national impact, agricultural development remains a state responsibility. This is particularly acute in states with a smaller population which, under the federal revenue allocation system receive a proportionately smaller share, yet have to meet the same costs of establishing a new capital. In some ways – although this may have been by default rather than design – the creation of more states tends to provide more government jobs for the educated elite and contractors rather than to generate more employment opportunities in the rural areas and curb the drift to the towns. Even where no State administrative centre has to be established, a further problem arises from the fact that the mere creation of a subnational unit does not guarantee equity in resource allocation at the new level. Thus, as is often the case, a few major urban centres and favoured rural areas have enjoyed a disproportionate share of the infrastructure and social services provided by the States.

Finally, administratively, State creation has given rise to some complications in the machinery of government at sub-federal levels. Already, prior to the creation of States, two or perhaps three incompatible models were discernible – a declining colonial line and staff-type field administration, represented by the Provincial Secretary and Divisional Officer, expanding functional ministries, and finally the subordinate local authorities. The creation of States complicated the situation in a number of ways, most notably in the North where scarce manpower resources to staff the new ministries led to the depletion and weakening of local authorities and the Provincial Administration. Furthermore, the new ministries established did not always base their field administration on areas corresponding to other ministries or the Provincial Administration. In the absence of any effective co-ordinative devices below the State level, extreme compartmentalization has resulted.

The last two years or so of the Gowon regime saw an increasing demand for yet more States. These were usually made on behalf of minority groups and areas in the existing States where discrimination was felt against the existing distribution of amenities and opportunities. In addition to these demands, there were also cases of States such as North-East which were clearly too large, ecologically unhomogeneous and in need of splitting up. Many of these demands and irrationalities were met by the creation of seven more states in 1976.

From the point of view of the needs of rural development administration, the remarks made about the 1976 creation of states still apply, and it will initially at least be simply a bonanza for the educated and urban elite and the contractors. Likewise, the motivations behind the demands for more states represent the interests of the few: those who, perhaps because of the favouritism of the former Military Governor were denied a scholarship, refused entry into the civil service or whose town was not provided with electricity, paved streets or a new hospital.[21]

References

1. Thus, for example, the Institute of Development Studies at the University of Sussex, England thought fit in 1972 to hold a six-week study seminar on this topic for high-level overseas administrators. For examples of the growing academic interest, see the bibliography at the end of this volume.
2. See the following chapter by Nelson Kasfir.
3. See B.B. Schaffer 'Deadlock in Development Administration', in C. Leys (ed.), *Politics and Change in Developing Countries* (Cambridge University Press, 1969), pp. 177–211.
4. An earlier study of Nigerian administration was the volume edited by David Murray, *Studies in Nigerian Administration* (Hutchinson for the Institute of Administration, Ife University, 1970). In that volume the only study which in any way addressed itself to the problem of 'bureaucracy' was Harrison's on the Western State agricultural extension service.
5. A twelve-State structure was created in 1967 at the outset of the civil war, in an eventually successful, if costly, attempt to split the four former Regions, two of which had been politically dominated by large, antagonistic ethnic groups – the Hausa in the North and the Ibo in the East. Seven more states were created out of the existing twelve in 1976.
6. Formally speaking, the machinery of government since the 1966 military coups has comprised Federal and State Executive Councils, bringing together militarily-appointed departmental Commissioners (mostly civilians) under the chairmanship of the Head of Federal Military Government and the State Military Governors respectively. The superior organ has been the Supreme Military Council, comprising the Head of the Federal Military Government, Military Governors and top military officers. In practice, policy-making has been dominated by Permanent Secretaries in direct working relations with the chief executives and their secretaries (the SMGs).
7. Tanzania, since the 1965 One-Party State Constitution, has made many fundamental changes in her civil service, likewise Zambia where the one-party system was also adopted. Milder reforms have been carried out in Kenya and Ghana by the Ndegwa and Mills-Odoi Commissions respectively.
8. Federal Republic of Nigeria, *Public Service Review Commission: Main Report* (Lagos, 1975).
9. See S. Osoba, 'Ideology and Planning for National Economic Development', in M. Tukur (ed.), *In Search of a New Political Community* (Kaduna, 1972), as well as the chapters in Part II of this volume.
10. A.H. Hanson: *Public Enterprise and Economic Development* (London, 1965), ch. 5.
11. See for example C. Teriba: 'Development Strategy, Investment

Decisions and Expenditure Patterns of a Public Development Institution,' *Nigerian Journal of Social and Economic Research* (July 1966); O. Teriba: 'Accountability and Public Control of Public Corporation – the Experience of Western Nigeria,' in Murray, *op. cit.*; O. Nwanwene: 'Public Corporations and State-Owned Companies', *Quarterly Journal of Administration*, 5, 1 (1970).

12. These features have been referred to in the literature as the problem of 'compartmentalization'. A recurrent theme of the essays in this section is the suitability of the inherited bureaucratic structures from implementing programmes of social and economic change at a level where administration and the public interact most closely. As the reading by Idusogie, Olayide and Olatunbosun on agricultural development administration shows, the machinery of government as it is presently organized has been characterised by lack of co-ordination and duplication of effort amongst departments. The result has been the ineffective use of resources by functionally overlapping departments, each of which carries heavy administrative overheads.
13. In the Nigerian case, however, less attention has been paid to patterns of rural stratification *within* administrative units and the emphasis has upon spatial aspects of access and distribution.
14. Unlike Tanzania, another country to have experimented boldly with adjusting central-local relationships but where inter-regional tensions are less marked, less attention has been paid to urban-rural disparities and none at all to patterns of rural stratification. See P. Collins, 'Public Policy, Rural Development, and Administrative Reform: a comparative study', *Working Paper 76–9*, School of Administration, Legon.
15. On this see: S.E. Oyovbaire, 'Geopolitics and political behaviour: some comments on the creation of States in Nigeria', paper presented to 1973 Annual Conference of Nigerian Political Science Association.
16. See the special number of the *Quarterly Journal of Administration* (April 1968).
17. See J.E. Elaigwu, 'Subnational Units & Political Development in New States. An African Experience' (Ph.D. dissertation, Stanford University).
18. Elaigwu, *op. cit.*
19. K. Barbour, 'Regional Planning in Nigeria', in K. Barbour (ed.), *Planning for Nigeria* (Ibadan University Press, 1972) p. 69.
20. Federal Republic of Nigeria, *Third National Development Plan, 1975–8 Vol. I* (Lagos, 1975).
21. Elaigwu, *op. cit.*

PART 1
Theoretical Perspectives

1. Theories of Administrative Behaviour in Africa
Nelson Kasfir

The study of administrative behaviour, one might assume, would be a central concern of researchers investigating the field of development administration. However, few aspects of the 'Dark Continent' have been the subject of less illumination than the international operating characteristics of African bureaucracies themselves. The natural opposition of any group of people to approval of studies into their own behaviour provides only part of the answer. Of equal importance has been the failure of theorists to work out conceptual guidelines around which meaningful research designs could be formulated. I am not suggesting that useless theorizing has been the problem (though that has been the consequence of many of the elaborate models constructed to explain other aspects of development administration). On the contrary, the absence of theorizing has been the difficulty.

Many who have struggled through the tortured prose of the model-builders of this subfield may regard this inattention as a welcome development. But the absence of theory means either the absence of research, or research that is based on older, half-forgotten, half-disproved conceptions.[1]

In this chapter I want to take a brief look at the failure to consider administrative behaviour as an important theoretical focus in developing countries, and then consider a variety of suggestions that could be united into two basic approaches to the examination of African administration. If research along these lines succeeds, the benefits that would follow from a better understanding of why civil servants act in the ways they do, could be extremely useful in improving the structure of policy formulation and implementation.

The Failure to Focus on Administrative Behaviour

Over the past ten years there has been a wide, and (until recently) increasing volume of discussion of how best to conceptualize administration in developing countries. However, the major writers have tended to focus on an older question in the public administration literature – the accountability of administrators to the government and ultimately to the public. Indeed, the question has been raised whether the performance of administrators *ought* to be improved (assuming we know how to do that), since it could increase their ability to evade public control.[2]

Consider three leading examples of development administration theory: the work of Ralph Braibanti, Milton Esman and Fred Riggs. Much of Braibanti's work is concerned with the question of external technical assistance and the effect it has on internal administrative reform.[3] Esman has initiated a major project to study 'institution-building' – the deliberate planning of new development-oriented institutions by leaders of new nations.[4] Riggs is well known for his formulations of the impact of 'ecological' factors stemming from the political, social and economic environment upon the behaviour of civil servants.[5]

Each of these three approaches could have been extended to conceptualise internal administrative activity in spite of its emphasis on external influences. But none was, save in cursory fashion. Riggs' general hypothesis that in the absence of public checks bureaucrats maximize private interests carries the argument about as far as any of these theorists have done. It is a relatively simplistic hypothesis, insensitive to many variations in internal administrative structure, and has not itself been tested.[6] Furthermore, given the fluid and changing nature of most political institutions in African countries, discussions which focus on external accountability are likely to lead to a dead end.

There are, however, sources from which we could construct guidelines to the study of African administration. In the first place there is an extensive body of literature on administrative behaviour and organisation theory based on studies carried out in Western Europe and United States. To test such propositions against African practices should not be dismissed out of hand, as many researchers and teachers in Africa have suggested. If local values and procedures differ from those of the West, the propositions considered will be falsified or restricted. If not, an enormous advantage is gained by being able to explain consequences through the existing literature without having to repeat all the studies which comprise it. In any event the use of existing studies tells us where we might find some interesting and useful results.[7] Furthermore, there are some investigations that have been carried out in African countries, as well as a variety of general observations on African administrative behaviour. From these sorts of materials we can outline the parameters of the problem and gain a sense of direction for further research.

Two general approaches which gather together many studies concerned with administrative behaviour could be called the 'productivity' approach and the 'decisional premises' approach. Each asks a different question about administrative activity. The productivity approach focuses on inputs and outputs in a manner parallel to the work of economists. The basic issue here is how to increase the output of administrators without increasing the input into the civil service structure by the same margin (if at all). The decisional premises approach focuses on the specific factors (or premises) that a particular administrator takes into account when he acts to formulate or implement a policy. The basic issue here is to determine what influences are actually governing administrative decisions. While the productivity approach focuses on the consequences of the administrative process, the decisional premises approach concentrates on the internal dynamics of a particular department, divisional office, or ministry headquarters. Naturally, the combination of both approaches will yield a more useful understanding of administrative behaviour. But it is better to avoid confusion at the beginning by separately examining the rather different problems that each must confront.

The Productivity Approach

If development means that significant changes in attitudes, demands and activities of large groups of citizens will constantly occur, the nature of effective administration may have to change as well. Bureaucracies established by colonial powers, and new administrative techniques mindlessly imported from them, may turn out to be unproductive. Or as suggested below below, an important distinction may have to be drawn between departments whose basic tasks are uncertain and constantly changing, and those whose tasks are relatively fixed and repetitive.

In order to reduce this question to manageable terms, it would be useful to consider how we might measure the productivity of administrative units. We need to find some way to relate the work civil servants do to its actual impact on the public, to link administrative inputs to governmental outputs.

In this sense productivity is measured by effectiveness and efficiency. The first question that any researcher, government official, or citizen wants answered is: 'Does it work? Is it a success'? That is, was the policy effective in achieving the goal government intended or, more completely, the goal government would have intended had it known what would happen? There is greater productivity when output is increasing. Effectiveness is a crude measure of productivity, because it does not take costs into account. Success at too high a price, however, is still success.

The next step is to compare input to output in order to develop a measure of the efficiency of the administration. If output goes up while input remains constant, productivity has risen in a more sophisticated sense than was possible to measure when considering effectiveness alone. Since most organisations – and government administration is no exception – tend to expand, that is the inputs consumed tend to rise over time, their output must rise at an even faster rate in order to increase productivity. The notion is directly parallel to wage negotiation in industry where workers demand higher wages due to inflation and management attempts to link increases to greater output per unit of time.

Unfortunately, unlike the industrial situation, administrative inputs and outputs are extremely difficult to measure. Improved agricultural production may result from higher prices offered to farmers, better weather or more effective assistance from extension agents. To sort out which of these inputs actually contributes to higher output will be problematic at best. The wider our field of comparison, the more complex this problem becomes, as new considerations of culture, governmental structure, education and language must be taken into account.

Administrative inputs can be measured in terms of their costs in money and time in spite of these problems. For example, the cost of tax collection can be compared with the revenue acquired. But, a government may be able to justify a tax whose administration costs more than the additional revenues collected. It may wish to demonstrate that it treats all of its citizens equally even though the additional effort costs more than it is 'worth'; or it may attempt to 'penetrate' a new area of the country. Thus while we must proceed cautiously, since governments employ a variety of criteria, it would be extremely useful to begin to assess productivity with the crude but clear measure that money provides.

The inputs into Kenyan administration have been quantified in preliminary fashion in order to show that 'general' administrative expenses declined slightly between 1964 and 1968 while salary and other payments relating to the administration of health and education rose in terms of total GDP.[8] These figures must be broken down into functional or 'program' categories and differentiated in terms of different types of regions to make them more meaningful. They could also be analyzed to compare different mixes of senior and junior officials in the same department but in different areas in terms of total salary and other payments.[9] The information on which to base such analyses is easily available in public documents in many African countries.[10]

Another way of conceiving of administrative inputs along a single measuring rod is to analyze the ways in which civil servants spend their time. There are many styles of administration at each level in the hierarchy. Taking a single level, it is possible to compare the administrators who spend most of their time in their offices (subdivided into those who see clients, and/or other officials and those who do not), those who are constantly touring their district, and those who return frequently to the capital city (perhaps subdivided into those who go back to consult senior officials and those who return to enjoy urban life). Which type of administrator is associated with successful and increasing policy outputs? By using time as the dependent variable to compare administrative inputs, we may gain insight into why certain areas adopt new crops faster than others, introduce more co-operative primary societies and the like.

Measuring output is no easier than measuring input but equally essential, if meaningful statements about productivity are to be made. Administrative output does not refer to the number of files examined or memoranda written. 'Paper productivity' is only a means (or sometimes a deterrent) to achieving policy goals in any field. True productivity means advances in agriculture, health, education or industry by governmental action. One test might be to ask knowledgeable civil servants to compare ministries in terms of their ability to handle problems. During the Obote years the Ministry of Animal Industry, Game and Fisheries often received praise as the most 'successful' ministry in Uganda. One could then, examine differences in administrative inputs between the 'successes' and the 'failures' for possible causes.

Often African administrators think in quantitative terms in expressing the productivity of a ministry or department. For example, the Director of Public Prosecutions in Uganda noted that the average detection and successful prosecution rate averaged 45% of the number of reported complaints to the police in developing countries, but amounted to only 20% in Uganda.[11] This is a statement about the productivity of the Ugandan Criminal Intelligence Department and the explanations of administrative inadequacy offered by the D.P.P. attempted to link inadequacies in administrative behaviour of officers to the low rate of crime control.

Ultimately input-output analysis can only spotlight significant relationships or deviations from expected norms. This approach to productivity offers no causal proposition to *explain* why those relationships exist. However, there are other approaches to the problem of productivity which attempt to do so. Riggs' argument that administrators tend to work inefficiently when political accountability by external institutions is low is an hypothesis about their productivity. It could be tested by comparing two parallel agencies – perhaps Co-operative Ministries – in countries with different levels of outside political controls. The amount of auditing per government official of the financial records of co-operative societies would provide a useful quantitative measure. Or, two regions in the same country staffed in different patterns might provide an interesting 'field experiment'.

A more radical perspective on productivity in developing countries is taken by those who argue that bureaucracy and development do not go together. The essence of this position is that bureaucracy works well in a society in which tasks have a high degree of predictability, clients are willing to accept decisions based on general rules rather than the merits of their cases, and officials are satisfied with incremental responses in adapting policy to a slowly changing environment.[12] If this 'bureaucratic style' is adopted by developing countries in which fundamental changes are anticipated, it will be unproductive, or even counterproductive. Administrative techniques that work well in an industrialized country consume a large fraction of skilled manpower with negligible results in developing countries according to this view.[13] Thus, in the case of Kenya – it is argued – the bureaucratic style will create problems for development administration when it characterizes technical ministries which bear a prime responsibility for initiating and managing the development process.[14]

While this argument has a certain surface plausibility, it mistakes change for development. Some aspects of development will require an administrative apparatus capable of turning out a predictable rule-oriented performance on a day-to-day basis. In other cases development will require a flexible agency capable of initiating large-scale changes. The two sides of the development process are related in complex ways which vary from one situation to another. Compare for example the problems involved in the introduction of a new cash crop involving small risks and small, but certain, material returns for farmer, and another new crop in which the risks are high and so is pay-off – if the farmer follows a complex routine carefully. If adoption of both is important enough to the government, it may opt for introducing the two crops through departments organized in entirely different ways – the former emphasizing a bureaucratic style, the latter focusing on a more *ad hoc* personalized approach using highly-trained senior officials in the field to 'sell' the program.

Thus, we might increase productivity by organizing administrative agencies in terms of two fundamentally different styles depending upon the task. Operating a successful telephone system, social security scheme, or tax office may require more bureaucracy than is now found in many African administrative structures. On the other hand, change-oriented agencies like development planning and national development corporations may require a great deal less. There is a limit, however, to the extent to which any African country is able or likes to organise change-oriented agencies. These 'rational-productivity bureaucracies'[15] are voracious consumers of the most highly-qualified professional people in the country and demand the greatest autonomy from direct governmental control.

The Decisional Premises Approach

If we turn from the issue of the contribution that administrators make toward the achievement of government goals to the internal dynamics of making and implementing policy, a new range of concerns must be examined. In this approach the premises of administrators are the considerations that enter their calculations, as each makes decisions – whether large or small. As Herbert Simon argued, these premises involve a mixture of facts and values.[16] To an important – though varying – extent they reflect the pattern of substantive policy, operating procedures, and the set of 'decision rules'[17] that have grown up over the previous period. Just as much of the government budget of any country cannot be changed from year to year, so fixed is the range of options available to a civil servant. The degree of available discretion will vary according to country, position, ministry and situation. Thus, the freedom of civil servants to personally determine the premises on which they base their decisions is a question for research.

The premises of different administrators are integrated in two ways. First, the process of decision-making requires that they co-ordinate their activities with those of other officials (and certain outsiders) who are involved in the same policy. There are two problems, though, that immediately complicate any approach that focuses on the decision as the unit of analysis. One is the difficulty in isolating the 'critical decision' from the many others that led up to it.[18] The other is that in many situations an administrator solves or copes with a problem by ignoring it, that is by making no decision. Unfortunately, the absence of a decision is rarely as clean-cut as the making of one. While these obstacles may be difficult to overcome, it would be foolish to dismiss an approach which focuses on the central activity – making decisions – for which servants are supposed to be responsible.

The second form of integration of the premises of administrators is the social system that grows out the formal administrative structure and that involves them as members. This system is the set of closely interrelated roles involved in the administrative activities being investigated by the researcher, and felt to cohere by a consensus of the participants. The existence of coherence does not necessarily mean that the level of harmony or the smooth co-operation of members of the unit will be high. The boundaries of this sort of system will probably be fuzzy, though the participants will usually know its limits. Thus, the overall problem is to determine what decisions are being made *within* a specified social system.[19]

However, external considerations will undoubtedly play an important role in the premises that an administrator brings with him to his work. In spite of strictures on the non-political nature of the civil service in several African countries, national political disputes will often find their way into policy formulation. Child-rearing practices, political socialization patterns in schools and client demands will affect the premises of administrators. Fundamental cultural patterns may vary among ethnic groups. These could condition administrative responses in ways that are easily overlooked. Ability to get along in a hierarchy may vary in terms of traditional political organization. Willingness to trust others and to take risks may also vary ethnically. Obviously, the level of education, religion and length of exposure to urban influence are only a few of the additional variables that may turn out to be important.

All of these considerations become important only insofar as they actually affect the premises on which an administrator is prepared to act. Of equal and perhaps greater importance – as a number of bodies in Western Europe and America have demonstrated – is the influence of internal arrangements: the way in which individual workers or civil servants interact among themselves. The work of the 'human relations' school and the 'dysfunctionalists'[20] has brought out the importance of informal organization in shaping decisions that superiors thought they were controlling.

For example, a study of miners working under hazardous conditions showed how they were able to evade many of the rules established by management.[21] In a state government office in America agents responded to the tighter supervision exercised by superiors who were responsible for assessing their performance by rarely consulting them for advice. Instead, they went to their less experienced co-workers.[22] In a third study workers who produced too much in order to gain extra pay were ostracized by their compatriots until they accepted the rate of production deemed a 'fair day's work'.[23]

These findings not only indicate that the social system may affect the behaviour of its members, but also have a special relevance to African administrative situations from which parallel examples can be put forward. Ugandan public servants assigned to the remote area of Bwamba (bordering on the

Republic of Zaire) during the Rwenzururu secession movement were likely to act in a different manner from their counterparts in more peaceful areas closer to ministry headquarters in Kampala. Tanzanian civil servants may be less willing to consult their superiors on professional questions when the latter are high party officials who must conform to changes in party policy. And, as everywhere else, African civil servants may find ways to make unpleasant the life of colleagues who insist on staying in their offices after official hours to complete their assignments.

There is a further consideration that makes these findings pertinent to the discussion here. All of them can be brought together in a general (though not comprehensive) explanation of administrative behaviour. In each example the actors attempted to retain as much freedom of manoeuvre as they could, while restricting other groups to as predictable a set of responses as they could manage.[24] In other words they are involved in power struggles and conflicts with other members of their social system. To examine these opens up a range of behaviour that has not been studied in African administration. Reliance on this approach requires the researcher to think of the administrative unit as a miniature political system which may or may not be concerned with the issues of national politics. The conflicts in which actors in this system find themselves and the ways in which they resolve those conflicts become the central focus of investigation. To the disputes each actor will bring the political resources he can amass.[25] These are often closely related to the areas of activity that are not restricted by rules (at least not by those that are actually enforced). In most cases the subordinate is trying to evade the control of his superior, while the superior is attempting to use regulations to determine that the subordinate does what he or higher authorities are demanding.[26] Control over critical points in the communications network and over expert knowledge are important resources. Thus, expatriates in technical positions whose knowledge cannot be challenged by local civil servants, and who enjoy preferential access to higher officials may exercise power out of proportion to their numbers.

The important question concerns the uses made of the power resources, not the resources themselves. They may be used to form bargaining strategies which permit the individual or the faction to which he belongs to gain additional power, carry out some desired objective, or avoid being involved in a policy that may have dangerous consequences for the civil servants administering it. Even where a strategy is engaged in for completely personal reasons, it is likely to be cloaked with a public policy rationale of some sort. Thus, a close reading of official actions taken, and justifications offered, by civil servants, may give insight into the manoeuvring for position by different groups.

From this perspective the question of policy innovation – a significant concern for development administration – takes on a new meaning. Innovation will almost always mean increasing the power of one administrative body while reducing that of another. Thus, it is threatening and therefore blocked by those who will be restricted by it. The conflict between the Tanzanian

Ministry of Agriculture and the planners over the adoption of the transformational or improvement approach to agricultural change involved just this issue. So did the planners' attempt to take the negotiation of foreign aid projects out of the hands of the Treasury.[27] If innovatory policies are not intended to die on the vine, national leaders have to give political muscle, that is, power resources, to the agency which is charged with pursuing the new goal.

Conclusion

The argument of this paper has been that little empirical investigation based on even the most minimal theory has been directed to questions of African administrative behaviour. The work of development administration theories has focused on the influence of environment on administration and not on administration itself. The two approaches suggested here – productivity and decisional premises – could serve as bases to study administrative behaviour.

Of the two, the productivity approach is more likely to interest national leaders and thus provide opportunities for research clearance. It has a more 'practical' and 'applied' cast to it than the decisional premises approach. The questions it raises mirror those raised by high political figures. Increasing output through government action is a good way to define development administration from their point of view.

But, if there are no short-cuts to development, there probably are few to certain knowledge of administrative performance.

Study of the influences that determine the premises on which civil servants act and how this affects their interaction will be necessary to explain why a particular pattern of organisation is more highly productive than another. This sort of research is extremely costly *to the government*. In addition to raising questions about the decision rules most African and other govern ments have regarding security, it may require an intensive investment of time by the administrators studied.

However, the successful execution of either approach creates a demand for the other. The linkage between input-output studies can only be supplied by studies of the social system integrating administrators' decisional premises, while explanation of internal administrative behaviour lacks application until related to differences in productivity. In the long run we can hope to combine the two into a more general theory of administrative behaviour that will be sufficiently useful to shape administrative reforms to the requirements of development.

References

This essay was first published in *The African Review*, 1, 3 (January 1972).

1. '. . . we all use models in our thinking all the time, even though we may

not stop to notice it. When we say that we 'understand' a situation, political or otherwise, we say in effect, that we have in our mind an abstract model, vague or specific, that permits us to parallel or predict such changes in that situation of interest to us.' Karl W. Deutsch, *The Nerves of Government* (New York: Free Press, 1963), p. 12.

2. Ferrel Heady, 'Bureaucracies in Developing Countries', in Fred Riggs (ed.), *Frontiers of Development Administration* (Durham: Duke University Press, 1970), p. 464.
3. 'External Inducement of Political-Administrative Development: An Institutional Strategy', in Ralph Braibanti (ed.), *Political and Administrative Development*, (Durham: Duke University Press 1969), and 'Transnational Inducement of Administrative Reform: A Survey of Scope and Critique of Issues,' in John D. Montgomery and William J. Siffin (eds.), *Approaches to Development: Policies, Administration and Change* (New York: McGraw-Hill, 1966).
4. *The Institution Building Concepts – An Interim Appraisal* (Pittsburgh: Inter-University Research Program in Institution Building, 1967)
5. The argument is most fully brought out in *Administration in Developing Countries* (Boston: Houghton Mifflin, 1964). He has recently restated his approach in 'The Structures of Government and Administrative Reform' in Braibanti, *Political and Administrative Development.*
6. See Nelson Kasfir, 'Prismatic Theory and African Administration', *World Politics*, 21, 2 (January 1969), pp. 311–13.
7. David Leonard has tested Theodore Caplow's theory of organizational effectiveness (which was developed in industrialized countries) in Kenya, and shows that it is useful, but must be modified to include size of work group before the relationships become statistically significant. 'A test of Organisation Theory on Agricultural Extension Work Group in Kenya.' (Conference on Comparative Administration, Arusha, September 1971).
8. Henry Bienen, 'The Economic Environment ' in Goran Hyden, Robert Jackson and John Okumu (eds.), *Development Administration: the Kenyan Experience* (Nairobi: Oxford University Press, 1970), pp. 53–4.
9. An interesting comparison of different ratios of agricultural officers and field extension agents (Agricultural and Field Assistants) in Uganda is presented in E.R. Watts, 'Extension Staff Organisation in Uganda' (Conference on Comparative Administration, Arusha, September 1971), pp. 11–12, 26–7.
10. Analysis of this data would be greatly enriched by a statistical analysis of the Government *Staff List*. A profile for the higher Ugandan Public Service is currently being worked out by Garth Glentworth and Nelson Kasfir.
11. *Uganda Argus*, 13 December 1971, p. 1. Mr. G.J. Masika, the D.P.P., might feel better about Uganda's seemingly poor performance in light of the record of the New York City police. 'In 1969, according to a report of the Mayor's Criminal Justice Coordinating Council, arrests were made in only 18 per cent of reported robberies, 7 per cent of burglaries and 6 per cent of grand larcenies. Only 32 per cent of those arrested were found guilty of any charge. Of these, only 7.4 per cent

received sentences of more than a year, and 42 per cent didn't go to jail at all, receiving suspended sentences.' Tom Buckley, 'Murphy among the "Meat-Eaters"' *New York Times Magazine* (19 December 1971), p. 47.

12. Bernard B. Schaffer, 'The Deadlock in Development Administration' in Colin Leys (ed.), *Politics and Change in Developing Countries* (Cambridge University Press, 1969).
13. Warren F. Ilchman, 'The Unproductive Study of Productivity: Public Administration in Developing Nations', *Comparative Political Studies,* 1, 2 (July 1968), pp. 234–36.
14. Robert H. Jackson, 'Administration and Development in Kenya: A Review of Problems Outstanding', in Hyden, Jackson and Okumu, *Development Administration: The Kenyan Experience,* p. 330, n. 8. See also pp. 324, 329–30.
15. Warren F. Ilchman, 'Productivity, Administrative Reform and Antipolitics: Dilemmas for Developing States,' in Braibanti, *Political and Administrative Development,* pp. 474–79.
16. *Administrative Behaviour [2nd ed.]* (New York: Free Press, 1965), pp. 45–60. See also Martin Landau, 'Development Administration and Decision Theory,' in Edward Weidner (ed.), *Development Administration in Asia* (Durham: Duke University Press, 1970), pp. 86–88.
17. For a discussion of decision rules (general principles for allocation resources without paying close attention to the specific of a program) see Warren F. Ilchman, 'Decision Rules and Decision Roles: Some thoughts on the Explanation of Productivity and the Productivity of Explanation' (Conference on Comparative Administration, Arusha, September 1971), pp. 39–49.
18. William R. Dill, 'Administrative Decision-Making', in Sidney Mailick and Edward H. Van Ness (eds.), *Concepts and Issues in Administrative Behaviour* (Englewood Cliffs: Prentice-Hall, 1962), pp. 34–6, 42–7.
19. See Nicos Mouzelis, *Organisation and Bureaucracy: An Analysis of Modern Theories* (London: Routledge & Kegan Paul, 1967), pp. 166–70.
20. Mouzelis, *ibid.*, contains a useful discussion of the theories of these two groups of investigators.
21. Alvin Gouldner, *Patterns of Industrial Bureaucracy* (New York: Free Press, 1964).
22. Peter Blau, *The Dynamics of Bureaucracy* (Chicago: The University of Chicago Press, 1955).
23. George C. Homans, *The Human Group* (New York: Harcourt, Brace, 1950), pp. 48–80.
24. This is the basic proposition put forward by Michael Crozier, *The Bureaucratic Phenomenon* (Chicago: The University of Chicago Press, 1963), p. 156.
25. For a discussion of the notion of 'political resources' see Robert A. Dahl, *Who Governs: Democracy and Power in an American City* (New Haven: Yale University Press, 1961), pp. 223–67.
26. The imposition of new decision rules is an important tactic that superiors can employ. See note 17 above.
27. See R. Cranford Pratt, 'The Administration of Economic Planning in a

Newly Independent State: The Tanzanian Experience 1963–1966', *Journal of Commonwealth Political Studies,* 5 (March 1967), pp. 38–59.

PART 2
Central Planning, Parastatals, and the Private Sector

Central Planning: An Introduction

Central planning is one area of development administration where the challenges of achieving national development goals are great. It is one of the most exciting and at the same time sometimes one of the most disillusioning areas, in that many of the planning experiences have been characterised by a wide gap between aspirations and achievements.

Part of the problem lies in the ambitious nature of the concept of planning. At its most abstract, planning has been conceived as the optimal use of resources and opportunities in countries where these tend to be used very inefficiently. It has been seen as an exercise, a form of rational organization whereby less resources are wasted, which leads to development. Waste results in particular from the pursuit of incompatible goals. Thus, the activity of planners in the formulation and co-ordination of societies' goals, and especially the determination of the ways and means by which the goals may be obtained. Put more concretely, planning simply refers to the design and execution of economic, social and political programmes in the less developed countries.

As a human exercise, the planning process comprises two major elements. First, there is the making of the plan, which comprises two stages – (1) selecting objectives and targets, and (2) identifying possible courses of action and means to achieve the objectives and targets. Second, there is the execution of the plan, the securing of action in conformity with the courses identified.

As far as the setting of targets is concerned, these are set at three levels. First, they are set at the national level where the plan document will indicate the fundamental shifts required in the economy in the given plan period. Second, they are set at the sectoral level. Here goals are set within the national framework for each of the major sectors: the public sector (agriculture, industry, education/manpower) and the private sector. The size of the latter will vary according to the desired extent of state intervention. Third, they may be set at the project level. Here the plan will specify particular enterprises and schemes to be established in each sector. At this level, usually only large projects of national or state 'impact' and significance are listed. Moreover, the projects included are normally public sector allocations only. It is difficult to get information on investment in the private sector, except where the state is giving a grant or credit to private enterprise. The process of drafting a plan can occupy varying lengths of time. The

Second Nigerian Plan was apparently put together in 8 months, while it took 18 months to prepare the Tanzanian Second Five-Year Plan.

A plan is both a political as well as a technical document. Thus its preamble or first chapter will include some outline of society's broad aspirations or ideology, followed by the goals to be attained in the planning period and the quantitative targets to be achieved. Apart from the intentions and priorities of the national leadership, a plan will also indicate a range and combination of policy instruments which may be used in achieving plan goals and targets.

In most countries eçonomic policy is a series of sectoral policies rather than a comprehensive model of economic growth. Thus the purpose of planning is to co-ordinate sectoral policies and instruments – checking them for mutual consistency. Targets are usually indicated at an early stage in the drafting of a Plan. The available resources are then estimated and provisionally allocated, and sectoral balances worked out. (The co-ordination of targets within a plan framework is the stage at which various quantitative techniques may be used. For example, 'input-output' tables may be used to ensure a balance of resources.) Finally, when the discussions on a draft plan are completed, the plan document goes to the political authorities for approval. After this, it is the task of the planning agency to oversee implementation and to secure conformity with plan objectives and targets. Co-ordination is also the essence of plan implementation as well as plan formulation; the soliciting of continuous co-operation amongst the various agencies, including the containment of a multitude of pressures which threaten to distort the plan – particularly from the private sector.

Plans differ as regards detail. Comprehensive plans are the most difficult to administer. As we shall see later, large sectors of the economy are outside, or only indirectly under, government control. Some countries, particularly federated states like Nigeria and the former Pakistan, or large and economically diverse countries like Tanzania, extend the planning process to the regional or state level. Essentially, regional or state plans translate the broad national objectives and policies into projects for execution, bearing in mind the amount of resources likely to be allocated to each region. Regional or state planning may be incorporated into national planning either by giving regional/state breakdowns of plan allocations, or by publishing or appending separate regional or state plans.

Finally, some planning systems provide the opportunity for mid-term appraisal and plan review. The planning process must be flexible to absorb changes in the circumstances of the economy or changes in policy at the level of political authority. A recent innovation is thus the 'rolling plan'. Tanzania, for example, has adopted Annual Plans within her current Five-Year Plan period. Aside from these innovations, the conventional short-term instrument of the planning process is the annual budget, which sets short-term targets and authorizes expenditures. The only problem of using the budgetary process as an instrument of development planning is first, that many budgetary systems are outdated, and second, that the budgetary process is usually in the hands of the Finance Ministry rather than the Planning agency. As we shall see shortly, the relations between these two departments are not always co-operative.

Turning to the machinery and organisation for plan implementation, the public service is obviously the key agency, except that in many ex-colonial countries it is not always well adapted to planning functions. Thus, new institutions are sometimes created for both plan preparation as well as implementation. Most countries engaged in planning have some kind of planning agency. The work of a planning agency is primarily the organization of information. Information is supplied from other departments of government, local government, and parastatals and private enterprise (where possible) during the preparation of the Plan. Likewise, when it comes to Plan implementation, the planning agency transmits information and instructions back. Thus the planning agency's role is to receive and impart information. A planning agency obviously cannot work alone, since it is dependent on information supplied by others. Likewise, in attempting to co-ordinate sectoral and local plans, the planning agency is dependent on other Ministries, groups and communities, (including also, co-operatives and trade unions) whose development efforts it is trying to stimulate in certain directions. The most difficult area is the relation between the planning agency and private groups (some foreign) and the ability of the government to persuade and induce private individuals to create enthusiasm and stimulate action amongst the mass of the population. Planning agencies sometimes deal with the private sector through a series of working groups and committees.

A universal problem of planning machineries is the status or authority of the planning agency within the system of government. The effectiveness of the planning agency will depend upon its location in the administrative hierarchy. There are two possibilities here. The first is to locate the planning function in or under the office of the Prime Minister or President. A planning authority must have the power to instruct other Ministries and its location in the office of the chief executive is the most effective way of ensuring this. On the other hand, planning, where it is located in political arena, can be distorted by political interference. For example, during the preparation of the Tanzanian First Five-Year Plan, individual Ministers put pressure on the President to secure their Ministries increased shares in the overall inter-departmental allocation of the development budget. The second possibility is to create a separate planning agency or commission.

Aside from the question of where the planning machinery should be located, the other problem area is the relationship between the planning agency and the finance ministry. Certain conflicts of interest arise between finance ministries on the one hand, traditionally conservative, cautious and restrictionist in policy orientation, and planning agencies on the other hand, which are essentially expansionist in outlook. For example, finance ministries will be more preoccupied with monetary, budgetary and foreign exchange matters, including inflation and balance of payments problems, whilst planning agencies are concerned with resource allocation and rates of growth. The relation between the finance ministry and the planning ministry will be particularly important in the context of the budget, particularly the development estimates, which is an important component or instrument of the planning process. Finance ministries are notoriously jealous of their powers of budgetary control, and it is only through executive backing that a planning agency can hope to influence the budgetary process. Planning agencies are not necessarily very large: Nigeria's contains 140 staff, Sri Lanka's 50, Turkey's 70, India's 200 and Tanzania's about 50, but these may include statisticians who may be under a separate department.

Finally, in considering the problem of plan implementation and performance, there are a number of parameters of what is possible. The most important of these is the degree of government control over the economy and the extent to which it can influence economic behaviour in given directions. That is to say, assuming that there are available enough skilled planners, and assuming also that sufficient statistical data (particularly in the rural/subsistence sector) is available to central planners, the extent of government control/influence will depend on the degree to which economic activity is concentrated in the public sector. Even where the resources and technical possibilities are known to central planners, the state usually has not the power to use them if they belong to the private sector. Only indirect techniques may be used here, although even these may be uncertain given the fluctuations in the world market for raw material exports. The possible range of direct means of government influence include ministry budgets, exchange rates, tariffs, subsidies, and quotas. Indirect means include the monetary system, private capital investments and education. Finally, outside government control are a range of social and political phenomena, including such things as mobility of labour, income distribution and population growth.

Common reasons for the shortcomings of contemporary planning efforts are three-fold. First, the economic models used have at times been inappropriate. Second, the data used have often been imperfect. Third, plan coordination has been distorted by conflicting demands of politicians. Possible ways of making the planning process more effective include first, the integration of planning and budgeting and the improvement of the integrated process through inter-ministerial committees. Second, the planning machinery may be made effective by obliging departments of government to justify their spending by broader arguments than narrow departmental needs. Third, there might be established a centralized comparison of information for policy choice.

2. The History of Planning in Nigeria
Gordon Idang

Nigeria's planning experience since 1946 has evoked considerable attention within and outside the country. There are several reasons for this widespread interest. First, Nigeria is a large and diversified country with vast economic and political potentialities. With an area of 336,759 square miles and a population of 55.7 million (according to the 1963 census) she is the most populous state in Africa and ranks thirteenth in the world. Besides, Nigeria is a model of a developing nation and shares some of the characteristics common to all new states – low income, investment and production; an underdeveloped and predominantly agricultural economy; an imperfectly integrated social structure; wide disparities in internal development and income distribution; and an inherited colonial administrative system with attendant bottlenecks in administrative and managerial capacity. While there is no universal model for economic planning, Nigeria's planning experience certainly has some relevance to other emerging nations, particularly to other African nations.

Secondly, and of considerable importance, the recent attempt by scholars to develop a valid body of middle-range empirical theories regarding the national development process in Africa has re-emphasised the need for detailed case studies of the administration of planned development in individual African countries. Until recently, much of the literature on development administration was related to Asian rather than African experience.[1] Although some of the case studies have some relevance to Africa, most of their findings cannot be directly imported without re-shaping them to handle problems that are unique to the new African states.

The main concern of this chapter therefore is to assess systematically the structure and performance of the Nigerian political system in the formulation and implementation of policies and programmes designed to promote accelerated economic development and social change. Throughout the chapter, the criteria of relevance will take the form of three research questions:[2]

(1) How did planning in Nigeria originate and what peculiar properties characterise it?

(2) What institutions and administrative organisations are involved in the planning process?

(3) What are the effects of the various development plans on Nigeria's overall development?

This chapter offers no conclusive answers to these questions. It does address them and in so doing provides an opportunity to understand development administration in Nigeria.

Pre-Independence Development Planning

Nigeria's planning effort can be traced back to 1946 when the Ten-Year Plan of Development and Welfare for Nigeria designed to guide the allocation of Colonial Development and Welfare Funds came into operation.[3] The Plan was divided into two five-year periods, the first with objectives more clearly defined and the second in more general perspectives. Both the formulation and implementation of the Plan up to 1954 were highly centralized and were carried out under the general direction and supervision of the Central Development Board, a small body consisting exclusively of senior colonial administrators in Lagos. In each of the three groups of provinces – North, East and West – that then constituted Nigeria, an Area Development Committee, again consisting mainly of top government officials, was set up to advise the Central Development Board.[4] Through these bodies, considerable effort was made to ensure both interdepartmental and central-provincial consultation and co-ordination in the entire planning process. However, this early Plan depended substantially for successful implementation on imported capital equipment and foreign personnel. Because of the post-war reconstruction shortage of men and materials in Britain and other European countries, these essential inputs were not forthcoming in the right quantity and quality.

The constitutional changes of 1951–54 under which Nigeria became a federation with four autonomous Regions – North, East, West and Southern Cameroons – and a Federal Territory of Lagos brought the Ten-Year Plan to a premature end, Accordingly, a new set of Economic Development Programmes (1955–60), formulated and presented jointly by the Federal and Regional Governments and based on the 1955 Report of the International Bank Economic Mission to Nigeria, was officially launched in April 1955.[5] The 1955–60 Development Programmes were revised in 1958 and extended to 1962.

In retrospect, the pre-independence development plans were not plans in the true sense of the term, but public investment programmes. Many of them proposed no more than an expansion of normal departmental activities and associated budgets for recurrent and capital expenditures. Furthermore, they constituted a random collection of projects which had not been co-ordinated or related to any overall economic targets.[6] The main emphasis in the plans was confined to building up the transportation and communications systems, while little provision was made for industrial development. In the agricultural sector, attention was concentrated on a limited range of export crops. Although the report of the International Bank Mission served as a common frame of reference for the 1955–62 Plan, the development programmes of the various governments of the Federation were competitive in character. There was also the problem of distortions and aberrations in plan execution (particularly after 1955), underspending on directly productive projects, and overspending on prestige or 'white elephant' projects not included in the plans. Consequently, these early development plans had only a limited effect in determining what developments actually occurred. Lack of public support and enthisiasm for the plans, inadequate executive capacity, and paucity of reliable data on which to base sound development policies also helped to make these early attempts at development planning sterile and ineffective. To quote one of Nigeria's leading planners: 'The 1955–60 Economic Programmes . . . were distinguished for their underfulfilment, distortions in projects implementation; substantial waste, administrative inefficiency, and [therefore] continued revision and extension.[7]

The First National Development Plan 1962–68

The 1962–68 Plan, officially launched in June 1962, was at least in theory the country's first national and comprehensive development programme with overall growth targets. According to the then Minister of Economic Development, Waziri Ibrahim, the programmes formulated by the Federal Government were later reformulated by the Central Planning Agency to ensure co-ordination with these of the Regional Governments. The resulting programmes were then integrated into the National Development Plan.[8] The main targets of the Plan included (1) a growth rate of the economy of at least 4% per annum; (2) an investment of 15% of the Gross Domestic Product estimated to raise the per capita consumption by about 1% per annum; and (3) the development, as rapidly as possible, of opportunities in education, health, and employment for all citizens.[9] Accelerated economic growth, optimum utilisation of the country's resources, and large-scale structural and institutional changes were thus the three main expressed aims of the Plan.[10] Of the projected sum of ₦ 1,356.6 million that was to be spent in economic development and social change over the six years, foreign economic assistance was to provide ₦ 678 million or just over one half.

Before the creation of the Mid-West Region in 1963, the Plan for the former Western Region included programmes for the areas which were later to constitute the Mid-West Region. Consequent upon the creation of the new Region, a separate Mid-West Plan was prepared to fit into the general framework of the National Development Plan and extended to cover the remaining four years of its life.

Achievements Under the 1962–68 Development Plan

In absolute terms, total annual fixed investment for the economy as a whole in the first two years fell short of the expected average level of ₦294.4 million. In subsequent years, however, the targets were considerably exceeded right up to and including 1965. The growth rate of recorded capital formation not only declined with the 1966 crisis, but was actually negative by 1967. This notwithstanding, actual investment in both public and private sectors combined in 1966 still exceeded the estimated annual average by about 37%. Similarly, 85% of the total planned investment for the economy as a whole during the Plan period was achieved as a result of the better performance of the private sector, where the target of ₦ 780 million for the Plan period was already exceeded by about 64 per cent in 1966.

Public investment, which in the first year of the Plan period amounted to ₦ 129.2 million, declined slightly to ₦ 126.8 million in 1963. Thereafter, it rose gradually to approximately ₦ 180 million in 1966. The expected annual average investment of ₦ 225.6 million was never achieved throughout the entire Plan period. The major projects successfully completed during the Plan period include the oil refinery, the Nigerian Security and Minting Plant, the paper mill, the Niger Dam, the sugar mill, the Niger Bridge and several trunk roads (including Gusau – Sokoto, Bauchi – Gombe – Yola, Shagamu – Benin and Kano – Zaria trunk roads).

The Second National Development Plan 1970–74

Although the First National Development Plan was due for completion on 31 March 1968, the political crisis of 1966–67 and the subsequent civil war made it impossible for the country to embark on the preparation of another plan until the end of the war in January 1970. Instead, annual capital budgets were employed by the various Governments of the Federation as the main instrument of effective allocation and utilization of the country's resources.

The Second National Development Plan 1970–74 was launched in November 1970 with 1 April 1970 as the commencement date. The five principal national objectives set out in the Plan were to establish Nigeria firmly as (1) a united, strong and self-reliant nation; (2) a great and dynamic economy; (3) a just and egalitarian society; (4) a land of bright and full opportunities for all citizens; and (5) a free and democratic society.[11] The achievement of these national objectives, according to the authors of the Plan, required not only the control of some key sectors of the economy by the state, but more important, the use of planning 'as a deliberate weapon of social change by correcting defects in existing social relations in various spheres of production, distribution and exchange'. Launched shortly after the end of the Nigerian civil war, the Plan was a development programme as well as a plan for the reconstruction of the war-damaged economy.

The biggest single sector in the Plan was transportation with 23.7% of the total public sector programme and 30.1% of the Federal Government's programme. For the States, education constituted the largest single sector

(19.1%), and the second largest (13.5%) for the public sector as a whole. This was followed by agriculture (10.5%), defence and security (9.4%), industry (8.4%), and general administration (5.1%). However, actual expenditure for the 1970–74 Plan period turned out as follows: transportation 23.1%, education 11%, agriculture 7.7%, defence and security 10.4%, industry 3.9%, and general administration 10.8%.[12]

It is important to note in passing that although the Second Plan envisaged a total expenditure of ₦3.2 billion, the actual amount of money spent during the 1970–74 Plan period was ₦5.5 billion while the Federal and State Governments had capital estimates of ₦2.6 billion for the 1974–75 financial year. When private sector spending for 1974–75 and the spending of the statutory corporations are added to these figures, then the total capital investment spending for the extended Second Plan period of 1970–75 for both the public and private sectors was approximately ₦10 billion.[13] Thus, the ₦30 billion investment planned for the 1973–80 Plan period is only three times the size of the Second Plan and not ten times as is often maintained.[14]

Major Achievements Under the 1970–74 Plan

In physical terms, the achievements of the 1970–74 Plan period were quite impressive. Aside from the fact that most of the damaged facilities and industrial establishments were fully reactivated and in some cases substantially expanded, the industrial sector witnessed the setting up of new ventures. These include the two salt refineries at Ijoke and Sapele, the Peugeot motor car assembly plant in Kaduna and the Volkswagen one in Lagos. The construction of both the superphosphate fertiliser plant at Kaduna and the fishing trawling projects has also reached an advanced stage. The period also saw the construction of about 2,200 miles of road while contracts for the construction of the airports at Kano, Lagos, Jos, Ilorin, Calabar and Enugu were awarded. In the field of education, the achievements during the Second Plan period were phenomenal. Primary school enrolment which stood at 3.5 million in 1970 rose to 4.5 million in 1973 while secondary school enrolment rose from 343,000 in 1971 to 649,000 in 1974. University enrolment which stood at 14,500 in 1971 also rose to about 25,000 in 1974.

The Third National Development Plan 1975–80

The Third National Development Plan (1975–80) is the largest, most ambitious and imaginative development programme ever launched, not only in Nigeria but in the whole of Black Africa. The Plan, which was formally launched on 29 March 1975 by the then Head of State, Yakubu Gowon, envisages a total capital investment programme of ₦30 billion (₦30,000 million).[15] Of this gigantic amount, the Federal and State Governments and their agencies will account for ₦20 billion, or two-thirds, of the planned total expenditure while the private sector will be responsible for ₦10 billion, or one-third, of the total investment programme. This massive investment programme is expected to accelerate economic growth and development and promote a good standard of living for all Nigerians. Among other things the Gross Domestic Product, valued at 1974/75 cost, will increase from ₦14,411 million in 1974/75 to ₦22,692 million in 1979/80.[16] Other major parameters are as follows:

(1) The growth rate of the economy in real terms will average 9.5% per annum during the Plan period.

(2) Per capita income, in real terms, will increase by 36% between 1975 and 1980, that is from ₦205 to ₦274.[17]

(3) Private consumption will increase in real terms by approximately 10.5% per annum. This is expected to lead to the doubling of the standard of living of the average Nigerian in about seven years.

(4) The value of oil exports is estimated to increase from ₦6,458 million in 1974/75 to ₦10,633 million in 1979/80. For non-oil merchandise the corresponding figures are ₦304.3 million and ₦396.0 million respectively.

(5) Imports are projected to increase in value from ₦1,637.4 million in 1974/75 to ₦7,085.1 million in 1979/80. The structure of imports is also expected to change significantly during the Plan period. Capital goods and intermediate goods will account for about 70% of total imports in 1979/80 with consumer goods totalling only 26%.

(6) By the end of the Plan period, agriculture and mining will contribute 55.5% to the GDP while the other sectors will contribute 44.5%. The corresponding figures for 1974/75 are 68.9% and 31.1% respectively.

(7) In terms of sectoral allocation, 63.2% of planned public investment during the Plan period goes to the economic sector (i.e. agriculture, livestock, forestry and fishing, mining, industry, commerce and finance, fuel and power, transport and communications); 23.3% to the social sector, (welfare, town and country planning, water supply, sewerage and drainage, housing, co-operative and community development, and information); and 13.5% to general administration, defence and security. In other words over 85% of total public investment has been allocated to the socio-economic sectors.

(8) As far as sector by sector growth rates are concerned, education will lead with an average growth rate of 21.8%, followed by electricity and water supply (21%), building and construction (20.1%), health (20%), manufacturing (18%), mining and quarrying (15.3%) distribution (11.3%) and agriculture (5%).[18]

The philosophy underlying the Third Plan is still the five broad national objectives enunciated in the Second National Development Plan. Within the frame of reference of these national objectives, the specific short-term objectives to be achieved during the 1975–80 Plan period are (1) increase in per capita income; (2) more even distribution of income; (3) reduction in the level of unemployment; (4) increase in the supply of high level manpower; (5) diversification of the economy; (6) balanced development; and

(7) indigenization of economic activities.[19] To achieve these short-term objectives, the highest priorities are accorded to transportation, education industry, agriculture, urban development, communications and health. Table 1 below shows the relative importance of major public sector programmes.

Table 1
The Relative Importance of Major Public Sector Programmes

Sector	*Amount in Million of Naira*	*% of Total Public Capital Investment*
Transport	7,300.0	37.5
Education	2,500.0	12.5
Industry	2,300.0	11.5
Agriculture	2,200.0	11.0
Urban Development	1,800.0	9.0
Communications	1,300.0	6.5
Health	759.9	3.8
Water	612.6	3.1
Information	380.2	1.9
Co-operatives and Community Development	193.3	1.0
Social Development and Sports	139.6	0.6
Labour	43.2	0.2

Perhaps the boldest and most imaginative single project included in the Plan is the introduction of Universal Free Primary Education in 1976. This scheme, when fully implemented, will provide equal educational opportunities (at the primary school level) for all Nigerians. Under the scheme, primary school enrolment which now stands at about 5 million will rise to 11.5 million by 1980. An estimated 150,000 classrooms will be provided during the Plan period for pupils at a cost of ₦300 million. In the training of teachers, over 6,600 additional classrooms will be provided in Teacher Training Colleges for primary school teachers at a cost of ₦ 200 million. Other important programmes included in the Plan are (1) the establishment of four new universities at Calabar, Jos, Sokoto and Maiduguri, and the doubling by 1980 of university enrolment which at present stands at over 26,000; (2) the opening of 800 new secondary schools and the trebling by 1980 of the secondary school enrolment which now stands at approximately half a million; (3) the full implementation of the iron and steel project; (4) the setting up of two petroleum refineries at Warri and Kaduna; (5) the building of two liquified natural gas plants (each with a capacity of one million cubic feet per day); (6) the estabiishment of a petrol chemical complex and a nitrogenous fertilizer plant; (7) the provision of four new berths in each of the ports at Warri, Calabari, and Port Harcourt; and (8) the establishment of 12 new teaching hospitals, 110 new general hospitals, 1,400 health centres, 6,000 health clinics, and 1,500 mobile health clinics.

On paper, the 1975–80 Development Plan looks incisive and grandiose, and when compared to the First and Second National Development Plans, its magnitude, scope and dimension and staggering. If successfully implemented, it is bound to drastically transform the Nigerian economy and promote accelerated socio-economic development in the country. What is more, it is launched at the end of the successful reconstruction of the war-damaged economy and at a time when increased oil production in the country and unprecedented high prices of oil have made available more than enough resources to finance such a gigantic development programme.

Post-Independence Development Plans: Major Shortcomings

Despite their technical detail and professional competence, the post-independence Development Plans (particularly the First and Second National Development Plans) are not without major shortcomings. According to the former Federal Commissioner for Economic Development and Reconstruction, Professor Adebayo Adedeji, 'our development plans have tended to be prepared rather hastily, kept secret from the public until they are published, and their publications have invariably taken place several months after the commencement of the plan period.'[20] For instance, the 1962–68 Plan was not published until October 1962 even though it was deemed to have become operational from April 1962, while the 1970–74 Plan was published in November 1970 with April 1970 as the commencement date. Consequently, very little attempt was made by their authors to enlist the interest of the average citizen in the planning process or to evolve suitable media for communicating the Plans – i.e. their aims and priorities – to the masses. Even the participation of the intellectuals, professionals and other non-governmental groups, whose activities and experience can assist and enrich the national planning effort, was greatly restricted. In this respect, the planning exercise in Nigeria has until recently failed to satisfy the most important requirement of good and effective planning process. Apart from the apparent shortcoming of 'planning from above', discussion in the press, in professional bodies, and in public meetings can help elicit useful suggestions and stimulate interest and enthusiasm for a national plan. In India, for instance, the Planning Commission maintains a service of advisory and consultative committees with representatives of industry, commerce, labour and agriculture as well as panels of experts drawn from various professional groups.[21]

The absence of a well-defined and inclusive national ideology on which to base an overall development policy is another major deficiency in Nigeria's planning process. Although the five cardinal principles of national objectives, as enunciated in the Second National Development Plan, can be regarded as the underlying philosophy, these objectives have neither been set in sufficiently operational terms nor taken seriously by the public policy makers. They represent more of statements of policy objectives than a plan for action. The fact that none of these objectives has been achieved to any significant extent lends weight to this proposition. It is hardly surprising that 'more often than not, the intellectual framework of the Plans and the stated overall and sectoral policy objectives are nothing more than *ex post facto* rationalisations of the project mix as submitted by the executing ministries, statutory corporations and other agencies of government.[22] Furthermore, partly because of the small number of feasibility studies actually carried out and partly because of the paucity of reliable data,[23] most of the projects included in the plans are often based on intelligent guesses or inferences drawn from rather limited and sometimes superficial evidence.

Perhaps the most conspicuous shortcoming of Nigeria's planning process is the seriour distortions in plan implementation. Indeed, a review of economic activities both during the 1962–68 and the 1970–74 Plan periods reveals that the various Governments of the Federation do not adhere strictly to the spirit of their plans. Aside from the general tendency to channel the bulk of the available resources to low priority sectors (i.e., social and administrative), the planned allocations and expenditures often differed significantly from actual allocations and expenditures. In a majority of cases, new prestige projects were inserted on an *ad hoc* basis without any plan review exercise having been undertaken. The widespread failure of the political leaders and state functionaries to maintain the self-discipline and integrity implicit in the Plans, the inter-regional conflict and rivalry on industrial and project location, the failure of the plans to emphasise the development of adequate executive capacity, and the lack of effective and dynamic political leadership to galvanise all organs of government in a co-ordinated and purposeful national development effort also accounted for shortfalls in plan targets during this period.

One further point about Nigeria's Development Plans is their excessive reliance on foreign aid. During the 1962–68 Plan period, for instance, it was assumed that 50% of the capital investment would be financed from abroad. Yet only ₦171 million (out of the accepted six-year total of ₦678 million) came from external sources during the first four years of the Plan.[24] Although the 1970–74 Plan tried to play down the need for foreign capital aid (only 19.4% of the public sector capital investment was to be financed from abroad), it emphasised the need for technical assistance. This is also true of the 1975–80 Plan which calls for large-scale importation of foreign technical and specialized manpower during the Plan period. This high reliance of the development plans on foreign aid not only introduces some element of uncertainty into the planning process, but also slows down the process of plan inplementation.

Although, as Adedeji shows, the Third Development Plan's preparation was a great improvement on the previous ones, some of its priorities are hardly justifiable in terms of allocations of available funds.[25] For instance, agriculture with a sectoral allocation of ₦2.2 billion looks quite impressive when compared to previous allocations. But when measured against the gigantic measures that should be taken to revolutionize agriculture, the allocation becomes less impressive. Besides, the measures proposed in the Plan such as loans to farmers, extension schemes and government's participation in agriculture are outdated methods which have not proved too successful in other places. Similarly, the allocation of ₦7.3 billion to transportation when health receives only ₦759.9 million and education ₦2.5 billion leaves much to be desired. One wonders how the authors of the Plan intend to implement the various health and educational projects spelled out in the Plan with these allocations. While we do not deny the need for massive investment in the transport sector, we find it difficult to justify the allocation to this sector, particularly when compared to other equally important sectors.

Allocations apart, the targets set out in the educational sector are not ambitious enough. Despite the fact that the manpower implications of the Plan are far-reaching, only primary education will be free from 1976. What is more, there is a great imbalance between secondary education on the one hand and primary education on the other. The Plan aims at only a total secondary school enrolment of 1.5 million in 1980 compared with 11.5 million primary school enrolment.[26] The university expansion programme which aims at increasing university enrolment to 53,000 in 1980 is, to say the least, quite modest.

The Planning Machinery

Although no universal formula for the administration of planned development exists, all empirical evidence tends to suggest that without adequate institutional and organizational arrangements for the formulation and execution of development programmes, even the most sophisticated development plan has little chance of being successfully carried out. Aside from the fact that planning is an integral part of the administrative process,[27] the dominant role played by the governments of developing countries in the national development process requires an immediate reorganization and revitalization of the bureaucratic system, as well as the creation of a multiplicity of planning and economic institutions and agencies. In Nigeria, the list of such institutions and agencies is quite impressive.

The National Economic Council

On the recommendation of the International Bank Mission to Nigeria, the National Economic Council (NEC) was set up in 1955 to provide 'a forum in which the Federation and the Regions might meet to discuss the many economic problems common to each . . . as many have consequences reaching beyond their respective constitutional spheres'.[28] In other words, the principal tasks of the Council were to co-ordinate the national development efforts and to examine the principal problems affecting the social and economic development of the country. It was composed of the Governor-General (and later the Prime Minister) as Chairman, all Regional Premiers, five Federal Ministers, four Ministers from each Region, together with the Economic Adviser to the Federal Government. It met infrequently and most of its functions was carried out by *ad hoc* inter-ministerial committees set up from time to time to deal with specific matters.

The Joint Planning Committee

Established under the aegis of the NEC in 1958 was the Joint Planning Committee (JPC). This body, which consisted exclusively of civil servants drawn from the Federal and Regional Public Services under the Chairmanship of the Federal Economic Adviser, was to (1) examine and report upon any matters remitted to it by the NEC or by individual governments of the Federation; (2) advise the NEC in particular in all matters related to economic planning and co-ordination; and (3) assist the various governments of the federation in the preparation of studies, reports and surveys, and in the collation, co-ordination and dissemination of information.[29] Among the important reports prepared by the Committee was the 1959 Economic Survey of Nigeria.

Other Planning Bodies

A variety of other bodies existed, though some met infrequently, and exercised little real power.[30] These included the Loan Advisory Council and the Ministerial Economic Committee. Composed of the Federal and Regional Ministers of Finance and their Permanent Secretaries, the Loan Advisory Council was set up as a consultative agency to consider the appointment for federal and regional purposes of money raised by loan, particularly foreign loan, all of which had to be raised by the Federal Government.[31] The Ministerial Economic Committee, a body of eight Cabinet ministers especially concerned with plan implementation, had important functions regarding the annual capital estimates and was the final authority with regard to their composition. The Committee was dissolved in 1964.

Ministry of Economic Development

Following the country's attainment of political independence in October 1960, a Ministry of Economic Development was set up both at the centre and in the regions. The Federal Ministry of Economic Development, apart from one of its divisions serving as the permanent secretariat to the NEC and JPC, is also the central planning agency and the chief co-ordinator of all technical assistance and external economic relations.[32] Its Economic Planning Unit (which has now been expanded into a central Planning Office staffed with a cadre of professional planners and economists outside the general pool of administrators, and headed by a Director) had only a skeleton staff of nine Nigerian economists, mostly very young and inexperienced, assisted by three foreign economic advisers when the 1962–68 Plan was being prepared.[33] It is this Unit that was (and still is) responsible for all the technical aspects of development policies including the preparation of plan documents, as well as for plan co-ordination and control. The Ministry however, has no constitutional or statutory authority to demand compliance with its directives. During its formative years, the Ministry suffered from frequent ministerial changes. It has, until recently, been faced with the formidable problem of recruiting staff, particularly trained economists, statisticians and professional planners.

Manpower Development Board

Following the recommendation of a Commission set up in 1961 by the Federal Government under the chairmanship of Sir Eric Ashby, the National Economic Council approved the establishment of a Manpower Development Board for the purpose of assessing the century's manpower need and formulating programmes for manpower development throughout the federation on a continuing basis.[34] The Board which came into existence in 1962 (with its secretariat as part of the Planning Unit of the Federal Ministry of Economic Development) is composed of the Permanent Secretary, Federal Ministry of Economic Development as Chairman, and the representatives of the Federal and Regional Ministries of Education, Labour, Economic Development as well as the representatives of the universities, the Employers' Association, and the trade unions. Under its terms of reference, the Board is responsible for both the determination of the nation's manpower needs in all occupations and the formulation of appropriate policies and programmes for manpower development and utilisation. Similar bodies were established at the regional (now state) level to act as feedback agents to the National Manpower Board.

Ministry of Finance

Another federal ministry that is directly connected with development planning is the Ministry of Finance. In addition to its wide powers of budgeting and expenditure, the Ministry is the final authority with regard to external borrowing and foreign financial aid.[35] The federal powers over company income tax, import and export duties, excise duties and royalties are also exercised through the Ministry. Furthermore, as provided in the Finance (Control and Management) Act of 1958, no federal ministry can spend funds without a warrant issued by the Ministry of Finance. Before the 1966 coup, the Ministry was also responsible for the preparation of the annual capital estimates. But unlike its exclusive control of the recurrent expenditure, it shared the responsibility for the capital estimates with two other bodies: the Permanent Committee of Officials (a small committee of top civil servants drawn from the Ministries of Works and Surveys, Economic Development and Finance under the chairmanship of the Secretary to the Prime Minister), and the Ministerial Economic Committee.

Other Federal ministries closely connected with economic development include Trade, Industry, Commerce, Works and Surveys, as well as Transport and Aviation. The latter has the final responsibility over four public corporations: the Ports Authority, Railways, Airways, and the National Shipping Line. In addition, all Federal and Regional (now state) Ministries are spending agencies in charge of projects and programmes which fall within their respective areas of jurisdiction.

Organisational Developments since 1966

Following the January 1966 military coup, both the National Economic Council and the Joint Planning Committee as well as similarly constituted bodies were formally abolished. One of the first institutional changes announced by the short-lived Ironsi Administration was the establishment in March 1966 of the National Economic Planning Advisory Group. Composed of 10 members selected mainly in their private capacities (there was no regional representation) under the chairmanship of Chief S.O. Adebo (then Nigeria's Permanent Representative at the UN), with Dr. P.N.C. Okigbe (then Economic Adviser to the Federal Military Government) as Deputy Chairman, the Group's Secretariat was located in the Cabinet Office. In addition to advising the Federal Government 'on the harmonious development of the national economy', the Group was specifically charged with the responsibility of (1) reviewing the progress of the economy since independence; (2) identifying the critical points that require urgent governmental action or modification of existing policies and recommending possible measures; and (3) making projections into the future and submitting recommendations about the direction of long-run economic policies.[36] Although the renewed political crisis and hostilities of July 1966 brought the activities of the Group to a premature end, it had during its short life advised the Federal Military Government on the 1966–67 capital estimates and on the Guidelines for the Second National Development Plan.

The creation of the 12 states in May 1967 by General Yakubu Gowon radically changed the political context of national planning and co-ordination. Since then, the Supreme Military Council, with all the state military governors and other top military and police personnel as members, and the Head of the Federal Military Government as Chairman, has assumed final authority for co-ordinating the state and the federal development plans and for laying down from time to time the broad guidelines for the national development planning.

At the official level, a Joint Planning Board has been established to (1) harmonize and co-ordinate the economic policies and development activities of the federal and state governments and their agencies; and (2) examine in detail all aspects of economic planning and make recommendations through the appropriate authorities to the Supreme Military Council or the respective state governments as the case may be.[37] The membership of the Board is made up of the Permanent Secretary, Federal Ministry of Economic Development and Reconstruction as Chairman; Director, Central Planning Office; the Chief Statistician, Federal Office of Statistics; the Director, Nigerian

Institute of Social and Economic Research; the Director of Research, Central Bank; the Permanent Secretary, Federal Ministry of Finance; and the Permanent Secretary, Ministry of Economic Planning from each of the states.[38]

Three advisory bodies have recently been established as part of the new planning machinery.[39] The first, the National Council for Management Education and Training, whose membership is drawn from among the senior officials of the Economic Development Ministries, the universities and the private sector, is set up to advise the Federal Military Government on all matters related to the development of administrative and managerial capacity in the country. The second, the National Economic Advisory Council composed of representatives of the employers' associations, the trade unions, the chambers of commerce, the universities, professional associations, research organisations, and a number of public and private agencies, is to advise the Federal Government on all matters related to economic planning, co-ordination and control. Finally, there is the National Advisory Committee on Statistics. Under the chairmanship of the Chief Statistician, this body is composed of representatives of the Federal Ministry of Economic Development and Reconstruction, the Nigerian Institute of Social and Economic Research, the National Manpower Board, the Central Bank, the chambers of commerce as well as representatives of industry and the universities. The Committee is to 'provide a forum for the review by producers and users of statistical data of the activities and other programmes of the Federal Office of Statistics and other agencies collecting and disseminating statistical information' and to 'advise the Federal Office of Statistics on questions relating to the scope and format of official statistics and other matters of statistical policy.[40]

Other bodies worth mentioning here are the regular meetings of the Commissioners responsible for economic development in the Federation, and the annual conferences of the senior planning officials from both the federal and state Ministries of Economic Development. The combined effect of all these institutions and agencies is to make for better quality planning, for participation by more people (particularly from the private sector) in the planning process, and for better and more effective co-ordination in the preparation and implementation of the development plans.[41]

General Appraisal of the Planning Machinery

The legal status and organizational structure of the central planning machinery and its relationship to economic policy-making and plan implementation are currently the subject of much discussion and controversy among leading students of economic and development administration.[42] It is not our intention here to deal with these problems extensively except in so far as they impinge on effective planning in Nigeria.

In a poly-ethnic society like Nigeria, unevenly developed and with a low degree of national unity, it is difficult for anyone to say that some of the above planning organisations and agencies played an effective and creative role in the national planning process during the 1955–62 and 1962–68 plan periods. In spite of the tremendous potential for economic leadership from the centre, both the National Economic Council and the Joint Planning Committee were little more than loose coalitions of vested and powerful individuals representing regional interests. There was also the problem of lack of effective feedback mechanism and continuity in personnel. Most of those who participated in their deliberations were not directly involved in the formulation and execution of the national development programmes. Furthermore, with the exception of the Federal Economic Adviser, no member of the JPC was at the same time a member of the N E C. An overlap in membership, as the authors of the Second National Development Plan have pointed out, would have greatly strengthened the two-way communication process between the two planning agencies.[43]

The Federal Ministry of Economic Development is also poorly organised to function effectively as the central planning agency. Not only does it lack clearly defined organizational precepts for its efficient responsibilities and inadequate constitutional or statutory authority. Although its Economic Planning Unit is solely responsible for the preparation of plan documents, the Ministry has no effective voice in the formulation of monetary and fiscal policies and in the design of administrative measures necessary for plan implementation. Even its responsibility for arranging external technical assistance is shared with the Ministry of Finance, while the latter is also the final authority with regard to foreign capital assistance. What is more, the Ministry is seriously handicapped by the acute shortage of qualified personnel. The low starting salaries and gradings make it rather difficult for the Ministry to attract and retain competent economists, statisticians and other planning personnel.

Another major deficiency of the planning machinery before 1966 was its inadequate provision for organizational arrangements for inter-ministerial and inter-governmental co-ordination and consultation. It is important to stress the fact that development planning puts a special premium on co-ordination and co-operation within and outside government. The NEC and JPC which could have performed these functions were ineffective because of their composition and lack of proper feedback mechanism. Furthermore, no attempt was made before the 1966 reorganisation of the Ministry of Economic Development to incorporate in the planning machinery special institutions charged with the responsibility for preparing high-quality feasibility studies on a continuing basis,[44] and ensuring that the sequence in which planned projects are put forward for foreign aid conforms to the national objectives and development priorities.

Summary and Conclusion

For the formulation and execution of economic development plans, Nigeria has, even before independence, established a network of administrative organizations and agencies which are directly or indirectly concerned with economic planning and policy co-ordination. It is important to note, however, that for a post-colonial state like Nigeria, and a federation which lacks any high concentration of power and institutions for enforcing compliance with development plans, the influence of planning on the overall national development is minimal. This is indicated by the gap between promise and performance.

Apart from the problem of lack of development-oriented administrative capacity and honest and dedicated political leadership, the cultural and ethnic diversities as well as inter-group tensions and animosities have prevented the emergence of a broadly-based political consensus or clearly perceived national objectives. The perennial problem of overlapping jurisdictions and conflicting sets of responsibilities among the government ministries and agencies concerned with planned development also reflects the practical difficulties in the way of ensuring inter-ministerial, inter-governmental, and inter-sectoral co-ordination and co-operation. Under such circumstances, development plans may be little more than 'symbolic ritualism' or 'utopian dreaming' – to borrow words from Bertram M. Gross.

Central to the correction of some of the problems facing planned development in Nigeria is the setting up of a small but powerful National Planning Commission to act as the final co-ordinating authority and to determine national objectives and development priorities. Such a body should consist of the Heads of the various governments of the Federation, their respective Commissioners (or Ministers) of Economic Development and Finance, elder statesmen, distinguished planners and economists, and representatives of labour, industry and agriculture. Under the chairmanship of the Head of State, it would be authoritative as well as persuasive. The Commission, to together with the recently-established Joint Planning Board, would provide high-level agencies to consider all questions relating to economic planning, and to ensure co-operation between the Federal and the State Governments, and between the public and the private sectors.

The second relevant lesson of Nigeria's planning experience is the fact that the preparation of a sophisticated macro-economic plan is of little significance unless the society concerned has the determination and the executive capacity to execute and operate development projects and programmes needed to give effect to the plan's targets. A rigorous examination of the adequacy of the governmental and administrative machinery should therefore be an essential part of the planning process. Once it is accepted that the political and administrative elements are as crucial for rapid economic development as the so-called hard economic facts, then it becomes imperative that administrative developments and institutional reforms should precede and set the necessary framework for economic and social development. Besides, planning must be regarded as a dynamic process in which any plans which may be developed must be monitored and revised as necessary in response to changing needs and circumstances.

Another important lesson to be drawn from Nigeria's past planning experience is the fact that she will have to rely more and more on domestic sources of revenue in the years ahead. The dramatic shortfall in foreign aid during the first plan period has already been noted. It is therefore imperative that the various governments of the Federation should increase their efforts to expand exports, mobilise and effectively utilise the country's scarce resources, and arrive at a better distribution of the national wealth. There is also the urgent need for a thorough re-examination of other public policies impinging on economic development. These include wages, income distribution policy, manpower development and utilisation, private foreign investment, indigenization and nationalization, and exchange control. Above all, there must be a radical change in the attitude of some Nigerian leaders towards the country's academics, the professionals and other talented individuals if the massive public investment is to bring the anticipated progress. In the past, highly qualified and outstanding Nigerians have not always been selected for important public offices because they are regarded either as non-conformists or as individuals who cannot be easily manipulated.

References

1. Compare Goran Hyden *et al*. (eds.); *Development Administration*: the *Kenyan experience* (Nairobi: Oxford University Press, 1970), p. xiii.
2. This analytical framework is adapted from Robert M. Jackson, 'Planning, Politics and Administration' in Hyden, *op. cit*., pp. 171–2;
3. The end of the Second World War witnessed the first serious attempts at colonial planning as expressed in the United Kingdom's Colonial Paper No. 3 on Development Planning (1944) and the Colonial Development and Welfare Act of 1945. The latter instructed each colony to prepare a ten-year development plan. For detailed treatment of the colonial planning, see Barbu Nicolescu, *Colonial Planning* (London: Allen and Unwin, 1958).
4. For detailed treatment of the origins of planning in Nigeria, see *Second National Development Plan 1970–74* (Lagos, 1970), p. 6; Sayre P. Schatz, 'The Influence of Planning on Development: The Nigerian Experience', *Social Research*, 27, 4 (Winter 1960); and Peter Kilby, *Industrialization in an Open Economy: Nigeria 1945–1966* (Cambridge: Cambridge University Press, 1969), Chapters 1 and 2.
5. The 1955–60 Plan consisted of five separate programmes – a Federal Government programme and four Regional programmes – without any pretensions at central co-ordination and control. See the 'Economic Programmes of the Governments of the Federation of Nigeria, 1955–60', *Sessional Paper No. 2 of 1956* (Lagos, 1956).
6. *National Development Plan, 1962–68* (Lagos 1962), p.6.
7. O. Aboyade, 'Problems in Plan Revision', *Nigerian Journal of Economic and Social Studies*, 7, 2 (1965), p. 126.
8. House of Representatives *Debates*, March 1962, p. 393.
9. *National Development Plan 1962–68*, p. 23.

10. For an excellent discussion of the main features of the 1962–68 Development Plan, see Peter B. Clark, 'Economic Planning for a Country in Transition: Nigeria', E.E. Hagen (ed.) *Planning Economic Development* (Homewood, III: Richard D. Irwin, 1963); S.P. Schatz, 'Nigeria's First National Development Plan (1962–68): An Appraisal', *Nigerian Journal of Economic and Social Studies*, 5, 2 (1963) and W.F. Stolper. 'The Main Features of the 1962–68 National Plan' *Nigerian Journal of Economic and Social Studies*, 4, 2 (July 1962).
11. *Second National Development Plan 1970–74*, p. 32.
12. V.P. Diejomach, 'Comparative Analysis of Second and Third Plans', *Daily Times*, 8 May 1973.
13. *Ibid.*
14. The ten-fold increase is derived by simply comparing the ₦3.2 billion originally planned for 1970–74 plan period to the ₦30 billion planned for 1975–80.
15. *Address by His Excellency General Yakubu Gowon on the Occasion of the Formal Launching of the Third National Development Plan, 1975–80* (Lagos, 1975).
16. At current prices the GDP will be ₦29.66 billion in 1979/80.
17. At current prices per capita income will be ₦371 in 1979/80.
18. Opening Statement by the Federal Commissioner for Economic Development and Reconstruction, Professor Adebayo Adedeji, at the Press Conference held in Lagos on 5th April 1975 on the Third National Development Plan 1975–80.
19. *Third National Development Plan* (Lagos, 1975).
20. See Chapter 4.
21. Albert Waterston, *Development Planning: Lessons of Experience* (Baltimore: The Johns Hopkins University Press, 1965), p. 579.
22. See Chapter 4.
23. For an extended exposition of this problem, see W.F. Stolper, *Planning Without Facts* (Harvard University Press, 1966).
24. Edwin Dean, 'Non-economic Barriers to Effective Planning in Nigeria, 1962–68', *Economic Development and Cultural Change*, 19, 4 (1971). However, this deficiency in foreign aid was partly due to the slow rate of disbursement of foreign aid funds offered because of the bottleneck in executive capacity.
25. For an extended exposition of this problem see S. Aluko. 'Third Plan: Consequences of Disproportionate Allocations', *Daily Times*, 23 April 1975.
26. For other deficiencies of the educational sector see Segun Adesina 'Is 3rd Plan's Educational Projection Realistic?', *Sunday Times*, 27 April 1975.
27. Planning was the first of the seven administrative processes in Luther Gulick's famous POSDCORE, i.e. Planning, Organising, Staffing, Directing, Co-ordinating, Reporting, Budgeting. It was also one of the five elements of administration identified by Henri Fayel: Planning and Forecasting, Organising, Commanding, Co-ordinating and Controlling.
28. *Second National Development Plan 1970–74*, p. 7.
29. *Ibid.*

30. Edwin Dean, *Plan Implementation in Nigeria, 1962–1966* (Ibadan: Oxford University Press, 1972), p. 42.
31. Taylor Cole, 'Emergent Federation in Nigeria', in Robert O. Tilman and Taylor Cole (eds.), *The Nigerian Political Scene* (Durham, N.C.: Duke University Press, 1968), p. 55.
32. The Federal Ministry of Economic Development is now known as the Ministry of Economic Development and Reconstruction.
33. United Nations, 'Administration of Planning in Nigeria' (Paper prepared for the Meeting of Experts on Administrative Aspects of National Development Planning, Paris, 8–11 June 1964, mimeo). Other important sections of the Ministry included the Economic Division (which until 1966 served as the Secretariat to the NEC and the JPC), the Technical Assistance Division, the Research Division, the National Manpower Board, and the Federal Office of Statistics. Following the 1966 administrative reorganisation of the Ministry, the Economic Division was abolished and, in its place,.the External Economic Relations Division was created. The Economic Planning Unit itself was sub-divided into six sections, including those concerned with Plan Coordination, Progress Report, Projects Evaluation, Resources, and Perspective Planning.
34. *Second National Development Plan 1970–74*, p. 7. The National Universities Commission, attached to the Cabinet Office, was also established in 1962.
35. 'Assignment of Responsibilities to (Federal) Ministries, Government Notice No. 748, Federal Republic of Nigeria', *Official Gazette*, Vol. 52, No. 33, 9 April 1965. The Ministry of Finance also shares with Economic Development the responsibility for arranging for external technical assistance.
36. *Second National Development Plan 1970–74*, pp. 8–9.
37. *Ibid.*, p. 10
38. *Ibid.*
39. Other bodies which have recently been established include the National Agricultural Council, the National Electric Power Authority, Kainji Lake Development Commission, the National Supply Company, the Iron and Steel Authority, the National Oil Corporation, the National Highway Authority, the National Agricultural Credit Bank, and the Bank of Commerce and Industry.
40. *Second National Development Plan 1970–74*, p. 8.
41. See Chapter 4.
42. See, for instance, Ronald Robinson (ed.), *African Development Planning; Impressions and Papers of the Cambridge Conference on Development Planning* (Queen's College, Cambridge, 1963), pp. 45–6 and 52–9.
43. *Second National Development Plan, 1970–74*, p. 7.
44. In this connection, E.R. Dean has suggested the use of the staff of universities and research institutions to reinforce the staff of the Economic Planning Unit of the Minstry of Economic Development and Reconstruction. See his 'Factors Impeding the Implementation of Nigeria's Six-Year Plan', pp. 127–8.

3. Political Constraints on Planning: The Second National Development Plan

James O'Connell

Introduction: Distinguishing Means and Ends

It is to some degree inevitable that the economic conditions of planning – ranging from feasbility studies of individual projects to the availability of foreign exchange – should dominate approaches to developmental planning. Yet where an economic outlook on planning dominates excessively, there is a tendency to regard political factors as either obstacles to rationality in planning that have to be overcome or as irrelevancies that are best diplomatically avoided. But in the last resort planning decisions are political. Political leaders (in or out of uniform) are normally limited by the technical possibilities that their economists present to them. But they tend to make their choice among those possibilities according to ideas on the use of power that include many factors besides the economic.

This paper sets out to concentrate on certain aspects of the politics of the planning process: political constraints on planning. Inevitably, this approach has an unsatisfying side because much of its emphasis is negative. However, though the politics of planning ranges wider than dealing with constraints (what politics is unlikely to let planners do), the constraints are worth reflecting on. They are not extrinsic to the planning process but enter into its setting of priorities and condition the implementing of priorities. Indeed only by taking constraints into account are economists likely to present political leaders and others involved in planning with alternatives that are socially feasible as well as technically sound.

A more positive way of presenting the approach of this paper is to say that it takes a look at what political resources are available for planning.[1] No economist would dare plan without mapping as best he could the available economic resources. But in the more emotive atmosphere of politics, methods and ends are more easily confused with one another than in economics. Hence, there is the temptation to assume that those political resources exist at the outset of a planning period which at best could only be hoped for towards the end of the period – and sometimes not even then. It is no small part of socio-economic planning to seek to deepen national unity, foster stable government, and improve administrative processes. One of the merits of the present Nigerian Plan is its conscious effort to reach such goals. But these ends are also means; they are resources that economists and others draw on to implement planning. If planners assume that these resource resources exist in a degree that exceeds their effective availability, they are likely to place burdens on government and administration that the latter cannot carry. Yet the fact is that planners in new countries are usually more willing to concede that economic resources are wanting than they are ready to acknowledge that political resources are scarce. Appealing to national sentiments, for example, is a most useful way to get populations to accept sacrifices for the sake of future progress. But it is unrealistic to assume that national sentiments exist as a driving force among leaders, civil servants and the general populace in countries where such primordial sentiments centre for most persons on the local communities rather than on the state. In short, it makes much sense to settle for existing resources such as they are and to try to expand them. If that is done, it is possible to avoid confusing the real with the ideal, what 'exists' with what 'should be', and means with ends.

The present Nigerian document[2] presents a picture of what is often called comprehensive planning. Its approach is, in fact, more ambitious than most:

> The Plan sets out clearly the National Objectives and Priorities of post-war Nigeria. It also outlines the general policy measures and programmes of action which flow from the Objectives as well as the agreed national scale of priorities.
> The Second National Development Plan has to be implemented by the Governments as well as the people of this country; all public sector institutions as well as private sector and individual initiatives will be involved in the execution of the Plan in one way or the other. Much sacrifice will be demanded of all sections of the community. The reward lies in the viable national economy which is expected to emerge half-way through the Plan period and from the years of the civil war. All Nigerians must be made to feel part of, and share from, the resultant buoyant economy . . .
> National Planning should be aimed at the transformation of the whole society, and must be directed at the power centres of economic and political decisions . . . The Plan views the whole national economy as one interdependent unit, growing through time in response to a set of mutually consistent policies and programmes. It starts from the position that total developmental resources must be mobilized and allocated by reference to common decision criteria that run through all sectors of the economy (pp. 5, 31, 39).

The Plan itself – not to mention a planning exercise that took place with little consultation[3] – does not bear out this concept of a mobilization and allocation of 'total developmental resources'. Moreover, it does not *demand* 'sacrifice' of all sections of the community – not least but because most sections of the community have bever even *heard* of the Plan, and hardly any of those who have know what is in it. Finally, the concept of government and administration suggested in the Plan for its implementation transcends what governmental leadership and administrative capacity Nigeria have up-to-date possessed and it does not at all fit the actual descriptions of existing government and administration that the Plan on occasion permits itself to give. Obviously, a Plan document may indulge in some rhetoric. But one might suggest that key passages that spell out approaches to objectives and methods mislead dangerously when they outline possibilities that are far beyond the power of planning to achieve.[4] One of the main contentions of this paper is that no plan in a developing country should be expected to reach such hyperbolic goals. If the second Plan does not reach them, it needs in no way be called a failure. But it would be better to state aims more modestly and more realistically. Flamboyance is sometimes defended in terms of political technique. But good politics tends to be flamboyant in style rather than in content.

If one were to take seriously the intentions outlined in this second Nigerian Plan, they would involve something like the following processes:
(1) Growth of the public sector to the point where it dominates the private sector;
(2) Extensive participation by government in directly growth-producing projects in industry and agriculture;
(3) Detailed control over the decisions of the private sector;
(4) Extensive development of the infrastructure by government – roads and communications, education, health, etc;
(5) Technical descriptions of how objectives are to be achieved;
(6) Consultation and projects at the level of the smallest social units – villages and clusters of villages.

But if this kind of planning is to be possible, certain basic political and administrative conditions need to be met. These conditions may be grouped under three headings:
(1) The political community needs already to possess a sense of solidarity such that trust exists between its various sections; and the uneven impact of development or competition for development must not be likely to deepen existing social cleavages.
(2) A basic affinity needs to exist between people and government such that the latter can ask citizens to make sacrifices and the latter will make the them without excessively reckoning the cost.
(3) A country has to possess a large, skilled and committed public service that strives to serve the population, that has a vivid sense of the urgency of economic growth,[5] and knows how to control private initiative without stifling it.

This paper argues that Nigeria fulfils none of these conditions: Nigeria is not a tight-knit political community; it cannot expect a deep attachment from its people to government; and it does not possess an exceptionally well-equipped administration. As Wolfgang Stolper has written with a slightly different emphasis: 'Government must operate under several limitations. There is first the recalcitrant nature of the economy. There is second the fact that we deal with plural societies. There is thirdly the lack of sufficient numbers of well-trained people, capable of running things'.[6] However, there does exist in Nigeria a sense of political community; its peoples are willing to accept being governed; and its administration is among the best in the developing world. In other words, this paper argues that it is in the proportion that political community exists, government is accepted, and administration is competent that planning is possible. What planning needs to do is to make its estimate of these factors and set its goals accordingly. In practice much of the second Plan, especially those parts of it that look as if the planners expect them to be implemented, conveys a realistic approach to planning possibilities. But a document does damage its general credibility when it asserts unrealistic objectives (like many in the passages already cited) and makes unrealistic assumptions.

In short, there is a good case for trying to spell out what kind of political community a country like Nigeria is, how much government is likely to be tried and accepted, and what administration may be able to take on. If this can be done with fair accuracy, economists may be able to propose economic development with a more conscious awareness of the possibilities and limits of planning.

The Body Politic and Planning

Planning is organized within the state – the political community in which people combine to pursue an ideal of welfare, maintain law and order, and carry on external relations with similarly constituted communities. In the Western World for about a century and a half until recently, a form of social solidarity has been generated around the state which has been called nationalism. Nationalistic sentiments of solidarity fostered beliefs in a convergence of interests among all members of the state (even where interests manifestly did not converge) and rationalized sacrifice on the part of all the members of the state to achieve ends proposed by the ruling groups as essential to the national good. Since planning of its essence requires that present consumption be subordinated to future growth and that private interests serve the public good, nationalism seems an obvious sentiment for planners to appeal to, even in the new countries of the developing world.

The Nigerian planners make their appeals to nationalism. They lament that what 'Nigeria lacked most in the past has been the national sense of purpose, particularly in economic matters' (p. 32). They want the 'new nation to march forward in progress' and to 'accept and work for the realization of a set of national objectives' (pp. 31–32). They rightly point out that the 'pursuit of a strong and united nation, as a fundamental social aim, is the very antithesis of secession or the exploitation of ethnic group, class and similar sentiments' (p.32). They frankly accept 'economic nationalism', and they also say that the 'uncompromising objective of a rising economic prosperity in Nigeria is the economic independence of the nation and the defeat of neo-colonial forces in Africa' (pp. 33, 32). The trouble is that ideals of this kind may make much sense to a planning and bureaucratic elite. They make much less sense to those parts of the intelligentsia that have done less well out of independence and they touch the common people even less. It is easier to borrow structures from the West than to borrow ideals. This kind of old-fashioned European nationalism has not developed in most new states. The 'reactive nationalism' of the colonial independence movements was a different variety from the European kind. And in historic fact it is almost certainly both too late and too soon to hope for or to seek to create state nationalism in West Africa.[7]

It is too late because in the modern inter-connected world political organization exclusively organized around the state is being profoundly modified – the European Economic Community is in this respect a symbol of the fundamental changes taking place in a part of the world where nationalism took its rise and enjoyed its hey-day. However, important as it is to realize that the sovereign state no longer exists – if ever it did – in a pure form, the state remains an important – and in the developing countries the most important form – of organization for achieving economic ends within the international system.[8] Planners may, in fact, be able to draw on sentiments that come from the period of 'reactive nationalism' and propose forms of self-respect and self-reliance to their citizens. But they cannot afford to ignore the inter-connected nature of the world economy or indulge in prestigeful forms of economic nationalism that impose unnecessary burdens on their own citizens. Moreover, scholarship, mass media and social contacts have conveyed to West Africans how cultural similarities and affinities stretch across frontiers in the sub-continent and how little foundation concepts of distinctiveness through the state possess. In short, more than ever before in history it is clear that the state is an organizational device for the sake of common order and social welfare (Aristotle's 'life' and 'good life'). We should hope for and expect fellowship to grow within it. But we should not put too much strain on this fellowship and not confuse it with the primordial sentiments of nationalism in the European past or believe it is in any way as strong as ethnicity or communalism in the Nigerian present.[9]

But it is also too soon for this kind of state nationalism in new countries for several simple reasons: the traditions and languages of the peoples differ too much from one another; they have not lived long enough together as have the Normans, the Bretons and the Burgundians; and they were not welded into a nation by their common colonial experience. Nigeria at best forms a multi-national state in which the basic, social and cultural traditions are national and in which nationalism (in the sense of sentimental attachment to the body politic), though it has begun to grow, is going to remain weak for years to come. Loyalty to the state will take a place behind several other social loyalties. The attempted secession by one people underlines this contention. It seems not unreasonable to think that only the absence of a suitable combination of political, economic, demographic and geographical circumstances (region, oil, population numbers and strategic location) prevented similar attempts by other nations or ethnic groups.[10]

Moreover, apart from the distinctiveness of many cultural traditions that radically impede the creation of a nation-state and its historical sentiment, the nations do not simply co-exist with one another within the state. Rather they compete – or, more accurately, their educated members compete – for jobs and promotions for themselves and amenities for their areas of origin. Ethnicity offers the most useful Group boundary on the state level for competitive social organization. Coinciding as this boundary does with language and culture, inter-ethnic competition or tribalism damages communication badly between socially mobilized persons and fossilizes the injured relations in group stereotypes. The result of poor inter-ethnic relations is a breakdown of trust that corrosively poisons relations between groups and that destroys any easy assumption that the growth in prosperity of the state involves a growth in prosperity of the various groups within the state. The Plan is perfectly right to say that the 'prospect of the citizen in the process of economic development and social change should not be determined by the mere accident of the circumstances of his birth (class, social status, ethnic group or state)' (p. 33). But given the communal cleavages in Nigeria and differing access to political power and representation in administration, it is very difficult to persuade Nigerian citizens or groups of them that social justice is readily available or that the national cake after it is baked is likely to be distributed equitably. Under such circumstances planners need to be careful in asking people to make sacrifices. And they clearly have been careful.

Yet though it does not seem to be too useful to appeal to a barely existent nationalism for solidarity in the development effort, at least, there is a rational basis for such solidarity since a minimum amount of it is needed to make social and economic co-operation possible in the state. Planning that is well thought out, that is the result of long consultation and hard-bargained give-and-take, and that can be shown to result in real growth may go a long way towards healing ethnic divisions and overcoming tribalism. 'Emphasis has been placed on growth as a pre-condition for a meaningful distribution of the fruits of development. . . But distribution is no less important for a country dedicated to the objectives of national unity and social integration. It also affects subsequent rates of growth in real output in terms of incentives for people to identify their interests with those of the nation and to give of their best to the development process' (p. 33). Some aspects of this may be put in another way. Tribalistic divisions are at their worst where the individuals think in terms of a static economy – a national cake baked once and for all and for whose slices persons are desperately scrambling before they disappear. The edge goes off bitterness where people realize that an economy is growing and that new opportunities are constantly becoming available. A well-thought-out and thoroughly carried out planning exercise may be a most useful political instrument of conciliation between ethnic groups as well as a most useful device in promoting economic growth.

Political Will-To-Rule and Planning[11]

In the previous section the newness of political community – or the untraditional company with which many groups find themselves in the state – was stressed. But government in its present form is itself new. Its impersonal and overriding capacity to adjudicate on all matters beyond the village (and in principle on matters even within the village) is new and strange. So is its considerable power of patronage in the distribution of amenities as well as its right to require taxes that do not always appear correlated with amenities.[12] Since little or no sentimental attachment to government – rather the contrary – existed during the colonial period, new governments have not only to create attachment to themselves but to reverse previous disaffection for government, especially in the terminal colonial period.

The vicissitudes of power after independence bring out clearly the fragile legitimacy of the new governments. These vicissitudes also do not help to deepen the attachment to government – though they may lead people to appreciate how delicate and necessary law and order is and how linked it is to stable government. In short, governments in new states can assert power more authoritatively than their colonial predecessors – they can, for example, impose in the first period of independence taxes heavier than ever colonial administrations dared dream of. But constantly in the post-colonial countries (as in the colonial regimes) submission to authority is balanced by forms of passive resistance that prevent communities from being easily mobilized by government. And sullen political alienation sometimes stamps entire peoples who have not yet accepted as their own and integrated into their lives non-traditional forms of authority and political organization.

Government can accomplish many tasks to the extent to which the educated groups accept that it should wield economic power and to the extent to which more traditional groups realize that it is needed for law and order. The educated groups are confirmed in their allegiance also by the fact that they benefit greatly from the posts and opportunities that government in its new forms creates. The traditional groups are confirmed in their submission by finding themselves incapable of opposing government. But government itself is seldom completely rational and well organized in its post-independence approaches. The biggest problem in this respect is that those who have taken over political power have been those who were foremost in the politics of agitation. For such men – who also often just under the surface embody deeply traditional attitudes – power is to be possessed rather than used. Moreover, they do not easily grasp a logic of politics that eschews communalism. And they seldom know that financial integrity and its appearances is needed to conciliate those groups who dislike paying taxes and who resent income differentials. Governments all over the continent which have failed to carry through policies manifesting competence, eschewing communalism and maintaining financial integrity have been falling like ninepins.[13]

The biggest single problem in political leadership is to find men in new states whose political psychology is oriented to development. Traditional attitudes in which power was geared especially to order and to adjudication slip gently into new constitutional and administrative structures and halt before development decisions. Hesitation before development decisions is aggravated by the time-consuming demands of politicking, by an unwillingness to resolve converging and competitive claims to benefits among the ruling groups, and by uneasiness in face of radical innovation, often urged by technicians who are less exposed politically than the politicians, not always wholly trusted by them, and too obviously more rational in their approach. Even military rulers seldom escape the carry-over of these more static traditional attitudes to power – and a reluctance to use power developmentally may be even more pronounced among soldiers unless the latter are deeply convinced that they have a popular mandate to rule.

But only the ablest technicians in new countries seem themselves to be sensitive to development and its urgency. Paradoxically, the relative indifference of a political or ruling class can sometimes leave the better technicians in the public service with more power to make decisions and more freedom to manoeuvre. But this power and freedom are counterbalanced by a final unwillingness for hard political decisions to be made and imaginative leadership to be given. Under these circumstances, only the ablest and most upright public servants can retain their morale. Often, they are not helped by a lack of support among their immediate colleagues in the bureaucracy.

What I am trying to say is that it is for the time being too much to expect to find in most countries a positive political will-to-plan.[14] But planning, especially if it seems to discriminate or to impose hardships, simply cannot be carried on without political leadership. Possibly the most that can be achieved at present in a country like Nigeria is a mitigated kind of planning – carefully worked out projects in the public sector, development of the infrastructure, selective controls over the private sector – that help the economy to grow, that demonstrate that government is serious about economic growth, and that at the same time do not impose too great demands on leadership or create too much obvious hardship for socially mobilized or politically alienated groups.

The position being defended here may seem minimalist to convinced planners.[15] But stronger measures proposed by technicians are unlikely to evoke political consent. Even where they seem initially to evoke such consent, its ineffectiveness is seen once hard measures have to be implemented. Import controls can be negatived in good measure by smuggling – Nigeria is a good example of this in recent times.[16] Government has been unwilling to implement measures that are resisted by powerful groups such as market-women. It has also been unwilling to move against influential persons who form part of social strata that are close to those in government and who use their political and social influence to evade, for example, levies on export crops. The failure of price controls parallels that of the failure to control smuggling: an occasional small dealer was prosecuted in court but every big contractor knew, for example, where he had to buy cement above the controlled price if he wanted to continue his construction work. That failures are not restricted only to a lack of political will but are sometimes compounded by stupid technical decisions is aptly illustrated by decisions on cement prices and the abolition of deposits on bottles.[17]

But to argue for restrained planning is not to argue against planning and its controls. Import controls, for example, that are implemented to a fair degree may be much better than none and may save a good deal of foreign exchange. But the economic gains made through such policies must constantly be measured against wider issues such as the appearance of ineffectiveness in governing and the corrupted integrity of public servants.[18]

If a political will-to-plan is only feebly available, what kind of strategy is politically open to planners? Conceivably one can have a planning approach in two broad – though not entirely chronologically separated – stages. In the first stage social welfare (including education), public works and general infrastructure offer choices acceptable to political leaders and the communities they represent. Concomitantly with this kind of programme can go strategic industrial development on a limited scale as well as organized efforts to help agriculture. In the second stage – which can advance as fast only as administrative competence and integrity improve – more complete planning (reaching down to the smaller community units), larger and more numerous public industrial projects, and more extensive and flexible controls over the private sector become possible. This second stage is likely to arise less out of positive political will or capacity (though as a country grows in skills political development may be hoped for) than out of the realization by political leaders that economic growth may be the only way they have of conciliating socially mobilized groups and of remaining in power. In the last resort, politicians everywhere in the world are men more moved by the will to hold power than stirred by the urge to use power in development. It is often up to good technical personnel to convince political leaders that where aspirations have mounted and frustrations are increasing economic development and the planning that underpins it are essential to the retention of power.

In many countries lack of administrative capacity, capital and other resources may impede even the best efforts to secure a growth that is commensurate with aspirations, especially in countries where global communication media have begun to tempt an intelligentsia to judge government by impossibly high and artificial standards. In such countries, government may do well to try to convince its educated citizens that law and order may be an even more basic value than economic growth and that freedom itself may also be a greater value. In this context, one lesson that government must learn is the proper use of the information media – using them to convey an image of constructive government, pressuring news media to avoid irresponsible approaches and yet not making the mistake of crushing the expression of popular sentiments and isolating itself.

There is a science of politics and an art of governing just as there is a science of economics and a strategy of economic growth. Planning has to draw on all these aspects of politics and economics. If governments plan well, they introduce more rationality into their operations and remain more sensitive to growing aspirations. In the process it is likely that more prosperity will be generated. But they can hope to stay in power only if they can identify the growth in prosperity with their own efforts. The attempt to identify governing and growth should also be part of the planning process. And in the long term the growth of planning may be the best index of the growth of effective government.

Bureaucracy and the Politics of Planning

The original political structure of Nigeria was built around a bureaucracy – or, if you wish, set of bureaucracies – alien and colonial. The successor politicians to the colonial rulers inherited their bureaucracy which by that time was largely Nigerianized. The Nigerian bureaucrats were the main group to keep the country functioning, first as the civilian regime fell, and then as one military regime gave way to another. Not least, certain civil servants played a key role in preserving unity in the prelude to the civil war and during the war. But the upset political period before 1966 and the unsettling strains of civil struggle and political re-organization have proved damaging to the morale of the public service in at least one region (West), have seen another region (North) unscrambled into six pieces, and have left still another (East) both unscrambled and reduced for long periods to a subsistence functioning. What is amazing is the resilience of both the federal and state public services at the present time so soon after the end of the war.

The key phrase in the thinking of the present Nigerian planners has heavy implications for public administration: '. . . Government cannot plan effectively what it does not control' (p. 23). Ignoring the ambiguity in the word 'control' (control includes anything from negative to positive measures and admits of everything from the most general to the most detailed capacity to give instructions and have them followed), the ideal behind this statement as well as others in the Plan would place impossible burdens on the public service. It would demand skills and experience that simply do not exist yet, especially in many of the states,[19] it would require a developmental outlook which the planning document tacitly concedes public servants do not have (p. 94); it suggests a form of nationalist commitment that some federal public servants possess but which remains a scarce commodity in the country;[20] it would imply that people throughout the federation and within each state accept that federal and state bureaucrats act according to an overall federal or state logic and not according to vested interests of their own or their areas of origin; and it would suggest that in the present relatively apolitical situation lower paid workers, peasants and small businessmen are ready to accept unpalatable decisions forced on them by relatively well-to-do public servants who are insulated from financial vicissitudes.

Longer organized and better equipped civil services than the Nigerian – the British civil service after World War II and the Indian one in its planning – found great difficulty in working an elaborate system of planning controls.[21] The Nigerian bureaucracy has not up to now shown that it has the capacity to operate a detailed system of controls. But the moral here is not that controls are unnecessary but simply that they should be kept to a minimum. Generally, in the developing countries a proliferation of positive and negative controls tends to leave bureaucrats unsure whether they have their foot on an administrative accelerator or brake. Moreover, inter-locking controls make heavy demands on collaboration between ministries and take up an enormous amount of time if they are not to bog down enterprise. And, not least, such controls offer serious temptations to corruption among civil servants – and for that reason, they contribute to damaging discipline within the service.

Together with looking after its own internal functioning a public service has to take into account the manner in which it is politically and socially visible in the country it serves. Comparisons are inevitably drawn, for example, between conditions of service in the public service and elsewhere in the economy. In a city like Lagos salaried workers as well as the lower ranks of the public service are increasingly comparing their standards of living with those of the upper civil servants.[22] For that reason it is doubtful if the latter can propose decisions that impose heavy sacrifices on unwilling sectors of society which are much less well-off than themselves. This unwillingness tends to be deepened among the general public by other factors that generate hostility to the civil service. In those lower sectors of the sectors civil service in particular that actually meet the public – the police, tax coll collectors, licensing clerks, etc. – there is a good deal of insensitivity, laziness, bullying and corruption which alienate people from the state generally. It would take a more popular as well as a more competent public service[23] to devise and implement a more comprehensive form of planning than Nigeria has enjoyed in the last decade.

A final word on the planning process itself: Though planning has been strengthened since Nigerians have taken over the controlling decisions and can ensure its administrative continuity, the planning unit is still too small and inexperienced.[24] Once one probes any single sector of the plan (the agricultural sector and its projects, for example), it shows itself to be a little thin. It is also heavily geared to public sector objectives and fiscal measures and does not work out measures needed to reach objectives. Moreover, there is no clear statement of priorities (except in the most general terms) and there are probably far too many projects in the Plan. This kind of planning approach falls under the reproach of Galbraith in his description of a situation where '. . . the plan easily becomes not a plan but a list of all the things that everyone would like to have done or that anyone believes ought to be done. Specification of the things of strategic urgency is lost.[25] And, not least, the planning units in the states are by and large much weaker even than the federal planning unit. The states were little enough consulted by the federal planners during the present planning exercise – and given their lack of capacity, it is doubtful if anything less than large-scale technical assistance from the centre could have brought them properly into the exercise. But the country is going to go on suffering from inadequate planning at state level and it is going to have to sort out the political and social unbalances that result from the lack of time allowed to and the lack of energy put into consulting the states during the formulation of the Plan.

What dismays one a little in the present planning is a technocratic attitude of a kind to be found principally – though not exclusively – among developmental economists. This attitude is impatient with labour, intends to tell big business what to do, is scornful of small business[26] and ignores the role of political leadership. It rejects conspicuous consumption in the shape of television stations and sports stadia but is apt to opt for fertilizer factories and steel mills which may prove to be much more expensive prestige symbols than the other baubles. On occasion also one gets the impression that this outlook considers that provided enough bright economic schemes in the public sector are started, some of them will work.[27] Obviously this mentality is not found in a pure state among Nigerian planners. The second Plan, for example, set out to offer modest help to smaller businessmen (though again in a country that has had poor luck with loans schemes, one would have liked more information on an extension scheme that might help loans to work).[28] But there are enough expressions of a technocratic mentality scattered throughout the Plan to make the reader uneasy. Not the least trouble with this mentality is that to stay pure it has constantly to take a more optimistic view of the economy than the meagre statistics available suggest should be taken.[29] It has also to ignore the discrepancy between official reporting, at best geared to actual spending, and the actual quality of the end product being provided, for example, in hospitals and schools. It takes refuge, finally, in macro-growth figures that translate badly into felt needs and existing living standards among different social classes and among communities in different parts of the country.

In short, technicians can figure too prominently in a planning exercise. They may with competence and in good conscience decide what is good for the country. But it may also be possible for other interested parties to argue that such planning furthers vested interests – including the building up of prestige and power – among the higher civil servants and planners. In a country also where in the public consciousness a principle of representation among bureaucrats and planners is most unevenly spread there can be a real crisis of confidence, and planners need to tread softly. And in a country where the use of power is constantly looked on with vigilant suspicion, they may need to tread more softly still. In practice Nigerian planners have tended to do this. Yet, one is tempted to think that planning might stretch further were some of its limitations more openly adverted to.

The Dilemma of Equality

One of the most admirably stated objectives in the second Plan is social equality. The entire planning exercise is justified in the document by a claim that it contributes not only to faster growth but to more equitable distribution (p. 37). Obviously, an over-all economic equality between persons of differing skills and responsibilities, between persons living in different parts of the country, and between persons living in the towns and the countryside is not attainable in the Plan period – and it is in any case an *ideal-limit* rather than a practical possibility in the present human condition. The most that a plan can be asked to do is to seek to reduce certain inequalities and to prevent other unreasonable differences from coming into being. But even these limited objectives can only be approached modestly.

There are few better known features of economic development than that those areas which are ahead of others are likely not only to remain ahead but to pull away. For this reason the coastal areas in Nigeria in fact grew much more rapidly than other areas (excepting two Northern towns: Kaduna and Kano) in the Plan period. The Plan rightly held that there was no sense in holding back any part of the country (p. 34) – apart from anything else the whole country is poor and whatever part can develop should be permitted to do so. So, too, those who are placed in strategic sectors of the economy – whether they be businessmen or bureaucrats – have always been much better able than others to profit from what growth takes place. Finally, though they may have to put up with a quality of life, particularly in the sense of strain, that is inferior to that of rural dwellers, town dwellers and workers have also by means of their organizational capacity to make more gains in crude economic terms than the farmers did.

It is well to recognize that not only did the Second Plan, in fact, do nothing to remove inequalities but that it helped to deepen existing inequalities. The patterns of spending have been such that they benefit the more developed areas – and this was accentuated as the better organized states, notably the East-Central, Mid-Western and Western states,[30] carried through projects more ably than other states. The Mid-Western State also benefited disproportionately from the revenue allocation system at that time.[31] Persons from the developed areas also tended to do better out of decisions to restrict certain economic functions – the distributive trade, for example – to nationals, and persons from the less-developed areas more than others bore, at least in the short run, costs involved in the transfer of functions.

What can primarily be done for the less-developed parts of Nigeria is to recognize and to break through the fundamental bottleneck which is their low possessions of skills. It is difficult to argue that the Plan came fully to terms with this problem. Indeed it was those areas that were and remain richer in the possession of skills that are planned to expand educational facilities: the Western and East Central States allocated proportionately and absolutely vastly greater sums than Kano, the Northwestern and

Northeastern States. In a sense, the hollowest note in the entire planning exercise was its failure to propose measures to close the educational gap in the country or to present it widening unduly. Declarations about equality do not in themselves reduce inequality.[32]

The other failure in moving towards equality lies in the provision of water supplies and electricity for the countryside. In large parts of the country the scarcity of water and the low quality of water during the dry season make life unpleasant and unhealthy (people often have to walk miles for water and then return carrying equal proportions of water and mud). Imaginative schemes to make cheap electricity available and more abundant water could transform rural living, lighten work and relieve tedium. But not only were the Plan's proposals for agriculture unimpressive but it is difficult to trace in its pages great concern for rural standards of living.[33] Yet only by raising such standards of living can we both hope to raise rural productivity and to slow down migration to the towns. Possibly, it is the farmers who lose most in a system without elected representatives. In a country where population is located mainly in the countryside, representatives tend to have, at least, a minimum concern for peasants – indeed such concern in a country like Turkey has caused tensions in governing. But technocrats seldom see the peasants as their constituents.

Conclusion

In the last resort it is difficult – except in a restrained and limited way – to carry on over-all planning in a country that is communally heterogeneous, uneasily led politically, inadequately administered and unevenly developed. But the effort has to be made. There are three basic aspects of planning that have carefully to be worked on. First, there is the planning of a programme of public spending. Political and social as well as economic considerations must influence this investment. Second, there is need to plan the means of implementing the investment programme. Otherwise even where money is spent, there is no guarantee that it is being well spent. Third, public policy needs most careful thinking out, especially in relation to the private sector. In taking these three factors together it is vital to stress implementation methods, not least so as to insist that policy must remain politically sensitive to the strains that socially mobilized groups are going to impose on government and administration during a planning period. It is important also to stress the need for a policy which formulates and prescribes only these controls that are within the reach of available administrative capacity, that do not lend themselves excessively to corruption, and that do not stifle private effort. Outside these aspects of planning the governments can best leave the Nigerian economy not with the planners but with the people.[34]

References

This essay was first published in the *Journal of Nigerian Economic and Social Studies,* 13, 1(1971). The author wishes to thank his former colleagues, Dr. P. Beckett and Dr. R. Gavin, for their comments and suggestions

1. Another way again of formulating the central preoccupation of the paper is to ask the question: How much planning is possible in a post-colonial and multi-national developing country?
2. *Second National Development Plan 1970–74,* Lagos, 1970.
3. I have written elsewhere on the weakness of a planning exercise in which the states were insufficiently consulted and taken into consideration: see 'Political Aspects', *Quarterly Journal of Administration,* 5, 3 (1971), pp. 313–28.
4. Since the Second Plan – like its predecessor – has been very little brought before the general Nigerian public, the point being made here is largely academic.
5. G.K. Helleiner's comments on the previous Plan are surely still relevant in large part to the Second Plan: 'The failure to start quickly, the remaining shortfalls in the foreign aid contribution, the rapid rate of population growth, upward wage pressures, the extra administrative costs of the establishment of a new Region, and the distortions likely to ensue from the growing pressure to create employment make it very unlikely that the aggregate, let along the *per capita* income targets established by the Plan for 1968 can be realized. There does not seem, however, to be a great concern among Nigerian policy-makers about this failure. The lack of urgency which has characterized development policy formation in the past seems to continue. Formerly produced by the healthy foreign exchange reserve position, it is now induced by buoyant expectations as to oil exports and capital inflows (public and private) for abroad.' *Peasant Agriculture, Government, and Economic Growth in Nigeria* (Yale, 1966), pp. 349–50. Thanks largely to the growth of the mining sector Helleiner is wrong about the aggregate targets – but the planning exercise had little to do with the actual growth attained.
6. W.F. Stolper, 'Economic Growth and Political Instability in Nigeria: On Growing Together Again' (Center for Research on Economic Development, University of Michigan, Ann Arbor), p. 14.
7. On 'nation' and 'state', 'multi-national state' and 'nationalism' in West Africa see James O'Connell, 'Senghor, Nkrumah and Azikiwe: Unity and Diversity in West African State', *Nigerian Journal of Economic and Social Studies* (1963), pp. 77–93.
8. Whatever the force of technology, it is clear that the growth of multinational corporations, by itself, tends to weaken nation states. Multinational corporations render ineffective many traditional policy instruments, the capacity to tax, to restrict credit, to plan investment, etc., because of their international flexibility. In addition, multinational corporations act as a vehicle for the intrusion of the policies of one country into another with the ultimate effect of lessening the power of both. These tendencies have long been recognized in developing

countries, but it is now also evident that even the United States, as a *nation-state*, is losing some of its 'independence' as it attempts to cope with the tangled web woven by its international business.' S. Ymer and R. Rowthorn, 'Multinational Corporations and International Oligopoly: The Non-American Challenge' in Charles P. Kindleberger (ed.), *The International Corporation: A Symposium* (Boston, 1970), p. 75.

9. The best single thing written on this subject is probably Clifford Geertz, 'The integrative revolution: Primordial sentiments and civil politics in the new states' in *Old Societies and New States* (New York, 1963), pp. 105–157.
10. On this see James O'Connell, 'Ibo Massacres and Secession', *Venture* (July, 1969).
11. This section describes what Gunnar Myrdal has called 'the soft state', *Asian Drama* (New York, 1968), pp. 66–9.
12. A speaker at a seminar on national integration held at the University of Lagos, December 1970 pointed out that villagers in a particular area who had rioted over a tax of £3. 1s. 0d. had been willing to subscribe £25 each to get a new secondary school under way in that area.
13. See James O'Connell, 'The Inevitability of Instability', *Journal of Modern Studies,* 5 (1968), pp. 181–91; more specifically on the Nigerian situation, 'The Fragility of Stability: the Fall of the Nigerian Federal Government, 1966' in Robert Rotberg and Ali Mazrui (eds.), *Protest and Power in Black Africa* (New York, 1970), pp. 1012–34.
14. Compare Myrdal's remarks on the 'paramount dilemma' of the soft state, *Asian Drama,* pp. 895–900.
15. These are political conditions of planning. Economists are going to be more directly concerned with factors such as the availability of capital. But in this context, it is worth remarking that the Plan (pp. 28–29, 47) consistently plays down the worth of petroleum revenue to the growth of the Nigerian economy. The planners seem to have a curiously bad conscience about petroleum revenues – deriving perhaps from the link with capitalist countries and companies, from a growth that is likely to take place without much intervention by the planners, and from a fear of growth without development. Yet the recent bargaining with Shell–BP in which the Nigerian government gained substantially higher prices and better terms for its oil (the contribution of the Libyans and the OPEC group to these gains can hardly be over estimated) brings with it much more growth than can be hoped from any part of the Plan. The point is that in an economy like the Nigerian, public policy in dealing with the private sector is often much more important than what government planning will achieve on its own. The moral may well be that planning public policy of this kind, is more important than any other kind of planning. As Kilby has written: 'The lack of impact of the 1962–8 and earlier plans can be traced to over-spending on administration, underspending on directly productive projects for lack of executive capacity, and investing in prestige projects not included in the plan. Moreover, the 1962–8 plan overestimated the availability of foreign aid and underestimated imports. While

economic planning as such has had little effect upon the course of events, government policies and public investment have been of critical importance in determining both the path and the speed of economic development'. *Industrialization in an Open Economy: Nigeria 1945–1966* (Cambridge, 1969), p. 23.

16. See the remarks of the Governor of the Central Bank on smuggling as reported in the *New Nigerian*, 8th and 9th March, 1971.
17. With considerable technical ineptitude the Prices Control Board imposed prices for cement in certain far Northern areas that were below anything that made commercial sense. Inevitably, cement supplies dried up. Price control has been lifted from cement. In the case of the bottles the Board evidently thought that there were political advantages in removing the unpopular deposit requirement. But it had not thought through the anomalies created in price structure and the effect on the circulation of bottles. It had also misjudged the determination of the companies involved to resist. The confusion caused and the untidy public dispute that took place forced the government finally to intervene and restore a (reduced) bottle deposit. But the prestige of the government was not enhanced by the affair
18. The 1971 federal budget was most sensitive to this issue and did its best to reduce unnecessary controls and to remove temptations from members of the public service.
19. One populous Northern state, for example, had in its planning unit one newly arrived expatriate and one recent graduate. The recent graduate has now gone for further training.
20. An attitudinal survey carried out by Paul Beckett and the present writer (which is still being processed) among university students suggests two conclusions that bear on issues in the text: students generally believe that (1) highly placed civil servants have done disproportionately well out of independence and that (2) very few of such civil servants are willing to put the public good before their own private good. This kind of image of civil servants hardly facilitates public co-operation with government.
21. On the Indian experience there are good comments and bibliographical references in Myrdal, *Asian Drama*, pp. 901–35, 1919–28.
22. Comparisons of earnings and standards of living of various groups run through the document presented by the United Committee of Central Labour Organization to the Adebo Salaries and Wages Review Commission, *Equitable Demand for Economic Growth and National Prosperity*, Lagos–Ibadan, 1970.
23. See the Plan's remarks on 'the apparent weakness in the administrative structure of the governments, both at the Federal and State levels' (p. 94) and the severe and recurring strictures on maladministration in the public corporations.
24. The best available description of recent Nigerian planning is given by O. Aboyade, 'Relations between Central and Local Institutions in the Development Process' in A. Rivkin (ed.), *Nations by Design* (New York, 1968), pp. 83–118. A book on the subject by E.R. Dean is expected soon.
25. *Economic Development in Perspective* (New York, 1962), p. 53. See

also A. Waterston's comments on the previous Nigerian Plan in 'What do We Know About Planning?', *International Development Review*, 7, 4 (December 1965), p.4.

26. Part of the trouble seems to be that civil servants partly take their antipathy to business from their colonial predecessors where the administrators not only looked down on the colonial businessmen but also on their P.W.D. (technical) colleagues and partly from their own entrenchment in a salaried system that is outside the kind of pressures that bear on businessmen and make the latter appear devious and dishonest to administrators with fixed revenues. The same phenomenon is observable elsewhere in the post-colonial world. Mason writes: 'A foreign observer in India and Pakistan cannot fail to be impressed with the strong anti-business sentiment that permeates the civil service in both countries. Despite salutations to private enterprise in the Pakistan Five-Year Plan, this is as true in Pakistan as in India . . . ' *Economic Planning in Underdeveloped Areas: Government and Business,* (New York, 1958), p. 74.

27. There is . . . some notion around that if only enough unprofitable enterprises are started somehow the economy will grow. Some vague and misunderstood concept of external economies and balanced growth will usually be mentioned . . . Moreover, there is never any virtue in investing money at a loss, even if the money is available and not at the time usable for other projects. Opportunity cost for funds is measured in interest rates which are quite high throughout the world. And losses mean that you come out with less resources than you started with, which means that you come out with less is not development'. W.F. Stolper, 'Comprehensive Development Planning' reproduced in G.M. Meier, *Leading Issues in Economic Development* (Stanford, 1970), p. 715. See Kilby's remarks, *Industrialization in an Open Economy: Nigeria 1945–1966,* pp. 24–5.

28. For remarks on Nigerian businessmen see A.E. Ekukinam, 'Economic Revolution that is Becoming', *Nigerian Business Digest,* 1, 1 (October/November 1970), pp. 12–14. See also the various studies by Schatz that take into account entrepreneurship, loans and extension assistance: he sums up his views in his last book, *Economics, Politics and Administration in Government Lending* (Ibadan, 1970), Schatz rightly points out the limits of the success of technical assistance to borrowers in situations where proper attitudes and skills are wanting.

29. This is the drive of the article by A. Adedeji and O. Teriba on the present Plan. Their language is quite strong: 'Overall, the planners' projection of fiscal means would seem to be more of a hoax based upon a chain of unrealistic assumptions regarding the availability and magnitude of domestic development finance and foreign aid, and designed mainly to persuade an unwary public that projected investment targets are within the capabilities of the nation's resources – indeed a perfect example of mistaking arithmetical consistency for truth'. 'An Appraisal of Fiscal and Monetary Policy', *Quarterly Journal Administration,* 5, 3 (1971), p. 356.

30. These states were subsequently split up and renamed in 1976. [Editor].

31. The decree which federalized revenue from off-shore oil sources has

redressed part of the present revenue imbalance.

32. The relatively well-developed Western State put £24.5m. capital expenditure into education while Kano State had planned for £8.1 and the North Eastern State only £4.4. This has subsequently been reviewed in the Third Plan period in the light of the 1976 target for Universal Primary Education.

33. There is often a strange bias among development economists against the intrinsic worth of agriculture for raising standards of living. Even as good economist as Helleiner and someone as sympathetic towards peasants as he is justifies agricultural development almost exclusively in terms of its contribution to other sectors: 'Peasant agriculture has contributed and will contribute to Nigerian economic development in six principal ways: (1) through the provision of foreign exchange and savings, both voluntary and involuntary, for the development effort; (2) through the provision of food, particularly to the growing proportion of the population which lives in urban areas; (3) through provision of labour for other "modern" sectors; (4) through the provision of linkages with domestic manufacturing industry; (5) through provision of markets for developing industry; and (6) through the external effects of infrastructure which was built to serve agriculture,' *op. cit.*, p. 140. One has no quarrel with the technical accuracy of these six ways but the emphasis is quite odd!

34. It seems worthwhile saying that the Second Nigerian Plan is in the direct line of the previous Plan. Much that was said in criticism of the previous Plan can be reiterated about this Plan: see the issue of the *Nigerian Journal of Economic and Social Studies*, 4, 2 (July 1962), that reviewed the 1962–8 Plan. And it looks as if even fewer feasibility studies – if that is possible – have been available to the architects of the Second Plan than to their immediate predecessors.

4. The Preparation of the Third National Development Plan
Adebayo Adedeji

It can be stated that almost invariably our development plans, particularly since Independence, have been (1) prepared rather hastily, and published several months after they were supposed to have become operative; (2) a little more than *ex post facto* rationalizations of the project mix submitted by executing agencies; (3) centrally prepared with very little grass-roots participation and equally insignificant participation by the people in the private sector; (4) nothing more than public sector capital expenditure programmes with some policy pronouncements affecting the private sector; (5) framed in such a way that targets are in financial expenditure terms rather than in terms of physical output; (6) distorted in the course of implementation and (7) under-implemented.

Our development plans have tended to be prepared rather hastily, kept secret from the public until they are published, and their publications have invariably taken place several months after the commencement of the plan period. Thus, the 1962–68 Plan was not published until October 1962 even though it was deemed to have become operational from April of that year. The 1970–74 plan was not published before November 1970 with the commencement date being 1 April 1970. In both cases the public had no inkling about their contents not only in terms of projects but also in terms of objectives and policies until the plan documents were published. This is not necessarily a criticism but a statement of fact that has to be mentioned. It is part of our planning experience to date and it has always had serious implications in terms of generating a sense of commitment on the part of the people and of whipping up public enthusiasm for implementation.

Our other planning experience is that, more often than not, the intellectual framework of the Plan and the stated overall and sectoral policy objectives are nothing more than *ex post facto* rationalizations of the projects as submitted by the executing ministries, statutory corporations, and other agencies of government. Because of the lack of any guidelines as to the framework, executing agencies were free to submit any package of capital proposals. The result of this omission was the emergence of sectoral programmes which were often not addressed to any coherent set of well-defined goals. Again this point is not made as a criticism. It is only fair to say that, given the circumstances in which our past planning efforts were being made, the outcome could not have been different. For example, the abnormal conditions under which the 1970–74 Plan was prepared precluded the advance publication of any policy and strategy guidelines to executing agencies. In the colonial era, development plans were merely an aggregate of proposals for spending money. They did not pretend to propound a strategy of development. Indeed, the story was told that when a colonial governor on home leave paid a courtesy visit to the British Colonial Office, he was informed that the Secretary of State had just sent a despatch to him to prepare a Five-Year Plan for the development of the territory under his charge. It was hoped that he would do this as soon as possible after his leave. As the governor did not see the necessity for returning to the territory before undertaking this assignment, he asked for a sheet of paper and pen. On half a foolscap sheet, the governor wrote the Five-Year Plan for his territory. This consisted of a dozen or so projects with the estimated 'costs' of implementing them. Of course we all know that this is not planning. It is not planning, because the various kinds of proposed expenditure were unrelated, although all of them – water supply, education, agriculture, forestry, etc. – were desirable and most of them were urgent. The point of criticism is that the execution of such a project-by-project Plan would not bring about any systematic development. And yet in spite of our delayed rationalizations, has the colonial legacy not died hard? In fairness to the colonialists, I must add that even they at that time appreciated the limitations of this type of planning.

Our third planning experience, it seems to me is the non-involvement, so far, of the mass of the people in the planning process. Everybody agrees that popular participation in the planning effort is most desirable as it will bring in its train mass involvement in Plan execution. But as yet no one has experimented in grass-roots planning in Nigeria. Admittedly, the federal nature of our system of government has broadened the base of participation through the involvement of the state governments in the planning process. But all our planning is still at governmental levels. We have not, until now, succeeded in involving the private sector, local government and most important of all the general populace.

Our fourth and fifth planning experiences need no amplification. Our development plans are basically public sector capital programmes and their targets are in expenditure terms rather than in terms of physical output. A Plan states how much government proposes to spend on each project or sector during the plan period. Sometimes these proposed expenditures are phased out annually. But it is very rare for target outputs to be stated.

Sixthly, there is abundant evidence that Plan objectives are often distorted in the course of execution; that planned allocations and expenditures differ significantly from actual allocations and expenditures and that new projects are inserted on an *ad hoc* basis without any Plan review exercise having been undertaken. The first Progress Report on the Second National Development Plan 1970–74 admits that during the first eighteen month of the plan period a 'wide departure' had occurred between planned and actual expenditures.

The Plan proportions among the three broad sectors – economic, social and administrative – have been distorted. 'The low priority administrative sector gained what the high priority economic sector lost. These distortions arise mainly from the fact that low priority projects in the administrative sector are relatively easier to prepare and execute than projects in the productive sector'.

The Progress Report first reminded Governments of the requirements of Plan discipline: 'Plan discipline demands that the annual proportions should be broadly respected. These annual proportions are meant to give priority to productive sectors so as to generate resources which in the later years of the plan would help to finance projects in the less productive sectors'. It then admonished them to guard against the danger of channelling the bulk of the available resources to low priority sectors.

It is of course realised that a development plan cannot be a rigid blueprint for the future to be followed blindly. As is admitted in the 1962–68 Plan, a plan cannot be conceived 'as a law akin to that of the Medes and Persians, but rather as a flexible instrument. Flexibility, however, cannot be equated with arbitrariness . . . the ultimate goal of development . . . can be achieved only if the overall Plan Priorities are strictly observed'. However, in practice this lofty principle was honoured in the breach than in the observance.

The final lesson of experience is the perennial under-implementation of the development plans. Allied to this is the dichotomy between the planners and the executors and the ineffective communication between them. Under-implementation is caused by a host of factors: (i) shortage of financial resources; (ii) shortage of skilled manpower; (iii) obstacles to the application of science and technology; (iv) lack of decision-making abilities and administrative capacity; and (v) lack of appropriate institutions. These are the determinants of executive capacity. They individually and severally have made the full implementation of development plans in Nigeria and indeed in nearly all parts of the developing world an unrealisable ideal.

Before discussing the arrangements for the preparation of the Third Plan in the light of the several lessons derived from the Nigerian experience in development planning since 1946, I would like first to highlight one particular achievement in the field of planning and plan implementation since the 1970–74 Plan was launched.

I have already stated that the Plan was prepared under abnormal circumstances and was launched six months late. It suffers from most of the deficiencies discussed earlier. But in spite of this we have under the circumstances made a satisfactory progress in implementation, although it is most unlikely that it will be fully implemented. However, in terms of the Third Plan, perhaps Nigeria's greatest achievement will be to realise the urgent need for institution building – particularly planning and economic institutions.

Accordingly, the Federal Military Government has set up the Central Planning Office, the Joint Planning Board and the Conference of Commissioners responsible for economic planning in the Federation and the National Economic Advisory Council. The combined effect of all these institutions is to make for better quality planning, for participation by more people, particularly from the private sector, in the planning process and for better and more effective co-ordination in the preparation and implementation of the development Plan. The private sector can no longer claim lack of involvement. Nor can state governments claim, as some of them did with regard to the Second Plan, non-effective participation in preparing the Third Plan.

The list of economic institutions suggested in the Third Plan is of course quite formidable. It includes the National Agricultural Council, the National Agricultural Credit Bank, the National Oil Corporation, the Standards Organisations, the Industrial Training Fund, Iron and Steel Authority, National Electric Power Authority, Highway Authority, Bank of Commerce and Industry, Centre for Management Development, Kainji Lake Development Commission, the National Supply Company and so on.

Most of them have since been established. Being relatively new institutions they inevitably encountered teething problems. The uncharitable or the cynical may call some of them lame ducks, toothless bulldogs, 'paper tigers' or what have you. But given proper leadership and good and imaginative staffing they can develop muscle and begin to make their existence felt. As they do, the quality of planning and administration is bound to improve significantly and our executive capacity enhanced.

Because of the improvement in the machinery for planning, it was the planners' intention to remove as many of the deficiencies as possible in the preparation of the Third Plan. For example, there was an early start made on the preparation of the Plan. The decision to publicize it in October 1974, though it did not become operative until April 1975, was itself evidence of a desire to ensure that the Nigerian public knew about their next development Plan before it became operative. This was also intended to enable the Government to embark on implementation immediately.

Nigerian planners have also learned their lesson about the need to provide guidelines and a policy framework within which context the executing agencies can articulate their development projects and programmes. Hence the Guidelines were published in August 1973. All the planning institutions mentioned earlier – the Joint Planning Board, the National Economic Advisory Council and the Commissioners' Conference – participated fully and effectively in the preparation of the Guidelines before they were subsequently considered and approved by the Federal Executive Council and the Supreme Military Council.

In the Guidelines it was assumed that the preparation of the Third Plan would be a two-way process – at national and state levels as well as at local levels. It was specifically suggested in the document that in order to ensure that the next plan encompassed activities at all levels of government it was essential that state governments specify sector by sector the Local Authority components of their programmes. This meant that the Local Authorities would have to be involved in the planning process. State governments were also urged to set up State Economic Advisory Committees with membership and terms of reference similar to the National Economic Advisory Council.

All of these were aimed at the involvement of many people at all levels of government and from the private sector in the preparation of the Plan, thus making it relatively easy for governments to mobilize support for implementation.

Perhaps the most important innovation in the preparation of the Third Plan was the 'sectoral consultancy' approach. The planners were determined to avoid, as much as possible, including projects which had not been fully articulated, studied, properly designed and ready for implementation in the Plan. At the same time they realised that given the manpower and technical know-how situation, neither the Federal Government nor, particularly, the state governments could undertake adequate projects preparation on their own. Accordingly, groups of consultants were appointed to be used for the identification, detailed study and preparation of projects in the key sectors of the economy, notably agriculture, transport, health, education and industry. The point of departure was that instead of each of the former twelve state governments employing a consulting team of its own, there were only five sectoral teams centrally appointed by the Federal Government and made available to any state governments and Federal Ministries that required their services. The advantage was that the team studying, say, industrial projects for all the governments of the Federation was in a position to spot and give early counsel against wasteful duplication in industrial development. Furthermore, such a team was in a position to identify projects with regional or national importance which otherwise would have been left out of consideration because their resource requirements were beyond the capacity of any single state.

By making portfolios of concrete projects available to state governments, the work of the Sectoral Consulting Teams was made easier. The Federal Government could then pick concrete projects to which federal grants could be directed, as the Federal Government then had a fairly clear idea as to what it was in fact assisting at the state level. As indicated in the First Progress Report, a number of state governments departed substantially from their development programme both in terms of overall magnitude as well as the scope and content of individual projects.

Thus the consultancy service was introduced to articulate and firm up specific projects in the course of preparing feasibility studies and preliminary designs, making it difficult thereafter to vary in a casual manner the scope and cost of projects. This was perhaps the most effective way of ensuring that the Third National Plan was not seriously distorted in the process of implementation. The Federal Government's effort in this field of consultancy was complementary to the effect of the state governments. It was not a substitute.

Some of these changes were already apparent in the Guidelines. Running through the policies enunciated in the document was the Government's awareness of the need to look beyond the rate of growth in the economy and concentrate more than ever before on the nature of this growth. Thus, governments were to concentrate during the Third Plan period not only in promoting the most rapid rate of economic growth but also in improving the quality of life of the individual generally. Accordingly, in the Guidelines the governments put much emphasis on food production, agro-allied industries, urban planning and provision of low-cost housing for workers, the human environment health and social welfare, and transportation, particularly intra-city transportation. These were all areas of public expenditure with income distribution effects. There was also to be an incomes policy.

Whatever criticisms there might have been of the document, it cannot be on the ground that it lacked candour. It was indeed remarkably frank and open about past and current shortcomings. Like the First Progress Report on the Second National Development Plan, it acknowledged openly weaknesses in plan implementation.

Finally, the collaboration between the planning and executing ministries at the federal and state levels remains crucial to the success of planning in Nigeria. An example of failures in this area has been the delay in implementing the petro-chemical and iron and steel industries. Here one can only be reminded of the political constraints on planners discussed in the previous chapter by James O'Connell.

Parastatals: An Introduction

In the parastatal sector, the working of public enterprise as agencies of development raises a number of issues in development administration.

Historically, public enterprises have been created in response to a perceived need for more national government control over the economy, but where the issue of the form and extent of state intervention in the economy has not yet been resolved. The issue is usually presented in terms of the balance between government control and autonomy that public enterprises require to make their maximum contribution to national development. Public enterprises, it is often argued, are set up by the State either to replace, supplement, stimulate or participate with private enterprise. If they are to do any of the things effectively, then they must be made to combine the efficiency and effectiveness of the best private enterprises with responsiveness to government controls, directives and goals in the policies they follow.

A range of political, economic and social motives have in fact been involved in the creation of public enterprises in the developing countries. Politically, they may be associated with ideologies of public ownership and control, or they may be simply symbols of government effort to develop the economy. Economically, they may have been justified on technical grounds. Socially, they may have been seen as providers of employment opportunities in industrial and agricultural sectors. The result has often been a lack of clear definition of the objectives of public enterprises. If anything, objectives – where stated – have been unrealistic given the resources available to public enterprises. Where a healthy balance sheet is stressed, management may spend half its time attempting to conceal its basic difficulties.

Public enterprises may be divided into three broad categories. The oldest are the public utilities, started in the colonial period for providing railways, roads, electricity, ports, harbours, waterworks and telecommunications – the infrastructure which private enterprise could not provide. The second, and more recent, are the public or development corporations set up in the late colonial period or the early years after independence for assisting large-scale industrial and agricultural development projects sponsored by the private sector. Third, and most recently, countries such as Tanzania have established state corporations to manage newly-nationalized enterprises. In cases like this, relative absence of any developed indigenous private sector has been coupled with a strong ideological commitment to public ownership and state sector development.

In the Nigerian context, the first and the second types are predominant, although state mining and oil corporations have recently been set up as a result of increased state financial participation in these sectors. The working of Nigerian development corporations has been particularly well investigated and documented.

For the student of development administration, the issues arising from the working of public enterprises as agencies of development may be summarized under two major headings: (i) the machinery for government control of public corporations and their relations to the planning process; and (ii) problems of internal organization and management.

Government Control of Public Corporations

The advantages of government control and direction are several, despite the prevalent view that a centralized system would destroy the advantages of autonomy and approximation to business practices for which public enterprises are said to have been established. There have been two standard ways of controlling public enterprises – through accountability to the legislature and through the Board of Directors of a public enterprise.

Accountability to the legislature, as during the Nigerian First Republic when the various regional development corporations were accountable to their respective Regional House of Assembly, has been minimal, involving the submission of annual reports to the legislature and on a day-to-day basis through the ministry supervising the public enterprise. Problems impeding effective legislative control have been both political and technical. Politically, parliamentary control through ministerial agencies may be limited where the Chairman and Board of Directors of the enterprise are influential in, or appointees of, the party in power. Technically, large public enterprises might in practice have a free hand to undertake projects without ministerial approval where no comprehensive staff and financial regulations or investment guidelines exist.

In non-parliamentary regimes, state control through the Board of Directors also raises a number of issues and problems. First, there is simply the question of the costs of maintaining a Board of Directors. It is often the case that Board members consume excessive administrative expenses and may even influence the enterprises decisions for personal benefit. The second problem area is the appointment of Board members. Appointment of civil servants, particularly senior ones, may be demanding time from those who are already overburdened. Some countries have moved towards mixed membership, including M.P.s, businessmen as well as civil servants.

Analysts of public enterprises in the developing countries have suggested that, alongside other forms of control, more effective government regulation could also be achieved through improving the statutory framework within which public enterprises have to operate. Basic to effective legal control is a clear definition of the objectives of the public enterprise – its policies and objectives (including performance criteria), activities and resources. The statute governing the enterprise should also lay down procedures to be followed in fixing capital structure, the responsible Minister and number of Board members. Finally, a statute should specify the relations between the responsible government Minister and the public enterprise, and the government Ministry Audit and Inspection and the public enterprise.

Co-ordination of Public Enterprises

Another issue raised by the expansion of the parastatal sector is the creation of areas of economic decision-making outside the normal experience of civil servants. At the same time the parastatal sector includes crucial areas of the developing economy and requires co-ordination with the central planning process. Such co-ordination can be effected in several ways. It need not necessarily be achieved through changes in structural inter-relationships. Indeed a balance may be struck between centralized direction and decentralized decision-making within centrally-supplied guidelines. One form of co-ordination may be effected through the supply of project selection criteria in order to bring parastatal investment programmes into line with government industrial and agricultural development strategy. This may involve priorities about the location and types of project to be embarked upon, for example, the rate of return and foreign exchange implications of a project, employment benefits as well as basic viability (its ability to generate revenue to meet recurrent expenses, loan repayments, and depreciation costs). Another form of co-ordination is through budgetary control. Some countries have actually included the parastatal investment programme in the central government development estimates. Where projects involve external loans, imported capital equipment or overseas management contracts, procedures may already exist whereby representative from Ministries like Finance, Economic Planning, Trade and Industry are involved in the negotiations with financial and technical partners. The same will obviously apply to projects involving a government capital loan or guarantee of a capital loan.

Internal Organization and Management

Internally the performance of public enterprises has been affected by a number of factors including recruitment and staff development, and internal management and organization.

Recruitment and Staff Development
More than any other branch of the government service, public enterprises require personnel with a range of skills and professional and managerial training. Essential to their working, then, is an administrative framework of procedures and policies which can ensure that they are able to recruit and retain the services of qualified, competent and motivated personnel who are able to plan and execute the enterprises programme.

Problems common to public enterprise recruitment are several. First, public enterprises have rather specialized manpower needs, in particular for technical cadres – maintenance engineers, storekeepers, accountants, etc. – without whom they cannot function at all. Second, there are often varying recruitment standards. Thus, some public enterprises have become overstaffed. In addition regularized conditions of service and salaries for senior (often expatriate) staff may be absent. In some cases they may attract away staff from the central civil service departments. Third, there is the problem of the irregular appointment of unqualified relatives of political influentials or Board members. The latter, together with the often very high salaries of senior staff, can weaken the moral of competent and middle or lower level staff. Finally, there is the problem of security of tenure and the location of hiring and firing power. Given the possible irregularities of appointment, security of tenure is probably less desirable, in order that incompetents may be removed. On the other hand, given the equal possibilities of political interference in staffing, security of tenure may also be desirable at times.

Management and Organization
The problem of internal organization and management have been well documented. They include financial mismanagement as well as poor decision-making. Apart from improvements which can result from external controls, direction, and support (accounting and inspection, planning guidelines and the provision of adequate manpower and financial resources), commentators have also stressed the need for specifying clear relationships between the principal organs of the public enterprise – the Board of Directors and the chief executive as well as the duties and spheres of responsibility and control of each.

On the one hand, the Board of Directors should be assigned the tasks of directing the affairs and policies of the enterprise and, through the managing director, managing its day-to-day affairs. This can be achieved through a schedule of duties of the Board, including periodic reporting and accounting to the responsible Minister. Statutes governing public enterprises might also elaborate on methods of appointment and dismissal, criteria of selection and duration of appointment of Board members. The Director, on the other hand should be assigned the tasks of calling Board meetings (as Chairman), hiring and firing staff and other duties. His method of appointment and its duration should also be specified.

One suggested solution to the problem of achieving effective working relations between organs of the enterprise is to have a managing director – one who is at the same time Chairman of the Board and the General Manager. Such a person can manage the day-to-day running of the corporation as well as shape the policy issues for the final decisions of the Board of Directors. Despite the dangers of concentrating powers in one man, this arrangement does link clearly the day-to-day management and decision-making of the corporation.

5. Nigerian Public Enterprises as an Organizational Dilemma

Ojetunji Aboyade

The development process of any economy is substantially determined by the way the productive forces in and around the economy are organized. This organization, in terms of dominant institutions and social production relations, in turn reflects the ideological bias of those who had hitherto ruled or are currently ruling the society. Economic control of the state apparatus offers one vantage point from which to view the historical evolution of these social production relations, as well as the current ideological predilections of the society. Public enterprises constitute only one segment of the economic control apparatus of the state. Because of the commonly-recognized differences between precept and practice, the philosophical foundation of public enterprises is also unlikely to be fully reflected empirically in the way they function on the ground. It follows from these two factors that neither can the size and pattern of public enterprises in a national economy be validly analyzed only from ideological perspectives, nor can the operation of the dominant economic ideology of a society be appreciated only in terms of the structure and performance of its public enterprises in the given period.

This chapter explores such general problems of the philosophy and strategy of public enterprises in one national economy over a given short period, namely the case of Nigeria against the background of the 1960s and 1970s. It argues that a philosophical approach is a necessary but not sufficient analytical frame of reference for an appreciation study of Nigerian public enterprises system.

After a sketchy view of the main historical forces that helped shape Nigerian public enterprises, especially during the late colonial period, an attempt is made to show the resulting policy confusion that is manifest in the current social scene. Part of these operational anomalies reflects the inevitable contradictions of post-colonial social transition, part arises from a defective appreciation of what a mixed economy truly means or should mean, and part is a residual of that universal (and probably eternal) genuine difference of view of how best to organize the productive forces of an underdeveloped economy. In the light of such avoidable ideological confusion and inevitable philosophical debate, the role of the State in the development process is reexamined against the empirical realities of the Nigerian case. A restatement of a more meaningful strategy of the development of Nigerian public enterprises system is attempted, while indicating a number of persistent unsettled questions of economic organization and social relations.

The Legacy of Colonial Experience

A great deal of research effort in economic history is still needed before anything definitive can be said about the organization and performance of public enterprises in the pre-colonial traditional society. But given the generous resource endowment (especially of land in relation to labour), peasant proprietorship as a basis for production organization in an essentially farming and trading community, and the efficacy of African Humanism as the ideological underpinning for social relations, we can hazard a guess that the domain of social ownership, social action and social goods was relatively large and that the public sector of the traditional economy was thus dominant. In a sense, this could be likened to the first stage of the Marxian conception of the historical development of society in five phases of production relations; namely, primitive communism, slavery, feudalism, capitalism and socialism. But apart from Marx's recognition that these are only dominant phases rather than organizational typologies likely to be found in their distinctive or pure forms, African Humanism is essentially different from primitive communism. By preventing self-alienation, it preserves individuality even if it does not encourage individualism as a system. Not content with *involvement* in the production process, it elevates the human factor of production to the level of *participation* in the development process by viewing production as an inseparable part of distributive relations. It rejects self-alienation in its conception of the totality of man's existence, and seeks to achieve egalitarianism through a deep sense of man's responsibility to his community. Through this holistic approach to economic and social relations, it attempts to blend individual and social morality as basis for social consensus and social action. Expanding trade tends to quicken the pace of social stratification. But within the pace of commercial growth in the pre-colonial economy African Humanism was able to contain the rapid formation of social classes with conflicting economic interests, at any rate as long as agriculture by a surplus-landed peasantry still dominated production and continued to provide the collective base for political power.

Colonial intrusion, however, changed this delicate balance, first by widening the scope and quickening the pace of commerce and then by altering the social foundation of political power. By intensifying and exploiting social strife in ethnically heterogeneous communities, it strengthened the naescent forces of slavery and feudalism. With the new range of goods demanded by international commerce and the new forms of administrative and financial institutions attendant upon it, the colonial impact also simultaneously gave impetus to the emergence of capitalist social formations.

On the political front, the colonial coercive forces broke up old empires and forged new political relationships, establishing the basis of the nation state as a unit of modern social organization for collective economic action. In the Nigerian case, that creation of the nation state did not come until 1914. Hitherto, the area had been thought of by the British Colonial Administration mainly as a haven for private commercial capital. But the necessity for amalgamation of the Northern and Southern Protectorates in 1914 was as much a result of political expediency as of economic necessity. And in that very event was to be found the philosophical genesis of the interventionist role of the State in the Nigerian development process. Forced to depend substantially on its own internally-generated resources to finance its administrative costs, the colonial government could not afford just to keep the ring as a passive referee for the capitalist operators. It had thus acquired a direct stake in their prosperity and orderly expansion.

The railways were probably the first major example of public enterprises in Nigeria. At first conceived mainly in terms of colonial strategic and administrative needs, they quickly acquired the dimension of welcomed economic utility for transporting the goods of international commerce. Given the structural nature of the colonial domestic economy as well as the contemporary experience of the private ownership and control of the railways in the metropolitan countries, it could hardly be expected that the Nigerian Railways could have been started other than as a public enterprise.

That kind of state intervention in economic activity, it may be noted, was also consistent with the dominant ideology of the metropolitan power at the time. The presumptive mode of economic organization was to be *laissez-faire* and the onus of justification, case by case, was on those advocating particular state intervention beyond its nominal or passive role of keeping the ring and refereeing the rules of the game. But even from the mid-Eighteenth Century, and certainly by the time of John Stuart Mill, the scope of state intervention had started to widen as more and more exceptions to the presumptive mode were rationalized on both philosophical and pragmatic grounds. As the full workings of Western industrial capitalism became evident through the Nineteenth Century, what started first as emotional reaction against the harshness, brutality, callousness, denigration and social injustices of private enterprise, progressively turned to a systematic and positive affirmation of public enterprise in its own right rather than as an exemptive special case that has to be justified at each turn.

But even in early Twentieth Century Britain, this reversal of intellectual attitudes had not permeated deeply the actual organization of investment decisions. So, it would be too much to expect that it would have radically affected thinking, not to say influenced action, far away in the colonies. The shift was nevertheless of real significance, in that direct state involvement in production could now be more readily justified on both practical and theoretical grounds. Much of course still hinged on the personality, convictions and dynamism of the bureaucratic figures who dominated the local administrative scene at any given time. But in general, the foundation was laid for direct state intervention on a broad front of economic activity in Nigeria during the inter-war years.

The colonial administration built the nucleus of necessary economic and social infrastructural capital that private enterprise could not or would not provide: railways, roads, electricity, ports and harbours, water works and telecommunication. Social services like education and health were still substantially left in the related hands of the Christian Missions. But even at this early stage, government itself moved positively into some of the directly productive sectors of the economy: the stone quarry of Aro, the colliery at Udi and the saw-milling and furniture factory at Ijora. True, the products of these plants were still substantially meant for the demand of the public sector itself; but there was little basis in their conception, structure or operation to confine their activities to such a straight-jacket. Government conducted agricultural production research, demonstrated and propagated improved production techniques, established farm extension services and attempted modest organized marketing institutions. As early as the 1920s, it had erected cotton ginneries at Gusau and Challowa, as well as a rice hulling factory at Sokoto. Even in the dark slump days of the 1930s, it established boat-building yards and marine shops, and laid the groundwork for the beginnings of civil aviation

In spite of this early-day state involvement in production, the hey-day for the establishment and expansion of public enterprises in Nigeria was the period between the end of the Second World War and the achievement of political independence. Beginning with the famous Commodity Produce Marketing Boards of the 1940s, both the central and all the regional governments created a plethora of public institutions to foster general development beyond providing the conventional scope of public utilities. By the middle of the 1960s, the range of Nigerian public enterprises had stretched from farm organizations to manufacturing, from municipal transport to mining, from housing to multi-purpose power, and from trading to banking and insurance.

The literature on the organizational problems and operational performance of these public enterprises is a rich one and is still growing.[1] What has generally emerged from these diverse studies, analyses, reports and comments can be characterized as a story of disillusionment. Whatever the laudable aims and however high the hopes at initiation, one after another the Nigerian enterprises have performed over the last two decades in a way that can only be described in polite language as disappointing.[2] Not only has there been a low (indeed, often a negative) return to capital invested, the low quality of management has compounded the high incidence of direct ministerial intervention in routine operation of the public enterprises. Poor internal administration and the pursuit, by arbitrary outside pressure, of non-economic policies of government had meant inadequate (and sometimes patently defective) pre-investment studies, even in many cases of so-called joint ventures. The extensive use of contractor finance and supplier's credit resulted not only in large leakages of public funds but hampered the operational viability of many public enterprises through an overburdened and unrealistic capital structure.

Admittedly, the degree of poor performance by public enterprises in Nigeria was unnecessarily high, and could obviously have been reduced if not eliminated by a more honest political and bureaucratic leadership. But the story of disillusionment with Nigerian public enterprises is not only paralleled by the contemporary experience of other underdeveloped countries, but would seem to be part of a basic disenchantment with public enterprises in general. Because, even in the advanced industrial countries, and especially in the liberal economies of Western Europe (including Britain), the actual performance experience of socialised industries is accepted even by the protagonists of public enterprises system as falling far short of expectation. Although a greater proportion of these cases do show economic and even greater financial surpluses than in Nigeria, they have scarcely realized the earlier hopes of safeguarding the interest of consumers against the hated discretionary behaviour of private monopoly. Nor have they much demonstrated the expected sense of civic responsibility, consistent with promotion of the public interest and of harmony between the potentially conflicting interests of capital and labour.

It is in the context of this lacklustre historical performance by public enterprises, especially in the under-developed countries, that the present disillusionment with direct public-sector dominance in the development process must be appreciated and re-evaluated. Some have challenged the operational validity of the underlying philosophy of public enterprises in the conditions of under-development and unsuitability for commercial activity of the inherited legacy of colonial bureaucratic structuve.[3] Some have even argued that public enterprises are unlikely to flourish where the private enterprise system is already entrenched and widespread, and are likely to succeed only in areas where the indigenous private sector is still weak.[4] Yet, others have sought particular explanations if not justifications for public enterprises performance in the structural context and policy environment in which they have been forced to operate.[5] The fact that remains, however, is that despite continued disappointing show on the ground, large and increasing investments continue to be made in public enterprises in Nigeria.[6] Could this be a reflection of policy inertia? Or is it grounded in a fundamental faith in the long-run structural supremacy of the public enterprises system as a means of fostering development?

Mixed Economy Dilemmas

In one sense, all economies of the world are mixed economies. There is almost no case that is absolutely, fully and completely run by public enterprises or by private enterprises. The degree of mixture, however, is not one of simple quantitative relationships, but a reflection of structured ideological perspectives. These perspectives may of course be a result of historical accident – as in the case of colonial and post-colonial economies – and may therefore themselves be undergoing much conscious and unconscious alterations.

Nigeria belongs to such case of historical accident in the process of ideological transition. In general, both official and non-official views tend to look at the public sector as performing essentially three interrelated sets of role:
(a) providing the necessary infrastructural facilities for private enterprise to operate,
(b) establishing a set of regulatory devices to make private enterprise conform as much as possible to standards of good behaviour, and
(c) supplementing private enterprise investment activity where this is not forthcoming adequately or promptly.
Most of the Nigerian public enterprises established before 1970 can be said to share one or other of these rationale. Irrespective of the quantitative magnitude (whether in absolute or relative terms) of public-sector investments, it is clear that the basic burden if not the initiative of development would rest with the private sector, whatever the rhetorical cloak in which government may wrap its programmes.

This conclusion of empirical observation derives from the hypothesis that in any given period there exists in any national economy a dominant type of production relations. The economic system functions in a way to reflect the predominance and over-riding influence of the particular type of production relations. Now, which production relations type is or is not dominant can be ascertained both from what the government does as well as what it refrains from doing. A government could, for example, enter directly into a given production itself; or cause others to enter into production; or prevent others from so doing; or just remain aloof from whether or not and how certain goods are produced. But not to intervene by government is really not a neutral act, but an implicit support for whatever power position may then carry out the production in lieu of government. At any given time, there exists in any national economy a production gap (or development potential) to be filled. Where the government is, so to say, development-passive and fills only the residual component of that gap, then it is clear that the dominant value system of society is that of private enterprise. This would be so, even where the government covers as efficiently as possible such traditional investment fields as natural public monopolies (railway, public utilities) and semi-public goods (roads, education).

The idea seems to have gained wide currency and is probably already entrenched that, given the great propensity of Nigerians to trade and exploit economic opportunities, the government should only intervene in the development process for the purpose of building and maintaining necessary infrastructural facilities suitably ahead of demand, and generally creating by indirect policies a healthy economic environment for competitive private enterprise to flourish. But, given the widely-recognized large development potential that exists in the economy, a government that restricts its intervention role to such a narrow range would be doing so out of free choice and not out of necessity. Hitherto, that is until the Second National Development Plan, successive Nigerian governments tended to regard their own public investment programmes and policies mainly as catalytic agents. It was only peripherally and uncertainly that they regarded them, if at all, as economically and ethically superior to private enterprises. So, we could conclude that whatever the relative share of investment or of aggregate national expenditure borne by the public sector, the mixed economy system followed in practice by Nigeria both during the colonial period and in the decade after Independence was really in essence a private enterprise system.

The quantitative magnitude of what the public sector does as one major (indeed the single largest) unit in the economy, and the wide publicity which for political reasons this tends to receive in the minds of the public, are a major cause of the mistaken belief that the mixed economy (*a la* Nigeria) is the existence of two parallel decision-making sectors with the government as the powerful partner. The unquestioned dominance of private enterprise ideology is reflected by the widespread notion that not only should government development infrastructures for the benefit of private enterprise and turn over successful public enterprises (which had been risked and developed by public resources) to a handful of private businessmen to accumulate more personal wealth, but that government should now proceed to delimit and announce its own area of production involvement!

The strength of the ideological confusion in Nigeria's mixed-economy system is additionally seen in the faulty appreciation of the real intentions and ultimate goals of the relentless indigenisation of the foreign enterprise sector. It has been hailed as a welcomed opportunity to strengthen indigenous capitalists in the development process, rather than more correctly as a necessary structural precondition for revamping social relations in a logical sequence. From a positive reformist viewpoint, it is a long road to that objective of progressive production relations. But whatever the social appearances of the workings of the indigenisation policy, it should really be seen (as indeed originally intended) as the first plank of a two-stage strategy of national economic independence and social distributive equity.

The question might then legitimately be asked: if the honest long-term aim of government is to subject the private sector effectively to the ascendancy of an economically and ethically superior public sector, then why can the government not say so in clear terms and avoid the present confusion? And how can the policy makers be sure that their long-term objective would not be preempted by the very indigenous private enterprise class which its present apparently confused policy is creating and strengthening?

Part of the answer to the first question is that a plan document, no matter how comprehensive and extensive, cannot spell out every action programme of government; nor is it evident that it should spell them out whatever the nature of the proposed action programme may be. Another part of the answer is that by the very nature of the socio-political problems that the plan was trying to solve, national integration of a more geographical dimension was of the utmost importance in the minds of the military-political leadership. The needs of establishing co-operative federalism within the twelve-state structure and the economic imperatives of post-war rehabilitation and reconstruction established the clear priorities of the early 1970s above the long-term issue of establishing new production relations. Again, there is the whole factor of style in the presentation of basic ideas. It is interesting in this respect how the chapter on 'National Objectives and Priorities' has been variously interpreted by different commentators, obviously trying to cast the ideas into their own ideological frame of reference. Or perhaps, the attempt to avoid the tyranny of well-known vocabularies and terms that sound more like noisy negative cliches than constructive positive and workable ideas has created more problems of understanding. But with particular reference to the central theme of this essay, a passage several chapters later in the Plan document probably sums up the position more neatly:

> The aim of Development Planning in Nigeria is that economic growth should be accompanied by general development. In other words, the benefits of economic advancement should be distributed as widely as possible over the entire society. Government, as the most important single institution for ensuring the translation of growth into development through the provision of economic and social services, must have at its disposal resources sufficient for achieving these goals of society. Today, industry and mining are the fastest growing sectors of the economy and are therefore likely to be important generators of resources for future development. It follows that Government must play a leading role in two sectors in order to harness the fruits of economic growth for the overall development of the Nigerian society. Government investment activities will no longer be limited to public corporations and 'dying industries' in which no private company can thrive, whilst leaving the virile, expansive and profitable industries to private enterprise. Private investors will, however, continue to be welcome in Nigeria as partners in progress led by the public sector.[7]

This ties up with consideration of the second question as to the translation of this idea into operational programmes such that are not likely to engender greater class stratification in society. At this level, it must be conceded that Nigeria is not yet in the fortunate historical situation of being blessed with a strong, disciplined, dedicated and honest leadership that is sufficiently committed to social development and whose style is able to catch the imagination of the population for inculcating a much-needed new system of values. But beyond that, there are real attempts to achieve structural shifts in the discretionary power balance between the public and private sectors. Although in terms of the mobilization and allocation of total available national resources for development there was little dramatic quantitative shift proposed in favour of the public sector share,[8] there were hosts of programmes, projects and policies designed to achieve a qualitative shift by the public sector to secure a greater control of the commanding heights of the national economy by increasing the effective points of collective leverage.

In any case, whatever the ideological predilections of a government might be at the philosophical level, practical commonsense would dictate recognition of certain practical realities on the ground. In the Nigerian case, some of these realities in the planning period included a general legacy of disappointing performance by public enterprises, continued poor administrative skills and management capability and the prerequisite need for certain institutional and policy reforms (e.g. more rational incomes policy) to attract quality resources to the public sector. All these are major programmes of reform and inevitably take time.

There is, furthermore, the conscious choice of policy priority in the domain of economic organization. The firm belief that the government of a nation could hardly control the institutions and resources which are outside the reach of its nationals meant that the battle of economic decolonization in the aggregate was judged to be more pressing. There was also the supplementary belief that economic nationalism offered at least one focal point of national consensus, and that the nation would need all its collective will for successful prosecution of the decolonization war. In this context, the critical question of economic organization has changed character from whether or not the public sector should be extensively involved in production, but rather one of at what points it should be immediately involved and with what instruments of policy.

It could very well be that in spite of these rationalizations (some might say apologia), the existence of internal contradictions in policy still persists. Such contradictions may be structural in the sense that change takes time to work itself out and in the dynamic sense of conflicts among the old, the changing and the new. Indeed, the essence of materialist dialectics is the acceptance of basic contradiction in opposing forces in the development process. In Marxism–Leninism, social development is nothing if not a continuous struggle of opposite tendencies, always provided of course that cumulative quantitative change ultimately results in a positive forward qualitative transformation in a new synthesis.

On the other hand, it could also well be that both the political-military leadership and influential power segments of the society have only a defective appreciation of the real ideological underpinning of the policies they are supposed to have designed. Such inadequacy in the level of appreciation can only lead to wrong and counter-productive implementation. Or they may have been genuinely convinced about the real ideological implications at the point of policy formation, but are no longer now so sure of their philosophical validity. The private sector, and especially the emerging indigenous capitalist class that sees itself as the main beneficiary of the new policy (and whose expectations are confirmed by the current fact of booming personal prosperity), is at least clearly at variance with such an ideological posture. For all these and more, and to raise the standard of social debate for the next round of national policy formation, it would be useful to restate if not re-examine the philosophical foundation of the role of the State in economic development.

The State and Production Relations

In the light of our discussion above, it is not necessary to re-examine at length the basic justification for intervention by the state in the economic affairs of a nation. Even the most rudimentary government anywhere controls its defence industry, seeks to influence its monetary system (monopolizes at least its Mint), collects tax, erects some infrastructural facilities and provides some minimum amenities for its citizens.

The more interesting question then is why a state should be directly involved in production activity through the establishment of public enterprises. The Western liberal view of this issue is essentially a negative one, namely to cover up gaps and deficiencies in a performance process dominated by private enterprises. Beyond the natural monopolies and semi-public goods ('gas and water' socialism of the Fabians), public enterprises are defended where private enterprise is unwilling or unable – considering the test of financial profitability – to undertake the production of certain goods and services which may be judged to be socially desirable. The existence of external economies which cannot be translated readily into private revenue is often the basis for a good case. Indivisibility of large capital requirement is offered as another ground for public enterprises to cover up a potential capacity leakage. Pressure of international competition in the home or external market, inability to perceive or wait for long-term benefits from a given investment programme with a long gestation period and the fear of large-scale unemployment in sensitive areas of the national economy are some of the other additional justifications made for public enterprises in directly productive activities.

For an underdeveloped country, however, the more relevant question should be: why not public enterprises? In other words, the presumption should not be private enterprise in the first instance. The theoretical supremacy of public enterprise as a model of production organization should be taken for granted, as implicitly justified by the very character of the existing state of underdevelopment. In this context, the relevant policy exercise becomes one of analysing and removing obstacles to expansion of the public sector as a standard production mode.

There are several reasons for this reversal of presumptive institutional hypothesis in the case of an underdeveloped economy. All the arguments made in support of public sector intervention to cover gaps and deficiencies by private enterprises in the advanced industrial economies remain with even greater validity in circumstances of underdevelopment. Additionally, the underdeveloped economy is typically dominated by neo-colonial economic relations; but the battle of economic decolonization can hardly be won without massive public sector intervention in all fronts. And subsequent to winning the battle of eliminating external control, there is the bigger internal battle for distributive equity as the only valid basis for long-term peaceful social relations. There is, furthermore, the well-known case that an underdeveloped economy with potential resources and markets can be defined in terms of its structural distortions, especially of the deviation of its revealed product and factor prices from their true equilibrium values. A successful translation of such shadow prices to real decision-making prices can hardly be made outside a set of progressive economic policies and of direct state involvement in production. Successful public sector investments also tend to have a kind of multiplier effect in generating the need for new and more public sector investments, not to mention the effect of shifts in and growth of private demand on public goods and services.

It is true that the adoption of economic planning as an approach to fostering development is not of the essence of public enterprises *per se*. In other words, it is conceivable to have public enterprises without planning the national economy. But the reverse is hardly valid, namely to have general equilibrium planning in an underdeveloped economy without the establishment and expansion of public enterprises. Now, once economic planning is accepted as a socially desirable and politically feasible frame of policy reference,the whole question of public enterprises takes a different turn.

The general aims of planned development are similar to and indeed reflected by the broad objectives of public enterprises: to maximize the relationship between social benefits and social costs of projects and programmes, to maximize potential growth of the social product and to equalise economic opportunities by eliminating unjustifiable inequalities of wealth. By the social ownership of the means of production, the inherent abuse of discretionary powers of private monopoly power is not only removed, but production relations take direct cognisance of distributive questions right from the base. An economic system dominated by public enterprises will facilitate direct economic controls and the pursuit of essential non-economic goals of economic development. They enhance the prospect of successful plan implementation. By inculcating the sense of community service in replacement of a myopic pursuit of self-interest, public enterprises attempt to eradicate the sense of class and create a consciousness of common interest and equal status. Improved ideological motivation makes possible higher individual and social productivities, facilitates the prediction and control of national economic trends, and helps to legitimatise government as an instrument of development. A new spirit of co-operation and fellowship replaces the brutal competitive struggle for personal gain, thereby transforming society to a higher level of values. An essential rationale of planning is the belief that certain social obligations transcend market considerations, and this is in itself the ultimate underlying purpose of public enterprises.

Public enterprises constitute a major instrument of plan design and plan fulfilment. Development planning, as well as the public enterprises system as an integral part of the planning process, share in common the basic assumption that the economic activities of a nation should generally be subject to democratic control of the community as represented by the state apparatus. This mutually inter-dependent relationship implies that successful general equilibrium planning, at any rate in the circumstances of underdevelopment, requires the creation and functioning of a large public sector sufficiently large to constitute the predominant force in the national economy.[9]

So we can now better appreciate our earlier point that although central planning is only tangentially related to the issue of public enterprises in the advanced industrial economies, the two are in fact inseparable in the circumstances of underdevelopment. In the former case, public enterprise can survive, indeed flourish, without a national plan; but in the latter, development planning without public enterprises would amount to little more than an academic exercise. For a country like Nigeria with so much widespread poverty matched both by growing resources and expanding market potential, meaningful development means total mobilization for speedy economic expansion and social reform. This implies that the productive forces of society must be related in such a way that the twin issues of economic growth and social equity (especially of income distribution) would be resolved simultaneously. Such a unique solution is provided by the concept of a large public sector engaged in directly productive activities.

Since all parts of the state machine must thus be geared to the process of planned development, it is futile to ask the question, how far should the state intervene in production? The only logical answer is that it could and it should intervene at *all* production points. For a planned developing economy, the whole process of development can be conceived as one massive movement of public enterprises. The interesting issue for policy then becomes not a defence of the public enterprises system, but an explanation of why the private enterprise sector exists. As the presumptive basis of production relations thus changes, the onus is reversed and existing private enterprise activities have to be explained in terms of the practical realities of the movement rather than as institutional ideal types with preemptive rights to dominate production organization.

The Third Restructuring

We have argued that on the philosophical plane, an underdeveloped economy should be dominated by a super-abundance of public enterprises. Yet, we recognized in our earlier discussion that their general performance hitherto has been far from inspiring at any rate in the development experience of Nigeria. Or, given the various organizational dilemmas which the mixed economy throws up, it might be asked how the internal contradictions can be resolved.

Actually, the necessary strategy of reconciling these apparent conflicts flows easily from our discourse. First, it is important to accept the principle of preemptive dominance of the public enterprises system on the grounds both of economic (not financial) efficiency and of moral superiority. Next, it is important to appreciate that current institutional performance can be very deceptive from the standpoint of long-run development. On the side of private enterprises, it is misplaced confidence to look at the bulging profits and apparently strong balance sheets as a measure of national development success. The simple truth is that much of these profits are themselves a function of past and current public-sector policies, patronage and ideological posture. We have argued that essentially, the so-called mixed economy in Nigeria at present tends in fact to little more than a private enterprise system, and that the state economic apparatus has hitherto been geared to nourishing precisely the interest of the private sector. In any case, we know that the national objectives as spelt out in the Second National Development Plan clearly went, in their combined effects, beyond the narrow scope of economic growth. So that even if it is assumed (and such an assumption is itself questionable) that the private enterprise system maximizes and is most likely to continue to maximize the growth opportunities, there would still be left other vital national developmental objectives to meet. Of the five principal national objectives – (i) a united, strong and self-reliant nation, (ii) a great and dynamic economy, (iii) a just and egalitarian society, (iv) a land of bright and full opportunities for all citizens, and (v) a free and democratic society[10] – only the second at best is likely to be achieved by dependence on a private enterprise system.

Now for the apparent failure of the public enterprise system. Although the Nigerian public enterprises have performed far worse than was necessary, it is important to note that in principle failure by public enterprises to cover their full costs is not a satisfactory indicator of worse performance relative to private enterprises. Marginal-cost pricing could be one explanation of lower aggregate revenue. Considering their investments pattern and the activity sectors in which they are typically concentrated, public enterprises are also likely to have very high ratios of capital to value added, capital to labour and excess capacity (by building infrastructure slightly ahead of demand as well as by greater lumpiness in the character of their technology). They generate a lot of external economies, the positive results of which are not reflected in their balance sheets but show up rather in the strengthened operational accounts of the private enterprises. These external economies become even more significant for private enterprise and more ruinous for public enterprise in respect of the training of a corps of skilled workers who then move out into private-sector employment in response to an irrational salary structure loaded against the public sector. Add to all these the social millieu, the political pressure, the resource constraint and the administrative environment surrounding public enterprise operation, it would then be clear why the severe criticisms of their performance must be tempered.

Unless the problems of public enterprises in Nigeria are put in a more objective perspective in this manner, policy makers stand the danger of throwing out the baby with the bath-water. Reactions against their poor and sometimes abysmal performance can lead to such strong condemnation that makes appeal for their abolition easily acceptable. Such a return to Western liberal orthodoxy is already being given analytical support in similar cases of poor performance by developing countries. The movement backwards and away from a progressive organizational philosophy is explained and justified by enlightened policy restructuring in the light of recent widespread historical experience. Although the second restructuring of Cohen and Ranis[11] was in terms of reaction against an inward-looking strategy of development and a return to a more open exposure to external trade, it is easy to see a parallel analysis in the post-war experience of developing countries of increasing use of public enterprises as a strategy of development.

The main argument of this essay is that Nigeria should move to the phase of third post-war restructuring and develop more confident and more positive attitudes to the public enterprise system. It is true that ideological factors alone cannot determine the size and pattern of public enterprises in an economy, but undoubtedly they do go a long way in creating the necessary frame of political faith and policy confidence. This is especially important if the scope of public enterprises is to be extended beyond the creation of new activities to direct intervention in existing private enterprises (by outright nationalization, joint ownership, production sharing and management control). A progressive government of a developing country would, at least, not deny itself the right if not the duty of such intervention with any private enterprise whatsoever, whether old or new and whether foreign or indigenous. It would, as a matter of clear policy regard, and cause all private enterprises to so regard, the organization of production for private (personal) profit only as a privilege rather than an inalienable right. This conclusion in fact flows directly from the concept of government as an institution of state with potential authority to control any human and social behaviour within its jurisdiction.[12]

In practice, of course, authority to do something does not mean that it is always exercised. At any given time, government would leave undone many things it could potentially do. The only justification for this could only be a practical one and would presumably be related to the government's effective administrative capacity. With not as deep an ideological commitment, this point about real capacity in relation to potential authority was put by Hanson in the following way: 'There is no difficulty in recognising the need for a particular public enterprise. The difficulty lies in establishing it, financing it, providing it with personnel, giving it a suitable organisational shape, ensuring that it attains the maximum possible efficiency, subjecting it to adequate – but not excessive – controls, etc.'[13]

Important as these constraints on capacity are, they are really operational in character and their consideration is outside the scope of this essay. The point may be made though that the degree of difficulty encountered in overcoming such operational constraints is a function of the mode of production relations in society, which in turn is a function of the dominant ideology of the ruling elite.

Now, in a society undergoing rapid change but with widely unequal distribution of economic power, it is not easy to determine who represents the legitimate interest of the state. Perhaps social stratification in Nigeria has not yet reached the situation in which the typical Marxian model of

open class struggles can offer a fitting description. But the question of governmental legitimacy would come more and more to the fore under the combined conditions of:
(a) increasing concentration of development resources in the hands of government,
(b) the absence of parliamentary institutions or of open competition for political power as an important factor in the principle of public accountability by public enterprises, and
(c) latent, even if unused, monopoly of violence as a force by a fraction of the population to coerce compliance with policies which the rulers may rightly or wrongly consider to be in the public interest.

In the third restructuring of public policy, therefore, new positive attitudes must not only be developed to public enterprises as the most potent force for achieving the national objectives, all arrangements that tend to make government act or appear as a pressure organization for a favoured group must be removed. The basic organizational dilemma of Nigerian public enterprises system can only be resolved when the basic philosophy is accepted that the public sector is at once an instrument for the planned production of goods and the opportunity for reallocating economic power relations in any society that claims to be progressive.

References

This essay was first published in *Public Enterprises in Nigeria: Proceedings of the 1973 Annual Congress of the Nigerian Economic Society* (Ibadan, 1974).

1. Some of the major sources include the following: Gerald K. Helleiner, *Peasant Agriculture, Government and Economic Growth in Nigeria* (Homewood, III: Richard D. Irwin, 1966), chs. 10 and 12; Peter Kilby, *Industrialization in an open Economy: Nigeria 1945–1966* (Cambridge University Press, 1969), ch. 5; R. O. Teriba, 'Development Strategy, Investment Decisions and Expenditure Patterns of a Public Development Institution: The case of the Western Nigeria Development Corporation 1949–1962', *Nigerian Journal of Economic and Social Studies,* 8, 2 (1966).
2. Several Reports of Official Commissions of Inquiry covering almost each of all the major public enterprises and over a period of about two decades. Case after case, the story seems to have followed the patterns established by two earlier famous reports: *Report of the Tribunal Appointed to Inquire into Allegations Reflecting in the Official Conduct of the Premier of, and certain Persons Holding Ministerial and other Public Offices in the Eastern Region of Nigeria* (London H.M.S.O., 1957); and *Report of the Coker Commission of Inquiry into the Affairs of certain Statutory Corporations* (Lagos: Federal Ministry of Information, 1962).
3. A.H. Hanson, *Public Enterprises and Economic Development* (London: Routledge and Kegan Paul, 1965), chs. 2 and 3.
4. See, for example, comments by Stephen H. Hymer on Charles R. Frank,

Jr. 'Public and Private Enterprise in Africa', Gustav Ranis (ed.), *Government and Economic Development* (New Haven: Yale University Press, 1971), pp. 123–25.

5. This would appear to be the general approach of Western liberal economists. See P. Sargant Florence, *Industry and the State* (London: Hutchinson's University Library, 1957), chs. 6 and 7. In this category also could be placed the essay by James W. Land,' The Role of Public Enterprise in Turkish Economic Development', Gustav Ranis, *op cit.*, pp. 53–79.
6. In the current Second National Development Plan, several new public enterprises are being started (Mining, Heavy Industry, Finance) and existing ones expanded (Transportation, Power, Communications).
7. Federal Republic of Nigeria, *Second National Development Plan, 1970–74* (Lagos: Federal Government Printer, 1970), p. 289.
8. See Chapter 6 of the Plan on 'National Accounts', especially Table 16 at p. 58.
9. Janus G. Zielenski, *On the Theory of Socialist Planning* (Ibadan: Oxford University Press for NISER, 1968), Lecture 11, pp. 116–26.
10. At page 32 of the Plan,
11. Benjamin I. Cohen and Gustav Ranis, 'The Second Postwar Restructuring', in Gustav Ranis *op. cit.*, ch. 12.
12. Alfred Kuhn, *The Study of Society* (London: Tavistock Publications, 1966), ch. 29.
13. Hanson, *op. cit.*, p. 204.

6. The Working of the Nigerian National Oil Corporation
Terisa Turner

This chapter has three objectives. First, it attempts to place the Nigerian National Oil Corporation (NNOC) in an historical and international context by comparing it with the national oil corporations of other societies. Second, it evaluates the role of the corporation in making policy on the generation of revenues through establishing oil prices. The assessment of oil price determination and the 1973 crude oil auction illustrate the position which officers of the oil corporation took in opposition to the oil ministry. Third, an attempt is made to show that the oil corporation was undergoing a transition from being an agency of a state geared to commerce to becoming the instrument of a technocratic state oriented towards capitalist production.

Types of State Oil Corporations

State oil corporations and agencies are common elements of virtually all modern states. Yet the functions of these state oil entities vary immensely. They may be active in one or all five phases of the oil industry (exploration, production, transport, refining and marketing). They may compete with or service large, integrated multinational oil firms. In order to appreciate the scope of this variation in state oil corporations' functions, it is useful to distinguish between capitalist and state capitalist societies according to whether or not the option for private ownership of wealth is kept open.

Capitalist societies can be divided into four categories depending on the presence and strength of these various classes: (1) commercial capitalism, (2) developing productive capitalism, (3) developed financial-industrial capitalism, and (4) over-developed or post-productive capitalism. The first two are the major concerns of this chapter.

The least developed capitalist society is the commercial political economy in which the indigenous bourgeoisie is engaged in commercial transactions with foreign producers, often via the state. There is little capitalist production. The local bourgeoisie is composed of middlemen who facilitate the access of foreign traders to the local market. There are a small number of professionals, a small proletarianized stratum and a large semi-proletariat of peasants. In many respects, this description applies to Nigerian society. A state oil corporation in commercial capitalist countries may act as a 'gate-keeper' governing the extraction of crude by foreign multinationals and the marketing of oil products.

Second are countries in which productive capitalism is developing and towards which the Nigerian possibilities are examined in this chapter. In oil-exporting countries such as Venezuela and Iran the indigenous property-owning bourgeoisie, while small, is more significant than in commercially-oriented countries. The state is the agency for developing capitalism given the dominance of multinationals and the absence of a strong indigenous bourgeoisie. Professionally skilled technocrats engage directly in fostering productive capitalism through state corporations. The links between the external bourgeoisie, state technocrats and private local capitalists are extensive. Under state capitalism, the professional stratum is expanding as is the class of less-skilled wage labourers. The semi-proletariat, while substantial, is declining. In these circumstances the state oil corporation competes with foreign oil companies, or it is the source of bargaining strength in securing maximum advantages in state-foreign oil partnerships.

To summarize, in commercial capitalist societies, state oil corporations facilitate extraction and marketing by multinational oil corporations. Developing productive capitalist states have oil corporations which, under technocratic control, speed industrialization by competing directly with foreign oil companies and forming short-term partnerships. In developed industrial-financial capitalist societies, such as the United States and to a lesser degree Germany and Japan, the state backs private oil firms either indirectly through overall policy or directly through state oil agencies. Finally, in over-developed, post-productive capitalist societies, such as the U.K., Italy and France, the state oil corporation seeks to give declining local capital a longer lease on life by appealing to both oil multinationals and the indigenous working class.

In state capitalist societies the option of private ownership of wealth by an indigenous bourgeoisie is ruled out. Developed state capitalist countries such as the Soviet Union are characterized by a large professional-technocratic stratum, a strong semi-skilled work force and a relatively small semi-proletariat. Second, state capitalist societies such as Algeria and Iraq are developing productive capacity. Here, the indigenous bourgeoisie is being expropriated. While much property owned by the external bourgeoisie has been nationalized, this class may retain influence through other channels. The professional-technocratic stratum is growing, the semi-skilled working class is expanding and the semi-proletariat is contracting. Finally, in peripheral state capitalist countries such as Tanzania and Somalia, foreign capital remains influential, for instance, through the terms of trade and aid. The professional and semi-skilled working classes are small and the semi-proletariat encompasses most of the population. The state capitalist corporation dominated by the professional-technocratic stratum may closely resemble its counterpart in developing, productive capitalist societies such as Iraq and Algeria where mass democracy is weak. For instance, Sonatrach and NIOC technocrats operate state oil corporations in much the same way as do managers of private and European state capitalist oil firms. The differences centre on their nationalism and their leading role in generating industrial development.

How does the Nigerian National Oil Corporation (NNOC) fit into this scheme? It may be argued that oil corporations are a means through which the middleman stratum in a commercial capitalist society facilitates the extractive operations of foreign oil companies. In the next section the NNOC's pricing activities are examined in order to assess the accuracy of this categorization in the Nigerian context.

The Campaign to Establish a National Oil Corporation

In November 1969 a fact-finding Mission on oil matters recommended that the Federal Military Government set about '. . . the immediate creation of a Nigerian National Oil Company.'[1] It was argued that a national oil corporation would (1) increase revenues from oil; (2) enable the state to participate in the operations of foreign oil exploration and production subsidiaries; (3) enable Nigeria to gain just as other prominent oil-exporting countries were benefiting from national oil corporations; and (4) fulfil an urgent need for the unification of Nigerian oil administration.

The 1969 Report emphasised that 'the all important question of the requisite manpower' had to be solved if the organization was to achieve its purpose. 'There can be no shortcut around this problem of adequate and appropriate staffing. There can be no question an attempt to conserve funds by understaffing or by poor and inappropriate remunerative arrangements.'[2] Despite widespread beliefs to the contrary, manpower shortages were not an obstacle to the establishment of an oil corporation as had been the earlier experience of the Algerian state firm Sonatrach.[3] The 1969 Report included organizational diagrams of the proposed 'professional arm' of oil affairs, including Directors of Petroleum Engineering, Economics and Utilisation, and Revenue. The range and organization of personnel was patterned on that of Sonatrach and suggests that its proposers viewed a national oil corporation as *the* single oil agency, which would report to the oil ministry as little more than a formality.

In the face of widespread opposition, three and a half years passed before a Nigerian oil corporation was functioning. The campaign for an oil corporation was centred in the Ministry of Finance's Petroleum Section. Officers there found that arguments based on increased oil revenues were more effective than appeals to nationalist sentiment or solidarity with OPEC member countries.[4]

Decree 18 of 1971 established the Nigerian National Oil Corporation as a statutory corporation 'empowered to engage in prospecting for mining and marketing oil, and in all other activities associated with the petroleum oil industry.'[5] The division of powers between the oil ministry and the Federal Executive Council effectively placed the corporation under the control of both. For example, the NNOC's General Manager was to be appointed by the Federal Executive Council (FEC) on the recommendation of the Commissioner of the Ministry of Mines and Power.[6] This key officer 'who shall be the chief executive officer of the Corporation, and who shall be responsible for the day to day running of the affairs of the Corporation'[7] was thus responsible to the FEC. The approval of the FEC was necessary before NNOC could enter into any transaction which exceeded ₦100,000 in value.[8] The Board of Directors consisted of nine members including the permanent Secretaries of the Ministries of Mines and Power, Economic Development, Industries, Finance; the Director of Petroleum Resources in the Ministry of Mines and Power; the Chief Executive Officer of NNOC (the General Manager); and three other persons appointed by the Commissioner on account of their specialized knowledge.[9] A measure of the Board's status was the inclusion of four Permanent Secretaries from the 'economic ministries'. Under the Gowon regime (1966–75) the powerful Permanent Secretaries overshadowed their 'political' chiefs, the Commissioners, and virtually controlled the FEC. Board decisions were to be taken by a majority vote with the Chairman, who is the Permanent Secretary of the Ministry of Mines and Power, having a casting or second vote.[10] The Board was empowered to appoint officers and servants of the NNOC and to fix their salaries and emoluments, thus removing the corporation from the jurisdiction of the Statutory Corporations Service Commission, which fixes appointments and salaries for personnel of many state corporations. The control structure of the NNOC, is shown in Chart 1. In practice no General Manager was appointed with the result that the Ministry of Mines and Power, and the Permanent Secretary in particular, controlled the NNOC.

The process of establishing the corporation as a functioning agency was slowed by difficulties with recruitment and a shortage of office space. The first Board meeting, held on 2 September 1971, was addressed by the Commissioner for Mines and Power, R.A.E. Dikko, and resolved to rely on the Common Services Unit of the Department of Petroleum Resources until staff and officers were acquired.[11] In connection with its responsibility to recruit principal and senior officers of the corporation, the Board constituted a committee charged with interviewing and selecting candidates for employment. In 1971 salary scales for NNOC management staff were fixed by the Board as a compromise between rates prevailing in the public services and those in the oil industry. The tasks of finding office space and recruiting staff were carried out by the Ministry of Mines and Power. A measure of the priority accorded the NNOC is indicated by the difficulties in finding office space. It proved impossible to find accommodation large enough to house the corporation in a single location.[12] This problem and a similar difficulty in arranging for telephone installation reflects in part the situation of infrastructure overload in Lagos. However, other firms are able to build, rent, and obtain functioning communication systems. The problem was that the NNOC's status was low with the Federal Government, which had leverage over the Lagos State Government, the major landlord in Nigeria's

Chart 1
Control of the Nigerian National Oil Corporation by the Federal Executive Council According to Decree 18 of 1971

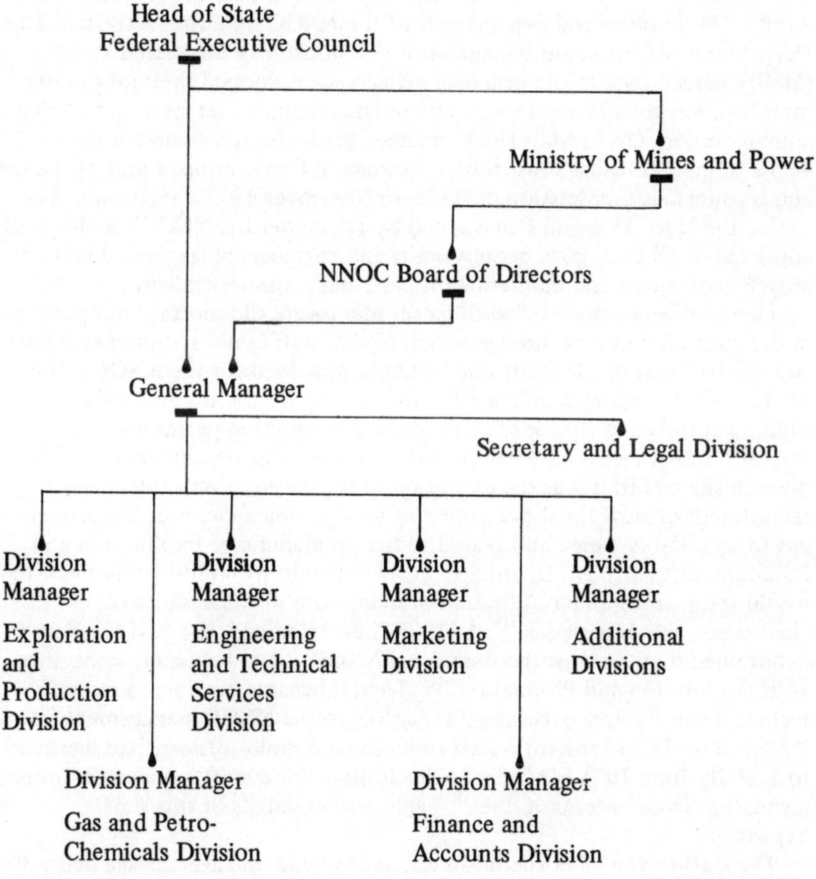

capital.[13]

Recruitment began in mid-1972 when the first intake of petroleum technologists occurred and specialized training was arranged. In July 1972 those securing training appointments were sent abroad or enrolled in courses in Nigeria. Twelve geologists and twelve engineers were sent to France for a year's training. A series of recruitments were spread over the rest of 1972. In April 1973 divisions and departments of the NNOC were first activated. The Department of Petroleum Resources of the Ministry of Mines and Power (MMP) handed over to the principal officers who assumed their jobs in that month all documents, equipment and outstanding matters relating to NNOC's administration. On 25 May 1973, nineteen graduates were sent for one year's training to India's Institute of Petroleum Exploration, a unit of the Oil and Natural Gas Commission of India. In November 1973 a recruiting panel visited the U.K., U.S. and Canada, and by December the NNOC's senior staff consisted of 64 geologists, geophysicists and engineers; 4 lawyers; 8 accountants; 8 economists and marketing officers, and 3 administrators.

Two problems associated with recruitment were the shortage of openings in the local oil industry through which NNOC staff could acquire experience and the fact that no clear-cut role had been approved for the NNOC to fulfil. The NNOC reported in late 1973 that 'currently the training effort is running at full capacity for exploration and production personnel. The biggest limiting factor has been facilities for practical attachments . . .'[14] A prerequisite to hiring was the definition of the corporation's role: 'The recruitment of staff for the Engineering and Technical Services Department has to be suitably timed and geared to the programme of Exploration and Production Department in order to avoid frustration and loss of morale which would result from under-utilisation of manpower or the absence of challenging job experience.'[15] As 1973 drew to an end, the NNOC's Board determined that ' . . . for the time being NNOC would be mainly concerned with Exploration and Production.'[16] 'Then it became possible to recruit technical and services personnel,' according to the NNOC management.[17] By the end of 1973 the total staff of junior and senior officers had increased to 159. By June 1975, a total of 178 additional new staff had been recruited giving the NNOC a total of 288.[18] Table 1 gives details of this staff expansion.

The staff of the oil corporation was very young, the average age being 30 years in 1975. NNOC staff were well-educated with 42% having a university degree or post-graduate degree. If we exclude the 145 officers in the administrative division, half of whom are messengers, drivers and office attendants,[19] of the remaining 143 staff members, 42% have post-graduate degrees, 33% have bachelor degrees and the remaining 25% have professional qualifications, the equivalent of high school education (or 'O' levels) or less. The remarkable fact is that a full 75% of NNOC's non-administrative personnel have post-graduate degrees.

The technicians and professionals in the NNOC with post-graduate degrees specialized in the following fields: petroleum technology, geophysics, petroleum geology, mechanical/civil/reservoir/pipeline and electrical engineering, business law, textile and chemical engineering, law, librarianship, zoology, and accountancy. The officers with bachelor degrees pursued similar courses but did not continue to the M.Sc., Ph.D. or diploma level. Those with professional qualifications obtained Higher National Diplomas (HND) in mechanical engineering and accountancy, or possessed statistical, secretarial or intermediate accountancy diplomas. Many draughtsmen and assistants in the geophysics department possessed the West African School Leaving Certificate (WASC), which is equivalent to a high school or Ordinary Level qualification. Finally there are several members of the administrative staff who have attempted the WASC or who have a minimum of six years formal education and have obtained the First School Leaving Certificate (FSLC) or the Modern III Certificate with three years experience.

Table 1
NNOC Staff 1973 and 1975

Function	*1973 December*	*1975 June*	*Increase*
Exploration and Production Division	65	77	12
Engineering and Technical Services Division	1	17	16
Administration Division	81	145	64
Marketing Division	8	12	4
Gas and Petrochemicals Division		1	1
Secretary and Legal Division	4	6	2
Finance and Accounts Division	9	17	8
Second Refinery Project Team		13	13
Less Wastage	–9		
Total	159	288	129

Source: *NNOC Annual Report 1971–1973,* Appendix I and NNOC Administration Division communication, 30 June 1975.

The Role of the NNOC

Revenue Determination

In recommending the creation of the NNOC, the 1969 Report emphasized its role in increasing oil revenues.[20] The state oil corporation was to secure participation in foreign oil companies and this was considered to be a means of increasing revenues, primarily through illuminating the 'grey area' between real production costs and high company declarations rather than through establishing state control and sale of oil. Participation via a national oil corporation would 'facilitate intimate contact with all activities [and] in turn enable the country to obtain a close approximation of costs and therefore make a better assessment of oil taxation and other oil revenue revenue . . .'[21]

In practice, the roles the NNOC came to play in revenue determination involved (1) calculating prices at which the state could sell its participation oil back to the producing companies, (2) assessing market prices and negotiating contracts for the direct sale of state oil to 'third party' buyers and (3) monitoring company operating costs with the objectives of maintaining a high taxable base and reducing the size of state contributions which were made towards operating costs in proportion to participation interests. The first and second roles are assessed in the following sections. However, the treatment of those latter roles is partial and selective given that this study's focus is on determining the function of Nigeria's oil corporation in what has been described as a commercial capitalist society.

The NNOC influenced the size of oil revenues mainly through pressing for high oil prices and urging that more oil be brought under state ownership. The corporation is empowered to recommend on, but not to decide, oil prices. Its role in revenue determination derives first from the fact that the state's participation interest, and therefore state oil, is vested in the corporation. Second, its authority is based on its possession of technical, market and financial expertise. This knowledge gives the corporation powers over revenue generation which go beyond the giving of advice. As is often the case when specialized information and final authority are held by different parties, it is sometimes difficult to attribute decisions to the oil corporation or to the ministry. But the evidence suggests that advice from the NNOC's marketing officials often was not accepted (rightly or wrongly) by the Permanent Secretary of the Ministry of Mines and Power who was also the Chairman of the NNOC.[22]

Between 1966 and 1973 when the corporation became operative, changes were made in legislation governing the financial operations of oil companies. The Petroleum Division of the Ministry of Finance initiated many of these reforms, which were aimed at bringing Nigerian oil regulations into line with those in Libya and in OPEC. The decision to revise expense royalties, base tax calculations on posted prices, reduce depreciation allowances, eliminate marketing allowances and add freight and other premiums on a posted price which was increasing with inflation, had the cumulative effect of increasing state income per barrel from $0.295 in 1966[23] to $1.87 in 1972,[24] an improvement of over 600%.

Income From the Sale of Buyback Oil

The increases in per barrel revenue secured through revision of financial terms between 1966 and 1972, significant though they were, were overshadowed by the huge boost to state income stemming from the sale of participation oil. The question of state participation involves two issues: financial involvement leading to control over oil on the one hand, and operational involvement on the other. The present concern is to assess the first issue: Under what conditions did the state acquire and sell buyback oil? Buyback oil is that part of production which is owned by the state as a result of the state taking an undivided interest[25] in the operations of oil firms and which is sold back to the producing companies.

Revenues from buyback oil were generated as early as June 1971 when the state acquired for $6,138,170 a 35% undivided interest in the French state oil company Safrap (renamed Elf in 1975) as a condition of the firm's resuming activity after the pro-Biafran stance of de Gaulle during the Civil War. Under the agreement Safrap was entitled to buy back 100% of the state's share of oil.[26] In October 1971 the government took up its option under a 1962 Agreement to acquire a third shareholding in the joint operation Agrip-Phillips. This involved a $33\frac{1}{3}$% undivided interest in the 50% share of Phillips Oil Company (Nigeria) Ltd., at a cost of $18,401,767 representing $16^2/_3$% participating interest in the Agrip-Phillips concessions. Because this is an undivided interest, a third of Phillips' oil or a sixth of the joint operation production accrued to the state. At the same time the state acquired $33^1/_3$% equity shares in Nigerian Agrip Oil Company at a consideration of $92,602. In effect, state interest in the total Agrip-Phillips holdings together produced only 75 million barrels of oil in 1973 or less than a fifth of Shell-BP's 431 million barrels. The volumes involved in the Safrap and Phillips participation deals were small compared to the amounts accruing to the state through the 35% Shell-BP participation arrangement which became effective 1 April 1973. In 1973 the state owned 8 million barrels of oil produced by Safrap, 6 million barrels from Phillips and 126 million barrels from Shell-BP.[27]

The acquisition of an undivided interest in Shell-BP was the first attempt by the Nigerian state to revise concession terms which had been established earlier. The move corresponded to initiatives in other oil-exporting countries to implement OPEC's 1968 policy of securing a participatory interest in long-established companies on 'the grounds of the principle of changing circumstances'.[28] The effect of OPEC participation was to place proportions of crude oil under state rather than company control from 1 January 1973. As a result, companies were unsure of their ability to supply refineries and marketing outlets. The issue of the energy crisis predates the October 1973 Middle East war and oil embargo and, in fact, is said by some students of the question to have started in 1968.[29] In April 1973 Shell urged the establishment of a contingency system of oil allocations in the case that shortages developed.[30] On 13 April 1973 a bill was introduced into the United States Senate to authorize the President 'to allocate energy and fuels when he determines and declares that extraordinary shortages or dislocations in the distribution of energy and fuels exists or are imminent . . .'[31]

As OPEC members gained participation, the demand for oil, especially in the United States, began to exceed the amounts allowed for by those planning supply levels. This context of shortage had implications for company-government negotiations over participation. The oil companies exerted every effort to delay the effective date of state participation, to minimize the extent of participation, to secure the buyback rights to maximum amounts of state oil and, finally, to secure low prices for the buy-back oil. The companies' success in achieving these objectives in Nigeria can be assessed by comparing Nigerian terms with those reached by other OPEC member countries. The actual terms may also be contrasted with those which appeared to be within the reach of the Nigerian state at the time. This assessment indicates that despite opposition from the NNOC, the oil industry presided over the implementation of terms which were very favourable to the oil companies with respect to the timing of participation acquisitions, the extent and cost of state ownership, and the volume and price of buyback oil.

The Timing of Participation Acquisition

In contrast to other oil-producing countries such as Algeria, Iraq and Libya who between 1971 and 1973 took ownership and control of their industries in the range of 51% to 100%, Nigerian participation in Shell-BP was not effective until 1 April 1973. Had Nigerian participation in Shell-BP been effective a year earlier, even at the lower level of 25% as was the case in Saudi Arabia and Abu Dhabi from 1 January 1973, revenues of $137 million would have been realized.[33] If a 35% interest had been acquired one quarter earlier, at the beginning of 1973, state income would have been augumented by $50 million.[34]

In 1973 the oil ministry did not secure participation in Gulf and Mobil which produce almost a third of Nigerian crude. On 6 December 1973 the Nigerian National Oil Corporation issued a protest to the oil ministry over low buyback prices charged to Shell-BP.[35] An interest in companies other than Shell-BP would have increased income from buyback sales by some 50%. It is clear that Nigerian participation came late. This cost the state, but benefited the oil companies.

The Extent and Cost of State Ownership

Also in contrast to other OPEC states who in early 1973 were seeking or had secured 51%, 60% or 100% ownership, the extent of state participation and control of oil in Nigeria was limited. Nigerian participation was increased by only 20% to 55% from 1 April 1974.

The delay in arranging state shares in Gulf, Mobil and Texaco has been noted.[36] Why were the American major oil companies able to retain 100%

ownership of their operations and their oil throughout the embargo shortage of 1974? This question is especially pertinent given that Gulf's subsidiary in Kuwait conceded 60% from the beginning of 1974 and a retroactive 25% interest for all of 1973. Furthermore, Nigeria had covenanted with Gulf and all operators that terms agreed to in other oil-exporting countries would similarly apply in Nigeria. Despite the strong position of the Nigerian government, the U.S. firms had open to them a strategy based on the denial of favoritism. In response to an NNOC call in late September 1973 for a 40% share in Gulf, Mobil and Texaco, the American firms demanded terms as favourable as those obtained by Shell-BP.[37] They sought to be compensated on the basis of book value updated for inflation rather than net book value. They rejected NNOC demands for buyback prices 'substantially above those agreed with Shell-BP.'[38] According to one report, 'it was assumed that the agreement reached with Shell-BP would form a basis of a settlement with the other large producers.'[39] Mobil and Gulf held out for several months by invoking the 'most favoured company' clause. This clause is part of the covenant accompanying oil production licences; it binds the government to treat one company no less favourably than another.[40] The settlement with the American majors, effective 1 April 1974, fell 5% short of the 60% OPEC minimum. Shell-BP, Safrap and Agrip-Phillips also conceded 55% undivided interest on 1 April 1974. However, in no case had the counterparts of the financial agreements which set out terms for operational involvement by the Nigerian state been signed. Nor had Mobil, Gulf and Texaco gone beyond agreement in principle to financial participation: in March 1976 they had yet to sign the agreements.[41] The Nigerian participation agreements did not include provisions for gradually increasing the state's share over a period of time. This was agreed by the oil ministry despite the trend in OPEC towards complete state ownership of oil-producing activities, which was accelerated in April 1974 by Aramco's offer of 100% ownership to the Saudi Arabian state.[42]

In contrast to other OPEC countries, Nigeria compensated Shell-BP for the 35% interest on the basis of updated rather than net book value.[43] terms in 1973. In 1974 payment for Nigeria's 55% interest in Gulf and Mobil and the 20% increase in Shell-BP participation was calculated on the lower net book value.

The Volume of Buyback Oil

The companies also obtained the right to buy back almost 100% of state oil in 1973 and 1974.[44] During its first year of participation, Shell-BP succeeded in buying back all state oil apart from 15,000 barrels a day.[45] The participation agreement gave the company the right to 99% of total production. In contrast, the Gulf states' 25% participation agreement made available to national oil corporations 6.25% of total production initially, rising to 12% by the third year.[46] This agreement, considered conservative at the time, was short-lived.[47] That even less oil was available to the NNOC is a measure of the passive character of Nigerian participation. From June and October 1971

Safrap and Agrip-Phillips respectively retained the right to buy back 100% of the state's 35% and 16⅔% of production. However, by special arrangement the state secured 10,000 barrels per day (bd) each from Phillips in August and from Agrip in September 1973.[48] Again, from 1 April 1974 the participation agreement with Shell-BP allowed the state to retain 13.75% of total production, of 25% of state oil, but in practice the company bought back 98% of production. Participation agreements specified company rights to buy back most of the oil. In addition during 1973 and 1974 the oil ministry, regardless of price, showed active preference for selling state oil to local producing firms rather than to outside buyers.[49]

The Price of Buyback Oil

The companies obtained buyback oil at favourable prices. Shell-BP paid less for buyback oil than did other companies in Nigeria. Overall, Nigerian buyback prices were lower than the OPEC norm. The April 1973 agreement through which NNOC acquired a 35% interest in Shell-BP specified that buyback prices could be re-negotiated[51] 'With effect from the date of any variation in Government take resulting from change in the posted prices for crude oil exported from Nigeria . . . the buyback price of any crude oil lifted after such date shall be adjusted for the amount of such variation expressed in U.S. cents per barrel payable by the Company on an identical barrel if sold by the Company for export'. But as posted prices rose sharply from $4.29 in October 1973 to $8.404 on 1 November, no commensurate increase was made in the price of buyback oil. Posted prices for 34.00–34.09 rose from $2.17 on 1 January 1970 to $2.42 in 1971, $3.176 in 1972, $3.561 in 1973, and to $14.691 on 1 January 1974. Table 2 indicates that the buyback price declined from about 84% of the posted price in the second quarter of 1973 to about 72% of the higher posted price at the end of the year. Table 3 compares the cost to Shell-BP of equity oil in 1973 with the actual buyback price paid and with the standard OPEC price for buyback oil which was half-way between the postings and the tax-paid cost. In the fourth quarter of 1973 the actual buyback price paid by Shell-BP was markedly lower than this standard half-way price. However, it is interesting to note that the buyback price did increase by the same number of cents in each quarter as the posted price. This indicates the mechanical nature of buyback escalation terms to which the oil ministry agreed. It is inherently contradictory for the Nigerian government to conform to OPEC's new posted price system while simultaneously retaining the rigid formula for buyback price increments. The oil ministry was challenged by NNOC for retaining these outdated price levels,[52] but the NNOC was unable to bring Shell-BP to the negotiating table.[53] If we consider a fair price for buyback oil to equal 93% of the posted price,[54] we can calculate that as a result of the oil ministry's refusal to revise buyback prices upwards for the fourth quarter of 1973, the gross value of buyback crude was reduced by some $53 million.[55] In 1974 average buyback prices for participation oil were between 82 and 88% of the posted price rather than the 93% which was standard in OPEC at that time. .

Table 2
Shell-BP Buyback Prices for 1973

Quarter and Month	*Barrels*	*Buyback Price ($)*	*Gross Monthly Value ($)*	*Posted Price ($)*	*Buyback Price % of Posted Price*
April	9,822,533	3.2102	31,532,158	3.806	84.35
May	13,000,872	3.2123	41,762,062	3.806	84.40
June	13,128,201	3.3249	43,649,787	4.003	83.06
Second quarter	35,951,606	3.2528	116,944,000	3.878	83.88
July	11,516,442	3.4057	39,221,263	3.806	89.48
August	11,840,151	3.5050	41,440,835	3.806	92.09
September	12,252,861	3.5067	42,966,857	4.291	81.72
Third quarter	35,609,454	3.4718	123,628,500	3.975	87.35
October	13,385,341	4.0003	53,546,003	4.287	93.31
November	13,438,686	6.0002	80,634,225	8.404	71.40
December	15,880,652	6.0029	95,329,293	8.404	71.43
Fourth quarter	42,704,679	5.3743	229,509,521	7.443	72.20
Total	114,265,739	4.1139	470,082,033	5.645	72.88

Source: *NNOC Annual Report 1971–1973*, Table 5.

Table 3
A Comparison Between 1973 Shell-BP Buyback Prices, Tax-Paid Cost, and 'Half-Way' Prices

Quarter and Month	*Tax-Paid Cost ($)**	*Posted Price ($)*	*Halfway Buyback Price ($)*	*Actual Buyback Price ($)*	*Difference Between Actual and Halfway Buyback Prices (cents)*	*Difference Between Actual Buyback Prices and Tax-Paid Cost (cents)*
Second						
April	2.4632	3.806	3.1342	3.2102	7.60	74.7
May	2.4623	3.806	3.1342	3.2123	7.60	75.0
June	2.5833	4.003	3.2932	3.3249	3.17	74.2
Third						
July	2.5833	4.003	3.2932	3.4057	11.25	82.2
August	2.5833	4.003	3.2932	3.5050	21.18	92.2
September	2.7579	4.291	3.5245	3.5067	–1.78	74.9
Fourth						
October	2.7554	4.287	3.5212	4.0003	47.91	124.5
November	5.2503	8.404	6.8272	6.0002	–82.70	75.0
December	5.2503	8.404	6.8272	6.0029	–82.43	75.3

Source: Calculated from *NNOC Annual Report 1971–1973*, Table 5

* 35 cents a barrel is assumed to be the cost of production. In 1974 the government allowed 40 cents a barrel to be claimed for production costs, so this estimate for 1973 is reasonable.

The buyback price regime accorded Shell-BP in the fourth quarter of 1973 is even more remarkable when it is noted that Safrap and Phillips were paying prices respectively $2.04 and $2.50 higher for state oil than those paid by the Anglo-Dutch major. If we compare the prices charged to Shell-BP, Safrap and Phillips for buyback oil to the end of 1973, for the month of December 1973 Shell-BP was paying $6.00 per barrel for government oil while Safrap paid $8.15 and Phillips $8.52.[56] These figures probably underestimate the price preferences enjoyed by Shell-BP. Given the small companies' higher production costs the difference in the cost of an average barrel of oil exported by these companies is probably even larger. In this connection, an oil corporation statement of December 1973 noted that companies like Agrip, Safrap, Phillips from whom they were getting a better basis of participation were paying over $3.40/bbl above Shell-BP for the same barrel of oil sold to the same market.[57]

Posted prices increased by 96% in the fourth quarter of 1973. While buyback prices charged to Safrap and Phillips were revised upwards 77% and 76% respectively, the price for Shell-BP was increased by only 55%. Throughout 1973 the average buyback price paid by Safrap was 11% higher than that paid by Shell-BP while Phillips paid 17% more on the average buyback barrel. Had all buyback crude for the fourth quarter of 1973 alone been charged at the price paid by Safrap ($7.42) the oil's gross value would have been increased by a third or $87 million. If the still higher price of $7.87 paid by Phillips applied similarly to Shell-BP and Safrap, the gross value of the quarter's buyback oil would be increased by two-fifths or $108 million. These calculations are detailed in Table 4.

Data on the buyback prices paid by individual companies in Nigeria during 1974–6 is not available. However, it appears that the price set for Shell-BP applied similarly to Gulf and Mobil from 1 April 1974, or from 1 January if a 35% interest was gained retroactively in those two firms. It is of considerable significance that throughout 1973 state revenues from Gulf and Mobil production were based on royalties and profits tax exclusively with no contribution from buyback sales. As a result these firms made major financial gains.

Oil which Shell-BP had the first opportunity to buy in 1973 is called option oil. Of the 114,265,739 barrels of state oil sold back to that company in 1973, 11% or 12,569,230 barrels fell into the category of option oil. The participation agreement specified that the price of this oil should equal offers made by third parties who were seeking allotments from the state:[58] 'The price for the (first option) crude oil to be sold and delivered under this paragraph and all other terms and conditions of such sale shall be established in negotiations between the parties, and shall be no less favourable than those at which a third party or parties would be prepared to purchase comparable quantities of comparable crude oil in firm bona fide offers.' While the actual price paid by Shell-BP for option oil in 1973 is not known, it is reasonable to assume that it is 20 cents above the price paid for the first 85% of state oil which was bought back.[59] Thus, for the

Table 4
Effect of Three Buyback Prices on Gross Value: Fourth Quarter 1973

	Shell-BP	*Safrap (Elf)*	*Phillips*	*Total (millions)*	*Increase in Gross Value ($)*	*% Increase*
Buyback barrels (millions)	42.705	2.158	1.090	45.953		
Gross value (actual prices)	229.510 ($5.3774)	16.009 ($7.4181)	8.576 ($7.8692)	254.094		
Gross value (Safrap price: $7.4181)	316.788	16.009	8.084	340.881	86.787	+34.16
Gross value (Phillips price: $7.8292)	336.052	16.982	8.576	361.610	107.516	+42.31

Source: Calculated from Tables 5 and 6, NNOC *Annual Report 1971–73*

three quarters in question, option oil was sold to Shell-BP for $3.23, $3.45 and $5.35. If Shell-BP had been required to pay the same price for option oil that third party buyers actually did pay, state income would have gained between 12 and 16 million dollars. If the option oil had been sold at prices offered by third parties, state income would have been increased by between 38 and 91 million dollars.

The oil companies benefited as a result of Nigerian participation terms which from April 1974 allowed the companies to retain 45% of production rather than only 40% as was the case in other oil-exporting countries. The companies were able to gain access to an extra 5% of oil at tax-paid cost in Nigeria. This amounted to some 30 million barrels in the last three quarters of 1974 when production reached 2.26 million bd. The companies lifted some 33 and 36 million barrels in 1975 and 1976 respectively when production averaged 1.79 and 2 million bd. In total some 100 million barrels of oil were released between April 1974 and December 1976 at tax-paid cost rather than at buyback prices.

Approximately $150 million was foregone by the state through treating 5% of production as equity rather than as participation oil. As a result the average cost to the companies of a barrel of Nigerian oil was lower than crude of comparable quality from other sources. This gave Nigerian oil a competitive edge on the world market. Another way of saying the same thing is that Nigeria was undercutting OPEC prices. This policy of Africa's largest producer created dissention within OPEC since Algerian oil was undersold. The overall effect of 55% rather than 60% participation in Nigeria was to exert a downward pressure on world oil prices from 1974.

This assessment of price indicates that oil companies secured buyback oil on terms favourable compared with those prevailing in other OPEC countries. Shell-BP paid less than the French and Italian state firms while the U.S. majors, Gulf and Mobil, secured all their oil at tax-paid cost at least until January 1974. This price policy cost the Nigerian state hundreds of millions of dollars. In addition it undermined OPEC efforts to maintain a high uniform price. The Nigerian state undercut OPEC prices by releasing buyback oil at reduced rates and also by maintaining the 45–55% participation pattern when other OPEC member countries had acquired 60% or 100% state ownership of production operations.

The 1973 Crude Auction

In late 1973 when international demand for oil reached unprecedented heights, the NNOC held a crude oil auction which failed to sell any oil. This attempt by the NNOC led to sharp corporation-ministry division. The 1973 crude auction was a dramatic event which formed part of an international crisis. Nigeria's oil auction illustrates the interests of the local private sector and major oil companies on the one hand and the interests of minor or independent oil companies on the other. Furthermore, the auction illustrates the connection between each of these three sets of actors and their respective home country states.

The oil auction was an attempt by the NNOC to sell state oil directly to purchasers on the basis of highest price. What would on the surface appear to be a straightforward technical exercise was in fact politically charged for three reasons. First, the companies producing oil in Nigeria sought to buy back state-owned oil rather than have it sold on the open market at higher prices. Second, private Nigerian middlemen competed to perform a role in the sale of oil and win a commission from the buyer. The lower the price, the higher the commission. The temptation for officials of state to allocate oil to local middlemen was considerable: it could mean substantial personal income. A successful oil middlemen could become fabulously wealthy overnight through nothing but patronage. A third sense in which direct state oil sales were politically charged has to do with the competition among international oil firms for access to oil in the late months of 1973. The large oil companies with integrated operations resisted crude auctions; in a shortage situation auctions would drive up the price of the marginal barrel.[60] The majors were reluctant to continue supplying small, non-integrated refiners and marketers with oil as 1973 unfolded. The Arab-Israeli war of October 1973 impeded the movement of oil supplies: by November Arab exporters cut back production. Under embargo and shortage conditions the large companies needed all the oil they could get for their own integrated systems. Consequently the small companies, which were active in only one or two phases of the oil business and which did not have access to cost crude, desperately sought oil and were willing to pay very high prices. Often these small operators approached state agencies of oil-exporting countries directly and sought to purchase crude. But they also worked through intermediaries. Many international market mediators appeared at this point.[61] These intermediaries aimed to buy crude from the producing states and sell it to refiners and other buyers at a higher price.

In sum, the Nigerian crude auction of late 1973 elicited great interest from Shell-BP and other Nigerian producers who stood to lose the oil, from Nigerian middlemen who sought fees, from international majors which opposed unconstrained price competition, from international intermediaries who sought commissions, and from independent oil firms (largely American and Japanese) which were desperate for oil at any price.

As mentioned above, the 1973 crude auction led to a sharp corporation-Ministry division. The divisive issues included the volume of oil available for direct sale, the role of middlemen, and the conduct of bidding.

Volume Available for Sale

Oil was available to the Nigerian state for direct sale from two sources. First, by virtue of state participation in the operations of Safrap, Agrip-Phillips and Shell-BP in 1973, the government owned crude. It has been stated that in practice almost all of this oil was bought back by the producing companies. Only 15,000 bd of state-owned oil from Shell-BP was retained by the state in 1973. Although the agreements with Phillips and Safrap specified that 100% of state-owned oil was to be bought back by the producing companies, special arrangements were made in August 1973 to retain 10,000 bd of Safrap's production and 10,000 bd of Phillips' production.[62] Thus, in 1973 the state had access to 15,000 bd of participation oil and 20,000 bd of 'special' oil for direct sale. Second, the agreements between the state and producing companies on royalty payments specified that the government could take royalties in cash or in oil. Cash royalty payments are calculated by multiplying the posted price by 12.5% for onshore production and by 10% for offshore production or by 14.5% for all production from 1 July 1974.[63] It is to the advantage of the state to receive royalties in cash as long as posted prices are higher than the going price for crude on the open market. But in 1973 the open market price of oil began to rise rapidly. By August 1973 there was no doubt that it was higher than posted prices.[64] While OPEC member countries increased posted prices in accord with the Tehran and Geneva agreements and in response to rising prices on the open market, these increases in postings were consistently overtaken by still larger rises in open market prices. Under these circumstances it was in the commercial interest of the state to take royalties in crude and sell the oil on the open market to a third party willing to pay prices higher than the posted prices. In 1973, according to the NNOC, some 250,000 bd of royalty oil were available for direct sale. But the volume of oil under NNOC control was itself a controversial issue. More oil was potentially available. The possibility existed for enlarging the amount of state oil retained from the Shell-BP participation share, for securing larger allotments of participation oil from Safrap and Agrip-Phillips, and most important, for establishing participation interests in Gulf, Mobil and Texaco and thereby obtaining more state oil for direct sales. One of the main motives behind NNOC's drive to obtain state participation in the U.S. oil companies in 1973 was to get access to oil. After months of frustration in this campaign the NNOC protested to the oil ministry that, because of the delay in finalizing the agreements with Gulf and Mobil, the latter were holding much of NNOC's crude.[65] As long as the international crude shortage persisted, tension over the availability of oil to NNOC continued to divide the ministry and the corporation.

The first direct sales of state oil were arranged by the Ministry of Mines and Power in early 1973. In March a contract was concluded to sell a million tons of oil or 15,000 bd to Tenneco, an American independent, over three years.[66] The 15,000 bd of crude from Shell-BP was committed to service this contract.[67] Another 20,000 bd was alloted by the ministry in April 1973 to the German firm, Gelsenberg.[68] Middlemen were involved in these first direct sales of Nigerian state oil. In the Gelsenberg contract the German firm was assisted by a Nigerian businessman who was a close relative of the Commissioner for Mines and Power.[69] The middlemen provided small services in the way of communication between Gelsenberg, Germany and officials in the ministry. He acted as a host when Gelsenberg representatives visited Lagos. Beyond this there is little role for a middleman since the buyer's chartered tankers collect the oil from the producing companies' terminals and the transaction is completed. Clearly no special knowledge of oil affairs is required of the middleman. In return for these slight services, Gelsenberg's middleman received handsome commissions ranging from 2¢ to 20¢ per contract barrel.[70] The variations in commission depend on the buyer's estimate of the value of the broker's services. The middleman has an interest in securing for his client allocation of crude at the lowest possible prices and under the most convenient terms. The criteria by which one Nigerian middleman is selected from the large number of aspirants are those of patronage and partnership. The role of middlemen in the 1973 crude auction was another issue over which NNOC and certain ministry officials were divided.

The first international announcement of the Nigerian crude auction, apparently initiated by NNOC alone,[71] appeared on 8 October 1973 when the oil trade journal *Petroleum Intelligence Weekly* published the standard reply which NNOC was issuing to those firms applying for state oil.[72] The standard reply indicated that the oil corporation in late September 1973 was not yet in possession of crude oil to sell.[73] The journal indicated in a commentary that the auction was likely to take place later in October, but also questioned whether oil would actually be made available to the oil corporation for sale.[74] The NNOC questioned the ministry's apparent reluctance to issue formal letters to the companies requesting them to release royalty crude; and was apparently concerned about the possibility that the oil ministry might merely channel the royalty oil back to producing companies.[75] Finally the NNOC announced that bids would be accepted until 19 October.

Table 5
Prices Offered for Oil Direct from Nigerian State: 1973-74 ($)

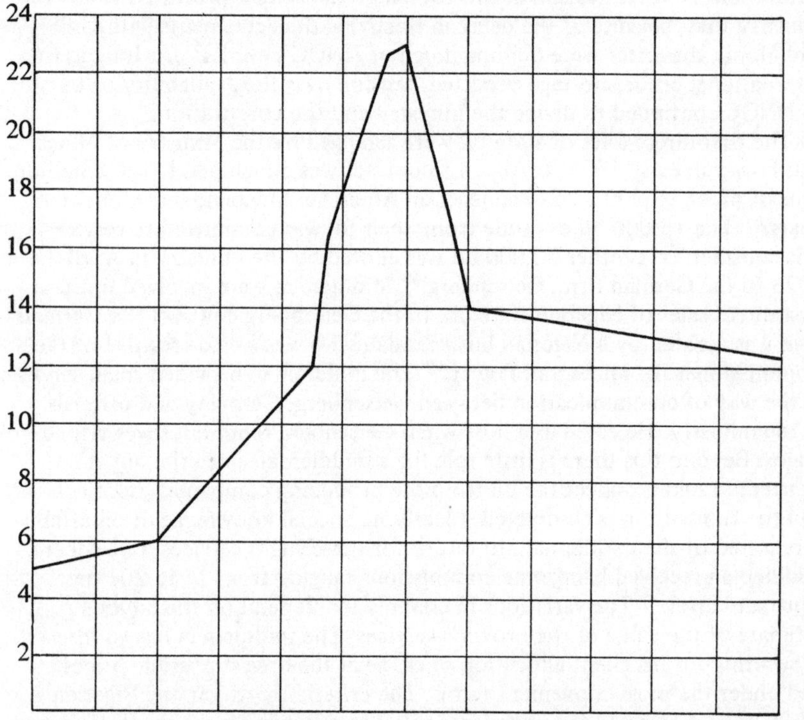

Source: Various national and international oil journals. The prices are f.o.b. Nigerian deepwater terminal for 34° API 0.14% sulphur crude oil.

The Role of Middlemen

The Commissioner, Shettima Ali Monguno, informed the Nigerian Chamber of Commerce in September 1973 that Nigerian intermediaries could compete with other buyers for allocations of state oil.[76] The Permanent Secretary of the oil ministry then denied that middlemen would be involved in state sales. He told the Chamber of Commerce only days after the Commissioner's address that oil would not be allotted to Nigerians for subsequent resale at higher prices to final users abroad.[77] The position of the oil corporation was emphatically against the involvement of middlemen:[78] 'Nigerian National Oil Corp. will not deal with middlemen or agents of whatever description be they Nigerians or any nationality whatsoever in negotiating or contracting for the purchase of crude oil.' Despite the corporation's efforts to 'make it abundantly clear that, for obvious reasons, it is the policy of . . . [NNOC] to deal directly with the ultimate refiners . . .'[79] the role of Nigerian businessmen in direct sales remained ambiguous. The success of a prominent businessman in the Gelsenberg and Tenneco sales had encouraged interest within the local business community. In the event, thirty-five Nigerian companies (not backed by foreign interests) submitted bids for crude oil purchases in the auction, the date of which had been set forward to 15 November. The issue of middlemen was not easily resolved. The division between the Ministry and the NNOC on this question continued into 1974.[80] Since those businessmen aspiring to become oil middlemen so vastly outnumbered the few who had any likelihood of succeeding, and since involvement was dependent on state patronage, the issue of direct oil sales aroused suspicion within the government and among members of Nigeria's commercial stratum.[81]

Oil to the Highest Bidder?

Another source of NNOC-ministry dissension was the basis on which crude oil allocations should be made. In organizing the auction, NNOC made it clear that prices offered from crude would determine which companies received oil.[82] 'Several rather persuasive factors' weighed on the oil corporation's decision to conduct a price-competitive bid:[83]

> (1) The rapidly changing circumstances – new posted prices, new supply/demand pattern created by the Embargo . . . [in which there was] no value to place on Nigerian crude oil rather than that which the market could offer and this can only be obtained if premium was placed on price offer.
> (2) The number of qualified companies bidding were so many that for justice and equity, there had to be a basis of elimination that starts them in the race on equal basis and this is the price a company, on its own free will, is prepared to offer.

The closing date for filing bids with the NNOC was originally 19 October, but with the Arab-Israeli war of 6 October and the subsequent oil shortages and increase[84] the oil corporation took steps to inform those who had filed bids with the NNOC to look out for new postings for Nigerian crude.[85] On 20

October Nigerian posted prices were doubled from $4.287 to $8.404 with effect from 31 October. As the new closing date (15 November) approached the bids flooded in.[86] On 19 November the NNOC opened 113 sealed bids from as many companies.[87] An elaborately formal procedure was deliberately followed in recording the bids in order that no question should arise as to irregularity.[88] The NNOC was attempting to set a precedent for the conduct of crude sale exercises.[89] Prices offered ranged from $16.50 by Texas Chemical and Plastic Corporation to Safrap's $5.10. Seventy-three of the 113 bids bunched between $9.00 and $11.99, reflecting the European and American realized prices in mid-November 1973. Of the 67 known companies seeking Nigerian oil, nearly two out of three were U.S.-based.

The auction drew bids from companies affiliated to the subsidiaries producing oil in Nigeria. In effect these firms were putting prices on their oil which was released to the state as royalty oil. On the list submitted to the oil ministry NNOC indicated that the local producers bid either as parent company, affiliate or subsidiary of a parent company.[90] Sohio and Shell Oil Company (US), affiliates of the same parent company as Shell-BP, bid $10.90 and $11.50 respectively for oil which Shell-BP would be required to release to the state. Phillips Petroleum Company, linked with Agip-Phillips in Nigeria, bid $14.00 while Safrap submitted a token offer of $5.10.[91] The fact of these affiliate bids and their levels are measures of the Nigerian producers' reluctance to yield royalty crude to the government, and the resistance offered by Mobil, Gulf and Texaco to the NNOC's efforts to acquire participation in 1973.

After the auction bids were opened the next step was the signing of contracts. The NNOC was urging the choice of buyers on the basis of highest price since a random allocation of crude could damage future Government efforts to secure high prices for its oil. The oil corporation argued against selling to firms of any particular nationality or only to the majors such as Shell-BP.

Nigeria's auction had international implications. In setting prices OPEC's Economic Commission Board was, in late 1973, relying largely on market realizations. Herein lay the importance of Nigeria's crude auction. NNOC's bid exercise was of considerable significance as a measure of the price the oil market would bear. If the Nigerian auction was concluded, it would produce an upper price limit and other OPEC crudes would be pegged accordingly.[92]

The ministry-corporation differences over the role of middlemen and prices in the sale of state oil were secondary to the fundamental disagreement over whether the auction should be held at all. Despite the NNOC's insistence, the oil ministry took no steps towards concluding the direct sale contracts. Eventually, on 19 December, the corporation proceeded on its own initiative to send invitations to companies to offer a final price. Seven companies responded on 21 December 1973 with offers ranging from $13.00 to $22.60. Four companies agreed on 22 December to pay $22.60 per barrel for about 40,000 b/d each over a two-year period. The buyers were invited to sign contracts on 24 December. When they arrived to conclude oil deals which would make pricing history, the foreign crude buyers were advised only to initial the agreements and sign after the holiday period. Prices plummeted in the last week of December and continued to fall in January. The four companies did not sign. The oil remained unsold except for 50,000 bd to the Ghana Supply Commission. Since the NNOC had 'failed' to sell the royalty oil it reverted to the producing companies. This turn of events was particularly beneficial to Shell-BP. The British and Dutch governments, beset by miners' strikes and embargo, were desperately seeking oil from their home-based majors, British Petroleum and Shell. The Nigerian state received payment at the level of posted prices which in effect meant that royalties were paid in cash rather than in crude. Because no direct sales were made, the producing companies paid the posted price of $14.691 for this royalty oil. A loss was sustained by the state since the oil could easily have been sold to companies bidding several dollars more than the postings. The direct sales prices to Tenneco and Gelsenberg were $14.904 and $15,517 respectively for the first quarter of 1974. But the companies viewed their payment at the level of posted prices as a concession to the government. This follows from the rules governing state liftings of royalty oil. If the state fails to lift its oil on time the companies are entitled to take it at buyback prices which for the majority was in the region of $9.797 a barrel in February 1974. The open market price of Nigerian oil had risen from $5.21 a barrel in July 1973 to $22.60 and even $23.00 by the end of 1973. By January 30 it had fallen to around $14.00. Why did prices fall?

The international price collapse followed from the U.S. Government's Mandatory Allocation Program[94] which limited all U.S. refiners' crude supplies to three-quarters of their 1972 throughput. This ensured that companies without their own producing fields were not driven out of business by the shortage. U.S. companies with excess oil had to sell it to a pool from which it could be purchased for around ten dollars a barrel by those in short supply. The incentive to import high-cost OPEC oil was thereby eliminated. If expensive oil was brought in, it could only be sold to the pool at a lower price.

After the buy/sell program had been in effect for six weeks, from 15 January 1973 to 28 February 1974, and had brought about a decisive and drastic plunge in world oil prices, it was discontinued. The Federal Energy Office 'recognized these disincentives to import oil'[95] and made a new rule that imported oil would 'not be subject to allocation to another refiner,'[96] The 'disincentives' to import crude which were written into the buy/sell program appear to be deliberate rather than the result of oversight. This conclusion follows from the fact that drafts of the plan were critically reviewed by the oil industry and concerned parties on three occasions prior to its becoming law on 15 January.[97] The evidence suggests that the oil majors achieved mastery of a critical international situation through the authoritative intervention of the United States Government via the buy/sell program.

The timing of the Mandatory Petroleum Allocation Program had implications for Nigeria's auction. World oil prices fell from late December 1973 when the buy/sell plan became common knowledge. But on 15 January when the plan became law, tankers loaded with high-cost oil bound for the United States changed course in mid-sea.[98] The embargoed Rotterdam bulk-barge market, a sensitive indicator of prices for freely-traded crude, was flooded with oil originally destined for the United States. Prices fell by a third overnight. By 18 January European prices were such that a barrel of 34°API Nigerian crude could fetch $16.78 in Rotterdam compared with $22.25 in December 1973. Not surprisingly, the companies which two weeks earlier had agreed to pay $22.60 for Nigerian oil declined to sign contracts at that price.

After the December 1973 auction, the NNOC's marketing department continued to receive requests for oil from crude buyers. The NNOC passed those on to the oil ministry with the recommendation that third party contracts be signed at the new, lower market prices. After three unsuccessful efforts to interest the ministry in concluding sales, the NNOC on 29 January cabled 13 firms asking them to confirm a price offer. The reaction of the Permanent Secretary to what was in effect a second effort by NNOC to auction Nigerial oil was to reprimand the Marketing Manager. The matter was dropped after the NNOC produced a memorandum on 11 February.[99] One result of the sharp disagreement between the NNOC and the ministry over the pricing and sale of state oil was the transfer of the marketing function from the corporation to the oil ministry. In July 1974 a Crude Oil Sales Committee was set up under the chairmanship of the chief engineer in the oil ministry.

The ministry's policy on direct oil sales cost the national treasury considerable sums in foregone income. Another cost was the loss of respect in oil circles where it was commonly known that Nigeria followed no coherent price policy and was open to company inducements. These implications were recorded by *African Development* where it was stated that '. . . again, it is not certain whether their [the government's] request [for royalty payments in crude] is being complied with, and if so whether the government is selling the oil for the top price available. Assuming it was disposing of all the oil available to it for independent sale, the government could be raising yet another $1,000m. on top of the estimated figure of $7,000 m.p.a. [for 1974–75].'[100]

The assessments of buyback price policy and the 1973 crude auction indicate that the oil ministry played what might be termed a 'comprador'[101] role in relation to oil companies operating in Nigeria. The ministry presided over company efforts to extract and export Nigerian crude oil on the most profitable terms. The oil corporation from its inception was geared towards replacing the foreign producers or at least establishing partnerships with them under which the 'national interest' would be better served. Despite thes these intentions of the NNOC management, the role which the state corporation played in practice was determined by the dominant officials of the oil ministry. The NNOC was less than effective in its efforts to ensure revenue benefits from oil sales. The technocratic management of the corporation had little more than an oppositional impact on comprador officials. But even in the expression of opposition to ministry oil policy, the NNOC was restrained by civil service practice; issues were never taken to the public. Opposition reached its height in March 1975 with a resignation threat by top management if the Federal Executive Council did not define lines of authority between the ministry and the corporation and remove the Chairman.[102]

Chart 2
Proposed Organization of a Nigerian Oil Authority (1976)

Head of State

FEDERAL EXECUTIVE COUNCIL

Board of Directors

Nine members, five of which are from the oil agency

Executive Manager

Managing Director

Executive Director(s) (Division) | Executive Director(s) (Division) | Executive Director(s) (Division)

This resignation threat followed a series of disagreements between NNOC and the oil ministry over oil policy.[103] In January 1975 after a Government White Paper endorsed the Udoji Public Service Review Commission's findings on remuneration in public corporations such as the NNOC,[104] the corporation mounted a major campaign to gain independence from the ministry. The revolt of some NNOC officials against the oil ministry under the Gowon Administration did not lead to clear-cut reforms under the short-lived regime of Murtala Muhammad. Between the end of July 1975 and 13 February when he was assassinated, Muhammad presided over a vacillating oil policy notable for its buyback price cuts in August when world prices were rising. However, the new Permanent Secretary in the oil ministry after the coup did call for a fundamental review of oil administration and the relations between NNOC and the ministry . In April 1976 the oil ministry formulated a plan to establish a strong, well-staffed oil corporation with safeguards to ensure its commercial independence. Chart 2 indicates the extent of this independence. How can we understand this apparent *volte face* by the ministry, hitherto soft in its line *vis-a-vis* the foreign companies and in conflict with the NNOC's technocratic policies? Ultimately, the move to award the NNOC more powers and independence within the Federal state may be seen as part of a shift of alliances which originated outside Nigeria.[105]

Technocrats in Transition

Our assessment of the NNOC's past efforts to develop strong state capabilities indicates that technocrats are in a weak position and carry little weight in the comprador state. The numbers of professionals and technicians in the Federal Service has, however, increased markedly since 1970 under the campaign to establish state corporations. In 1975 half of those working in the federal and state civil services (or 160,000 people) were employed by statutory corporations.[106]

Technocrats then are those technically-skilled professionals who were hired to put into effect the regime's post-civil war policy of state intervention to foster capitalist economic development. Their jobs involve combining technology, finance and managerial skills in a commercial organization to produce a tangible result (for example, a steel mill for the National Steel Authority). The division of labour in such an economic agency requires an interdependence among specialists, the success of which is measured in terms of actual production and in terms of profits.

Members of the technocratic stratum are relatively uncorrupt, not because they possess special moral qualities, but because their formal function is to replace national dependence on foreign production by building local units of production. Therefore they do not enter into triangular relationships and they lead the campaign to exclude middlemen from government transactions. In contrast, comprador officials in charge of the new state corporations are engaged in organizing the access of foreign businessmen to the local market. Technocrats come into conflict with compradors because this new stratum seeks to alter the terms of the relations between international capital and the Nigerian state in such a way as to increase the bargaining strength of the state and secure for 'the nation' maximum benefits from the operations of international firms.

The defining characteristic of technocrats in oil and elsewhere is their capacity for organizing productive activities. In contrast, compradors are concerned with commerce. Over one third of the NNOC's staff were drawn from private foreign oil companies. All are professionals and the NNOC has pursued training programmes with vigor. Most important, the corporation was, in theory at least, structured as an agency of state capitalist production. It was designed as a corporate means of displacing foreign oil subsidiaries in the Nigerian milieu. In this respect it resembles state oil corporations in countries where capitalist productions is developing. The key point about technocrats is that, in a sense, they are 'produced' by foreign capitalist production. They are the local state counterparts of foreign production just as the comprador-middleman stratus is the historical creation of foreign trade and currently acts as the local counterpart to international commerce.

The fact remains that today the dominant socio-economic relations in Nigeria are commercial, not productive. Technocrats have not been allowed to function. The conception of national interest embodied in NNOC policies was akin to the aims of technicians and professionals in other federal state corporations. Professionals in the Nigerian Electrical Power Authority were unable to achieve job objectives in the face of ministry obstruction; the National Supply Company was unable to undertake bulk imports due to middleman opposition; similar difficulties faced other state bodies Across the Federal spectrum, state corporation technocrats shared the task of establishing functioning productive ventures. They were frustrated in the performance of these state capitalist roles by the 'gatekeeper' pattern of state interaction with foreign firms.

What does this mean for the oil industry? On an international scale, companies have transferred ownership of oil exploration and production operations to oil-producing states.[107] In virtually all OPEC member countries, the state oil corporation owns 100% of exploration and production activities. Under the present circumstances this arrangement is favoured by international oil majors since it is more profitable, secure and stable. Oil companies are divesting 'upstream', but the state heirs must satisfy minimum criteria of experience, efficiency and commercial independence if the West is to rely on oil supplies from those sources.

While foreign oil corporations are interested in signing service contracts to develop new lines of business in the provision of technical advice and support , and in injecting Nigerian rather than multinational finances to work in exploration and production, the state lacks an institution with which oil firms can confidentially deal. Those oil companies with an eye to the future have reason to foster the emergence of a competent national oil corporation in Nigeria and make gains in partnership. From this perspective, the April 1976 proposal to confer on the NNOC substantial independent powers can be understood as one step in the transformation of the Nigerian state from a comprador to a technocratic organization.

Postscript

On April 21 1977 events took a dramatic turn with the promulgation of a Federal decree which abolished both the Ministry of Petroleum Resources and the NNOC, replacing them both with the Nigerian National Petroleum

Corporation. According to the decree, the functions of the new corporation include the following:

(1) The refining, treating, processing and generally engaging in the handling of petroleum for the manufacture and production of petroleum products and its derivatives;

(2) To engage in purchasing and marketing of petroleum products and by-products;

(3) To provide and operate pipelines, tanker ships or other facilities for carriage or conveyance of crude oil, natural gas, their products and derivatives, water or any other liquids or commodities related to the corporations operations;

(4) To construct, equip and maintain tank farms and other facilities for the handling and treatment of petroleum, its products and derivatives, are well as to carry out research in connection with petroleum or anything derived from it;

(5) To do anything for the purpose of giving effect to agreements entered into by the Federal Military Government with a view to securing participation by the government or the corporation connected with petroleum and enhance the petroleum interest for the overall interest of Nigeria.

The Corporation is run by a Board of Directors whose Chairman is now to be known as the Federal Commissioner for Petroleum. Other members of the Board are the Permanent Secretaries of the Ministries of Finance and Economic Development; the Managing Director of the Corporation; and three other members appointed by the Federal Executive Council.

The decree also provides for an inspectorate department in the Corporation independent of the Board and directly responsible to the Commissioner. The department carries out such duties as the issuance of licences for all activities connected with petroleum exploration and exploitation, the refining, storage, marketing, transportation and distribution of petroleum, as well as the enforcement of the provisions of the decree.

Announcing the decree, the then Commissioner of the defunct Ministry of Petroleum Resources, Col. Mohammed Buhari, stated that the changes were to bring the activities of the oil sector under close and more direct scrutiny by the government. The single oil administration would make optimal use of the scarce indigenous manpower resources in the oil sector and would also, as the sole authority, remove 'confusion in the minds of the members of the public and of the oil companies and other investors as to where responsibility for various functions of oil lies'.[108]

References

1. *Report of the Fact-Finding Mission on Petroleum Taxation, Problems Affecting Petroleum Revenue and Miscellaneous Matters on the Oil Industry*, (Lagos: Federal Ministry of Justice, 24 November 1969).

Hereafter cited as the *1969 Report*. The report was the result of lobbying by the Ministry of Finance. On 27 November 1968 the Federal Executive Council in its conclusion EC. 39(68)4 gave approval to the request of the Honourable Commissioner of Finance to send out a mission to Libya, Algeria and the OPEC Secretariat in Vienna. Nominees from the ministries of Finance, Mines and Power, Justice and the Federal Board of Inland Revenue made up the mission, p. 27.

2. *Ibid.*, pp. 26–7.
3. *Ibid.*, p. 34.
4. Interviews with officials involved in the process of establishing the NNOC, Lagos, 1974–5.
5. 'NNOC Decree No. 18 of April 1971, Explanatory Note', *Official Gazette*, Vol. 58, No. 21, 22nd April 1971.
6. *Ibid.*, Section 4(1).
7. *Ibid.*
8. *Ibid.*, Section 9(1) and (2). This was the limit then applied to all statutory corporations.
9. *Ibid.*, Schedule: supplementary provisions (1).
10. *Ibid.*, Schedule: supplementary provisions (Proceedings) 4.
11. This and subsequent information is drawn from the Nigerian National Oil Corporation, *First Annual Report*, 1 April 1971–31 December 1973.
12. *Ibid.* From September 1972 the temporary head office location was the United Bank for Africa (UBA) Building where the NNOC occupied 8,000 sq. ft., but was used to capacity by February 1973. In October 1973 the Finance and Accounts Division was housed in Western House near the UBA headquarters. By mid-1974 the corporation had rented office space in Apapa.
13. The *First Annual Report* emphasised 'the urgent need for acquisition of land or for its allocation by government for the erection of a head office in Lagos and operation based in the Midwest (now Bendel) State and Rivers State. Representations have been made to state governments with no immediate success.' The *New Nigeria* of 7 November 1975 editorialized that 'prestigious projects' such as 'the headquarters for the National Oil Corporation . . . should be postponed to the next plan (which begins in 1981).'
14. *Ibid.*, p. 10
15. *Ibid.*, p. 11.
16. *Ibid.*
17. *Ibid.*
18. Personnel information provided by the NNOC, 30 June 1975.
19. The Administrative Division includes 14 personnel supervisors, 24 secretaries and typists, 21 clerical officers, 22 office attendants, 33 drivers and machine operators and 31 security guard or watchmen.
20. *1969 Report*, p. 27.
21. *Ibid.*, p. 37.
22. See Terisa Turner, *State Capitalism: the Case of the Nigerian National Oil Corporation* (London, forthcoming). This work provides the full background and details on which this case study is based.
23. For a discussion of these legislative revisions see L.H. Schatzl,

Petroleum in Nigeria (Ibadan: Oxford University Press, 1969), and S.R. Pearson, *Petroleum and the Nigerian Economy* (Stanford: Stanford University Press; 1970). For the OPEC financial gains of the early 1970s see A.A. Kubbah, *OPEC: Past and Present* (Vienna: Petro-economic Consultants, 1974).

The 1966 per barrel income is listed in the *1969 Report,* Annex I. The figure of 29.5 cents is based on Shell-BP returns only. The *Petroleum Press Services,* 34, 7 (July 1967), p. 246 gives the per barrel revenue for 1966 as 34.61 cents.

24. IBRD, *Nigeria: Economic Memorandum,* Report Number 1235 UNI, July 1976, Table 21, p. 5. The United Nations report quotes Mission estimates based on various national and international publications as the sources for its figures.
25. These are two common kinds of participation: undivided interest and shareholding. In the first kind all past expenditure, all real property and all oil in the ground is divided between the partners. All costs are shared in proportion to their interest, and most important, all operating decisions are made by the partners. In contrast, a shareholding gives its owner a voice on the Board of Directors and a cut in the dividend issue. Shareholders have no opportunity to engage directly in operations or to control day-to-day activities. Prior to the activation of the NNOC, these interests were held by a state holding company, the Ministry of Finance Incorporated.
26. *NNOC Annual Report,* p. 17. The cost of the 35% interest was not paid to Safrap Oil Company *en bloc.* Rather, 'a current account was opened for this amount in favour of the Company. Safrap financed the operations and took credit for the sales of our crude oil entitlements until the current account was completely liquidated during the second quarter of the year 1972.' *Ibid.,* p. 30.
27. *Ibid.,* Table 1C.
28. 'OPEC Resolution XVI. 90 of 25 June 1968', *OPEC Documents 1968,* (Vienna: OPEC Secretariat, 1969).
29. Joe Stork, *Middle East Oil and the Energy Crisis,* (New York and London: Monthly Review Press, 1975).
30. F. McFadzean, Chairman of Shell Transport and Trading Company Limited, in his speech accompanying the 1972 *Annual Report,* (London: Shell Transport and Trading Co. Ltd., 1973).
31. S. 1570, 93rd Congress, 1st Session, Report No. 93–159, Calender No. 152. This bill was made law on November 27, 1973 and is known as the *Emergency Petroleum Allocation Act.*
32. Government of Algeria, *Background Information on the Relationship Between Algeria and the French Oil Companies* (Algiers, 1971). Also see Stork, *op. cit.,* pp. 185–194 and 202–4.
33. The income foregone through delaying participation in Shell-BP is estimated, first by calculating the proceeds from buyback sales of 25% of Shell-BP production (not exports) at 83.9% of actual posted prices from April 1972 to 31 March 1973. From this figure the income which profit tax and royalties on that oil would have generated is deducted.
34. *Ibid.* The same procedure is used for estimating the income foregone

through delaying participation one quarter in 1973. The cost of production in 1972 is assumed to be 30 cents a barrel and 35 cents a barrel in 1973. These estimations of foregone revenue are indications of magnitude rather than precise amounts.

35. For full details of the conflict between the NNOC and the oil ministry over pricing policy *vis-a-vis* Shell-BP and other oil majors, see Turner, *State Capitalism.*
36. See Ministry of Mines and Power's *First Five-Year Development Programme for NNOC,* dated 17 July 1974, and the *Nigerian National Oil Corporation Budget – 1974* which appears as Appendix 4 to the NNOC's submission to the Udoji Review Panel, January 1975.
37. NNOC, *Annual Report,* p. 23. The report notes that NNOC's legal department, set up after the conclusion of the Shell-BP participation negotiations had been 'involved in various other negotiations and joint venture undertakings with other oil companies. . .' For more evidence of the corporation's effort to acquire an interest in the U.S. firms, see note 2, p. 50.
38. *The Times* (London), 24 September 1973. 'Nigeria stiffens oil stake demands,' by Roger Vielvoye.
39. *Ibid.* The *Times* report touches on a reason for Shell-BP's preference for a continuation of the *status quo* for 1973 with regard to the U.S. firms' 100% ownership: 'there are now underlying fears within the industry that the Nigerians may also want renegotiations of the Shell-BP deal including higher buyback prices. Renegotiation of the Shell-BP agreement would have more serious implications for prices in Europe since the European group produces over 1.2 million barrels of oil a day compared with a combined output of around 527,000 barrels a day from Mobil, Gulf and Texaco.'
40. The Letters of Agreement between the companies and the government stipulate that the Deeds of Covenant can be revised in favour of the Government if the shareholders of an oil company operating in Nigeria, or any company which they directly or indirectly control, concludes a contract or recognizes a law in any other African state under which the other country's share in profits is higher than Nigeria's. *Shell-BP's Financial Arrangements with Government* (Port Harcourt: Shell-BP Petroleum Development Co. Ltd., 1965), p. 1. In 1967 this 'most favoured nation' clause was broadened to include not only African but all countries.
41. Interview information, London, March 1976.
42. *Middle East Economic Digest,* 5 April 1974.
43. Stork, *op. cit.* p. 200
44. *NNOC Annual Report, 1971–73,* p 18
45. *Participation Agreement* between the Government of the Federal Republic of Nigeria and the Shell-BP Petroleum Development Company of Nigeria Limited, 6 June 1973, Article 6 and Annex 4. The agreement restricted the total volume of oil the government could claim, taking into account the possibility that the state might want to lift its royalty oil.
46. Stork, *op. cit.,* p. 200.
47. *Ibid.,* p. 202. 'The fact that independent purchases were already lining

up in December [1973] to purchase the crude made available to the national companies under the [October 1972 Gulf 25% participation] agreement, indicated that the companies could indeed market more crude than the participation agreement allowed them.'

48. NNOC *Annual Report,* p. 17.
49. See various issues of the *Petroleum Economist,* 1974–6: e.g. (Sept. 1974), p. 323; (Jan. 1975), p. 14.
50. The discussion on third party sales in the subsequent sections provides details of the oil ministry's willingness to take prices from producers which were lower than other firms were offering.
51. *Participation Agreement,* Annex 4, 'Retained crude and buy-back crude oil', para. 4.
52. Due to the dynamic supply and price situation by the end of 1973 the grounds on which buyback prices were determined had changed. On 6 December NNOC drew the ministry's attention to the revised basis of participation in Saudi Arabia both on the matter of buyback volume volumes and the principle reached on buyback prices.
53. See Turner, *State capitalism.*
54. Saudi Arabia set the pattern by taking 60% undivided interest in Aramco, effective 1 January 1974, and charging $10.80 or 93% of the posted price for 34° API buyback oil. Kuwait's buyback price for June–December 1974 was 95% of posted price. Terms are subject to quarterly revision. *Petroleum Economist,* September 1974, p. 323. An internal paper from Shell International notes that 'In November 1974 a meeting called by Saudi Arabia, Qatar and Abu Dhabi resulted in steps towards another rise in revenue, of 40¢ per barrel to $10.00 (assuming 40 per cent company ownership of crude oil sources and buyback terms at 93 per cent of postings.) This policy was subsequently adopted by all OPEC members at their meeting in December 1974.' 'The Economic Consequences of High Oil Prices', London, December 1974, p. 3.
55. See NNOC, *Annual Report 1971–1973,* Table 5.
56. *Ibid.*
57. Turner, *State Capitalism.*
58. *Participation Agreement,* art. 6, para. 3. [Editor] – However, according to the former Permanent Secretary of the oil ministry, neither the ministry or the NNOC could have imposed 'buyback' or 'option' prices on Shell-BP which were different from those resulting from the application of the Participation Formula. In the wake of the 1973 Middle East War and petroleum crisis Nigeria, like other OPEC countries, renegotiated its participation agreements and agreed on new prices backdated on a new formula to 1 January 1974. Likewise, according to the former Permanent Secretary, Shell-BP (and Gulf and Mobil later) could not have been made to pay the same price for 'participation oil' as Safrap, Agrip-Phillips, Tenneco, and Gelsenberg. (Participation oil was that accruing from the participation agreements negotiated in 1973 in the wake of the OPEC resolution on participation in old concessions). See P.C. Asiodu, 'Aspects of Nigerian Oil Policy 1971–75', mimeo (Lagos, February 1977), p. 4, para 3.4 and p. 5, paras. 3.13 – 3.15.

59. This differential was specified in *Participation Agreement*, art. 6, para. 3. The agreement makes reference to buyback oil at $3.05 and to first option oil at $3.25. The same 20 cents difference distinguished buyback from first option oil in the first two quarters of 1974.
60. The 'marginal barrel' is that barrel of oil which if available for sale will fetch a price either higher or lower than the price paid for the last barrel sold. Therefore, the price of the marginal barrel has implications for 'going' prices at any moment. Its role in the international price structure is given more importance by the fact that little oil had hitherto been bought or sold outside of integrated company channels.
61. There were some established crude buying firms involved in the international market at this point, often representing several refiners. But in practice, businessmen whose normal activities involved the sale of general commodities to oil-producing countries merely added another activity to their portfolios. They sought allotments of oil through the network of contracts already established. They would then sell the oil to refiners in the industrialized countries at a profit.
62. NNOC, *Annual Report 1971–1973, op. cit.*, p. 19.
63. A 'generally accepted mean between on and offshore production' is 11.8% for early 1974. Alan Hutchinson, 'An Economy Floating on Oil,' *African Development* (March 1974). Effective 1 July 1974 royalties of 14.5% were levied on all production, regardless of location.
64. The most dramatic evidence that the market price of oil was higher than postings was Libya's third party sales at 30¢ above the posted price in mid-1973. In August when Libya took 51% of Oasis and established a buyback price of $4.90, the same as the market price for direct sales of Libyan oil, the commercial good sense of accepting royalty payments in crude rather than cash was indisputable. These high market prices simultaneously created strong commercial incentives to sell maximum amounts of state-owned participation oil. The July 16 1973 issue of *Petroleum Intelligence Weekly* reported that Nigeria intended to market royalty crude and had signed contracts for $4.25 or 11.5 above the 1 July posted price.
65. See Turner, *State Capitalism.*
66. NNOC, *Annual Report*, p. 19 and Table 6.
67. *Ibid.*
68. *Ibid.*, Table 7. The April 1973 agreement was with Gelsenberg Mineral Oil GMBH for delivery by NNOC of 20,000 barrels per day in 1973, 25,000 bd in 1974 and 30,000 bd in 1975.
69. Interviews with the Nigerian 'crude broker' as he terms himself, and the crude buyer for Gelsenberg, Lagos, 1974 and 1975.
70. This information was provided by the crude buyer for Gelsenberg in an interview, August 1974, Lagos.
71. NNOC, *Annual Report*, 1971–1973, p. 20.
72. *Petroleum Intelligence Weekly*, 8 October, 1973, p. 6. 'Don't call us for oil, we'll call you, Nigeria says.'
73. *Ibid.*, The text of NNOC's letter to prospective oil purchasers is reprinted in the weekly trade journal.
74. *Ibid.*, Commentary on the text of NNOC's response.

75. For full background details of the corporation – ministry relationship over the auction, see Turner, *State Capitalism.*
76. *Daily Times* (Nigeria), 30 September 1973. A statement that it was 'advisable for all foreign companies engaged in the Nigerian oil industry to promote meaningful indigenous participation in their operations' was issued after a meeting between the Commissioner of the Ministry of Mines and Power and representatives of the Nigerian Association of Chambers of Commerce, Industry and Mines in Lagos. Text of a telegram from BBC Monitoring, Caversham to BP London, 30 September 1973.
77. *Daily Times,* October 1973. Interviews confirmed that Commissioner Monguno gave several Nigerian businessmen the assurance that they would receive consideration in the allocation of state oil.
78. Text of the standard response which NNOC sent to firms inquiring about the purchase of crude in late September 1973, printed in the *Petroleum Intelligence Weekly,* 8 October 1973. The vehemence of the NNOC's stance against the involvement of agents is underscored by its refusal to allow foreign companies to employ local representatives even for the negotiations. In short, NNOC was willing to speak with full-time employees of the final crude-using firm.
79. *Ibid.*
80. See Turner, *State Capitalism*
81. None of the 35 Nigerians bidding in the 15 November auction received allocations, nor did any of the dozens of middlemen representing foreign firms secure commissions since their principles received no oil. It was hard to reconcile the widespread knowledge that a great demand existed for Nigerian oil with the fact that no sales had been made.
82. 'On the basis of your assessment of the foregoing information, especially with regard to the base price level or base price formulation, the price escalation and price reopener provisions, we shall let you know when we are in a position to make firm offers of crude oil for sale. In the circumstance you would be given an opportunity of updating or revising your offers especially with regards to the price level and other financial considerations. Our ultimate consideration would be based on such revised proposal.' *Petroleum Intelligence Weekly,* 8 October 1973.
83. *Ibid.*
84. An OPEC Ministerial Committee representing four Gulf states met in Kuwait on 16 October to unilaterally fix crude oil posted prices at $5.110 for Saudi Arabian light crude, an increase of 70%. On 18 October Iraq, Abu Dhabi and Iran announced similar increases with Libya following on the 19th.
85. Announcements about the postponed date of the Nigerian auction appeared in the local media, *Platts' Oilgram* and the *Petroleum Intelligence Weekly.*
86. In the words of an officer of NNOC, 'What had started as a simple exercise almost got out of hand. . . given the great international and local public interest.' *Ibid.*
87. *Ibid.* If the 35 private Nigerian bids are included a total of 148 bids were received in the 15 November 1973 crude auction.

88. Turner, *State Capitalism.*
89. Interview information, Lagos, 1974. For full details, see Turner, *State Capitalism.*
90. See Turner, *State Capitalism.*
91. Gulf International Chemical Inc., which bid $9.45, may be linked with Gulf which is producing in Nigeria. Information available on participants in the auction is insufficient to say whether affiliates of Mobil and Texaco sought to buy Nigeria's oil. Tenneco had signed the sales contract in early 1973 with the oil ministry, and in this way a Texaco affiliate was able to buy Nigerian oil at very low prices.
92. *The Guardian,* 6 December 1973, 'Suddenly Nigeria has the Limelight' by David Ottaway.
93. Interview data. NNOC's *Annual Report 1971–1973* states that after the 15 November bid: 'Fourteen companies were then selected from the bid list and requested to submit final offers on 29th December, 1973. The highest offer was $22.60/bbl. which was then taken as the selling price for Nigerian crude. Four companies agreed to buy at this price but by the second half of January 1974, due to the combination of factors stated at paragraph 6.5 *amongst others,* none of these four who had signed provisions agreements [the ones they initialled] was willing to conclude a deal.' Paragraph 6.5 contains no statement of factors which might indicate why the four potential oil buyers decided not to buy Nigerian oil. Paragraph 6.5 states only that prices increased from $3.805 in May 1973 to $14.691 in January 1974, pp. 19–20. [Editor] – According to the Permanent Secretary of the oil ministry at the time, the directive to initial but not sign the contracts was from the Head of State to the Commissioner, who then relayed it to the Permanent Secretary who in turn passed it on to the Head of the Auction Panel. See P.C. Asiodu, 'Aspects of Nigerian Oil Policy 1971–75', Lagos, February 1977 (mimeo), p. 1, para. 1.11.
94. The Allocation Program, part of which was the buy-sell regulations, was itself the means of implementing the Emergency Petroleum Allocation Act of 27 November 1973. The U.S. Congress enacted Public Law 93–159, 87 Stat. 627, on recognizing the existence of 'severe economic dislocations and hardships' caused by a shortage of oil. *Staff Report to the Federal Trade Commission,* 15 March 1974. 'An Evaluation of the Mandatory Petroleum Allocation Program,' 15 January–28 February 1974. Serial No. 93–95 (92–70) Appendix A. See also Stork, *op. cit.*
95. *FTC Report,* p. A–146.
96. *Ibid.,* p. A–49–50.
97. Drafts were prepared and available on 12 December, 27 December and finally on 15 January 1974. Critics within the U.S. charged that the shortage was deliberately engineered. See Joel Andreas, *The Incredible Rocky vs. the Power of the People,* (New York and San Francisco: NACLA, 1975).
98. The FTC report stated that '. . . there are claims that some companies may have diverted shipments and reduced imports.' p. 187.
99. See below.
100. Alan Hutchinson, 'An economy floating on oil,' in a special supplement on Nigeria, *African Development* (London), March 1974, p. 27.

101. 'Comprador' is a Portuguese word used to describe those performing the function of organizing foreign traders' access to local markets. Typical examples in West Africa in earlier periods were slave merchants and cocoa middlemen. With political independence, and the development of the state as a major market, the comprador role was assumed by public officials. The position of officials of state allows them to influence state spending and government policy and to use this position to assist foreign capital in its dealings with the state and indigenous society. Not all state officials are compradors: the group includes only those who can and do benefit from using their position to assist selected foreign businessmen in securing a profit.
102. [Editor] – There appears to some controversy over the details of these events. According to the former Permanent Secretary of the ministry, the latter, on 11 February 1975, submitted to his Commissioner his comments on a memorandum signed by 2 members of NNOC staff dated 11 February 1975, which had been improperly copied to all members of the Federal Executive Council and some officials. As the Commissioner took no action, the Permanent Secretary copied his comments on 17 February 1975 to recipients of the memorandum. Later, on 8 April 1975, the Head of State directed that the two NNOC officials who through the memorandum had petitioned against the Chairman (the Permanent Secretary) should be de-seconded from the NNOC and a General Manager appointed. Delay over this appointment had apparently centred on the issue of the availability of a suitably experienced indigenous candidate for the post. See P.C. Asiodu, 'Aspects of Nigerian Oil Policy, 1971–75', Lagos, February 1977, mimeo, p. 6 paras 5.3 and 5.4 and p. 7, para 5.15.
103. [Editor] – According to the former Permanent Secretary, the ministry saw the divisive issues rather differently. The basic disagreement, according to him, was over priority areas for NNOC development. The Chairman wanted the NNOC to acquire skills and competence primarily as an oil exploration and production company, whilst the managers preferred NNOC to act straight away as the policy planning and co-ordinating arm of the Government in all oil related matters – presumably with other bodies to develop actual expertise in exploration and production. See Asiodu, *op. cit.*, p. 6 para. 4.2 and p. 7 para 5.8.
104. [Editor] – Apparently, there had also been opposition by many Federal Executive Council members to the earlier 1973 grading by the NNOC Board of certain managers on 150% of the highest salaries prevailing in the public sector. Asiodu, *op. cit.*, p. 9 para. 9.2.
105. See below.
106. *Third National Development Plan,* (Lagos, 1975), p. 371.
107. See M. Tanzer, *The Energy Crisis* (London, 1975); Z. Mikdashi, *The Community of Oil Exporting Countries* (London, 1975); A. Sampson, *The Seven Sisters* (London, 1975).
108. Reported in the *New Nigerian,* 30 April 1977.

Government and Private Sector: An Introduction

The relations between government and private sector in the 'mixed' economies of Africa are complex, particularly in the context of national efforts to plan for accelerated industrialization. In mixed economies where the private sector plays a significant role, the economic decisions made therein may also affect the course and extent of the implementation of public sector programmes. For example, the private sector might supply substantial proportions of capital goods such as plant, machinery, and cement which the public sector requires for the construction of major infrastructure projects like roads, dams, electricity and water plants. Other ways in which private sector decisions can affect the public sector's plan implementation capacity are through levels of investments, profits and employment. Data concerning such variables would be necessary, for example, in planning targets in respect of development revenues, anticipated customs duties, imports of raw materials and equipment, exports, as well as tax revenues from company profits and incomes from the increased labour force.

Relating private sector activity to the national planning process poses formidable tasks. Reliable data is often absent and consultative machinery and enforcement agencies weak. Even where consultative machinery is established, the task remains hard. Central planners are faced with the sheer physical exercise of contacting thousands of private enterprises in the industrial, commercial and agricultural sectors, spatially scattered and in some cases (particularly where indigenous and small) lacking adequate records and accounting procedures, or in other cases, expatriate and reluctant to furnish information about the policies of the company.

Nevertheless, efforts have been made in this direction. In general, the consultative machinery developed has depended upon the distribution of production points as well as the extent to which private sector decisions affect the national economy. In a country with few industries, the contact points would be few and consultation could be established at the national level. In other cases, a first step might be the selection of a few key industries for more comprehensive consultation. Where problems related to identifying points of contact and determining bases of representation have been surmounted, multi-sectoral consultative committees have been established as part of the central planning machinery, supplemented by *ad hoc* consultation on a project basis. The agricultural sector poses the severest problems of contact for obvious reasons of the scattered and often sparse rural population. As we shall see in Part III of the Reader, one solution commonly adopted by government is to set up and work through farmers co-operatives as intermediary organizations.

On the control and enforcement side, the challenges of ensuring conformity in the private sector with national plan objectives are even greater. Examples are the achievement of certain levels and areas of investment or, in the case of the Second Nigerian Development Plan, increased indigenization of management. Control mechanisms available are theoretically two-fold. First, there is direct control which involves the use of obligatory mechanisms. Here non-compliance would invoke sanctions or penalties, for example, by the Expatriate Quota Allocation Board or the powers invested in the officials of federal and state Ministries of Trade and Industry by the Nigerian Enterprises Promotion decree in the case of efforts to indigenize the private sector. With the exception of political priority programmes like indigenization, government efforts to control the private sector usually suffer from the lack of an enforcement agency, particularly as regards acquiring the relevant information. But even in the case of indigenization, the possibilities for evading the arms of government are great and it may take a cadre of inspectors to monitor and verify what is actually happening in certain private enterprises. Another example of the enforcement problem would be price control. The second broad type of control mechanism is indirect and non-obligatory. As such it works through incentives and rewards for compliance, particularly for the fulfilment of quantitative targets such as gross capital formation and gross output. Again, it would require the working out of concrete measures of performance of particular types of enterprise as well as appropriate incentives for this to be effective.

Apart from the basic organizational problems of operating effective consultative and control mechanisms in the private sector, a second and related factor complicating planning relations between government and private sector stems from the whole or part ownership and control of enterprises in that sector by non-nationals. A high proportion of private firms in Africa are in alien hands, because indigenous private interests lack the necessary capital, technology and other skills for large-scale industry and commerce. Some of the alien firms may have been dominant since the early colonial period when government primarily represented the interests of foreign firms. A good example is the United Africa Company, now a giant company operating in several spheres (finance, manufacturing, distribution), whose origins are intertwined with the economic history of Nigeria itself. In the period immediately after independence these firms, as well as new ones in some cases, were encouraged to continue to invest. This was achieved through a variety of mechanisms, including the construction of essential infrastructure, the granting of tax-free holidays, the establishment of tariffs to prevent competition from imported goods, the lending of funds by fully or partly-owned state development banks, and the granting of free transfers of profits and capital abroad.

Thus, although most new national governments established central planning agencies, which prepared development plans ranging over periods from three to six years, the initial years of Africa's first decade of independence were not generally ones in which policymakers come to grips with the problems of dependency and the challenges of economic decolonization. The reasons for the general lack of policy initiatives in this area probably lay in more pressing political problems, particularly the tasks of rapid localization of the public service itself and, in some cases, the search for more effective political institutions. Towards the end of the 1960s the situation began to change. With the tasks of political institution-building largely over, economic nationalist feelings began to rise. People began to realize that political independence had not meant economic independence. A number of countries began to reject the dependency syndrome and to demonstrate that in fact they had a certain margin of choice or area of manoeuvre through the exercise of public policy in creating successful indigenous capitalist economic development, or at least ensuring that the activities of foreign enterprises dominating certain areas of the economy were moulded to the national interest. A range of policy instruments were increasingly adopted to enhance national control over foreign investments and to give opportunities to indigenous public and private enterprise to grow side by side.

Amongst the various policy initiatives taken, two broad patterns are discernible. On the one hand there have been countries where programmes of outright nationalization of foreign private enterprise have taken place. The most notable example of this pattern is Tanzania where after the 1967 Arusha Declaration a range of enterprises in manufacturing, banking, insurance and import-export sectors were taken over by the state to be managed by state corporations. In contrast, the other pattern is exemplified by the recent indigenization programme undertaken in Nigeria, where state intervention is limited to providing the legal framework and financial resources for private indigenous businessmen to acquire part or whole ownership of a specified range of alien enterprises. Other variations on these two contrasting patterns do of course exist. An example of such is the 'joint-venture' type enterprise. The State enters into partnership (usually as a passive financial participant) with a foreign company. Such ventures are often welcomed by foreign investors because of the obvious guarantees they involve. Governments committed to a 'mixed economy' may eventually want to hand over such enterprises to the indigenous private sector. Also, of course, particular countries may contain a mixture of all three institutional patterns. Recent Ghanaian industrialization and investment policies allocated subsectors to various institutional forms: exclusive indigenous private enterprise, exclusive state enterprise, joint ventures between the state and foreign private enterprise, and a subsector open to any investor.

The determinants of these various policy options are fairly clear. In the Tanzanian case, there was no alternative to state management of the former foreign companies. Historically, Tanzania was neglected by Britain as the colonial power. Consequently, there was comparatively little foreign investment at Independence. Also, as a result of the relatively low level of development, there was absent any sizeable indigenous capitalist class to form the backbone of a private sector. Given these factors, together with the ideological preference of the leadership for public ownership, nationalization was a scarcely surprising consequence of the basic commitment to attain more economic independence. The Nigerian case is a contrasting one in several respects. Levels of foreign investment are high and the indigenous private sector is more developed. In addition, Nigeria has had a rather poor experience with public enterprise since Independence.

In all cases however, the role of government is a clear one. It lies in adjusting the relations between foreign capital and local (or a national) economic interests. The basic problem in all countries is that of gaining control over the surplus wealth generated in the economy in order that it may be reinvested for local benefit and development rather than being expropriated by aliens. The public enterprise approach has the advantage that the benefits will be redistributed for the good of all, whilst the private enterprise approach can mean that a set of foreign monopolists are simply replaced by a set of indigenous ones. Thus, as the analysis of the beneficiaries of Nigeria's indigenisation programme in the following chapter shows, state action has undoubtedly contributed to an overall concentration of ownership (albeit nominal) of the means of production and distribution and has marked the emergence of new strata in Nigerian society.

On the labour front, a range of parallel strategic issues and organizational problems arise in relation to government control over the private sector. Politically, organized labour is an important group in any less developed economy. Though trade unions in Africa may often have appeared weak and divided, it is their potential power that is sometimes feared by the ruling group and their policy-makers. First, the trade unions are one of the few national organizations outside the political system itself having their own finances and leadership. Second, some of the latter have demonstrated political consciousness – a threatening development to those concerned with monopolizing state power, especially when one considers the way in which organized labour is easily mobilized and tends to be concentrated in the urban areas close to the seats of government. Third, trade union leaders – though more rarely – have at times exhibited 'radical' tendencies, extending themselves beyond simple bargaining in their narrow sphere of self-interest to activities aimed at articulating or activating the grievances of other less organized and less consulted groups such as urban employees and farmers. Economically, trades unions, especially where labour is employed in large numbers, have a unique disruptive capacity. Thus strikes and stoppages can be applied at key points in the economy, for example, ports and railways during the early colonial period and even the banks as witnessed in Nigeria after the Udoji public sector increases. Likewise, 'excessive' wage claims may cause inflation and undermine government planning efforts. Finally, trades union militancy may increase labour costs (all of which may not be passed onto the consumer) and hence discourage private investment (particularly foreign investment) in industrial development.

Organizationally, relations between government and unionized labour have featured some of the general problems mentioned above of planning the private sector. One of these is the frequent absence of any single trade union organization. This presents obvious dilemmas in determining the representation of labour interests on any formal government machinery for consulting the private sector. A parallel in Nigeria has been the representation of indigenous entrepreneurs drawn from sectors like transport, contracting and other service and small-scale industrial activities where a number of rival association associations may exist. This has created difficulties, for example, in inviting private business representation on the State Enterprise Promotion Committees set up to facilitate the buying of foreign companies under the 'indigenization' Decree.

From a governmental point of view, controlling organized labour has been seen as a question of imposing a 'proper role' on 'recalcitrant' unions, particularly in relation to political activities. Government has preferred that they confine themselves to economic bargaining – 'industrial relations'. 'Responsibility' in these matters has been fostered by a range of regulations and supervisory roles inherited from the colonial state and more industrialized societies.

According to the prescriptive model of the early period, the role of state was a *laissez-faire* one, rather as it remains in respect to the recent indigenization programme. That is, the state 'simply' provides the framework for private treaty between the two parties – between management and labour (free collective bargaining) and between foreign owner and prospective indigenous buyer in the case of selling a business or shares in a business under the Nigerian Enterprises Promotion Decree. Since Independence, government – labour relations in many African countries have moved into a new 'corporativist' phase, either through restrictive legislation or through informal tactics such as co-option of key union leaders by government patronage, or simply through outright coercion.

7. Public Policy and the Development of Indigenous Capitalism: The Nigerian Experience

Paul Collins

Nigeria provides, *par excellence*, an example of an independent African country where, at least in terms of size and resources, the possibilities of creating a successful national or indigenous capitalist development appear great.[1] As a major oil producer, Nigeria possesses an international strategic resource[2] which gives her scope for initiative in the exercise of public policy as well as the financial means of developing through state or indigenous private enterprise her huge internal market.[3] In reality, as the experience of the 1972 Nigerian Enterprises Promotion Decree shows, the implementation of public policy in Nigeria has been less than effective in regulating patterns of direct foreign private investment. One major effect has been to promote the development of indigenous 'capitalism' within a framework of continued dependence[4] on foreign enterprise in many sectors.

This article attempts to show how and why this has happened. It also assesses some of the social and political consequences of the recent policies, in so far as they have created increasing inequalities amongst Nigerians – with opportunities for profit, through partnerships or share holdings in foreign enterprises, being restricted to a relatively small privileged circle – and may thereby affect political stability.[5]

The 1972 Nigerian Enterprises Promotion ('Indigenisation') Decree and its Implementation

A major change in public policy towards foreign private investment had been indicated by the 1968 Companies Decree. This required the local incorporation of all foreign companies doing business in Nigeria. As such it marked a shift away from the earlier 'accommodationist' attitude towards foreign capital, although still within the framework of the 'free enterprise' economy. Prior to this,[6] since 1945, Nigeria had pursued an 'open door' policy towards foreign investment in common with Kenya[7] and most of the francophone African countries.[8] The Second National Development Plan launched in 1970 confirmed this shift, declaring: 'The government will seek to acquire, by law of necessity, equity participation in a number of strategic industries that will be specified from time to time. In order to ensure that the economic destiny of Nigeria is determined by Nigerians themselves, the Government will seek to widen and intensify its positive participation in industrial development'.[9] In pursuit of this objective, the Nigerian Enterprises Promotion ('Indigenisation') Decree (NEPD) was announced in February 1972.[10] Its provisions required that by March 1974, a range of economic activities, then dominated to varying degrees by non-nationals, should be partly or wholly owned by indigenes.[11] Indigenisation of industrial ownership had been hinted at as early as June 1971 and several important expatriate firms had already offered ordinary shares to the Nigerian public.

Factors accounting for this policy shift are fairly clear. Indigenous businessmen had been keen to break expatriate dominance of certain sectors, particularly retail trade, and pressures have been exerted on successive governments since the 1950s.[12] Other factors include the civil war experience, the advent of military government, and the demonstration effect of other African states, all of which have contributed to the growth of economic nationalism. Parallel indigenisation measures in the management of foreign-owned or controlled enterprises had been started in 1966–67 when the Expatriate Quota Allocation Board was established.[13]

The provisions of the Decree reserved for Nigerians certain types of business with effect from 31 March 1974. Aliens were to be excluded entirely from some 22 businesses listed in Schedule I, whilst 33 other businesses listed in Schedule II were to be reserved for Nigerians only if they were below a certain size. Continued alien activity in larger businesses included in Schedule II was to be governed by two conditions. First, it must be a sufficiently large business with capital of over ₦4,000,000 or turnover exceeding ₦1,000,000.[14] Second, there must be 40 per cent Nigerian participation. Three enterprises originally included in Schedule I were subsequently transferred to Schedule II. They were: electronics assembly, clearing and forwarding agencies, and haulage of petroleum products by road.[15] Schedule I included some six activities in the small scale industry sector (such as brick and bread making, garment and candle manufacture), four in entertainment and the media (pools, cinemas, casinos, and newspaper printing and publishing), four in local processing/ assembly (rice milling, tyre retreading, and the blending and bottling of alcoholic drinks), three in the service sector (hairdressing, road haulage, and dry cleaning) and finally the retail trades. Schedule II included thirteen major manufacturing industries (such as furniture, matches, paints and cement), seven activities in the service sector (such as shipping construction and travel agencies), five in local processing (such as beer brewing and paper conversion), four in the food industry (including poultry, fish and meat), three in commerce (wholesale distribution, department stores and supermarkets, and distribution agencies for machines, technical equipment, and vehicles) and finally the production of sawn timber and plywood.[16]

Affected enterprises, as listed by the Nigerian Enterprises Promotion Board (NEPB), totalled some 950: 357 under Schedule I and 593 under Schedule II.[17] The financial assets of these enterprises have been estimated in the range of ₦100m–₦500m. As at 30 June 1975, only 57 per cent of Schedule I enterprises and 89 per cent of Schedule II enterprises had provisionally complied. Confirmed cases of compliance after proper inspection numbered 314, that is about 33 per cent. The enterprises exempted from the Decree numbered 81. The British are the most heavily involved in Nigeria, although it is the Lebanese who have borne the initial brunt, entrenched as they were in the retail and distributive trades under Schedule I which Nigerian businessmen were most keen to get into.[18] Alien involvement in Schedules I and II is not, of course, exclusive. In 1967, for example, 56 per cent of paid up capital in Schedule I enterprises was already Nigerian-owned, while in Schedule II the figure was 32.4 per cent.[19] Alien companies are involved in a range of manufacturing, distributive, and service activities. They include the old established trading companies like the United Africa Company (UAC), CFAO, and John Holt as well as large multinationals like ICI, Lever Brothers, and Dunlop.

In terms of location, most of the large foreign companies affected under Schedule II are based in Lagos, with branches in the nineteen states. As far as Schedule I is concerned, affected enterprises within the northern states tend to be concentrated in a few major centres, particularly Kano State, with a lesser number in Kaduna and Jos, the capitals of Kaduna and Plateau States respectively. Within the remaining 'southern' states there is a similar large concentration of Schedule I enterprises in Lagos State, with a lesser number in Ibadan, Oyo State. In the eastern states of Anambra and Imo, foreign enterprise (in the trading and service sector) never got a foothold as elsewhere while in other fields all enterprise remains hampered by the infrastructure damaged in the civil war.

Implementation of the NEPD

The Machinery: The machinery for implementing the Decree was located under the Federal and State Ministries of Trade and Industry, and comprised a central NEPB under the Chairmanship of the Federal Permanent Secretary with Enterprises Promotion Committees at the State ministry level.[20] The machinery was charged with identifying affected enterprises and monitoring and verifying transfers of ownership, while the Federal Commissioner was vested with discretionary powers in granting extensions and exemptions. The issue of shares in public companies was handled separately by the Capital Issues Commission and Stock Exchange. Inspectors were appointed to verify compliance in selling or closing down enterprises and procedures for capital repatriation announced.

The Federal Government also took supporting measures to make available the necessary capital for the takeover. The first was the acquisition of a 40 per cent share in the foreign-owned commercial banks. Banks are now required, under Central Bank guidelines, to allocate at least 40 per cent of their total loans to Nigerian businessmen. Before the Central Bank directive, expatriate banks were found to be granting, on average, less than 20 per cent of their loans and advances to indigenous borrowers. It was for this reason that many of the indigenous banks were established, in order to liberalise credit to African borrowers. Expatriate commercial banks have lent only against marketable securities such as government bonds, the shares of well established companies, life insurance policies, and documents of title to imported or exported stocks or those awaiting sale. They have been extremely cautious in accepting titles to land and real estate – the major assets available locally.

The overall result of the measure was an increase in the proportion of bank loans to indigenous borrowers from 48.8 per cent of total bank loans at the end of December 1970 to 66 per cent at the end of December 1972. This increase was very much related to commercial bank participation in financing indigenisation where, as pointed out below, they have been mainly interested in advancing money to buy shares.[21] Later the establishment of the Nigerian Bank of Industry and Commerce was announced and detailed. Under the NBIC Decree No. 22 of 1973, the principal functions of the Bank include the provision of equity capital and funds by way of loans to indigenous persons, institutions, and organisations for medium and long-term investments in industry and commerce, the performance of aspects of merchant banking, and the conduct of other banking and commercial business as deemed appropriate. The authorised capital of the Bank is ₦50m which comprises 500,000 shares of ₦100 each. Of this, ₦10m has been paid up by its shareholders – the Federal Government (60 per cent) and the Central Bank (40 per cent). During the first phase of the Bank's operations medium and long-term loans to indigenous persons and institutions are to be granted, especially in furtherance of the NEPD.

Public Companies Under Schedule II: Since the NEPD some eighteen of the larger and more profitable companies have gone public. In 1971 only ten companies were quoted in the Lagos Stock Exchange. In April 1977 there were thirty-four. Under manufacturing are now listed some eighteen companies, such as Bata (Nigeria) Limited, Nigerian Breweries Limited, and Tate and Lyle (Nigeria) Limited. Under distributive activities are listed some six companies, including the United Trading Company of Nigeria and Leventis Motors. Finally, service sector companies quoted include Blackwood Hodge, Costain (WA) Limited, and the Daily Times of Nigeria Limited. Four banks and John Investment Company are also quoted.

The last companies to go public were Boots and the UAC group. The UAC was given an extension by the Federal Military Government in view of its size and the consequent complexity of arrangements to be made. The giant UAC group now includes seventeen former companies as subsidiaries, including GB Ollivant (NIgeria) Limited, (major importers and wholesalers), Pan Electric Limited, Kingsway Stores of Nigeria Limited, and African Timber and Plywood (Nigeria) Limited. Share offers ranged from Metal Box, who offered 1,440,000 units of ₦0.50 at ₦0,51 each, to the United Africa Company, who offered 7,000,000 units of ₦0.40 each. The Stock Exchange fixed the minimum subscription low at ₦25.

Investment-conscious members of the salary-earning stratum responded impressively to equity share issues of many public companies, particularly those with a reputation for efficient management and a long record of profit. The high level of profit of the large foreign companies is also, of course, related to the element of monopoly and protection in their operations. Even allowing for multiple applications and for inflated applications induced by anticipated rationing, there was public over-subscription to share issues in many cases. These included, for example, UAC, Guinness, Briscoe, the Nigerian Bottling Company, Costain, Metal Box, and Paterson Zochonis.[22] The total market value of these issues has been estimated at ₦30 million. Nearly 50 per cent of the purchases were financed by the banks who made loans totalling ₦13.8 million for these purposes.[23] Apart from the general public, including employees of the issuing companies, state governments also bought on the Lagos Stock Exchange. UAC in fact set aside blocks of one million shares for each state government.

The Purchase of and Equity Participation in Private Companies Under Schedules I and II: By the nature of the case, there is less hard data readily available about this category. Most of these sales were carried out by private treaty. The Stock Exchange and Capital Issues Commission were not involved. At the state level transactions (equity participation and outright purchase) were sometimes carried out without reference to the State Enterprises Promotion Committees, which was only informed afterwards through the NEPB. Furthermore, some of the shares of businesses purportedly 'sold' appeared to be held in trust for aliens. Funds were sometimes difficult to obtain, in the case of bank loans because the shares of companies for sale had not been properly valued. More often, it was part of a collaborative arrangement between an affected alien and one or more of his former customers or retailers. This was particularly the case in the wholesale and distributive trade discussed below. Total private sales conducted have been estimated at a total nominal value of ₦53 million and a market value of ₦70 million. Less than 10 per cent of private companies shares were purchased with help from banks. For *all* purchases, private savings put up have been estimated at ₦14 million.[24]

Among the northern states, Kano State was the location of the bulk of the enterprises affected. Of the 179 enterprises under Schedule I, the majority were small, Lebanese, family-owned retail businesses (116), most of these were closed down and the stock sold. Of the remainder, twelve were sold. Four of the cinemas were bought by the Kano State Investment Company. Road haulage was the other major area of alien involvement in Schedule I. There few of the 34 enterprises were sold and extensions were granted, despite protests from indigenous transporters. In Schedule II, of the 152 Kano-based firms, 16 were closed down and the rest made arrangements (mostly by private treaty) to sell shares in their enterprises. Schedule II also included four enterprises with capital less than the ₦400,000 minimum requirement. These – a travel agent and manufacturers of suitcases, nails, and matches – were sold outright to indigenous businessmen. Buyers of entire enterprises included leading industrialists (Alhaji Sanusi Dantata, Alhaji

Inuwa Wada, and Alhaji Isiyaka Rabiu for example), emergent conglomerates like Birma General Supplies and Ibru Limited, as well as lesser indigenous businessmen and certain well-connected individuals in public service or private sector employment. The Kano State Investment Company bought ₦3.2 million worth of shares in Schedule II enterprises including a steelwork factory, a sawmill and furniture manufacturing company, a steel construction company, and a trading company. The private purchase of shares in the remaining Kano-based Schedule II companies benefited a diverse range of individuals – leading businessmen, State Commissioners, civil servants, members of traditional ruling families, as well as smaller scale businessmen (distributors, transporters, general merchants). During the last ten years, the Lebanese and local business communities have become closely associated in many cases.[23] Lines of distinction have become blurred. Apart from those Lebanese who were already exempt from the Decree as Nigerian nationals, some 40 or 50 more also eventually acquired citizenship as a result of legislative changes. Pending that outcome they continued in business under extensions from the authorities. Others stayed on in management positions in fully indigenised enterprises.

Among the southern States – indeed the whole federation – the bulk of enterprises affected were in Lagos State. There the tasks of indigenisation were far greater than in Kano. This is reflected in the fact that a final figure about the number of enterprises closed or sold was never released by the NEPB. The main contrast with Kano was with respect to the distribution of enterprises between Schedules. In Lagos, because of the existence of a very active and competitive indigenous private sector, most aliens were already in Schedule II activities. Of the few in Schedule I, most were small, non-limited, family-owned businesses – in textile retailing, transport, entertainment, and services – and as such were closed down and the assets sold. Among the private companies which issued shares under Schedule II, several patterns of ownership emerge. In the case of manufacturing companies, most of those acquiring shares were connected with the alien company's major indigenous competitor and/or its major indigenous distributors. This was also the pattern in the case of expatriate import and wholesale companies. Examples of both cases include the Odutola Group, S.B. Bakare, Chief Johnson, Chief Edu, Alhaji Hamza, Chief Ajanaku, and Chief Henry Fajemirokun. A smaller number of notables (ex-politicians, individuals well connected in the public sector) also received shares, as they did some of the few enterprises (mostly service) sold under Schedule I.

The Impact of Nigeria's Indigenisation Policies on Economic Institutions

In assessing the impact of Nigeria's indigenisation policies on economic institutions, this section examines first the relation of state action to the continued dominance of foreign capital and, second and more ambiguously, to the dependent position of indigenous capitalism.

The Dominance of Foreign Capital

In its original conception, the NEPD would have affected the Lebanese most. The tacit decision to prefer western capital was an understandable one in terms of buying political support. The Lebanese were entrenched in the trading and service sectors which Africans had long been wanting to dominate and the bulk of press publicity in the earlier stages of indigenisation was directed towards alleged acts of alien sabotage, usually but not always in sectors monopolised by the Lebanese.[26] The most serious of these were the extensions granted to some Lebanese born in Nigeria pending their applications for citizenship and to some firms which had genuine difficulties in finding buyers. There was also some evasive behaviour on the part of alien owners. For example, prices of businesses were inflated to deter buyers in the hope that the Decree might be eventually changed or its deadline postponed.

The position of many Lebanese businessmen in Nigeria has in some ways been different to their Asian counterparts in East Africa. True many have shared characteristics with the latter: their businesses have been small family concerns concentrated in the wholesale, retail, transport, and (in Nigeria) produce buying subsectors. Also, a certain insecurity has discouraged them from local investment, except in urban real estate. The bulk of enterprises sold under Schedule I of the NEPD were of this kind, although some Lebanese subsequently returned to Nigeria in the hope of being favoured by the changed naturalisation laws. Some political repercussions of these events are discussed below.

On the other hand, some of the more successful Lebanese businessmen have moved into manufacturing. In the northern State of Kano, for example, where indigenous entrepreneurship is less competitive than in the southern States, certain Lebanese families (for example Fawaz and Akle) own a range of light industries as well as a major proportion of the north-south haulage business. Some have gone into partnership either with the State Government or with one of the few Nigerian industrialists. A Lebanese even occupies the position of President of the Kano Chamber of Commerce and Industry. Interconnections between the Lebanese business community and higher government circles have been many. The State Military Governor under the Gowon administration was well known for his accessibility to the foreign business community and his negative attitude towards local businessmen. The State Ministry of Trade and Industry, the main public agency for assisting the latter, remained weak. A seminar to inform businessmen about buying a business under the NEPD took place only a few months before the deadline and complaints made at the seminar were bitter. Later, controversy reached the press about transport businesses and a cinema allegedly reserved for top state officials and their friends.[27]

The interests of non-Lebanese foreign capital have also been well represented in the higher circles of government. The Nigerian Chamber of

Commerce and Industry – by far the most influential and recognised business organisation in Nigeria – is dominated by Nigerian senior executives of large European Companies.[28] Its President, Chief Henry Fajemirokum, holds multiple directorships in several foreign companies and a leading foreign bank. In the absence of any official statement, it was the Chief who, after the July 1975 coup, reassured foreign investors of a continued welcome.[29]

A measure of the influence of foreign business, as an organised pressure group, can be obtained from the drafting of the NEPD itself. Apparently there were originally some 26 businesses listed under Schedule I, but as the result of 'behind the scenes manoeuvres' these were reduced to 22. Some of these – shipping, for example – might have been reclassified on economic merit. Thus, shipping was divorced from the less capital intensive clearing and forwarding agencies and placed under Schedule II. Of the remainder, however, doubts have been case about the deletion of printing, travel agencies, poultry farming, and the soft drinks bottling industry. In the last case an 'open secret' was reported that a few top brass civil servants allowed themselves to be courted by some of the companies most affected in the industry and that some nine government functionaries had retired to a virtual sinecure in the industry.[30]

In the light of the post-1975 coup revelations about irregular contracting and acquisition of land and property by top government officials,[31] there can be little doubt about this. In addition, a number of exemptions were subsequently made (for example for publishing companies) for undisclosed reasons. Also, a massive merger took place of some 17 companies to form the UAC group and pressures on government resulted in the transfer of petrol haulage (mainly Lebanese controlled) to Schedule II.

At the outset of this article, it was suggested that in practice the 'indigenisation' Decree has created continued opportunities for foreign capital, whilst (albeit in a defined way) increasing the fruits of collaboration for certain members of the local bourgeoisie. One basic factor working in favour of the interests of foreign capital has been the *laissez-faire* or *ad hoc* approach of public policy in this area and in particular the choice of organisation for the implementation of indigenisation. This approach ensures the dominance of foreign capital in various ways. First, it gives foreign capital a free hand in picking its indigenous auxiliaries. Thus, as this article illustrates elsewhere, foreign private companies may select as their major shareholders (often giving them the title of 'Director'), indigenous notables who can give political protection, as well as 'tie in' indigenous distributors and sometimes competitors in various ways. The only transactions resulting from the NEPD which were regulated were the sale of shares in 'public' companies and this was done by pre-existing government machinery – the Capital Issues Commission.

The second way is through direct manipulation of the machinery of government. While the broad indigenisation policies, starting with the economic nationalist rhetoric of the Second National Development Plan, may have been formed at the centre by far-sighted strategists,[32] those occupying key decision-making points in the machinery for implementing the NEPD were not always of the same outlook. Important in this respect are the *de jure* powers of Federal and State Commissioners for Trade and Industry to change the Schedules of the Decree or grant exemptions, as well as the practical discretion of civil servants at the NEPB in deciding whether a company falls under Schedule I or II. The returns made by foreign companies are now in fact being independently assessed by the tax authorities. The Decree itself has assisted manipulation by its lack of precision; it failed, for example, to make clear the difference between wholesale and retail activity.

In some ways, much of this is not particularly surprising. Most governments have a limited capacity for controlling foreign companies whose resources and ingenuity can assist evasion. (An earlier parallel in Nigeria would be the Expatriate Quota Allocation Board, established to promote the indigenisation of management.) Also in their accounting procedures goreign companies have developed various practices, and mention has already been made of companies which inflated their capital over ₦400,000 so as to qualify for Schedule II of the Decree and so sell 40 per cent only of their shares. Since the NEPD, the declared local dividends of some companies which have gone public have shown a marked decline. Buyers of shares in private companies under Schedule II have received low dividends and complained about lack of access to company records (particularly in relation to the pricing of imported items) and sometimes even about the failure to call shareholders' meetings.

Finally, obstacles to implementation apart, the compromising nature of state action can be discerned from the Decree itself. Larger enterprises are unaffected, apart from 40 per cent Nigerian equity participation. The Decree requires the transfer of ownership and control of specified industries within the given period and, moreover, to an indigenous private sector rather than to an expanded public sector. What the Federal Government has in mind is thus the establishment of a clearer division of labour between foreign private capital and an emerging indigenous sector. In other words indigenisation is an attempt to secure a certain position for a growing local elite of private entrepreneurs while at the same time preserving the dominant place for foreign capital elsewhere in the industrial sector. Indeed it is officially argued that one of the effects of indigenisation should be to encourage foreign private investors to move out of their traditional sectors into new ventures with high technology, management and risks. With respect to the Decree's requirement of 40 per cent equity participation for Nigerians in Schedule II enterprises, early critics had already pointed out that under certain circumstances ordinary shareholders in this category might in practice lose out, for example, where there was reduced company profit and what there was was sent to alien preference shareholders. In short, it was foreseen that 40 per cent of the share capital did not necessarily mean 40 per cent of the profits. It was also questioned how much of a voice the 40 per cent Nigerian participants would have in the running of a company.[33] The Nigerian Companies Decree of 1958 apparently does not prohibit the issuing of non-voting shares. Finally, the way in which shares could be spread widely among large numbers of applications is likely to weaken further the position of the minority of indigenous shareholders. These forewarnings have proved to be justified and the NEPD has thus restructured ownership without creating effective indigenous control.[34] A point to add, however, would be that even majority shareholding within the present framework would not make any qualitative difference, since the option remains one for passive financial participation in what is an overwhelmingly foreign-dominated private enterprise system. What is more, these very limited achievements have been made at the cost of additional capital export through the switch to local sources of capital in companies required to invite 40 per cent Nigerian equity participation.

Indigenous Capitalism: Conflict and Dependence

Given the continuing domination of foreign capital – aided and abetted by modes of state action – the indigenisation process has given rise to conflicts of interest among sections of the local hourgeoisie, sometimes competing with each other for the fruits of collaboration and sometimes in conflict with the state itself over the extent of public sector intervention and expansion. The relation of the emerging local bourgeoisie to the state is thus an ambiguous one. This is rooted on the dependent character of the economic system and the limits it imposes on options and opportunities.[35] Sometimes the local bourgeoisie supports the state in its efforts to increase opportunities. This has been the attitude of businessmen who have benefited from various forms of state patronage since independence – the Licensed Buying Agents (who profit as middlemen between the farmer and the marketing boards),[36] those who took advantage of import substitution during the civil war (especially in textiles), and more recently the contractors in the supply, transport, and construction sectors who have benefited from increased military and public expenditure since the oil boom. It also applies to most categories at the outset of the indigenisation exercise.

On other occasions, elements of the bourgeoisie have been in conflict with the state. This is discussed more fully below in the context of controversies over government proposals to take over indigenised businesses remaining unsold as well as government weakness in the face of the organised interests of foreign capital.

A third category includes those who in various ways join the foreign capitalists because of the latter's monopoly over technology and supplies. In the context of the formal indigenisation process, there have been first the civil servants, managers, and other professionals who, because of the physical restrictions of their office on business activity, are limited to passive financial participation as shareholders in foreign companies. Second, there are those businessmen, also discussed below, who provide political protection for foreign companies (as nominal shareholders) in return for a share in the profits or as sole distributors of their imported or locally manufactured goods. A more parasitical variant of this form of collaboration is the appointment of a prominent indigenous personality as 'Director'. These have included civilian Commissioners, members of traditional ruling families, retired politicians and civil servants, and leading businessmen. Some companies affected under Schedule II combined these two forms. Major distributors were allocated shares, while a well-known and/or well-connected Nigerian was made a 'Director'.

Against this background, the conflicts of interest that have arisen in the course of implementing the NEPD may be grouped in two major categories – sectional and geopolitical. The major issue of sectional conflict was the role of the public sector *vis-a-vis* the indigenous private sector in terms of allocating activities to public and private enterprise respectively, as well as *vis-a-vis* foreign capital in terms of the distribution of opportunities among the latter and its growing indigenous counterpart.[37] Conflicts in the second issue area arose mainly in the context of changes in the schedules of the indigenisation Decree in favour of foreign enterprise, while in the first case they were occasioned by official hints that the government might take over companies remaining unsold to indigenes when the Decree deadline expired. In addition to conflicts between public and private sectors was a certain amount of factionalism within the indigenous private sector itself, mainly over differential access among the various businessmen's associations to the government machinery supervising the indigenisation exercise. At a more informal level, the public-private sector rivalry was also expressed in terms of personal resentment on the part of Nigerian entrepreneurs who, as well as being in competition among themselves for state patronage, now found themselves in competition with enterprising state officials. Jealousies about the advantageous position of certain officials with respect to the control of information, patronage, and channels to foreign companies were central to many of the dismissals following the July 1975 coup. Pressures on General Gowon during the two years preceding his fall for a return to civilian politics may also be interpreted in this way.

The other major category of conflict was of a geo-political nature, where state interests attempted to keep resources in local hands by excluding businessmen from other areas (particularly the richer and historically more-favoured ones) from opportunities accruing from the Decree. Hence state governments bought shares and businesses and large expatriate companies shrewdly set aside equal blocs of their public shares for state governments. Fears of minority or underprivileged areas continued to be articulated and have to some extent been accommodated by the creation of 7 more states in 1976.

This should not necessarily be interpreted as an indicator of the continued pervasiveness of 'tribalism' in Nigeria. Such instances have mainly been in the petty trading and service sectors where there will always be more intense competition for opportunities among businessmen and where factors such as language and place of birth will be brought into play. At its upper levels, however, the emergent capital-owning class in Nigeria is characterised by unity of interest, A glance at the patterns of indigenous shareholding and directorships in individual foreign companies reveals a diverse geographical spread. Doubtless this also serves the interests of the companies in protecting and furthering their activities in all parts. But also, among the bigger Nigerian businessmen, many have offices in several states.

The competitive element may be taken at its face value where it takes place between states for opportunities, a pattern which is reinforced by the politics of federal revenue allocation. An example here would be the National Bank for Commerce and Industry, set up, *inter alia,* to finance indigenisation. Some resentment was caused by the way in which Lagos-based businessmen had obvious advantages over businessmen in the northern states where a branch has yet to open. The former Benue-Plateau State for example reported that out of 300 applications made by its businessmen only one was assisted. Likewise, Lagos businessmen had direct access to the NEPB where they could personally pilot through their takeovers. In the case of many northern businessmen, this was serious. The machinery charged with implementation was characterised by a high degree of centralisation at the NEPB in Lagos. Consequently, the processing of applications for the purchase of enterprises took some time. Also, ambiguities in the Decree required State Enterprises Promotion Committees to refer individual cases to Lagos.

These conflicts apart, it was the trading and service sectors towards which most indigenous businessmen's interest was directed in Schedule I. For those outside the shareholding category, these sectors represented the real substance of what the Decree affected. Indeed, historically, they are areas where the presence of aliens has been long resented.

Outside popular activities like transport, entertainment, and retail trading indigenous businessmen have been less keen to invest their capital in new and unfamiliar ventures. The NEPD did not help there in that it forbade expatriates to stay on as managers after the deadline. In other cases businessmen preferred to wait for loan capital, particularly from government sources with low rates of interest. Where foreign enterprises were small sole proprietorships or partnerships, with strong elements of personal control and direction, these factors were particularly acute. Buying such enterprises does not always guarantee the continuity of supplies, contracts, orders, and customers or the goodwill the former owner had with banking and financial institutions. The success of the business may have been tied up with the personal managerial efforts and contracts (particularly overseas) of the former owner. The situation varies of course according to type of enterprise. The Kano survey of indigenised enterprises revealed that these problems tend to be less acute in the entertainment, (cinemas, gaming machines, casinos, clubs, etc.) transport, and service (dry cleaning, haridressing etc) sectors. They are most acute in the case of the wholesale and distributive trades and manufacturing where supplies and essential raw materials come from overseas.

In some ways, indigenisation came at a particularly disadvantageous time for Kano-based businessmen. First, the recent drought had been a major set-back, biting deep into the pockets of businessmen whose core activity in many cases was produce-buying and transportation. Second, the economic mismanagement of the last years of the Gowon regime also affected business performance. Ports became congested, delaying supplies; the availability of petrol and diesel oil was irregular; and labour costs rose 30–100 per cent as a result of wage demands precipitated by the 'Udoji' round of public sector salary increases.

Against this background it was not surprising that considerable frustration built up as a result of the way indigenisation was implemented. Three instances may be cited. In one, an indigenous transporters' association in Kano made a public protest over the extensions granted to Lebanese transport companies, with the allegation that private arrangements were being made to sell them to public officials. Already, Nigerian transporters had been denied the most lucrative and guaranteed sub-sector – petrol haulage – which was removed to Schedule II. In the second, again in Kano, a similar delay over the sale of a Lebanese-owned cinema provoked a public controversy. The underlying issue was favouritism, in this case a move by the State Governor to set aside the business for a colleague. The other cinemas in Kano had already been taken over by the State Investment Company in partnership with a senior official in the Emir's Palace.[38] The third instance is that of the distributive trades both in Kano and in Lagos. As a result of changed immigration legislation, some Lebanese formerly engaged in retain trading had returned to resume their businesses in the hope that citizenship might eventually be granted. This caused frustration among certain sections of Nigerian businessmen who had in the meantime moved into this activity. They were again facing competition from aliens whose relations still dominated the wholesaling of textiles, and were unable to get adequate supplies. Furthermore, with the return of the Lebanese, some landlords increased the rent for their shops. An abortive delegation went to the Emir's Palace in Kano, as a result of which police action was taken against some of the organisers. Since then citizenship has been approved for many Lebanese who have re-established themselves.

In Schedule II, where some businessmen bought shares in wholesale companies, other frustrations were experienced. Many complained about the failure of partially indigenised companies to call shareholders' meetings to pay satisfactory dividends, and even to disclose information about the companies' internal operations. With the exception of a few well-known and well-connected shareholders, the general picture was one of lack of shareholders' involvement.

In Lagos, by way of contrast, the problems of indigenising the distributive trades were of a slightly different kind. As might be expected in a relatively sophisticated business centre, shareholders were more informed about their rights. Most appeared to be the major customers and distributors of the company. It was difficult, however, to ascertain whether the shares had actually been bought, but many respondents complained they had no choice but to associate themselves with the alien enterprise, otherwise they would get no supplies or goods for retail. In the case of textile wholesalers who were also engaged in retailing before the Decree, the latter activity appeared on occasions to have been 'spun off' to an indigene who would sell the goods (obtained on credit) on behalf of the alien.

One feature that stood out in contrast to Kano was the absence of 'goodwill' on the part of aliens towards their successors or partners. A quite common behaviour was for an alien to threaten to cut off overseas supplies and contracts as a means of muting effective indigenous participation. One such case was a small company whose capital had been inflated to qualify it for Schedule II. The indigenous prospective buyers had to opt for 40 per cent shareholding instead of outright purchase since the latter would have provoked the severance of overseas contacts. Where indigenous shareholders were also customers or distributors, a similar tactic has been applied.

Commenting on the nature of economic nationalism in the early 1960s, Wrigley stated: 'The late colonial period produced a curious and explosive blend of colonial paternalism, welfare socialism and mercantilism natural to the stage of economic transition which Nigeria had reached. The already prevalent conviction that "government" had the duty to promote economic development, that is primarily to provide jobs, was confirmed and enhanced. "Nationalism" became almost synonymous with Nigerianisation and appropriation of the white men's jobs.'[39] The mode of state action in the indigenisation of the economy has not been essentially different. It has been to assert formal ownership over, or create new occupational roles or niches by reserving, certain activities for indigenes, but in ways which do not deter the foreigner. Such an approach serves to reinforce the tendency of many Nigerian businessmen to seek activities where profits can be made through fixed concessions and monopolies much in the fashion of the licensed buying agent system. Thus it was not surprising that some Nigerian businessmen expected the government to finance the whole indigenisation exercise and simply hand over alien enterprises to them.

Unfortunately, because of the dominance and ingenuity of some of the aliens operating in the reserved sectors, an informal process of co-optation has taken place, with the aliens themselves creating roles for would-be Nigerian capitalists. Because of the difficulties of removing the aliens, Nigerians have had to instal themselves alongside the former – to mutual advantage. Certain Nigerians have been able to secure for themselves a concessionary niche inside the circle of protected and largely foreign-owned industry and commerce – gaining access to supplies as sole distributors. Aliens for their part have been able further to secure their dominant position by 'locking in' indigenous entrepreneurs through their superior abilities in manipulating the government machinery (by bogus shareholding arrangements), reinforced by their monopoly of overseas contacts and supplies. In these ways, some Nigerian businessmen remain dependent clients rather than entrepreneurs.

The Socio-economic Impact of Indigenisation: The Beneficiaries of Indigenisation

The main thrust of state intervention, it will be recalled, has been to facilitate the purchase by certain privileged Nigerians of minority shares in a range of large expatriate companies in manufacturing and wholesale activities and to confine productive indigenous investment to a limited range of complementary and dependent activities in the service, retailing, and 'small-scale industry' sectors. One major socio-economic effect of recent state action is the emergence of what in a comparable context has been called an 'auxiliary bourgeoisie'.[40] The auxiliary bourgeoisie and their allies are drawn from a number of sectors – bureaucratic, managerial, and commercial. In the course of indigenisation, sections of Nigerian society have been auxiliary to foreign capital in a number of ways, according to the position and interests of each.

The first section of the auxiliary bourgeoisie comprises the category of individuals who have acquired shares in large public companies affected under Schedule II. Prominent among these have of course been state officials themselves, who through privileged access to credit, information, and sometimes the foreign companies have formed the core of the Nigerian emergent share-owning class. A major shift of resources in favour of this group took place in early 1975 with the payment of a massive backdated pay increase to civil servants. It was greatly regretted amongst some of the latter that these came too late to be used to secure more benefits under the indigenisation Decree. Consequently what was invested went mainly into urban real estate speculation. The higher civil service in fact comprises a growing element of the Nigerian rentier class. Property and shareholding are clearly the most convenient types of business activity for those confined to the office desk. The extent of property speculation among top civil servants (as well as other public figures) was dramatically revealed after the July 1975 coup when lists of extensive and lucrative land acquisitions in Lagos were published in the press.

The second group of shareholders comprises the top Nigerian executives of large foreign-owned companies. Some of these companies guaranteed bank loans to employees in managerial grades to buy shares. They included Nigerian Breweries, CFAO, Paterson Zochonis, Vono, Bata, Metal Box, Blackwood Hodge, Wiggins Teape, the *Daily Times*, Berger Paints, and John Holt The issue of UAC shares gave preferential consideration to applications from company employees up to 700,800 ordinary shares. Apart from common shareholding, the Nigerian bureaucratic and managerial elites have a growing community of interest. This was underscored by the 'Udoji' Public Service Review Commission which sought to create inter-sectoral mobility between public and private enterprise by 'harmonising' the salaries of civil servants and the executives of top private (and usually foreign) companies.[41] To the civil servant, the private sector executive symbolises 'technical efficiency' and an internationalised life style. State Enterprises Promotion

Committees co-opted these executives to their membership, for example, in the former North Central (now Kaduna) State the General Manager of Dunlop (Nigeria) Limited and in Kano an official of New Nigerian Investments Limited. Top Nigerian executives of leading foreign companies also dominated the Chambers of Commerce and Industry. Throughout the indigenisation exercise the alleged incompetence and even the lack of integrity of smaller Nigerian businessmen was a constant theme in the speeches and harangues of public officials.[42]

In an under-developed economy such as Nigeria's, where the state and a few large (and mostly foreign owned) private enterprises are the major employees and sources of profit, it is to some extent inevitable that the shareholding class should be dominated by the bureaucratic and managerial elites. Other numerically smaller groups include some of the larger-scale Nigerian businessmen who have an appreciation of modern corporate structure, and various professionals in education, medicine, and the church. With some exceptions, most notably the State Military Governors, the regular military do not appear to have been taken any significant or direct advantage of indigenisation, probably because the outlets for their particular brand of entrepreneurial zeal lie elsewhere – in 'quick gain' sectors such as contracting.

Publicly the issue of shares in partially indigenised companies was much discussed in the national press, in particular the alleged restrictive allocation of shares to certain sections of the public and the apparent transfer of a very large blocks of shares to single individuals. With almost no degree of risk, some argued, a few rich Nigerians who had been able to buy shares were placed in a position of reaping unearned income to supplement their incomes from real estate and financial investment.[43] More systematic analysis of at least 'public' issues does suggest, however, that with some exceptions, shares were distributed among more than the proverbial 'handful'.[44] For example, the basis of allotment of UAC shares, the largest issue, is shown in Table 1.

A total of 85,488 applications were received for 58,966,735 shares, the offer being subscribed 8.4 times. A total of 934 applications for 10,990,645 shares were rejected because they were considered ineligible under the terms of the offer and 700,800 shares reserved for employees of the Company were taken up in full. A numerically wide distribution of shares would in fact make sense although this would not necessarily mean any wide distribution from a *social class* view point. Atomistic shareholding would further reduce the influence of minority indigenous shareholders. Most significant from the point of view of concentration ownership have been the mergers as a result of indigenisation – most notably the UAC group, now embracing some seventeen subsidiaries – as well as the multiple directorships held by a few prominent Nigerians in the large alien companies and banks.

The second area where Nigerians, as a result of the 'indigenisation' Decree, have assumed auxiliary roles is in the smaller private foreign companies also affected under Schedule II where various collaborative arrangements have been made. The issue of shares in these companies was transacted bilaterally

Table 1
Allotment of UAC Shares

Number of shares applied for	*Number of Applicants*	*Actual allocation of shares*
50	7,208	In full
100–500	60,436	80
550–950	2,153	100
1,000–5,000	5,198	130
5,050–10,000	247	250
10,050–20,000	104	600
22,500–50,000	78	1,500
60,000–100,000	14	2,200
125,000–250,000	11	3,800
500,000	1	7,130

Source: *Daily Times* (Nigeria)

(and often secretly) without any reference to public bodies. Private companies do not fall under the purview of the Capital Issues Commission or the Stock Exchange and buyers and sellers have only had to notify the NEPB. The basis of returns reveal a preponderance of top civil servants, professionals, big businessmen (often competitors), occasional members of the armed forces, members of traditional ruling families, former politicians, State Commissioners, and the employees and the leading distributors of companies selling the shares. Since the Stock Exchange and Capital Issues Commissions have no control over private company transactions, there is nothing to prevent a further concentration of share ownership through resale and transfer. To this group should be added first the state officials, who, as illustrated above, have abetted in the manipulation of the formal machinery of indigenisation. A second and related group of beneficiaries are the privileged workers who continue to enjoy high wages and security in the high profit, oligopolistic, and foreign-dominated capitalist sector. Some of these campaigned against the complete indigenisation of the particular sector, fearing either redundancy or lower wages and loss of security under Nigerian ownership.

The overall picture which thus emerges from these various patterns of co-operation and clientage is one of a tightening nexus between government and foreign capital. On the one hand important sections of the bureaucratic and managerial bourgeoisie have been co-opted as shareholders, while on the other chosen members of the commercial bourgeoisie have secured a niche in the alien-dominated distributive network and therefore tied in, as satellites, through the latters' monopoly of supplies and credit.[45] The state must now protect even more the interests of foreign capital in which the local bourgeoisie has a stake.

It would be a mistake, however, to exaggerate the impostance of the auxiliary bourgeoisie which has lately emerged through state action and the manipulation of changing economic institutions. As we have seen, the Nigerian commercial bourgeoisie is not always the 'willing partner' that others have identified.[46] Dependent though it might remain in most cases, the role it now has to play is not necessarily readily assumed, and survey data suggests considerable antagonism towards the nexus between government and foreign capital.[47] A common complaint among interviewees who had bought shares directly in private companies was that the expatriate owner/manager continued to exercise total control over the enterprise. This was achieved through tactics such as the suppression of information on company activity or not calling shareholders' meetings in order to limit indigenous participation, but also by using as a threat the discontinuation of the expatriate's overseas sources of supply and credit. For example, of 29 partially-indigenised commercial enterprises in Lagos, Nigerian partners or principal shareholders interviewed from some 12 expressed bitter frustation with the way in which the NEPD had been implemented. One stated: 'Even if you are successful in taking an enterprise from an alien [i.e. through instigating official action where he has evaded the NEPD] he can always block supplies from abroad'. Another declared: 'If we dare show our dissatisfaction [i.e. with the way in which the NEPD had been manipulated] the owner of the enterprise will invite others, who may subsequently dismiss us as agents'. Third, a number of intervening variables, notably the weak enforcement machinery of the state and the continued dominance of foreign capital and its accommodation by a manipulable local partner, further reduced the impact of indigenisation policies on existing economic institutions. Fourth, in addition to creating increased social inequalities among Nigerians as beneficiaries, the implementation of indigenisation policies has also been a divisive issue within the ruling group itself.

As in other policy areas, the Gowon regime displayed weakness in its implementation of the NEPD. At th outset, Schedules were altered as a result of pressures from affected foreign interests and finally formal changes in Nigeria's citizenship laws, coupled with individual exemptions from the Decree, further reduced its scope. At the same time the regime became increasingly defensive, particularly about its performance in relation to the distribution of benefits, and during his 1974 Budget Speech, General Gowon declared 'It has never been, and it cannot be, the intention of the Federal Military Government merely to crease avenues for a few individuals to grow rich excessively and easily on account of the indigenisation decree . . .'[48] In addition, the economic mismanagement of the Gowon regime resulted in conditions which any enterprise, whether foreign or indigenous, found trying. This had, to some extent, been caused by the unplanned Udoji public sector wage increases, resulting in inflation, ports congestion, and shortage of petrol and supplies.[49] It was characteristic of a regime which had increasingly resorted to buying short-term political support (through public sector wage increases, and the giving out of lucrative supply and construction contracts) rather than attempting to create the framework for strengthening the productive capacity of the economy. Consequently, important elements of Nigerian society became increasingly disunited and alienated as benefits were eroded and opportunities restricted to a small controlling clique of military leaders, selected bureaucrats, and foreign businessmen and their clients, and pressures were mounted on the military for a change in leadership.[50]

Since the July 1975 coup, which replaced the Gowon administration, the incoming leadership of first General Murtala Muhammed (until his assassination) and his successor Lt-General Obasanjo has carried out a major investigation of the indigenisation exercise through the Industrial Enterprises Panel. The latter scrutinised most of the compromising acts of the previous regime, including the extent of enterprises allowed to default, the original placement of affected enterprises by the Board in Schedules I and II (especially in relation to their declared value) and regrouping of companies to evade the Decree. Its recommendations included limiting the shares taken by individuals in future indigenisation exercises, more public sector participation in Schedule II, and the laying down of basic pricing, spread of ownership, employees' interest, and indigenisation of management. The Board is now to be involved in negotiations related to the selling and buying of affected enterprises. The Panel also covered the role of the Stock Exchange, the National Bank for Commerce and Industry, the National Industrial Development Bank, and the Expatriate Quota System. As regards the Stock Exchange a Council was recommended, a process to ensure a less nepotistic transfer and wider spread of shares, and greater use of the Stock Exchange by companies. The suggestion for accelerating the expatriate quota system was rejected by the Federal Government as too idealistic.[51] The outcome of the Panel's report and the Government's acceptance of most of its recommendations has been the promulgation of the Nigerian Enterprises Promotion Decree No. 3 of 1977, considerably wider in scope and tighter in machinery than its predecessor.

It remains to consider, in the light of post-1975 coup policy trends, the prospects for any future genuine indigenous industrialisation in Nigeria.[52] Critical to such a possibility are the relative strengths of two groups: the emergent industrial elite in the indigenous private sector and their counterparts within the public policy-making process and supportive organs of government.[53] The indigenous industrial elite, as indicated above, is at present not entirely distinct from other categories. For example, it overlaps consierably with the indigenous commercial stratum, being divided from the latter by its relative access to patronage and opportunities. Nor is it entirely independent of foreign enterprise.

The 1976 Industrial Enterprises Panel Report and the government White Paper on it takes cognisance of the absence of any clear industrial development strategy in Nigeria. The Report's recommendations, most of which were accepted by the federal government and embodied in the 1977 Decree, ranged beyond diagnoses of the late indigenisation exercise and its shortcomings. They included the expansion of the scope of Schedules I and II, with an increase in Nigerian equity participation from 40 per cent to 60 per cent and the addition of a Schedule III where the equity participation requirement is 40 per cent. The deadline for the implementation of these new Schedules is 31 December 1978. But more pertinent to our point here, they also included suggestions about possible criteria to be laid down for the creation of new enterprises: value-added, technological transfer, and conformity to national plan priorities.[54] The 1977–78 Federal Budget indicates some degree of appreciation of these suggestions in so far as it announces a package of incentives and protections for local manufacturing industries.[55] On the other hand, there appears as yet no clear official position as regards the distribution of these new industrial opportunities between foreign and indigenous private sectors. For example, of the activities added to Schedule I (100 per cent Nigerian ownership) by the 1977 Decree, only two are in manufacturing (suitcases and furniture, which in themselves are fairly light), and the rest are in commerce, processing, and the service sector. While further manufacturing activities have been added to Schedule II and minimum Nigerian equity participation raised from 40 to 60 per cent, there is no guarantee that indigenous participation will not be of the passive character it has in the past.

The strategic alternative of direct state intervention in manufacturing appears even remoter. Public policy towards state sector expansion remains ambivalent.[56] For example, the 1976 Industrial Enterprises Panel Report places strong emphasis on the weakness of government machinery and its 'soft' approach to implementation as well as the role of 'some misguided Nigerian citizens' in 'fronting' for foreign business interests.[57] However, the response of the federal government was ambiguous, particularly to the recommendation that a reorganised, expanded and upgraded NEPB should spearhead the 'fresh approach to new enterprises creation'.[58] The federal government preferred that the Board should remain as a 'regulatory' organisation. Debate on the control of the economy caused an open rift within the Constitutional Drafting Committee over the public ownership/ 'mixed' economy issue. Finally, the subcommittee responsible opted for the compromise formula that: 'the state shall . . . control and operate the major sectors of the economy while individual and groups rights to operate the means of production, distribution and exchange shall be protected by law'. This was essentially a formula to preserve the status quo since the Constitutional Drafting Committee went on to define the state sector in term terms of what is currently being operated exclusively by the federal government.[59]

References

This essay was first published in the *Journal of Commonwealth and Comparative Politics*, 15, 2 (July 1977).

1. This point derives from certain recent literature which has made the controversial suggestion that in certain less industrialised nations the state, through the exercise of public policy, has begun to demonstrate the possibilities of creating a successful national capitalist development or at least of ensuring that the activities of foreign companies dominating the economy are moulded to the national interest and that opportunities are given to indigenous private and public enterprise to grow side by side. See Brian van Arkadie, 'Foreign Investment and State Enterprise: An African Context', paper presented to IDEP-IDS-CLACSO Conference on 'Strategies of Economic Development in Africa compared with Latin America', UN Institute for Economic Development and Planning, Dakar, 4–17 September 1972, esp. pp. 20–2. Bill Warren, 'Myths of Underdevelopment, Imperialism and Capitalist Industrialisation', *New Left Review,* 81 (1973), pp. 3–45.
2. For some preliminary findings of a penetrating political economy of Nigerian oil, see Terisa Turner, 'Multinational Corporations and the Instability of the Nigerian State', *Review of African Political Economy,* 5 (1976), pp. 63–79. Also her 'The Working of the Nigerian National Oil Corporation', Chapter 6 above.
3. A tempting parallel is Brazil, an example which has not gone without notice in Nigerian policy-making circles. For example, the Industrial Enterprises Panel made a one-week study tour of Brazil in 1975 and made recommendations to the government, based on its observations of the working of the Bank of Brazil. See *Federal Military Government Views on the Report of the Industrial Enterprises Panel* (Lagos, 1976) p. 25, paras. 80–81.
4. A substantial literature has now accumulated using the concept of 'dependency' as a focus for the study of underdevelopment. For a useful review, see P. O'Brien, 'A critique of Latin American theories of dependency', in I. Oxaal, T. Barnett and D. Booth (eds), *Beyond the Sociology of Development* (London, 1975), pp. 7–27.
5. See Dos Santos and Cardoso who have argued (in the Latin American context) that dependency is the conditioning context for certain types of internal structure. Thus, new forms of dependency give rise to novel social adaptations and reactions inside dependent countries. The major consequences of dependency is internal differentiation and fragmentation of interests. See Theotonio Dos Santos, 'The Crisis of Development Theory and the Problem of Dependence in Latin America', in H. Bernstein (ed), *Development and Underdevelopment* (London, 1972) pp. 188–9, 203, 209, and 213; F.H. Cardoso, 'Dependency and Development in Latin America', *New Left Review,* 74 (1972), pp. 83–95; also his *Estado y Sociedad en America Latina* (Buenos Aires, 1972), pp. 184–91.
6. For full details of the evaluation of public policy in this earlier period, see P.D. Collins, 'The Policy of Indigenization: An Overall View', *Quarterly Journal of Administration,* 9 (1975), pp. 137–40.

7. See for example, C. Leys, *Underdevelopment in Kenya: The Politics of Neo-Colonialism* (London, 1975).
8. See for example, R. Joseph, 'The Gaullist Legacy: Patterns of French Neo-Colonialism', *Review of African Political Economy*, 6 (1976), pp. 4–13.
9. Federal Republic of Nigeria, *Second National Development Plan, 1970–4* (Lagos, 1970), p. 289.
10. Federal Military Government. *Supplement to Official Gazette Extra-ordinary*, 58 (1972), Part A. Prior to the Decree expatriate commercial and industrial enterprise was governed by the Immigration Policy of 1952 (Amended 1956), according to which Nigerians were protected only from 'additional competition'. Those already in Nigeria before October 1960 were not affected by the immigration legislation.
11. The NEPD was apparently modelled on the Ghana Business (Promotion) Act, 1970.
12. E.O. Akerdolu-Ale, *The Underdevelopment of Indigenous Enterprise in Nigeria* (Ibadan, 1975).
13. See G. Rimlinger, 'The Indigenisation of Industry', *Quarterly Journal of Administration*, 7 (1973), pp. 205–15.
14. ₦1 (Naira) = 72p or $1.58.
15. Federal Military Government, *Official Gazette* (26 March 1974), NEPD (Amendment) No 2 Decree 1974.
16. For a full reproduction of the Schedules, see P.D. Collins, 'The Political Economy of Indigenization: The Case of the Nigerian Enterprises Promotion Decree', *The African Review*, 4 (1976), pp. 493–4.
17. Alien enterprises submitting returns but not affected by the Decree included some 805 others, 231 in various manufacturing activities, 61 in property investment and management and real estate, 51 in oil exploration, services and production, 42 in hotels, entertainment and catering, 29 in insurance, pensions and life assurance brokerage, 25 in food and confectionery manufacturing and processing, 27 manufacturers' representatives, 23 finance and investment companies, 18 in technical services, 17 engineering consultants, as well as smaller numbers in a range of other activities. These were distributed among the former 12 states as follows: Lagos 612, Kano 57, West 41, North-Central 21, Rivers 20, Benue-Plateau 19, Mid-West 11, South-East 11, East-Central 8, North-East 5, Kwara 3, and North-West 1.
18. For example, of the 556 affected enterprises listed by the Nigerian Enterprises Promotion Board in July 1974 as not yet having complied, 179 were Lebanese, 94 were British, 64 were Indian, 54 were continental European, 18 were Arabs (other than Lebanese), 13 were American, 6 were Oriental, 2 were Israeli, with 126 others miscellaneous or unspecified.
19. Federal Military Government, *Guidelines for the Third National Development Plan, 1975–80* (Lagos, 1973).
20. For full details of the machinery, see Collins, 'The Political Economy of Indigenization, pp. 497–8.
21. See O. Teriba, 'Financing Indigenisation', *Quarterly Journal of Administration*, 9 (1975), pp. 159–76.

22. All public share issues were advertised in the national press as required by law. Companies also later published details of applications received and shares allocated.
23. S.A.Asabia, 'Share Valuation: the Nigerian Experience', paper presented to Nigerian Economics Society Symposium on 'Indigenisation', Lagos, 9 November 1974. Mr Asabia was Deputy Governor of the Central Bank at the time.
24. *Ibid.*
25. See J. Paden, *Religion and Political Culture in Kano* (Berkeley, 1973), p. 365. More generally, see R. Bayley Winder, 'The Lebanese in West Africa', in L. Fallers (ed), *Immigrants and Associations* (The Hague, 1967), pp. 103–53; *Kroniek van Afrika,* 3 (New Series) (1975), special issue on 'Asian Minorities in Africa: Indians and Lebanese'.
26. For example, *Daily Sketch* (Ibadan), 17 March 1972; *New Nigerian* (Kaduna), 11 July 1972; *Daily Sketch,* 7 November 1972; *Daily Times* (Lagos), 2 March 1973; *Daily Times,* 27 April 1973; *Daily Sketch,* 13 June 1973; *New Nigerian,* 23 June 1973.
27. See note 38.
28. Hence it has sometimes been the object of strong criticism by rival indigenous businessmen's organisations. For example the Nigerian Chamber of Indigenous Contractors has attacked the Chamber of Commerce as unrepresentative of Nigerian businessmen and as 'watch-dogs of foreigners' over the expatriate quota system. *Daily Sketch,* 9 May 1972.
29. *Daily Times,* 13 August 1975.
30. *Afriscope* (Lagos), 7 May 1972.
31. See, for example, *Daily Times,* 16 September 1975.
32. See E. Akeredolu-Ale, 'The "Competitive threshold" hypothesis and Nigeria's industrialisation process', *Nigerian Journal of Social and Economic Studies,* 14 (1974), p. 116.
33. J. Cottrell, 'A legal approach to the indigenisation Decree', *New Nigerian,* 23 March 1973. In addition to the provisions of the Decree, the official statements made since in clarification of its policy goals indicate the absence of any intention on the part of the majority of the Nigerian leadership basically to alter the dependence situation. See Collins, 'The Political Economy of Indigenization', pp. 501–2.
34. See *Government's Views on the Report of the Industrial Enterprises Panel* (Lagos, 1976), para. 36.
35. See F.H. Cardoso, 'The Industrial Elite', in Bernstein, *Development and Underdevelopment,* pp. 191–204.
36. See G.K. Helleiner, *Peasant Agriculture, Government and Economic Growth* (Homewood, Illinois, 1966).
37. For a full account of these conflicts, see Collins, 'The Political Economy of Indigenization', pp. 504–5.
38. These events have now been publicly revealed in the *Report on the Kano State-owned Organisations and Companies Commission of Inquiry* (Kano, 1975), esp. pp. 136–45.
39. C. Wrigley, 'Some Aspects of the Political Economy of Nigeria', seminar paper, Institute of Commonwealth Studies, University of London, 13 June 1968.

40. Leys, *Underdevelopment in Kenya*, p. 147 *et seq.*
41. See P. Collins, 'Current Issues of Administrative Reform in the Nigerian Public Services: the 'Udoji'' Review Commission', Chapter 16 below.
42. See, for example, *Rennaissance*, 12 July 1972 and *Daily Sketch*, 8 March 1972 ('individualism' and 'lack of cooperative spirit'); *Rennaissance*, 2 December 1972 and *Daily Sketch*, 26 January 1973 ('conspicuous consumption'); *Daily Sketch*, 26 January 1973, 8 March 1972; *New Nigerian*, 17 June 1972 'low managerial competence and productivity'); *Rennaissance*, 24 August 1972; *Daily Sketch*, 22 May 1972; *Rennaissance*, 11 June 1972 ('poor workmanship'); *Daily Sketch*, 19 January 1973; *Rennaissance*, 30 October 1972 ('dishonesty').
43. See Teriba, *op. cit.*, p. 174.
44. I am grateful to Dr Neil Cohen, formerly of Ahmadu Bello University, Zaria, for showing me his tabulations and statistical tables bearing on this. A similar observation has been made by Holger Enberg who also quotes a Lagos Stock Exchange Secretariat estimate that Nigerian shareholders are far in excess of 200,000. The prevalent procedure in allocating NEPD shares appears to have been to accept as many applications for the minimum number of shares (usually 50) as possible and to cut down drastically the allotment of shares to large applicants. See Holger Engberg. 'Indigenisation of the Business Sector Through the Organized Capital Market: The Lagos Stock Exchange', *Journal of Management Studies*, 7 (1975), p. 6.
45. For example, Paterson Zochonis allocated most of their shares to their distributors, following a pattern established by many expatriate companies even before the NEPD. An example is Nigerian Breweries which is reported to have sold some ₦400,000 of its shares in this way. See Engberg, *op. cit.*, p. 4, note 3. In other sectors such as construction, however, a reverse pattern of clientage is prevalent. For example indigenous construction companies often win contracts and then pass them on to large expatriate companies for execution.
46. See Leys, *op. cit.*, Chapter 5.
47. P. Collins, *Surveys of Indigenised and Partially Indigenised Enterprises, Lagos and Kano, 1975*, Research Reports presented to the Institute of Administration, Ife University.
48. Reprinted in *New Nigerian*, 2 April 1974.
49. See Collins, 'Current Issues of Adminstrative Reform'.
50. The two most celebrated episodes of the sequence of events were first the successful campaign to unseat first J.S. Tarka as Federal Commissioner and second, but unsuccessfully, J.D. Gommwalk as Military Governor of the former Benue-Plateau State. Both were accused of shady business deals while in public office. Gommwalk was later shot for his complicity in the alleged plot to bring back General Gowon after the assassination of Muhammed.
51. *Federal Military Government's Views of the Report of the Industrial Enterprises Promoting Panel* (Lagos, 1976).
52. Thus referring back to the literature by Warren *et al* cited at the outset of this article.
53. Some political economists have advocated a role for the state in industrialising non-socialist societies which centres on adjusting the

relations between foreign and domestic national/private capital, thereby creating new opportunities for certain sections of the growing local bourgeoisie. See J. Weeks, 'Uneven Sectoral Development and the Role of the State', *The Bulletin* (Institute of Development Studies at the University of Sussex), 5 (October 1973). p. 76. However, others have doubted whether this can lead to the emergence of a genuine local capitalist class. Wrigley has pointed out for example that in the first Nigerian Republic new business elites have relied far less on constructive enterprise than on the easier methods of political intrigue. 'Why', he asks, 'as a lorry owner bother to cut one's costs when, as a client or colleague of a Minister, one can secure a monopoly profit on the transport of the Marketing produce?' Thus the 1972 Nigerian Enterprises Promotion Decree, by and large, led to patterns of nominal ownership only (i.e. permission to draw 'dividends as shareholders), control remaining in foreign hands. Wrigley, 'Some aspects of the political economy of Nigeria'.

54. *Federal Military Government's Views on the Report of the Industrial Enterprises Panel,* p. 17, para. 49.

55. These include a ban on the import of certain items (beer bottles, lace, all cars over 2500 cc, carbon paper, galvanised buckets, food items such as meat, cheese and fruit, and travel goods including handbags and briefcases), licensed importation for a further range of goods (canned beer, soft drinks, furniture, carpets, common salt, cars from 2000 cc to 2500 cc, stockfish, and bicycle tyres), increased duty of certain competing imported goods (textiles, garments), and the reduction or elimination of duty on certain raw materials used in local manufacture (synthetic rubber, refractory goods, latex, barley and hops, parts used in manufacturing electrical goods, and animal feed).

56. Students of some sectors of the Nigerian economy have seen the possibilities of a 'technocratic' revolution in the state sector. For example, Terisa Turner's political economy of Nigerian oil and its relation to the instability of the state has placed much emphasis on the diverse effect of Gowon's and his associates' personalised control of the sharing of oil revenues and company kick-backs, rather than more institutionalised forms of national control, such as through a really effective National Oil Corporation. Backing the creation of such, the argument runs, was an increasingly self-conscious and ambitious group of technocratically-minded civil servants enthused with the idea of a real national industrial policy based on public investment rather than the frittering away of the surplus on the buying of short-term political support and seeing themselves in control of an expanded public sector. Such an interpretation carries some degree of plausibility when seen in conjunction with other recent events. For example, the 1975 'Udoji' Commission Report, containing *inter alia* a package of the latest management techniques and procedures, may be seen as a step towards the consolidation of a more technocratic (as well as better paid) public service as the organisational basis of a more successful national capitalism. Likewise, some parts of the 1976 Industrial Enterprises Panel Report, discussed below, hint at stronger public sector agencies and a more interventionist industrial development strategy, although the

ambiguous government response to the report at these points suggests that the 'technocratic' element (if that is how it is to be characterised) has yet to dominate the state sector. On Nigerian oil, see Turner, 'The Working of the Nigerian National Oil Corporation'; on the 'Udoji' Commission, see Collins, 'Current Issues of Administrative Reform'.

57. *Federal Military Government's Views* . . . p. 4, para. 4.
58. *Ibid.*, para. 59.
59. *Report of Constitutional Drafting Committee* (Lagos, 1977), Volume 1, Section 3.7, p. xiii. When the new Constitution is adopted and operative, additional areas may be included in the state sector by a resolution of each of the Houses of the National Assembly. A third 'radical' view however contested the whole basis of the debate arguing that control by the state of 'major sectors' would only transfer control of the other sectors of the economy from the foreign multinational corporations (if Nigeria were to succeed in wresting control from them) to domination by the political party elite. They also objected to the implied competition between public and private sector (*Report,* p. xv).

8. The State and the Control of Labour: The Case of the Lagos Port Cargo Handling Industry

Peter Waterman

Introduction

Of the three major sectors of the labouring poor in Nigeria – farmers, workers, self-employed craftsmen, traders and service-offerers – only the workers have demonstrated the capacity to organize themselves on a continuing basis – nationally, with distinct class strategies, and with the ability to take effective mass action against the controllers of the economic surplus and holders of political power in the country. The latter therefore have every motive to wish to control them. The purpose of this chapter is to reveal the ways in which those who control the Nigerian state seek to do this. 'Control' is to be understood here not simply as restraining, but also, more positively, as forming and guiding. In this activity the state has at its disposal a wide range of practices and devices inherited from the colonial state or drawn from the experience of more industrialized societies.

This control of labour will be examined through the case of Lagos Port. The Port has particular interest because of the existence within it of two distinct sectors that can be taken as in some way representing two of the major wage employment sectors in Nigeria and elsewhere in Africa. The two sectors are the foreign private and the state sector on the one hand, and the local capitalist sector on the other.[1] The first is capital intensive, large scale, combines semi-skilled and high-level labour, and practices bureaucratized labour relations. The second is labour intensive, small scale, mixes unskilled and skilled labour, and practices personalized labour relations.[2]

The two sectors are represented here by the government-owned Nigerian Ports Authority (NPA) and the dock labour contractors. The NPA workers not only appear to be typical of other public sector employees in Nigeria, but evidently consider themselves to be so, and in early 1975 took combined action together with other public corporation employees in a major wage conflict. The dock workers can be compared with workers in the Nigerian-owned construction or mining companies. But they differ from workers in other local capitalist employment by their numbers, their concentration and their visibility. Whilst this might limit the generalizability of the Port case, it should nonetheless enable us to see in sharpened form the general relationship of the state to labour and its different relationship to the two types of

Nigerian worker.

The Industrial Structure

The Nigerian state first appears as the creator of the industrial structure within the Port. This is evidently so in the case of the NPA, a large, monopolistic, state-owned corporation. The NPA is responsible for the physical structure of the Port, for pilotage, the storing and handling of goods on their way to or from the quayside, and for other commercial and technical services. In April 1975, it employed over ten thousand workers in the 'junior staff' grade. The NPA is descended from the colonial Harbours Department. Its public corporation status was intended to ensure its accountability in both the general sense and the specifically financial one. The NPA Board consists of representatives of the interested ministries, of the Railway Corporation and other harbour users. A place is reserved for 'labour interests'.

Critical light on the management and functioning of the NPA was thrown by one of the series of inquiries into public corporations ordered by the new military rulers of Nigeria in 1966. The Report of the tribunal headed by Justice Beckley stated that the NPA had at all times functioned 'in the best interests of the State and . . . the general public'.[3] But it in fact uncovered a series of gross inefficiencies and malpractices, the one being often difficult to distinguish from the other. Problem areas concerned the nature of the Board, the behaviour of the General Manager and top management, the powers of management *vis-a-vis* the Board, the award of contracts, organization of dock labour, financial and land policy, and relations with staff.

The evidence in the Report suggests that the function of the NPA at that time was not only its public and formal one, but also that of providing sources of illegitimate revenue and patronage to leading politicians and ministers. It was further suggested that a series of graded perquisites of office existed down to the level of clerks, some of whom could receive 'dash' by speeding goods through, undercharging, or even clearing without charging. The Inquiry revealed that during one three-month period in 1965, the Board Chairman had deposited £24,457 in his bank account at a time that a witness declared he had paid bribes to obtain a dock labour contract. Another area of dubious behaviour was that of recruitment and promotion. The Inquiry found that in one month 80 clients of the Assistant General Manager, Board Members, Ministers, Parliamentary Secretaries and other outside parties had received preference in recruiting. The Report also mentioned the problem of over-staffing within the NPA, of a too-rapid rate of advancement and an 'appalling lack of basic qualifications'.[4]

In the absence of another such inquiry, one cannot know to what extent the situation has changed today. But the NPA has been continually subject to criticism for inefficiency. The problem has appeared to the public eye (literally, since the Port is in the middle of Lagos and is even at one point overlooked by a public footbridge) in the form of queues of ships waiting to load or unload, disorganized quays, breakdowns in vital equipment, and bureaucratic delays in the clearing of goods. During the Civil War, when Lagos was virtually the only port in Nigeria, the situation became so grave that the power of the Board and management was temporarily suspended. Colonel Benjamin Adekumle, notorious in the frontline as the 'Black Scorpion', was appointed Port Commandant. Treating the problem as a purely physical one, and touring the Port area daily, he actually managed to clear the backlog, although questions were raised about where the backlog went and about the considerable loss in uncollected revenues. In the post-war period the problem of docking delays reached astronomical proportions, with each month in 1975 being marked by the number of ships – two, three, four and five hundred – being recorded as joining the floating city just beyond the harbour entrance. The Lagos Port scandal became one of the issues that brought the Gowon regime into disrepute and led to its downfall. The Port Manager denied his responsibility for the mess, stating 'it is not the fault of anybody. It is the fault of the system'.[5] This is a fair statement. The ships were full of goods purchased with Nigeria's new-found oil wealth – lavatory bowls, ten different brands of canned beer, Mercedes cars, steel rods, turbines, paper, baby foods and cement.[6] The cement was ordered by the state, either by civil agencies for building the schools necessary for universal primary education, or by the army itself for building barracks. Once again, the issue of inefficiency and corruption were intertwined. According to *The Guardian,* shipowners were quite happy to sit around collecting a profit of $1,000 per day. But 'for reasons known only to some Nigerians', one vessel, for example, was receiving $4,100 per day when it should only have been receiving $200. The inability of either civilian or military powerholders to effectively control and operate such an essential national resource, and the corruption or inefficiency of the top state agents within the Port, not only throw a light on the nature of the state but also must have an effect on worker attitudes.

Whilst state responsibility for the NPA is overt and recognized, its hegemony over the contract labour companies may not be so. Nonetheless, the private sector is a state creation, dependent upon the state not only for its changing size and structure, but also for a large part of its daily revenue. The function of the industry is to carry out the stevedoring (on-board) and quayside labour on behalf of either the NPA, or one of the mostly foreign-owned shipping companies and agencies. The industry contains a few large contractors and a large number of smaller ones. At present there are around 35 in all. Apart from their own small staffs, they were said in mid-1975 to be employing 6,500 men. In the late 1960s there were some 27 recognised contractors. These included four big ones employing around one thousand or so workers on a more or less regular basis, and others that might receive just one small contract every few months. Neither the increase from one or two in the early 1960s, nor the mooted decrease to 16 registered companies, has been due to the spontaneous working of the market economy. The increase was due to a state decision to introduce 'competitive tendering' (a convenient fiction); the mooted decrease will also be a government decision. During the civilian period contracts were awarded on party, regional or ethnic grounds. Contractors bribed Board members for contracts; they failed to bid competitively. Having received contracts, they breached them, avoided settlement of debts to the NPA, and paid labour below the officially-agreed rates.[8]

The structure of the dock labour contract industry is of a type already outmoded when it was created. The problem is not simply the large number of contractors for the small number of berths (17 in all), but the existence of the 'divided contract' system. The latter implies that one cargo may be handled by two different contractors, one on board and one on the quay. The disorganization this leads to can be imagined. Yet, despite the recommendations of the Beckley Report, of a later inquiry headed by A.A. Ayida,[9] and an UNCTAD study commissioned by the government,[10] the state has still not taken action on rationalization. Following the UNCTAD study, a government-owned National Cargo Handling Company was brought into existence, and given offices and equipment. The intention was that it would provide a model of efficiency and good labour relations to just *four* other private contractors, to be selected from amongst 16 approved in late 1964. In the absence of hard information, one can only speculate about state reluctance to act when the principle is officially accepted, the machinery exists, and nothing remains but to choose the four contractors with the best records. Given the evidently non-competitive behaviour of the contractors, it cannot be because of attachment of the policymakers to the principle of free enterprise. Neither, given their notorious disorganization, can it be on grounds of efficiency. Nor, given the continued labour unrest to be dealt with below, can it be on grounds of good man-management. The last possibility is that of personal financial interest in the contract labour industry by those with the power to decimate its ranks. Popular rumour at all levels within the industry supports this speculation, but it can provide no substitute for hard evidence.[11]

The Labour Force Structure

The decision to divide the cargo-handling industry into a public and private part was also a decision to divide the labour force into two quite distinct segments. When the NPA was first set up it was the idea that while ships' labour would remain the responsibility of the shipping companies, dock labour would be decasualized and come under the NPA itself. The advantages of this were said to include standardization of shore-handling, possibility of training a stabilized work force, and the reduction of pilferage.[12] In 1955 the NPA did take over direct employment of dock labour in Port Harcourt, but in 1963 it concluded that contract labour was more efficient and less expensive. The trade unions had refused to cut gang sizes, had pressed for more senior posts for members, and opposed attempts to 'weed out those that had become incapable from age or deformity of doing a good day's work'. Contract labour had higher output by all measures, and 'Labourers employed by contractors were more amenable to discipline and more adaptable to changes!'[13]

Three consecutive reports treated this issue. The Beckley Report favoured continuation of a contract labour system in principle. The Urhobo Report, which followed a significant dock strike, argued in favour of a direct labour system.[14] But the Ayida Report of 1969 seems to have been the most influential. Its argument against nationalisation (which it saw as part of a possible programme of 'socialising the national economy') was that a government monopoly would not only increase the incidence of strikes but that 'powerful shipping interests would place deliberate impediments' in its way since they obviously preferred to deal with several companies rather than with one.[15] Government eventually favoured the proposal of Ayida for a scheme under which a government company would operate along with five private ones, with workers employed directly by them. It argued against a central pool system on the grounds that it 'will deny the dockworkers the employee/employer relationship which alone can secure for him certain privileges which dock-workers now enjoy, viz., annual leave, medical attention and other benefits'.[16]

Dockworkers, in fact, enjoy no such privileges, a matter of which they have complained, and about which they have gone on strike for some thirty years. Despite changes over time, contract labour continues to be of a basically 19th-century carrying, lifting and pushing type. Labour is divided into five main categories, with a differential of but 1:1.2 between the labourer at the bottom and the tally clerk at the top. Employment is casual, even for the tally clerks and security-men registered in the pool run by the Port Labour Office. The official decasualization schemes have never been systematically carried out. Although an obligatory registration scheme was introduced in the mid-1960s, the number of 'preference' workers (guaranteed 15 days work or wage equivalent by the employers against whom they were registered) never reached the official two-thirds. And, although the official rate for dock labour is above the government minimum for unskilled labour in Lagos, anything up to 74% of registered dockers were earning between 10 and 40% less than this. Moreover, they are subject to a whole series of illegal wage-reducing or labour-exploitative practices by contractors and their agents. Dockers have to pay anything from 18 to 30% of the officially listed wages in bribes in order to obtain and hold a job. They have paid obligatory contributions to the National Provident Fund, only to have this pocketed by contractors (who also pocketed the employer contribution paid to them by the NPA). Although at great risk from accident or injury, they have no access to first aid and have great difficulty in getting legal compensation. They lack toilet, refreshment and washing facilities, and even drinking water. And, despite the Dock Labour Scheme, they are subject to arbitrary hire-and-fire by the contractors.

The contrast with the position of even the unskilled grades within the

NPA could hardly be greater. NPA labour is highly structured and stratified by designation (job), skill, wage grade, department and employment status. In 1973 the five main wage grades were themselves sub-divided, and there existed the 'daily-rated' stratum below that. Differentials between this stratum and those at the top of the junior staff scale (which excludes the managerial, professional and technical 'officers' who have their own respective scales!) amounted to at least 1:5. Employment status varies from the 'hire-and fire' workers taken on for a particular contract, through the regular 'daily-paid', to the 'established servants' and 'officers'. However, 'hire-and-fire' apart, even the lowest daily-paid worker is protected by a series of formal rights far removed from the primitive wage-contract relationship. Such benefits, which evidently vary greatly between employees of different status and wage grade, include annual salary reviews, free health treatment, sick pay, paid leave, loans for vehicle purchase, possibilities for housing, and formal appeal procedures against arbitrary dismissal.

Most dock work is physical labour of the simplest and most primitive kind. Most port work requires skill and literacy. The different skill level and composition would itself imply a gulf between dockworkers and portworkers, although there are overlapping categories. What state policy has done has been to create a gulf where there was a gap. Interviews in 1975 suggested that the two labour forces inhabit different universes, do not know one another, and do not communicate with one another. Commenting on this last point, a prominent port union leader confirmed it when he declared: 'We do communicate with them; we give them orders'.

The division of the labour force in the Lagos cargo-handling industry should not be considered simply as determined by the interest of would-be entrepreneurs in opportunities provided by the creation of a private sector. We see here entrepreneurial rationality operating in its more general sense. There is an assumption that those employed by government will not work efficiently, whilst no consideration is given to non-economic reasons for lack of worker commitment. There is a calculation that contract labour is more efficient that ignores the social costs (in terms of industrial disorganization affecting the whole economy), not to mention the human costs in terms of over-worked men, damaged limbs and shortened lives. There is action to submit not all employees of the NPA to the whip of the market, but only those least able to defend themselves from it. The effect of state activity has thus been to create two industries within the one, each with its own distinct labour force.

Worker Organization, Demands and Action

Within NPA there is a high rate of unionization. As long ago as 1968, 8,000 of the NPA's national junior staff force of 9,875 were said to have signed check-off forms for one union or another.[17] In 1973 there existed some 10 or more unions or associations within the NPA, distinguished from one another by names referring to particular grades, departments, or department and grade. A major one was based partly on a department of the NPA, partly on a section of the railways. Only one had a name that at least suggested it was open to all NPA workers. A protracted merger process during the 1970s still leaves in existence two major unions – the NPA Workers Union (based largely on workers in the engineering and mechanical departments), and the Railways and Ports Transport and Clerical Staff Union (based within the NPA largely on the clerks and operators of the traffic department). A somewhat smaller but still significant union is the Nigerian Maritime Workers Union, based on the 'floating' workers of the Harbours Department.[18]

These unions, as well as most of the smaller ones, were long affiliated nationally with the moderate United Labour Congress of Nigeria.[19] And this was in its turn long affiliated to the reformist, Brussels-based, International Confederation of Free Trade Unions. The major unions have had direct affiliation to one or other of the specialised trade union internationals (such as the International Transport Workers Federation) that are associated with the ICFTU. Several have had bilateral relations with the American unions and their African-American Labour Centre. Despite the common orientation to moderation, reformism and the 'West' that these affiliations suggest, and despite the existence on paper of a projected Nigerian Transport Workers Union since at least 1973, the unions have been unable to unite. Moreover, they have been in quite serious conflict at various times over the poaching of members, representation within the NPA Board and other matters. They are, however, all members of the Nigerian Maritime Trades Union Federation which acts as a co-ordinating committee and as a negotiating agent when dealing with the Port or the NPA at top level.

Amongst the multifarious demands made by the various unions we may distinguish several main types. The first are those which are (at least in principle) generalizable to the workers as a whole, even though they may in practice be made on behalf of grades or departments. These are demands concerning rates of pay, overtime, hours of work, security of employment, health, housing, canteens, training and principles regarding regrading and promotion.

The second are those that by their nature are limited to small groups or even individuals. In the most extreme case, unions have disputed amongst themselves on which has the 'right' to nominate a candidate for the post of one Labour Relations Officer. Through the 1950s and '60s the unions made a major issue out of Nigerianization of the top managerial and technical posts within the NPA, although the number of such positions going to individual union members or even leaders must have been few.[20] Larger numbers, though still in principle limited, must have benefited in the continuous struggle for regrading and promotion. At one time Nigerianization was considered to imply that 'the management becomes the people's management',[21] and even today it is reported with pride that 'management offered our union six new posts of Senior Wharf Plant Supervisors on salary scale (A) . . .'[22] But certain reaction seems to have set in. One union report complains that although 85% of Nigerians holding 'Senior Service' posts had risen from the rank and file, they had been 'callous and indifferent' to their less fortunate brothers and sisters. The report implies that the unions' attitude towards Nigerianization has been in error. Speaking of promotions and regrading, it says that, 'While wages are central to problems of industrial relations in other advanced countries, promotions appear to be central to problems of industrial relations in this country . . . Many people who struggle for promotions do . . . so . . . because . . . the higher people go, the less work they do and more salaries and fringe benefits they get . . . What is really needed is to reduce the existing multiplicity of worthless grades for promotion in the service and to improve the purchasing power of the workers . . .'[23]

A third type of demand is one that questions or impinges on managerial prerogatives. Rather than assuming that management can be transformed by promoting individuals into it, these demands challenge – at least potentially – the powers and competence of the NPA officers. The Beckley Tribunal provided a public opportunity for attacks on the honesty and efficiency of management by the unions. Whilst this activity was largely of a negative and limited nature, the unions have on occasion demanded the right to comment on Port management structure,[24] and in 1975 produced a detailed set of criticisms and suggestions on Port decongestion.[25] The right to participate in management has, however, been barely breached within the NPA. But there has been criticism of management's 'having never . . . taken the Unions into confidence'.[26] And the constitution of the projected Nigerian Transport and General Workers Union does contain amongst its aims 'the securing of a real measure of control in industry and participation by the workers in the Management, in the interests of Labour and the general community.'[27]

Portworker protest activity seems to be comparatively limited in both frequency and extent. The Ministry of Labour's own records for 1971–4 record thirteen disputes involving various unions, only two of which are reported as having led to strikes. One of these was of 1,000 men for one day, the other of 300 for three days. Additionally, there is recorded a 'go-slow' action, of which there are no further details.[28] There were, however, more significant disputes recorded either by the unions or the NPA itself. Amongst these are said to have been a one-day stoppage of all workers in November 1972, and a go-slow action of over 3,000 workers for a day or so at the end of June 1973.[29] Although this suggests slightly more activity than the Ministry admits to, it does not affect the overall image of infrequent and limited recourse to collective protest action. And such general impression is reinforced by a survey of some 200 portworkers carried out in mid-1975. This suggested that only 50% of them had ever been on strike, although 64% had taken part in some other kind of protest – overwhelmingly go-slow activity.[30]

Impressionistically, it would seem that there are significant differences between the NPA unions. The Railways and Ports Transport and Clerical

Staffs Union is led by Alhaji H.P. Adebola, who has a reputation for industrial militancy and did, indeed, appear to have made the running for a wage increase in 1971–2 that was later followed up by the more moderate leaders of the NPAWU and NMWU, and generalized throughout NPA. However, the militancy of Adebola is of a distinctly sectionalist kind, and he has been frequently and pointedly criticized by other leaders of the Federation for poaching members and for tribalism. It is, paradoxically, the more moderate O. Zodonu, leader of the Nigerian Maritime Workers Union, who made the criticisms of the Senior Service and struggle for promotions cited in the last section. What we would seem to have within the NPA are two types of reformist trade unionism and economistic action. That of Adebola seems to be that of American-type business unionism, aggressively seeking a rather narrow interest, and that of Zodonu, more of a West European, social-democratic type that has, perhaps, some view of a broader worker interest. In the face of the multiplicity of contractors within the Port, the problem amongst the dockers has been that of establishing a body that could speak for them as a whole. Whilst one or two grade-based unions (the Tally Clerks and the Security Workers), and one enterprise union (Biney's) would seem to have been founded as long as 1950 or earlier, no general dockworker organization seems to have been able to survive more than five years or so. The story until 1968 was one of bitter personal and ideological conflict, extreme dependence on external finance, and frequent 'carpet-crossing' as individual leaders shifted from one sponsor to another. In 1967, on the basis of considerable financial donations from the USA and organizational support from the moderate UCLN, there was finally created a new Amalgamated Dockworkers Transport and General Workers Union. It was immediately rent by internal disputes, accusations of corruption and misuse of the American money, charges of thuggery and inefficiency. The public inquiry into the union held following a dock strike in 1968 confirmed this picture and elaborated on it, thus showing dramatically the problems of creating a stable and inclusive organisation in such an industry.[31] Despite the factionalism, dependence and incoherence of dockworker unionism, however, there clearly exists a labour movement and trade union tradition in the docks, its bearers being the trade union officers, paid or volunteer, whose names and activities can be traced over a period of ten or fifteen years. Furthermore, most of these leaders appear to have come from within the industry, though few are labourers or ex-labourers.

Since 1966 there has been some stabilization, with the appearance of two organizations claiming the title of the ADWT & GWU. The first, which will be referred to as the ADWT & GWU(R)[32] is led by the veteran Jonas Abam. Abam's organization, however, appeared in 1975 to have little following in the docks, being heavily dependent on the International Transport Workers Federation and on official government recognition for the preservation of even a shadow existence. The second, which will be called the ADWT & GWU, is headed by Bernard Odulana, a national officer of the Communist-led NTUC.[33] Since 1968 Odulana seems to have been able to build up an effective Lagos-level leadership amongst the dockworkers. This consists of a team of paid and volunteer officers, some veteran and some young, who meet almost daily at the Call Office, dividing amongst themselves the responsibility for organizing the dockworkers within the different companies. In 1975, and following a series of actions in which Odulana and his organisation had been able to establish themselves in the eyes of the workers, the organization was collecting considerable sums of money from dockers, and had a register showing names of cardholders and membership dues. The extent of unionization amongst the dockworkers is difficult to establish, but of Odulana's following there can be little doubt.

If we try to distinguish amongst dockworker union demands what do we find? There have, of course, been general protests about pay and conditions ever since the beginning of dock labour in Lagos. The first wage demand recorded was in 1919.[34] We find specific demands or complaints concerning overtime, meal breaks, protective equipment, lavatories and drinking water, medical facilities, short-ganging, under-paying and many other abuses. Sectional or small-group demands seem to be less frequent than in the Port, but they do nonetheless appear. Tally clerks and winchmen have in the past pressed their own special interests. But they seem today to seek these through the ADWT & GWU rather than through separate demands and organization.

On the other hand, protests and demands threatening the rights of management are rather extensive. Dockers have continually and violently attacked the contractors as exploitative and callous. Interviewed in mid-1975 on whom, if anybody, they considered their enemies, they mostly answered simply, 'the contractors'.[35] The solution to this problem has been seen in terms of the establishment of a government-operated dock labour scheme of one kind or another. Although in the limited form in which this was first demanded (as a voluntary scheme in the 1950s), this would not seem to – and did not in fact – affect employer control of the industry or the labour force. There have been more radical demands. As early as 1964 the following different demands were expressed by dockworker leaders: (1) that a Board should be the virtual employer of the dockers, whilst contractors should be retained; and (2) that 'dock worker organisations . . . take over the dock labour industry and manage it for themselves'.[36] Although this last may seem like a demand for worker self-management, it more likely represents the petty-entrepreneurial aspirations of dockworker leaders at that time. In 1975 only Odulana spoke up clearly for complete nationalization. However, one finds this specific demand neither in the documents of his own organization, nor in the minds of ordinary dockworkers. The ADWT & GWU simply demands a Dock Labour Board and integrated cargo-handling scheme, pressing for implementation of government's own declared intentions. And dockworkers interviewed in 1975 mostly declared for government takeover in an unspecified form. Dockworker protest activity seems to be both frequent and more extensive than that of portworkers. Although the Ministry's records for 1971–4 include only seven disputes amongst Lagos dockworkers, these include two two-day strikes, each involving the whole body of dockers. Dock strikes have historically been more visible than port strikes. There was a major, radical-led, but unsuccessful strike in 1963.[37] There was another three-day stoppage in the middle of the war, in 1968, led by disgruntled militants of the original ADWT & GWU. Since that time, disputes and strikes seem to have not only continued but to have increased in number and intensity. This activity is frequently of a rowdy or violent nature, with the police being drawn in and making arrests. After the 1968 strike a prominent leader was found dead in Lagos Lagoon. Factions are prepared to use strong-arm methods with opponents. On one occasion supporters of the radical ADWT & GWU threw a leader of the moderate ADWT & GWU (R) into the harbour. All strikes organised in Nigeria since 1968 have been in breach of the law. But even after Odulana has been called in and warned against striking by the Assistant Director of Labour, he has led the dockers in a 'work to rule' action involving 6,000 dockers.[38] In January 1975, after a seven-day ultimatum he brought out the dockers in a successful three-day strike, demanding that the 'Udoji Award' made to public sector workers be extended to them.

We may at present identify three patterns of union activity amongst the dockworkers. These are represented by the two Amalgamateds and by the Biney Staff Association (BSA) – an organisation of at least historical interest, though its present significance might be limited. The BSA is a classical company union. When Chief Biney calls for rationalization in the industry, the BSA calls for it. When the May 1974 strike began, the BSA disassociated itself and promised to carry on working, stating it was strengthened in its stand by 'the continued sacrifices made by the management of the company which it invites other dock labour employers to emulate . . .'[39]

Abam's ADWT & GWU (R) is of more significance, not only because it is heir to a long tradition, but also because of its continued official recognition. The tradition, going back to the 1950s, is one of attempting to build up a pattern of 'responsible trade unionism' on the British pattern, constantly urging the creation of industrial relations machinery, and an end to casual labour in the docks. Abam is continually calling for pay increases 'in the interest of the national harmony', demanding a 'high-powered inquiry', and denouncing Odulana for his 'violence' or 'unscrupulousness'. The susceptibility of this approach to external threat, internal collapse, or impotence, would seem arise from the irrelevance of its strategy to crudely exploitative and oppressive entrepreneurs totally uninterested in playing industrial relations according to 'Westminster' rules.

The comparative success of Odulana's ADWT & GWU on the other hand, is evidently due to his readiness to play the game according to the local terrain. In this he had no doubt been assisted by the Communist ideology of the NTUC,[40] an ideology which presents employer-worker relations in stark class terms. These terms correspond with the perceptions of workers in the industry. We should note, however, that the difference between the ADWT & GWU and the ADWT & GWU(R) is one of comparative militancy, not of programme. Indeed, one's impression is that it is the former that formulates the demands having greater access to international trade union expertise and advice on all kinds of policy and technical problems concerning ports ,[41] and the latter that fights for them. Whilst the ADWT & GWU(R) falls into the same category as the 'West European social democratic' type identified in the Port (although its predecessor in 1966–8 was decidedly of the 'business union type'), the ADWT & GWU of Odulana should, perhaps, be distinguished from them as 'radical reformist'. And, in the BSA, a 'company union', we have a fourth (if peripheral) type of trade unionism in the industry.

In calling the ADWT & GWU 'radical reformist' one is stressing that it shares a perspective with at least the two types of unionism identified in the Port. This is important to recognise if one is not to oppose the one type to the other. Having said this, of course, one cannot fail to recognise that just as the style and ideology of the old NTUC has a fit with dockworker conditions, so does that of the two 'moderate reformist' types with those of the Port. 'Moderate reformism' (with its sub-types) and 'radical reformism' are then, the distinct types of worker organisation and protest that we find dominating the two sections of the industry.

'Industrial Relations' and the Control of Labour Protest[42]

The National Pattern

By 'industrial relations' is meant here the ideology, laws and regulations, institutions and procedures intended to incorporate workers, their values and behaviour into a society controlled by others. Taken in this sense, we can identify the existence of two periods within the history of Nigerian industrial relations. The first is that of the 'Anglo-Saxon model' identified by Peter Kilby,[43] although it should more properly be described as the 'Anglo-Saxon colonial model' because of its differences from the British original.[44] This model, which was in operation from colonial days through till the middle of the Civil War in 1968, was marked by the following featuers:

1. The ideology was one of 'free collective bargaining' between the 'representatives of labour' and the 'representatives of management'. As the archetypal statement of this ideology we may take this always cited one of the Federal Minister of Labour to the International Labour Conference in 1955:

> Can the various types of collective bargaining familiar to older industrial societies thrive in the different conditions of underdeveloped countries today? This is an important question which in the view of my government permits of only one answer. We have followed in Nigeria the voluntary principles which are so important an element in industrial relations in the United Kingdom . . . Compulsory methods might occasionally produce a better economic or political result, but labour-management must, I think think, find greater possibilities of mutual harmony where results have been voluntarily arrived at by free dicsussion between the two parties. We in

Nigeria, at any rate, are pinning our faith on voluntary methods.[45]

Although this policy is traced back to the 18th-century philosophy of *laissez-faire,*[46] and does indeed rest on concepts of free contract, free association, etc., its roots can rather be found in late 19th-century British state paternalism. The ideology has it that social conditions in Nigeria 'tilt the scales so much in favour of the employer that there is need for control on the reputed freedom of the parties to agree on the terms and conditions of employment.'[47] The *laissez-faire* and the paternalist element in the ideology of industrial relations at that time echoed dominant social ideologies in Nigeria during the transition from colonial to post-colonial rule.[48]

2. The legislation and regulations were of a 'permissive' character where trade unions were concerned. They did not make trade union registration obligatory and did exclude the police and prisons staff from union membership, but they permitted any five persons to form a union, and they provided unions with protection from common law doctrine on restraint of trade. It is significant that when 'check-off' legislation (under which the employer substracts dues from wages on union behalf) was introduced in 1961, it was in no sense made obligatory (as in other African countries) but required agreement between union and employer, and the signed consent of the member.[49] The law was of a 'protective' character where minimum conditions of employment were concerned. The Labour Code laid down conditions on contracts of employment, length of notice, forms of wage payment, hours of work, the employment of women and children, etc. The Factories Act laid down regulations concerning safety, and the Workmen's Compensation Act, the right to compensation in case of injury.[50] The National Provident Fund Act of 1961 provided small benefits in case of age, invalidity or death. It conflicted with the voluntary principle in so far as it was made compulsory for large numbers of workers and their employers. Since 1932 the State has had the power to fix minimum wages in industries where wages are considered too low. The legislation was supplemented in 1943 and by the Wages Board Act of 1958. The justification was that of intervening on behalf of unorganised workers too weak to bargain collectively with the employers. By 1964, however, this power had been invoked only nine times, even in Lagos state.

3. The institutions created by the State were largely of a more positive or 'stimulative' character, intended to provide a framework for voluntary bipartite collective bargaining between workers and managers. The base, of course, was the Department of Labour established in 1942, to which a trade union division was added in 1946. This latter section has always played an active role in assisting, advising and training trade unions.[52] Whitley Councils, a British institution for negotiation in the public service, were tried out once or twice in the late 1940s and early 1950s,[53] but seem to have never caught on except, possibly, in Eastern Nigeria.[54] The above-mentioned Wages Boards were meant to be a substitute for Joint Industrial Councils, within which it was hoped that unions in each industry would collectively negotiate with

employers collectively. The latter have been most successful in the banking industry,[55] at least for a limited period, and have played a role of some importance in the Jos minefields, rubber, shipping, building, civil engineering and other industries.[56] Despite the ideology of free collective bargaining, there has always been an element of tripartite negotiation and direct state intervention in the bargaining process. In 1941 there was passed a Trade Disputes (Arbitration and Inquiry) Ordinance providing for conciliation and arbitration – but on the basis of the voluntary agreement of both parties, and their voluntary acceptance of the findings.[57] In 1965 two tripartite bodies were created, the National Labour Advisory Council and the National Wages Council. The purpose of the former is to advise Government on labour and social security legislation, that of the latter to advise on wages and incomes policy.[58]

The official encouragement to industry-wide collective bargaining, and the creation of tripartite institutions, implied the existence of bodies that could speak collectively for workers and the private sector on both the industrial and national level. National trade union centres (united usually only for brief periods) have existed continually since the early 1940s. The public sector workers have had industrial federations since the mid-1940s. An early attempt to meet the dominant foreign private company (the United Africa Company) and the dominant private company type (the commercial companies) on an industrial basis through an Amalgamated Union of UAC African Workers and Mercantile Workers Union was short-lived in its success.[59] With the growing expansion of foreign private industry and the diversification of such companies as the UAC itself, there was created the Nigerian Employers Consultative Association in 1957. Although through the years NECA has gained Nigerian member companies, its values, membership standards (and – still in 1975 – its British Secretary) indicate clearly that it is primarily the spokesman of foreign private capital. It had been strongly in favour of collective bargaining, has encouraged (since 1962) the formation of trade groups that can bargain collectively with unions on an industrial basis, and it refused membership to employers and employers' associations that do not meet certain standards in labour conditions.

Finally, we must not forget the existence in Nigeria (as elsewhere) of an institution the role of which is simply repressive – the police. This is always available if this is desired by the management concerned, the police itself or the government to deal not so much with infringements of industrial relations legislation as with strikers, pickets and demonstrators, the actions of whom can usually be constructed as being in breach of the peace or obstructive.

4. The practice, finally, was so different from the ideal and so subversive of the institutional framework described above, that Kilby rightly spoke of the 'failure of the Anglo-Saxon model'. The key area of breakdown was in that of wage-bargaining. This has always taken place basically through the reports and recommendations every three to five years of national (occasionally regional) wage commissions. Since the early 1940s the pattern has been one of union agitation and demands in the predominant public sector for a

general upward revision of wages. The state eventually appoints a commission and ends up making a general adjustment of rates throughout the public sector. Agitation in the foreign private sector either results in individual increases there, or obliges the government to recommend payment of analogous increases throughout the private sector. Finally, the less-organised workers in the local capitalist sector will agitate – often for years – for their increases too. This traditional practice has been universally considered to be due to the weakness of trade unions. It could also, however, be interpreted as representing the recognition by the trade union movement of the weakness of the colonial and post-colonial political structure, and of the existence in Nigeria of a highly political economy! This pattern has been reinforced by the major strike waves that do not so much precede the reports of the major commissions as accompany or follow them. Such development of company or industry-wide negotiations as may have taken place has not yet significantly changed the dominant pattern.

Other common practices of this period must be described if the definition of industrial relations given above is to be filled out. The existence of the 'promote or fire' syndrome at enterprise level is often mentioned by enterprise-level union leaders in Nigeria. A successful agitator or union organizer is offered promotion or threatened with dismissal. The effect is to prevent or to undermine or to domesticate trade unionism at the enterprise level.[60] At higher levels in the trade union movement this pattern was repeated during the first period by what might be called the 'appointment or arrest' syndrome. Trade union leaders at regional level who were willing to ally themselves with one or other of the elite parties, were favoured with posts on government boards, parliamentary seats, and memberships of delegations abroad. Furthermore, government recognition was ceded to the 'moderate and responsible' wing of the trade union movement, the ULC, this implying access to numerous foreign scholarships, places on ILO delegations, etc. During this period the leaders of the radical trade unions established their own sources of benefits through contacts with the U.S.S.R. the World Federation of Trade Unions, and the Nkrumah-backed All-African Trade Union Federation. But their radical ideology and militant opposition to the regime meant that they were continually in danger of arrest (particularly for illegal border crossing en route to Ghana and Eastern Europe), as well as to actual arrest, loss of passports and other forms of harassment. Although political and other privileges for moderate union leaders have always been an important (if unstated and unlegislated) element in the Anglo-Saxon model, the crude bias of managers and the state towards moderate leaders – plus the privileges which such leaders evidently reaped – further undermined its legitimacy in Nigeria. The second period is that of a corporativism that began with the legislation during the Civil War and was still intensifying, although uncompleted, in 1975. This new tendency is marked by the following features:

Ideology: The old ideology changed only slowly. The first clear indication of change here was a declaration on labour policy made by the Commissioner of Labour just before the formation of the NLC.[61] This not only indicated a future orientation, it was also in many ways a comment on the changes in labour relations that had been taking place since 1968. The two key emphases were on 'the right to take the necessary measures to guarantee public order and national security', and on the active role of the Labour Department where there is a 'development-oriented administration and greater government involvement in social and economic development'. Commissioner Adefope declared the necessity for 'limited government intervention' in order to provide for the 'effective prevention and expeditious settlement of labour disputes'. He proposed positive action to restructure unions on industrial lines, introduced the compulsory check-off, and proscribe all activities and influence of the internationals in Nigeria – the Organisation of African Trade Union Unity excepted. For the rest, the declaration was largely one of intentions, concerning the effective policing of existing labour legislation and of sanctions against its breaching. It may be noted that the innovatory and positive action is almost totally in the trade union sphere, whilst the part concerning employers is largely in terms of a general intention to apply already existing legislation. Although the government stopped short at 'politicizing' the unions (administratively incorporating them into the machinery of state?), this remains the next and last step in the road from *laissez-faire* to state corporatism.

Directive and Restrictive Legislation: This has been increasingly the case since 1968.[62] The Trades Disputes (Emergency Provisions) Decree No. 21 of 1968 gave the Commissioner of Labour the right to intervene in any dispute, set out a clear procedure for their settlement, and made the reporting of disputes obligatory after a set period. Decree No. 53 of 1969 cleared up the ambiguity over whether there remained a right to strike. It had become known as the 'strike ban' and, in addition to making strikes illegal, it also made it an offence to instigate them, or to present them in the press in such a manner as to cause public alarm.[63] The Decree further gave extensive powers to the police, permitting them to detain anyone who had been, was, or was likely to be engaged in acts prejudicial to industrial peace. Such persons, moreover, were specifically denied the protection provided by habeas corpus.[64] Although introduced during the Civil War for a 12-month period, Decree 53 has continually been extended, marking a sharp break with the previous period and a turning away from the International Labour Organisation model. Decree 53 created a standing Industrial Arbitration Tribunal. The Tribunal was to act upon the request of the Commissioner for Labour, who also has the power to either confirm its decisions or refer them back. The decision thus made is binding on both parties, who have no appeal against it.[65] Decree 1 of 1973 on Wages Boards and Industrial Councils, and Decree 21 of 1974 on Labour, were essentially consolidating and rationalizing acts bringing together old legislation. Decree 1, however, innovated in providing for the establishment of Wages Boards to set minimum wages nationally and regionally, as well as in allowing for joint industrial councils, the decisions of which could be extended throughout the industry by government order.[66] Decree 31 of 1973, the Trade Union Decree, was also in part a piece of consolidating legislation, but it pointed clearly towards greater legal controls on the unions. It was, however, also clearly intended to push the unions towards a simplification and rationalization of their structures. The minimum number of persons required to form a trade union was raised from five to fifty. Not only were soldiers, policemen and certain key state financial and communications employees prohibited from joining unions, but there was also a provision permitting extension of this ban to other establishments as required. The Registrar's powers were extended, enabling him to refuse a new registration when it appeared that an existing union covered the particular category. For the first time there is a clause that hedges with restrictions the political activities of unions and union financing of political activities, although it does not ban them outright. Registered unions for the first time can apply to the Commissioner for a compulsory recognition order. The right to recognition is accorded firstly to unions able to demonstrate that they organise 60% of the relevant labour force, and there are provisions covering the recognition where rival unions exist. For the first time, also, there is statutory regulation of federations of unions, these being obliged to register and fulfil other detailed requirements. The same applies to central labour organizations. Additionally however, the decree recognized only four existing centres (thus excluding from legal existence two very minor bodies). And it provided for the future existence of only such centres as could demonstrate coverage of 40% of the membership of currently registered trade unions.[67] This last feature of the Trade Union Decree makes it symptomatic of the legislation in Nigeria during this period. Whilst many other African countries have legislated for just one official trade union centre, Nigeria's new law provided, by implication, for not more than two.

The Industrial Arbitration Tribunal: This was probably the major institutional innovation of the period. This has had to deal with such issues as mass dismissals, victimization for trade union activities, breach of agreement, adjustment of salary structure, etc. By the end of 1973, 52 disputes had been referred to the Tribunal by the Commissioner and 39 had been confirmed by his order. Although the minimum period for dealing with these cases is about two months, some have taken as much as thirteen or fifteen months. Moreover, delays in confirmation by the Commissioner have taken between four and twelve months. These delays have themselves led to strike action, action which is not only illegal but which it was the very purpose of the IAT to avoid![68] Despite this shortcoming and a dependency of the IAT on the Commissioner, the key importance of the IAT was clearly demonstrated during the 1975 strike wave following the Udoji Award.[69]

Anarchic Industrial Relations: Disruption of the Nigerian political economy was as marked in this period as during the earlier one, and this despite the gradual change in government attitudes and the formidable array of new legislation. A wartime wage-freeze (accompanying the 1968 legislation) did not prevent demands for fringe benefits and regrading. Nor did the strike ban prevent strikes, which occurred with increasing frequency and were usually dealt with in the way customary when they were previously legal. The Reports of the Adebo Commission in 1970–71 and the Udoji Commission in 1975 both led to large-scale and widespread strike action, in each case forcing government to make important concessions. In the latter case, the strike wave continued for some three months, included large numbers of public sector workers and salaried professionals, and was so disruptive in practice and implication that it can be considered a major contribution to the discrediting of the Gowon regime. Despite this continuity, however, there was certainly an increase in state administrative and repressive action. In 1971 a number of NTUC leaders were arrested and detained for 18 to 22 months. In 1972 one or two ULC leaders were detained for three to four weeks for having displeased the regime by a press statement. Occasionally – and arbitrarily – strikers or strike leaders are arrested, detained and released. During the Udoji strikes, arrests were carried out more selectively, particularly in the banking sector. And it was due to disruptive strikes in this sector that the government amended the Banking Act (by Decree 18 in 1975) so as to make it possible to ban trade unionism within it. The pattern of arrests above suggests a continuation of the traditional bias against the radicals and in favour of the moderates in the unions. This is confirmed by the continuation of the practice of appointments to board posts and regional commissionerships of leading moderates. In general, however, the military regimes have abandoned the favoured treatment given the moderates, granting equal recognition (and ILO conference places) to the different tendencies. This was in line with its attempts to encourage union rationalization by persuasion. However, the spectre of a united national trade union centre coordinating the kind of protest potential shown in the disruptive – and illegal – strikes of early 1975, must have been a factor causing the regime to produce its 'interventionist' declaration in December.

The NPA Pattern

Ideology: Over time, the ideology and attitudes of top NPA management seem to have come in line with those of government generally. Complaints of past authoritarian and arbitrary behaviour by the NPA were recognized by the Beckley Report, which stated that 'a lot of unrest in the Authority could have been avoided if Management adopted the correct attitude towards the Unions in certain respects. There were instances of unilateral abrogation of agreements reached between Management and the Unions, by Management and without due consultation.'[70] Since then, top management seems to have become increasingly favourable to the notion of formalized collective bargaining with well-organized trade unions. One union itself reported on the 'highly commendable' attitude of the NPA, noting that a new General Manager, M.A. Tokunboh (himself a one-time trade unionist and Commissioner of Labour) had 'declared his preparedness to assist in all possible measures for all unions to work towards unity and fusion of disintegrated ones, with the full realisation of the fact that such united fronts (though some unrealistic employers and labour exploiters might not like to see), would be of immense help for the day-to-day running of our Ports.'[71]

Regulations and Institutions: In evidence to the Beckley Tribunal, the then NPA Chairman, A.L. Wilson, advised the creation of effective industrial relations processes within the organisation: 'A Labour or Industrial Relations machinery should be created possessing some scientific equipment and able to operate with more than hit and miss primitive techniques. While the directive force of this machinery should be pitched at top management cadre, it should be clearly understood that the usefulness of this equipment depends entirely on its operation independence. Its function is to liaise between the various groups in the Authority; it does not belong to either group and it is not its business to defend any group. Its responsibility is to smoothen relations between groups.'[72] The intention was clearly to replicate at NPA level the self-image of the state as a neutral arbiter between the interests of management and workers. Whilst this might seem to have been a somewhat utopian ideal, there has been clearly an attempt to set up an effective industrial relations department, and this department has been for a considerable part staffed by ex-unionists. This policy began well before Beckley. Already in 1956, Francis Nyong Inok, one-time President of the Nigerian Ports Authority Workers Union, was Personnel Officer. In 1975 the Assistant General Manager (Industrial Relations) and another Industrial Relations Officer were former union officers. Before Beckley, furthermore, there had already existed a National Industrial Whitley Council,[73] although it seems not to have had a long or significant life. There has always been machinery for consultation and bargaining within the NPA of a voluntary kind. In 1974, for example, the finalized version of the 'Memorandum of Agreement on the Negotiating and Consultative Procedure in the Nigerian Ports Authority', to give it its full title, was drawn up with the Nigerian Maritime Trade Union Federation, with the aim of establishing 'peaceful and harmonious industrial relationship . . . for the settlement of any dispute or grievence and the avoidance of industrial unrest in the interest of all parties'.[74] This granted recognition to the Federation and its members for collective bargaining purposes. It set up joint consultative committees at all levels. It committed the unions to 'not order withdrawal of labour of their members or cause a slow-down of work or organise demonstration in any form until all stages provided for in the Negotiating and Consultative Procedures stipulated in this Agreement and in the Trade Disputes Decree or any other relevant law for the settlement of disputes and removal of grievance shall have been completely exhausted.'

Each department was to have a Joint Consultative Committee, chaired by the departmental head, with advisory and consultative functions on welfare safety and productivity questions. Each port was to have a similar committee, the function of which was to consult on both welfare and on the 'proper and correct application of the general conditions of service (staff) of the Authority'. Matters of disagreement and possible trade disputes were to be referred to the National Joint Negotiating Council. Trade Disputes raised in this highest body were deemed not to exist until further examined by the General Manager and the federation within one month, whereupon the issue could by mutual agreement be submitted to a Referee as a basis for further discussion. A dispute still unsolved could then be reported to the Ministry of Labour in accord with national law. Finally, the Agreement stated that, 'Neither party to a dispute shall resort to any direct action in the form of strike, lock-out, demonstration or litigation until the provisions . . . have been exhausted'. With the creation of this machinery, replicating and extending down to each department the state-created institutions for the channelling of worker protest, the unions would seem to have been successfully incorporated. However, to judge this, we have to consider their attitude toward and behaviour in respect of the collective bargaining machinery within the NPA.

The Trade Union Response: The trade unions have always been in favour of collective bargaining, accepting the ideology of 'peaceful and harmonious industrial relations', whilst complaining of management's failure to fully apply the implied practice. Thus, the NPAWU in 1961 spoke of its 'cordial' relationship with management whilst complaining that the 'Personnel Department is fettered somehow by the other departments'.[75] Such complaints were also made to the Beckley Tribunal and forcefully expressed once again by the Nigerian Maritime Workers Union in 1973: 'It is sad . . . to state here that after so many years since the inception of the NPA, with all the advantages of in-service and overseas training of the industrial relations officers, coupled with the old brigade of Trade Unionists who have crossed the carpet to the Management in the industrial relations department, the relationship between the Management and its Staff can still be likened to the primitive type between a master and his servant.'[76] The same statement criticised in detail the department for failing to act as a 'Liaison Officer', and instead taking on the powers of the General Manager, as well as going round the unions to negotiate directly with the workers. In its reaction to the appointment of the Udoji Commission, the statement revealed, however, the close attachment of the union to collective bargaining. 'In actual fact the practice of appointing Commissions to review wages and conditions of employment in this country is in variance with the . . . principles of the right to organise and to bargain collectively. Consequently appointment of such Commissions has not provided the opportunity for the development of industrial democracy in a developing economy.' Whilst the criticism is expressive of the continual tension in union-management relations (despite the evidently increasing institutionalization over time) it is to be noted that it is expressed in terms of an official ideology of liberal industrial relations that the government was already beginning to abandon at that time.

In the absence of an adequate account of union behaviour with regard to the new procedure, we will have to make do with a case from the period 1970–73.[77] This was a long drawn-out dispute, principally between the Railway and Ports Transport and Clerical Staffs Union (led by Adebola) and the NPA, although the other port unions, grouped within the Nigerian

Maritime Trade Union Federation, were drawn in in the later stages. Although the dispute covered a whole range of issues it became known in its critical phase as the 'one-eighth dispute', since the most contentious issue was apparently that of a demand of one-eighth pay increase to cover the difference between the official minimum 38 hours and the actual minimum of 44 hours being worked. The dispute began with issues postponed by the R & PT & CSU during the civil war, and which it claimed to have taken through negotiation, conciliation and arbitration with NPA. Although agreement was apparently reached in negotiations in March 1970, action taken did not satisfy the union, which accordingly declared a dispute in June. The absence of action (by the Ministry?) brought the union to demonstrate in March 1971, and this resulted in the issue being sent to the Industrial Arbitration Tribunal.

In May 1971 management claimed that settlement had been held up by the Statutory Corporations Service Commission which had not acknowledged a letter for six months. The union ridiculed this (the SCSC being next door but one to NPA) and on June 9 issued a long public statement in advertisement form,[78] giving its account of the matter and threatening 'any action we deem fit' from July 1. The Ministry of Transport instructed NPA to settle the issues outstanding, but this did not apparently occur because on July 1 a work-to-rule action began. This lasted at least three days[79] and was called off after a tripartite meeting, the official apprehension of a dispute, and its reference to Mr. A.C.S. Boardman, a Ministry official, as conciliator. On July 13, at a mass meeting, Adebola attacked workers for laziness, asserting that wage demands were only justified by higher productivity,[80] a statement perhaps addressed as much to Boardman as to his members. In August he was denouncing the NPA before the IAT for recruiting outside 'people with better connections' rather than promoting NPA staff.[81]

One year later, on August 24, 1972, a ministerial order confirmed the payment of the one-eighth to those categories (basically Traffic Department clerks) for whom it had been demanded by Adebola's union. The other NPA unions, through the NMTUF, then demanded that payment be extended to all staff engaged on a 44-hour week. When management refused on the grounds that it could not vary a government award, the NMTUF addressed an ultimatum to the Ministry of Labour. Dated October 2, this demanded payment of the one-eighth to all relevant categories, threatening that it would otherwise 'ask its members to revert to 39-hour week in conformity with present salary scale'.[82] On October 10, one thousand members of the NPAWU took industrial action for the one-eighth. And on November 1, there was a general one-day strike making the same demand. Negotiations between management and the unions took place on the same day, as a result of which management proposed to reduce hours to 39 throughout the Port, paying overtime rates for any excess. This left Adebola's members still on their 44-hour week, and it left unsettled the question of arrears for the excess hours unpaid for in the past. Disputes were declared by different unions over this last issue. Management proclaimed its inability to pay the increases implied.

It also distinguished its 'most smoothing relationship' with the NMTUF in general with the lack of restraint and responsibility of an unnamed union clearly identifiable as the R & PT & SCU.[83]

In early 1973 one union was calling 1972 'a most revolutionary year' because of the reduction in hours, while mentioning that aspects of the issue were still in dispute.[84] The R & PT & SCU, however, seemed to be much less satisfied, complaining forcefully and at length about the failure of the NPA to implement the decisions of the IAT – as well as of delays in the processing of matters referred to the IAT.[85] Although, according to the NPA, the introduction of monthly meetings with the unions led in 1974 to a calmer industrial relations climate, this climate did not prevent Adebola's union again taking action from June 30 to July 1. The go-slow was apparently effective, for an agreement was signed in the presence of a Ministry officer to the effect that management would within 30 days implement an agreement of 9 October 1972 relating to the extension of the one-eighth allowance to 'all employees of the Traffic Department'.

This case suggests that although the unions accept the ideology of collective bargaining, and although they are in favour of formalized bargaining procedures, they do not necessarily confine themselves within them. Whilst making full use of the procedures which exist at enterprise and national level, the unions have exploited differences in interest between these two levels and repeatedly taken strike action to back up their demands. This is most evidently the case with Adebola's R & PT &CSU, but even the more moderate and 'responsible' majority within the NMTUF have been prepared to take action that directly flouts the laws of the country.

The Contractor Pattern

Ideology; Here it is essential to distinguish between the official ideology of employer spokesmen and unofficial attitudes of the contractors themselves. The Association of Nigerian Dock Labour Contractors, which existed in the 1960s, echoed the official ideology of industrial relations. Thus, in 1966, it was 'seeking . . . a means whereby participants in the Dock Industry would meet in a cordial atmosphere to resolve whatever problems confront them, without working themselves into conflict and hate.' It believed that given the right institutions the trade union leader would 'see himself more as a Nigerian who must take pride for the building, promoting, preserving and sustaining Nigerian industrial organisations from where he must derive his sustenance.'[87] The ANDLC, however, existed only briefly and was never a determining influence on contractor attitudes. The real attitudes of the latter can be inferred from action or pieced together from indirect evidence. Much of the latter is to be found in a pamphlet written by U.U. Nkamare, at that time himself a contractor, a former dock labour officer and the future Secretary of the ANDLC.[88] Nkamare deals in turn with four dock contractors, easily recognisable to specialists behind their designations as Company A, B, C, D.[89] In Company A, the general labour assistant was 'learned in the art of cheating' and bullied the men without opposition. In Company B, 'the average worker did not seem to count. He was constantly made aware of this by frequent dismissals and threats of dismissal . . . The proprietor . . . delighted in running the business like petty trading. The worker himself realised that so many more were at the gate and jobless, and any one of them would be glad to step into his worthless shoes.'

In Company C, the proprietor had the reputation outside his company as a 'philanthropist of magnitude', but inside he earned 'the odium of paying low wages'. However: 'His personal touch with employees, placed him not so much in the position of an employer but much more in the status of a chief in a comitatus. He received marrying employees with their brides and donated gifts; babies born to employees engaged his attention and so did deaths or other domestic problems. Fringe benefits provided a bond of loyalty to the company rather than wages.' Under the son of the founder, things changed for the worse. The new director would assume the managerial roles one after the other, personally employing workers, fixing their wages arbitrarily and dismissing them at will. Moreover, 'A distinguishing feature of this company . . . was the keeping of a paid cortege of organised gangsters who were scattered among the workers and who, when occasion presented itself, were quickly formed into fighting squads. Some members of the fighting squad enjoyed privileges that were denied to the senior staff . . . The personnel manager was asked to leave . . . and the squad actually took personnel job such as the recruitment of workers . . . The squad haunted the gangs like the mafia and workers dreaded to be summoned before its secret tribunal.'

Allowing for the passage of some ten or fifteen years, this inside picture enables us to obtain an image of the combination of throat-cutting, free enterprise attitudes and of the arbitrary and personalized relations with employees typical of a new capitalist class.

Regulations and Institutions: One has here to distinguish between those laws and institutions directly introduced by the state and urged on the contractors and those requiring the initiative of the contractors themselves. Amongst the former are the various dock labour boards and schemes, particularly the obligatory ones. Amongst the latter are the ANDLC itself and the Joint Industrial Council. The development of both types is detailed chronologically below.

It was in 1947 that the colonial government in Nigeria first created special labour relations machinery for the docks. This was a Labour Advisory Board, the function of which was to look into employment, wage rates, methods of payment, methods of labour supply and control. On the recommendation of this Board there were passed in 1949 Orders in Council Nos. 26 and 27, respectively the Minimum Wage Fixing (Stevedors and Dock Labour in the Port of Lagos) Order and the Conditions of Employment (Stevedore and Dock Labour in Port of Lagos) Order. The passing of such orders implied official recognition that the dockers were too weak to defend themselves by collective bargaining with employers.

In 1949 the Sealy-Langford Commission was appointed to investigate the problems created for stevedoring in Nigeria by the import of foreign labour into Nigerian ports.[90] The Commission had been brought into existence as a result of agitation by the British National Union of Seamen and the complaints of Nigerian dockers. The Commission recommended continuation of stevedoring recruitment in Sierra Leone and the Gold Coast on efficiency grounds, but recommended creation of a pool of registered dockworkers in Lagos, so as to lead to development of an experienced force of stevedoring and dock workers there. On the basis of the Commission's recommendations there was created in 1951 an Ad Hoc Committee to advise on the setting up, constitution and functions of a Dock Labour Board. The work of this Committee was taken over by the Nigerian Ports Authority, the planning for which began in 1952.[91]

In 1962 there was put into operation a voluntary Dock Labour Registration (and Control of Employment) Scheme. This brought government more deeply and directly into dock labour relations than had previously been the case. Henceforward, the relationship between dockworker and contractor was to be in large part mediated by the Port Labour Officer. However, the Scheme was evidently not intended to do away with bilateral collective bargaining. Clause 8 made wages and conditions dependent upon this when it stated that: 'It shall be an implied condition of the contract between a registered dockworker available for work and a registered employer that the rates of remuneration and conditions of service shall be in accordance with any agreements reached between representatives of the workers and their respective employer.' Supervision of the Scheme was put into the hands of a Lagos Dock Labour Advisory Board consisting of 12 members appointed for one year by the Minister of Labour on the following basis: two members from the Ministry (Chairman and Secretary); one from NPA; one from shipping interests; four from dock employers; four from dockworkers. The functions of the Board included advising on efficient utilization of dock labour, reviewing and advising on the numbers registered against employers, advising on the quota or preference workers; recommending on additions and removals from the worker or employer registers. The Board met 18 times in 1962–3, its recommendations including the putting of 60% of registered dockworkers on the Preference List, and the establishment of a pool for tally clerks.[92]

Under the Board there was also created a Disciplinary Committee, consisting of the Port Labour Officer (Chairman), an Assistant Labour Inspector (Secretary), and two representatives each of the NPA, dock employers, tally clerks, other dockworkers, and the shipping companies. Its function was to examine complaints against workers and employers. It had the power *vis-a-vis* employers 'to recommend written warning or any other appropriate action'.[93]

In 1963 the contractors formed the ANDLC. This apparently had difficulty in overcoming the prejudice of the Ministry in favour of the NECA,[94] a body which both then and now seems to have considered the dock labour employers unqualified by their labour relations practices for membership. In 1967 the ANDLC had established itself and was engaged in negotiations with the Ministry and the ADWT & GWU over the creation of a Joint Industrial Council for the docks.

In 1967 the voluntary Dock Labour Scheme was made compulsory through the Dock Labour (Registration and Control of Employment) Rules brought into operation in Lagos on July 5. The restriction of cargo-handling to registered employers and workers, and the guarantee of 15 days' pay for two-thirds of registered workers, now became legally enforceable. The Advisory Board now became the Lagos Zonal Dock Labour Committee (LZDLC). On August 30 there was launched the first Joint Industrial Council for the docks. This managed to issue a Memorandum of Agreement on the two-shift system being introduced as a result of the Civil War, but seems not to have met after 21 May 1968.

In 1968 strict enforcement of the Dock Labour Rules officially began. But some workers covered complained that they were ineffective; others not covered complained of being deprived of a 'means of livelihood however meagre that might have been'.[95] The same year saw the major dock strike which indicated a virtually total breakdown of the industrial relations machinery in the docks. Amongst the causes of the strike listed in the Urhobo Report were breaches of the Factory Acts and Labour Code, failure of the National Joint Industrial Council, ineffectiveness of the Dock Labour Scheme, of the Lagos Zonal Dock Labour Committee, and of the Lagos Zonal Dock Labour Disciplinary Sub-Committee. Of the LZDLC it was said that it had not met frequently from March 1967, delegating most of its functions to a sub-committee. Of the Disciplinary Sub-Committee it was stated that: 'We find it was ineffective because the Sub-Committee had no final authority to deal with any matter. Although it recommended disciplinary action against employees, there was no evidence that any allegation proved against an employer ever resulted in discipline of the employer This situation weakened the effectiveness of the Sub-Committee to both employers and particularly the dockworkers who lost confidence in it.'[96]

As far as industrial relations were concerned, the Report recommended an enhanced role for the Ministry of Labour. It should be consulted more adequately by other bodies involved in dock affairs and should preferably have an official with Senior Labour Officer rank in the docks. The LZDLC should be revived and should itself exercise powers to equally discipline contractors and dockworkers. As for the Joint Industrial Council, the Report recommended its immediate reconstitution.[97] The Government accepted these recommendations and reaffirmed its faith in collective bargaining. Commenting on the considerable difference between the wage rate of 1971 and that laid down in Order in Council No. 26 of 1949, it stated that: 'The improvement was achieved through the process of voluntary collective bargaining. Government does not regard the obstacles in the way of the effective functioning of the Amalgamated Union as well as of the Joint Industrial Council highlighted in this report as a permanent disability and sincerely hopes that as soon as they are removed, it will again be possible to reach a negotiated agreement on this important issue between the Union and the Association of Dock Labour Contractors.'[98] Despite the sanguine hopes expressed, little was done to revive either the machinery of industrial relations or the practices of collective bargaining. In late 1974 one union was complaining that the 'employers don't want to hear about it', and that neither the JIC nor the LZDLC had been revived.[99]

Despite its unlimited faith in the virtues and achievements of free collective bargaining, the state has done little in intervening years to re-establish it, or to overcome the causes of the strike as listed above. In the belief that it has been the split in dockworker unionism that has prevented re-establishment of a dock labour scheme and effective collective bargaining,[100] energy has been concentrated on bringing about a re-unification. An attempt to achieve this in April 1973 failed, and as a result of this failure, the Ministry interpreted the Urhobo Report recommendations as implying recognition of the leaders of the old 1967 Amalgamation – now forming the ADWT & GWU(R) – rather than the new one led by Odulana! There is no evidence that either the Ministry or the NPA has yet used the immense powers they wield to discipline the contractors for flouting the Factory Acts or Labour Code, the NPA contract clause on fair wages, or the Dock Labour Rules. The only state organ that since 1969 seems to have gone so far as to take legal action against contractors has been the National Provident Fund. This has on occasion taken an employer to court for non-payment of NPF contributions,but this was only after a prolonged period of persuasion had failed, and the 'punishment' was a requirement that the company concerned re-pay the Fund within a given period.[101] The last state organ with direct responsibility is the Registrar of Trade Unions. Since 1973 there has been a clear new regulation on the registration of federations. Yet, despite the fact that Abam's ADWT & GWU(R) has been unable to make a financial return, and despite the fact that only one of its constituents (Okon's Akere Dockworkers Union) appears to exist in the Registrar's files, the ADWT & GWU(R) was in 1975 still treated as having full legal existence.[102]

What one must note here is not only the contrast between NPA practices and contractor practices, but also the contrast between the state-employer relationship in the two sectors. State labour control ideology and practices are reproduced or extended in the NPA. NPA workers are directly involved and incorporated into a more or less homogeneous industrial relations system. State labour control ideology and practices are rejected by contractors. The workers are faced not only by the contrast between the crude 'master and man' techniques of the contractors and the sophisticated bureaucratic practices of the state, but also by the support effectively given by this state (through acts of both commission or omission) to this pattern. How do their organizations react?

The Trade Union Response: Faced with the above situation, worker organizations would seem to have had three options open to them. These were (1) to recognise the limits implied by contractor attitudes and to work within them; (2) to appeal to government to impose official national industrial relations policies and practices on the contractors; (3) to make government enforce national policies and practices on the contractors. These three options have been taken respectively by the Biney Staff Association (BSA), the ADWT & GWU(R) and the ADWT & GWU.

When the ADWT & GWU called workers out on strike in May 1974, the BSA not only dissociated itself but declared 'that should any industrial action be precipitated, it is prepared to carry on and ensure the smooth flow of traffic through the major ports of the country, provided it is given adequate and continued protection by the law-enforcing agencies.'[103] The ADWT & GWU(R) of Jonas Abam revealed its own orientation in reaction to the same strike: 'As long as there is no National Joint Industrial Council for collective bargaining, so will industrial harmony continue to evade us in the industry and chaos shall continue.'[104] On the occasion of another strike threat by Odulana's union in September 1974, Abam warned workers against it, stating: 'The wage talks will start when the dock labour scheme is introduced and accredited dock labour contractors registered with the government are known.' He stressed that it was wrong to make workers feel that they could improve their conditions without such a scheme and a JIC and 'emphasised that violence was not the best method of settling industrial disputes and would not be to the best interest of dock workers.'[105]

The attitude of the increasingly dominant ADWT & GWU is difficult to find so clearly expressed. It is, however, easy to read it out of the forms of action taken to achieve its demands. The importance of the organization justifies devoting the remainder of this section to it.

The general aim of Odulana's organization since 1973 seems to have been that of (1) winning dockworker demands by militant action, including frequent illegal strikes; (2) bringing pressure to bear directly on government, seen as having both the power and the responsibility for dockworker conditions; and (3) by such action to force effective recognition of itself by the government, the NPA and the contractors as the representative organization of the dockers. This comes out of the following narrative of the union's activities in 1974–5.[106]

In early 1974 the ADWT & GWU was demanding government-union negotiations on the proposed dock labour scheme and stating that 'the dockers would not accept responsibilities for any industrial situation created by the refusal'.[107] It further demanded an interim pay rise of 80%. On May 9 Odulana issued a seven-day strike warning. On May 15 he and three of his officers were invited to the Ministry of Labour and treated to a dressing-down. The Ministry's statement contained the following significant elements: (1) there was a wage freeze on; (2) there was no evidence of an attempt by the ADWT & GWU at collective bargaining with the employers on the issues raised; (3) that, given the existence of three registered unions in the docks, the declaration of a dispute by such an unregistered group was not provided for; (4) that strikes were illegal. He appealed to the union leaders to await government action on integration and wages. In response: 'Mr Bernard Odulana promised to convey the advice of the Assistant Director of Labour to the dock workers and to ensure that they pursue their claims in accordance with the provisions of the law and without resort to the threatened industrial action.'[108] On May 20 there nonetheless began a work-to-rule action which three days later involved 6,000 workers. Police were called in and 25 demonstrators were arrested.[109] Negotiations with the NPA took place on May 23, at which it became evident that the major issue was that of non-recognition of the union. Port Manager Tukur promised to take up the issue, to ensure wage payment for the day on strike, and to attempt to get the arrested dockers released.[110] Following the strike the Ministry signed a joint communique with the Amalgamation, and in mid-June the union was referring to this in calling urgently for a tripartite meeting in the docks. In July there were negotiations between Odulana and the Port Labour Officer.[111] Despite all this activity there was, nonetheless, another four-day dock strike at the beginning of September.[112] And by the end of the month, Odulana was again giving a seven-day ultimatum to the contractors. In this case, the threatened action seems not to have taken place.

In December there finally appeared the report of the Udoji Commission and the government White Paper on it.[113] This established a new official minimum wage for public sector workers in Nigeria amounting to ₦2.00 per day. On January 1, Odulana addressed an ultimatum to the Ministry of Labour demanding it 'open negotiation with them on the implementation of the government White Paper.'[114] The Port Labour Officer advised the union that they were supposed to negotiate increases with the employers.[115] However, 'Odulana stated that his men rejected the idea of negotiation with dock employers of labour as being suggested in some quarters. He explained that since 1947, the government had always been responsible for negotiating the salaries and wages of dockworkers. Mr Odulana further stated that during the Morgan and Adebo awards, the Federal Ministry of Labour negotiated the salaries and wages of the dockworkers and later directed the dock employers of labour to pay.'[116] Following another 24 hours of grace on January 7, the dockers struck work for some three days in January 8. On this occasion there was no violence because the union advised all dockworkers to stay at home apart from a few pickets. The strike was immediately effective. On January 10 the Port Manager wrote to the union that 'in accordance with the tradition of the Port in matters of Government Salaries and Wages Awards', he could assure it that the award and arrears would be paid partly at the end of January and the rest by February 15.[117] On January 11 eight of the dock employers signed a confirming agreement in the presence of the PLO, ensuring also that there would be no victimization and that workers would be paid for the strike days.[118] On January 23 the NPA management presented the Amalgamation with the new rates. These implied an increase for labourers from ₦1.26 to ₦2.42 per day, with the rates backdated to April 1974.[119] A labourer who had worked 100 days since April would be getting a lump sum of around ₦116. The *Daily Times* of February 17 carried a photo of some of the many Biney workers queuing for their arrears.

In the following weeks a number of negotiations ensued between the employers and the Amalgamation, suggesting that informal bilateral bargaining was becoming established. At one of these, on May 28, Odulana made a statement to the contractors that is worth quoting at length:

> 'We welcome you to this important meeting which we summon to find ways and means of achieving industrial peace in the docks . . . we are not abandoning our militancy. But we consider the country first and we know fully well that the gigantic programme of the Federal Military Government can only be successfully carried out if we have smoothworking conditions in the docks. Our stand, like all other Nigerians, is that we are committed to the fulfilment of the Third National Plan . . . We call on you to cooperate. For this period we can assure all concerned that there will be not stoppage of work. Any contractor whose behaviour is capable of leading to industrial unrest in the docks, rather than stopping work we shall call for his removal . . . We are happy to report that when we met the Commissioner for Transport on the provision of facilities, e.g. adequate toilets, water, etc., he promised taking action and we are convinced that he meant business. Please let us discuss frankly with view to achieving our objectives.'[120]

It is striking to recognize from this case that even the most radical of the trade unions, basing itself on the workers with the most consciousness of oppression, nonetheless seems to accept the government's ideology of industrial peace as well as the general developmentalist ideology of the power-holders in Nigeria. From the ease with which Odulana moves between such professions and activity which undermines it, it might be concluded that his declarations are pretensions, or mere forms of words without significance. But the public adoption of the strategic aims and ideology of the state by a leader of the workers signifies the absence of an autonomous ideology and strategy. On the other hand, however, one cannot but recognize the extent to which in the docks the ADWT & GWU has imposed its pattern of labour relations on the contractors, the NPA and the central organs of an extremely reluctant state.

Conclusion

The purpose of the proceeding text has been to de-mystify the relationship of the state to wage labour, concentrating on the legal-administrative-political-ideological level whilst revealing the relationships of ownership and control that underlie these. It may be as well to collect together the most significant concepts, findings and arguments before concluding the chapter.

The initial purpose was to reveal through the case of Lagos Port the ways in which the Nigerian state sought to control the only sector of the labouring poor which is able to organize continuous, nationwide and effective opposition. It was shown that control began with a created industrial organization, dividing it in this case into a state-owned and private entrepreneurial sector. Each of these, it was argued, was marked by inefficiency and/or corruption, with the central state authorities being unwilling or unable to solve the basic structural problems of the industry. It was further argued that the division of the labour force implied by this organization should not be considered simply a consequence of capitalist interest, but also a consequence of a market rationality of a more general nature. In treating next the pattern of labour organization, demands and action, I implied that these followed from the structure of the industry and the organization and nature of the respective work-force. Two industrial patterns were shown, but it was argued that the various union types identified – company, business, social-democratic and radical-reformist – should be seen as lying within a spectrum of consciousness and protest. The existence of polar oppositions in the demands and actions of the two distinct work-forces was denied.

In moving onto the terrain more conventionally assigned to 'industrial relations', the term itself was given a highly specific and unconventional definition as meaning the political and ideological means for the incorporation of workers into a society controlled by others.[121] Two distinct periods were identified in the official national doctrine and practice of industrial relations, the first being dubbed '*laissez-faire*/paternalist', the second the 'corporativist'. The second strategy – still taking shape as this chapter was being written – was seen as resulting from the failure of the first to effectively subordinate labour.

In dealing with the labour control strategy in the two parts of the cargo-handling industry, there was identified the increasing fit over time of NPA strategy with that of those state, and the continuing lack of fit of contractor strategy with that of the state. In each case an attempt was made to identify the extent to which labour has been incorporated. In the case of the NPA, stress was laid on the extent of the incorporation of the unions into a single and consistent set of national and industrial norms and practices. It was, however, pointed out that the encapsulation was incomplete and that the unions persisted in oppositional activity subversive of the strategy. In the case of the contractors, stress was laid rather on this latter aspect – the extent of oppositional activity in a situation in which industrial control practices conflict with the official national ones. But here, too, it was pointed out the extent to which the union concerned nonetheless accepted the official national ideology.

One's conclusions from this case are likely to depend on one's position and one's purpose. Let us consider the perspective of the administrator. The administrator might conclude that there is indeed a major labour 'problem' in the industry and that the 'solution' to it is to apply national standards and practices within the contractor sector as they have been in the NPA. The 'problem' would then be reduced to the 'reasonable' proportions it has there. It is, indeed, probable that in so far as the long-delayed reorganization of the dock labour industry is at last carried out, the situation will be transformed. There is nothing that dockers want more than to be employed on 'government job' (with all that that implies in terms of good conditions, security, possibilities for advancement, and more civilized supervision). There is no reason to assume that once within the charmed circle they would behave any more militantly – or any less militantly for that matter – than the port workers. Thus, a 'solution' for the labour 'problem' is the cargo-handling industry. But for the nation?

Here the administrator is obliged to consider the relevance of the cargo-handling case for labour control in Nigeria nationally. It has already been said that the division that exists in the Port exists throughout Nigeria. Indeed, it may well be that the pattern within the NPA in Lagos is a model in the sense of being the best of the type. My impression is that the model is successively less valid as one moves away from (1) the public sector, (2) large-scale employers in general, and (3) Lagos. The other extreme should therefore be provided by small-scale private employers in Maiduguri (this being the major town furthest from Lagos). In the absence of information on that city, we nonetheless have some on Kano that supports the hypothesis. Here, in December 1975, we could find a large foreign-owned company following far more primitive practices than those in the South. We could also find large private Nigerian firms ignoring the implications of the Udoji award and practising the lock-out with impunity.[122]

The possible solution for Lagos Port looks an unlikely one for Nigeria as a whole. So long as the Nigerian state persists in its intention to permit the entry of foreign private capital and to stimulate the development of local private capital, so long will they be producing heterogeneous industrial sectors within which any national 'industrial relations policy' will have heterogeneous effects. So long as they persist in this intention, so long will they also produce regional heterogeneity, raising similar problems for the application of national legislation and practice. Since, however, there is carved over the door of every administrator the dictum of Keynes that 'in the long run we are all dead', we may expect to see Nigerian labour administrators continuing to seek short-run 'solutions' to immediate 'problems'. Where workers outside the state and large foreign-private sector prove themselves capable of effective industrial action – as in the docks – they will move to institutionalize the forms of protest. Where institutionalization into a pattern of 'free collective bargaining' proves insufficient – as in the NPA – they will move towards a corporative pattern. The impossibility of producing national homogeneity within a market economy means that we are likely to see the present syndrome continue in the future, although in a more advanced form. This means that there will continue to be a sector within which national policy applies fully and other sectors that follow their own practices to a greater or lesser extent.

A differentiated policy for different industries and types of labour is more or less forced on administrators by the nature of the market economy. But even 'divide and rule' has its limits as a strategy. The policy that Nigeria is moving toward has been long-practised in Latin America. In Argentina – perhaps the most industrialized country of the Third World – it appears to be breaking down. Corporative strategies of one kind or another were practised by both the populist Peron in the 1940's and by his conservative successors in the 1960s. The 1969 general strike in Cordoba in 1969, and the generalized labour unrest since, was brought about by the widespread discontent of the workers in the 'informal sector' fusing with, and coming under, the leadership of the 'privileged' workers in the big factories and the public services. There are other features of this example – the incapacities of local entrepreneurs, the regional imbalances, the absence of political parties – that are highly suggestive for a Nigeria of ten or twenty years hence.[123] From the perspective of the administrator the worker is an object. He is to be manipulated by one or other strategy of control, to be dominated by one or other 'industrializing elite'.[124] And, indeed, this chapter and the conclusions above have done no more than suggest the dissatisfaction of the workers, their capacity to destabilize the *status quo*. There is neither in the Port – nor in Nigeria as a whole – an ideology, a strategy of an organization amongst the workers that suggests that their interest lies in the destruction of a system based on the market, on competition and hierarchy. Even the occasional – and admittedly ritualistic – cries of the old NTUC leaders for 'worker power' as an alternative to military rule seem to have been abandoned.

Yet, from the perspective of political economy, the contradiction between the working class and the capitalist class (or whomsoever plays its role) is the primary one under capitalism. This is an 'antagonistic' contradiction, the victory of the working class implying not simply the defeat of the capitalist class, but the destruction of the labour-capital relationship and therefore of capitalist society. At present workers within the Port do not see themselves as one class or, rather, as part of one class, i.e. the labouring masses. And they do not define their interests in terms of the overthrow of capitalism and the state.[125]

References

1. The third sector is currently called the 'informal' sector in most writing on the subject. It may account for as much employment as the two others combined, but the labourers within it are neither unionized nor potentially so, and merge in their status and behaviour with the petty entrepreneurs.
2. Compare the distinctions made in the seminal article on industrialization in Africa by Giovanni Arrighi; 'International Corporations, Labour Aristocracies and Economic Development in Tropical Africa', in G. Arrighi and J. Saul, *Essays on the Political Economy of Africa* (New York: Monthly Review Press, 1973). Arrighi considers that the workers in the first sector are a 'labour aristocracy', privileged in position and conservating in behaviour. This is a conclusion against which I have argued. See 'The "Labour Aristocracy" in Africa. Introduction to a Controversy', *Development and Change*, 6, 3 (1975), pp. 57–73. I hope this essay may further undermine such simplistic analysis.
3. *Report of the Tribunal of Inquiry into the Affairs of the Nigerian Ports*

Authority for the Period October 1, 1960 to December 31, 1965 (Lagos: Federal Ministry of Information, 1967), p. 233. Further cited as *Beckley Report*.

4. *Op. cit.*, pp. 197–200.
5. Gabriel Oviogbudu, 'The Multi-Million Naira Plan and Port Congestion', *Management in Nigeria* (May–June 1975), p. 23.
6. I mention only some of the items I personally witnessed being off-loaded in August 1975.
8. *Beckley Report*, Chapter 3.
9. *Report on the Reorganisation of the Dock Labour Industry in Nigerian Ports*, (Lagos: Federal Ministry of Information, 1969). Further cited as *Ayida Report*.
10. Peter G. Patinson, *UNCTAD Technical Assistance Project to Assist the Government of Nigeria to Form a National Cargo-Handling Company*. (Draft Final Report: UNCTAD/NIR/70/8), Lagos, 1970. Further cited as *Patinson Report*.
11. Since popular belief, true or false, is a social fact that influences popular behaviour, the most widespread rumours may be at least noted. In 1975 these were: (1) that a former Federal Commissioner was married into one of the big contracting companies, and (2) that a major contractor with a bad name was on first-name terms with General Gowon and presented him with a Mercedes on the birth of the latter's son.
12. This latter seems to be such an accepted part of the scene that it was possible in August 1975 to witness two men jump down from the dock wall, dropping one or two from the bundles of cycle bells they carried, and trot steadily, but not too speedily, past a policeman, several soldiers, and an amused and encouraging crowd.
13. *Beckley Report*, p. 55.
14. *Report of the Board of Inquiry into the Affairs of the Amalgamated Dockworkers Transport and General Workers Union* (Lagos: Federal Ministry of Information, 1971), pp. 70–3. Further cited as *Urhobo Report*.
15. Ayida Report, pp. 22–3. The felt impotence of the Nigerian state *vis-a-vis* one foreign industry is here exposed. It is, perhaps, more typical of the era of civilian rule than that of military rule. For further evidence on this relationship in the earlier period, see Segun Osoba, 'The Nigerian "Power Elite", 1952–65: A Study in some Problems of Modernisation', paper to the Historical Society of Nigeria, 16th Annual Congress, Ibadan, 1970.
16. Comments of the Federal Military Government on the Report of the *Board of Inquiry into the Affairs of the Amalgamated Dockworkers Union* (Lagos: Federal Ministry of Information, 1971).
17. *Nigerian Ports Authority Annual Report* (Lagos: NPA, 1963), p. 71. The 'check-off' is a procedure of American origin by which the employer acts on the union behalf to subtract membership dues from salaries.
18. The unions are comparatively stable and well organized. Each of the big three has a General Secretary of long standing. They are amongst the oldest unions in Nigeria. The organizational maturity of the unions

is suggested by the survival of the General Secretary of th. NPAWU despite his absence in the East during the Civil War, and his disciplining (by three months suspension) for overstepping his brief in 1972. The unions keep up their returns to the Registrar of Trade Unions make statements of account, hold regular conferences, and have proven capable of weathering the internal disputes that have shattered so many unions in Nigeria.

19. In December 1975 the existing national trade union centres in Nigeria merged, forming the Nigerian Labour Conference (NLC). This has no formal affiliation with the major internationsls.
20. In the period 1961–8, the total number of Nigerians in the officer grades rose from 205–451. See *NPA Annual Reports 1962, 1970*. Many of these must have come from outside the NPA.
21. 'Nigerian Ports Authority Workers Union 14th Annual Conference, Hotel Majestic, Sure Lere, Yaba, Lagos, Wednesday 23rd to Friday 25th October 1963', mimeo.
22. 'Nigerian Maritime Workers Union 15th Delegate's Conference, 16th–18th April, 1973', mimeo.
23. *Ibid.*
24. 'Observations of the Nigerian Maritime Trade Unions Federation on the Re-organisation Proposal of the Management Structure', August 27, 1974. mimeo.
25. NMTUF Letter, 'Views and Proposals of the Nigerian Maritime Trade Unions Federation on the Decongestion of the Posts', to the Cabinet Committee for Ports Operation, 20 May 1975, mimeo.
26. 'Minutes of Meeting Between the Management and Representatives of all the Trade Unions Operating in the Nigerian Ports Authority Held on Wednesday November 19, 1972 in the Board Room, NPA Headquarters, Marina, Lagos, at 3.30pm', mimeo.
27. 'Nigerian Transport and General Workers Union. Draft Consultation, 1973', mimeo.
28. Source: Register of Trade Disputes, Ministry of Labour, Lagos.
29. 'Annual Report for the Year Ended March 31, 1974. NPA Industrial Relations Division', mimeo.
30. The survey was limited to a sample of the two lowest grades of workers in the Engineering and Traffic Departments.
31. See *Urhobo Report*.
32. The organization has at various times referred to itself as the 'reconstituted' ADWT & GWU.
33. The NTUC merged into the broader Nigerian Trade Union Federation in 1973, and this into the Nigerian Labour Congress in December 1975.
34. Arnold Hughes and Robin Cohen, 'Towards the Emergence of a Nigerian Working Class: The Social Identity of the Lagos Labour Force, 1897–1939'. Occasional Paper D7, Faculty of Commerce and Social Science, Birmingham University, 1971, mimeo.
35. Portworkers asked the same question usually responded to the effect that they had no enemies.
36. U.U. Nkamare, *Lagos Dock Labour Problems (Lagos: Ribway Printers, 1964), pp. 22–7.*
37. Wogu Ananaba, *The Trade Union Movement in Nigeria* (London:

Hurst, 1969), p. 230.
38. *Daily Times* (Lagos) 17, 23 May, 1974.
39. *Ibid.* 20 May 1974.
40. Peter Waterman, 'Communist Theory in the Nigerian Trade Union Movement', *Politics and Society* (Spring, 1973) and 'Neo-Colonialism, Communism and the Nigerian Trade Union Congress' (M.Soc.Sci. dissertation, Birmingham University, 1972).
41. See, for instance, the detailed technical questions dealt with in the documents of the International Transport Workers Federation West African Seminar for Port Workers, Freetown, Sierra Leone, 7–11 April 1975.
42. This section has benefited from discussions with Sylvester Ejiofoh, a Nigerian trade union leader studying at the Institute of Social Studies, 1975–6.
43. *Industrialisation in an Open Economy: Nigeria 1945–66* (Cambridge: Cambridge University Press, 1969).
44. The significant difference from Britain at that time was the colonial requirement of compulsory registration for trade unions. See A. Adeogun, 'The Legal Framework of Industrial Relations in Nigeria', *Nigerian Law Journal*, 3 (1969), p.16.
45. Cited in Robin Cohen, *Organised Labour in the Nigerian Political Process* (London: Heinemann, 1974).
46. S.S. Ameh, 'Workers Protection: a Focus on the Labour Decree and the Wages Boards and Industrial Councils Decree', paper to National Seminar on the Union the Law and National Development, Kano, Sept. 1975, mimeo.
47. Adeogun, *op. cit*, p. 13.
48. See Segun Osoba, 'Ideological Trends in the Nigerian National Liberation Movement and the Problems of National Identity, Solidarity and Motivation, 1934–65: A Preliminary Assessment', Ibadan 27, 1969, and P. Waterman, 'Conservatism Amongst Nigerian Workers', Occasional Paper 48, Institute of Social Studies, The Hague, 1975.
49. Cohen, *op. cit.*, p. 185.
50. Adeogun, *op. cit.*, p. 13.
51. Cohen, *op. cit.*, p. 182.
52. Kilby, *op. cit.*, p. 268.
53. A. Akpala, 'Industrial Relations Policies in Nigeria', *Acta Africana*, 10,1 (1971), p. 35.
54. David Ojeli, 'The Development of Trade Unionism in Eastern Nigeria' (M.S.S. dissertation, Institute of Social Studies, The Hague, 1975).
55. Akanimo Etukudo, *Multi-Employer Bargaining: Industrial Relations System in the Banking Industry in Nigeria* (Arthur: Ilfracombe Stockwell, 1971).
56. Cohen, *op. cit.*, p. 184.
57. Akpala, *op. cit.*, p.39.
58. See *Ibid.*, p. 38. Also 'Address by the Commissioner of Labour to the First Meeting of the Reconstituted National Labour Advisory Council', *NECA News* (March 1973).
59. Kilby, *op. cit.*, p. 291–2.
60. For cases, see Dorothy Renny, 'Economic Security and Industrial

Unionism: a Nigerian Case Study' and Paul Lubeck, 'Unions, Workers and Consciousness in Kano, Nigeria: a View from Below', both in R. Sandbrook and R. Cohen (eds), *The Development of an African Working Class* (London: Longmans, 1975). For a general comment on domestication, see Cohen, *op. cit.*, pp. 116–7.

61. 'Address . . . to Representatives of the Four Central Labour Organisations and the NECA on the new National Policy on Labour . . . December 4, 1975, at 11.00 a.m.', Lagos, mimeo.
62. For a clear, precise and complete description of Nigeria's Labour legislation in terms comprehensible to the layman, see R.B. Davison, 'Industrial Relation in Nigeria: The Legal Framework: 100 Questions and Answers', paper to the National Seminar on the Unions, the Law and National Development, Kano, September 1975, mimeo.
63. As a result of this clause, during the spontaneous strike wave of 1970–1, the Northern press reported the Southern strikes and vice versa.
64. A.A. Adegun, 'Industrial Relations and the Unions in Nigerian Law', paper to the National Seminar on the Unions, the Law and National Development, Kano, September 1975, pp. 27–30.
65. *Ibid.*, pp. 32–5. See also 'Statement of the Federatl Commission of Labour at the Commissioning of the Second Chamber of the Industrial Arbitration Tribunal, December 28, 1974', *NECA News* (December 1974).
66. Ameh, *op. cit.*, p. 11.
67. Adeogun, 'Industrial Relations', pp. 7–24.
68. *Ibid*, pp. 32–40.
69. For more on both the IAT and the government's attitude towards it, see the Commissioner's statement referred to in note 65 above.
70. *Beckley Report*, p. 160.
71. NPAWU 10th Annual Conference Documents, 1956.
72. *Beckley Report*, p. 160.
73. 'Welcome Address at the Reunification Party of the NPAWU . . . Apa . . . July 26, 1974', mimeo.
74. 'Memorandum of Agreement on the Negotiating and Consulting Procedure in the NPA, October 24, 1974', mimeo.
75. NPAWU 12th Annual Conference Documents, 1956.
76. NMWU 15th Delegates' Conference Documents, 1973.
77. This account is pieced together from newspaper reports, union, government and management documents, and interview notes, none of which cover the issue from beginning to end. It must be considered a makeshift substitute for a full and detailed account.
78. *Daily Times,* 9 June 1971.
79. Six days according to the *Daily Times,* 8 July 1971.
80. *Daily Times*, 16 July 1971.
81. *Ibid.*, 23 August 1971.
82. Letter, 'On the Implementation of the IAT Award in Reference to the 44-Hour Week', October 2, 1972, mimeo.
83. NMTUF Conference Documents, Warri, December 1972, mimeo.
84. NMWU, *op. cit.*
85. 'R & PT &CSU: Report of Activities by General Secretary to the 25th Conference, Lagos, January 22–5, 1973', mimeo.

86. 'NPA Industrial Relations Division: Annual Report for the Year Ended March 31, 1974', mimeo.
87 ANDLC letter, 'Joint Industrial Council for the Dock Industry', 17 August 1976.
88. Nkamare, *op. cit*.
89. An interview with Nkamare in 1975 revealed that company D was his own company at that time. Whilst his favourable account of it might be quite fair, I have thought it best not to include it here.
90. Labour Department, *Annual Report, 1950–51.*
91. William Knight, *The History of the Ports of Nigeria* (Lagos: NPA, 1965).
92. Ministry of Labour, *Annual Report, 1963–4*, pp. 28–32.
93. *Ibid*., p. 33.
94. ANDLC letter to the Dock Labour Board: 'Representation in the Dock Labour Advisory Board', 5 April 1967.
95. *Urhobo Report*, p. 7.
96. *Ibid*., p. 67.
97. *Ibid*., pp. 72–3.
98. *Comments of the Federal Military Government*, p. 11.
99. ADWT & GWU(R) Petition, 'Petition Submitted to the Head of State', 21 September 1974.
100. Source: Interview with Ministry of Labour Officer, 1975.
101. Source: Files of the NPF Offices, Apapa, 1975.
102. Source: Files of the Registrar of Trade Unions, Lagos, 1975.
103. *Daily Times*, 20 May 1974.
104. ADWT & GWU(R), *op. cit.*
105. *Daily Times,* 30 September 1974.
106. Once again, the piecemeal nature of the account must be admitted.
107. *Nigerian Tribune*, 27 February 1974.
108. 'Threatened Industrial Action at the Docks', Ministry of Labour Press Release, 15 May 1974.
109. *Daily Times*, 17 May 1974.
110. 'Meeting Held with the Representatives of Striking Dockworkers in the Lagos Port Complex over their Demands', NPA Statement, 23 May 1974.
111. *Daily Times*, 26 July 1974.
112. *Daily Express*, 6 September 1974.
113. *Public Service Review Commission: Main Report* (Lagos: Federal Ministry of Information, 1974), and *The Public Service of Nigeria: Government Views on the Report of the Public Service Review Commission* (Lagos: Federal Ministry of INformation, 1974).
114. *New Nigerian*, 10 January 1975.
115. Source: Interview with Port Labour Officer, 1975.
116. *New Nigerian*, 10 January 1975.
117. 'Udoji Award', letter of the NPA to the ADWT & GWU, 10 January 1975.
118. 'Agreement Reached at the Meeting of Dock Employers and the ADWT & GWU on the Udoji Award Which led to Industrial Disturbances in the Docks on January 11, 1975', mimeo.
119. 'Minutes of Meeting Between Management of NPA and Representatives

of the Dockworkers on January 23 1975', mimeo.

120. See 'Address Delivered by Bernard Odulana, General Secretary of the ADWT & GWU on May 28, 1975, at the Meeting With the Dock Employers', mimeo.

121. Contract this, for example, with just one of the wide variety of contemporary non-Machiavellian formulations' 'An industrial relations system . . . is . . . comprised of certain actors, certain contexts, and ideology which binds the . . . system together, and a body of rules created to govern the actors at the work place and work community', J.T. Dunlop, *Industrial Relations Systems* (New York: Holt, 1958), p. 7. Dunlop's view of industrial relations as a set of roles that can be variously filled, with the power of role players varying under different relationship which my definition stresses. Dunlop is currently Secretary of Labour in the United States. His definition is evidently functional to those seeking to control labour in that country.

122. Personal communication, January 1976.

123. See the fascinating analysis of Roberto Massari, 'Le "Cordobazo"', *Sociologie de Travail*, 4 (1975). This article proposes the term 'corbobazo' as a generic one for revolutionary worker upheavals in dualistic and dependent economies, implying that similar conditions elsewhere could lead to analogous uprisings. Although of a far more limited extent and significance, Nigeria's strike movements of 1964, 1970–71 and 1975 could be considered forerunners of future cordobazos.

124. The term and the concept of Clark Kerr and his associates, social scientists who have well articulated and shaped the attitudes of administrators. See C. Kerr *et al.*, *Industrialism and Industrial Man* (Harmondsworth: Penguin, 1973).

125. Yet, it is evident that they already play a significant role not only in this case, but also in the analogous cases mentioned in the chapters by Collins and Turner.

PART 3
Local Administration for Development

Local Government: An Introduction

In a spending sense local government institutions are not usually very important development agencies, although in other senses they might be focal institutions at the local level. The use of local government for 'development' purposes has mainly been confined to the collection of taxes on behalf of central government. In terms of the organization of development projects and agricultural production, it is the technical departments of government like Agriculture and Community Development who alone penetrate down to the community or farm level, although the low ratio of field staff to the farming population or communities tends to minimize severely the scope of their impact. For various reasons, local government in the Anglophone countries in the post-independence period has declined in relation to other parts of the machinery of government. In Nigeria, its financial position has deteriorated, coupled with a loss of staff to other parts of the public service, particularly in the localization drive and more recently to meet the staffing needs of new State civil services in Nigeria. Thus, in an atmosphere of declining confidence in local government, 'reforms' have ranged from a virtual abolition of independent local government – in the sense of democratically-elected bodies with powers of taxation and spending – or have subordinated it to the field administration of central government.

Some of these points (as well as others) were subsequently taken up by the 1974 (Udoji) Public Service Review Commission. The findings of the Commission met with a varied official response. The major recommendation of the Udoji Report, in its chapter on Local Government, is for a single tier system. In some States the earlier changes had multiplied levels of government below the centre. Where manpower has been limited, the creation of a new level (with staff increases) has weakened structures at all levels. Moreover, the administrative costs of new levels has diverted already scarce resources away from development projects. The general plea of the Udoji Commission is that the allocation of responsibilities should be consistent with the resources and abilities of the level of government. The other structural aspect of local government is that of choosing an appropriate unit. Here the Udoji Commission leaves the matter to the state concerned to decide in view of the prevalent local conditions. Three considerations which usually inform such decisions are; (i) synonymity with traditional authority patterns; (ii) economic viability; (iii) suitability as a unit of popular participation.

The second aspect of local government treated in the Udoji Report is functions and services. Here it is recommended that the States set up investigating committees. However, the Commission cautions against the further erosion of local government functions because it does not believe that central governments are better equipped to provide all services at the local level. Some nine, mainly minor non-technical, functions are mentioned in this respect. Towards the urban areas, however, where poor provision of local services is often most acutely felt, the Report is less clear. The third aspect is staffing and manpower. A perennial problem of local government in Africa is the attraction of suitable staff. In line with its recommendations for other areas of the public service, the Udoji Report puts forward the 'harmonisation' of salaries and conditions of service between central and local government as a solution. In the case of local government, the problem has been the loss of better staff to other branches of the public service. This measure may not be sufficient *per se*, however, since part of the problem is related to the more general status of local authorities within the total machinery of government.

The fourth area treated by the Udoji Commission is finance, where a single personal tax system and more federal aid to the states is urged. Both the Report and the resulting Government White Paper see aspects of finance as key factors in the decline of local government. They include: (i) poor financial management (ii) inadequate grants, and (iii) frequent changes in the revenue-sharing arrangements between central governments and local authorities.

In sum, the main thinking of Nigerian policy makers in the area of local government – at least as expressed in the White Paper reactions to the Udoji Report – has been in terms of structural changes. Relatively less has been acknowledged about procedural aspects and indeed the desired future role of local authorities within the total machinery of government. In general, Nigerian policy makers seemed to have acquiesced in the present trend towards local government as an agent of tax collection and law and order administration, although even the tax collection function has become less important now that federal and state governments have oil-derived revenues as an alternative source. With the exception of the Udoji Commission's discussion of the methods of selection of Councillors, relatively little attention has been given to the participation (i.e. the procedural) aspects of local government. The Commission's proposals for the democratization of local government were in fact rejected. Official emphasis has thus been more upon the distribution of powers and resources between levels of government (Federal-State-Local Authority) than on the relationship of local government to its electorate. In other words, policy makers have tended to prefer 'technical' and 'administrative' solutions rather than to tackle fundamental political questions.

9. The Reorganization of Local Government Under Military Rule in Nigeria, 1966-74

Belle Harris

Introduction

The twelve states system, which existed in Nigeria until the addition of seven more in 1976, legally came into being on 17 May 1967 by authority of the States Creation and Transitional Provision Decree No. 14[1] Prior to the decree all units of elected representative governments had been suspended, including the elected local government councils in those relatively few areas where they had survived.[2] Indeed, as recent as December 1974, the Government had reiterated the non-elected principle by declaring that the states should continue to decide who should be appointed to serve as members of local authorities for the duration of the military regime.[3]

Between 1968 and 1970 each of the existing twelve states had authorized a committee to examine proposals for the reform of its local government system. By 1972 all had issued edicts promulgating changes – in one case to the extent of nominally abolishing local government.[4] The need for these reforms was not legally dictated by the establishment of the states *per se*; the constitutional relationship between the responsible governments (formerly the regions, now the states) had not fundamentally altered. What had necessitated the change had been the corresponding reduction in size, scope of activities and resources available to the now more numerous states. In the light of this situation most states had incorporated, in one form or another, the following three objectives in their proposals: (i) to bring government closer to the people, (ii) to accelerate development, (iii) to re-allocate functions. It was the third objective which was to be the key factor leading to immediate observable change. A common result of the proposals has been the *de facto* transfer of functions, resources and, therefore, power from local governments to the newly established state ministries. This characteristic was particularly pronounced in those states where large local authorities dominated the area.[5] Moreover, this trend had already been enhanced under military rule with the transfer of the residual law and order functions, including police, customary courts and prisons, from the Local Authorities (hereafter referred to as L.A.s) to the federal state governments. Thus, it would seem that the changes in Nigeria have mirrored the world-wide trend of legislating for a weaker local government *vis-a-vis* central government under the label of 'reforming' local government. What has taken place in Nigeria, as elsewhere, is a shift of power from local government to the decentralized arm of the central bureaucracies or to other central government agencies.

On the other hand, it should not be assumed that the common trend towards greater centralization has created uniformity. The legislation which followed the reform proposals illustrated marked diversities for which two major reasons have been put forward. First, each state has tended to interpret in a different manner the reform objectives relating to the 'representative' and 'development' elements. Secondly, and more importantly, each state still operates within an inherited regional legislative framework which in turn had been heavily influenced by its own particular history.

The legislative details emanating from the twelve states show that there emerged a patchwork of local administrative institutions each with differing terminologies.

Yet, it is also suggested that the state systems had more in common than the readings of the legislation would perhaps indicate – largely due to historical events. It is proposed, therefore, to include in this study a brief historical survey followed by a summary of the local administrative systems in each of the twelve states. From the formal structural details an attempt will then be made to classify and group the separate systems into identifiable comparative models. Finally, and on the assumption that models are only in part useful for understanding the operational behaviour of institutions, a more detailed study will be made of three former states: East-Central, Kano and Western.

Historical Perspective

To obtain an adequate perspective, it is necessary to examine (i) the nature of the pre-colonial political system, (ii) the method of rule adopted by the British and its consequent impact, (iii) how this influenced the choice of local government system made during the period prior to independence, and (iv) finally, the subsequent perceived success or failure of this choice and its influence upon the post-military reforms.

Much has been written about the early local administration systems, particularly from the structural point of view.[6] Most of the commentators have agreed that it was the British choice of the northern emirate system as the 'ideal' model to export throughout Nigeria that provided the single most important moulding influence upon all subsequent local government matters. The emirate system was said to have satisfied all political, administrative and judicial attributes of 'states' – at least prior to colonial rule.[7] Internally, the system was characterised as authoritarian and hierarchial; each sub-unit – the districts and villages – was strictly subordinate to the centre. Social security, underpinned by religious sanctions, was to offset the obligations of levies and tribute. Based on the emirate system the British or, more accurately, Lord Lugard was said to have adopted the 'pure' model of 'indirect rule'.[8] Its application made it inevitable that the boundaries of local authorities would follow large-scale traditional lines, be dominated by the rural areas, and administered by a designated emir or chief legally authorised as the Native Authority (hereafter referred to as N.A.). Each of the large N.A.s were armed with wide 'paper' powers and each allowed, under the 'indirect rule' principle, a great deal of discretionary power where this did not conflict with the interest of the colonial state. It also allowed the relationship between the emir/chief and the colonial government to be visually maintained as 'partnership' rule long after the establishment of British control.

The existence of large subordinate administrations – whether already existing or artificially created – enabled the British to rule with a minimum of staff.[9] Small numbers of British staff in the field were in a position to be the 'eyes and ears' of central government. In all cases the designated N.A. was expected to act as the intermediary between the British administrative/divisional officers (hereafter referred to as D.O.s) and their people. The D.O. still remained an essential feature of the local administrative system in at least ten of the twelve post-1967 states. The system has been described by Ronald Wraith as the 'dual' system of government and by Brian Smith as the 'unintegrated prefectorial system'.[10] Powers of the D.O., then and now, included all supervisory and default functions over the N.A.s/L.A.s. Also, they were empowered to attend meetings, inspect accounts and assist in preparing budgets. In the last resort they could be designated the 'Sole Authority' of a dissolved N.A./L.A. and the Sole Administrator for all Townships, except for the first class township of Lagos – a point that will be taken up later.

Native Authority System in Southern Nigeria

From the beginning it was felt in many parts of Western Nigeria, and almost all parts of Eastern Nigeria, that the N.A. system had been imposed upon them. In many areas of the West it was a relatively easy task to identify an accepted paramount chief as the N.A. Yet, it was also observed that the necessary pyramidical relationships were particularly lacking in the numerous urbanized areas where 'strong dispersed powers' had developed outside of the N.A. headquarters.[11] The lack of an overall urban policy – inherent in the N.A. system – was to remain an integral weakness of local government both in the former West and elsewhere. As for Eastern Nigeria, the pattern of non-centralized political systems and the fragmented economy that had developed by the 1920s presented problems for colonial and post-colonial governments.[12] Here, the imported N.A. policy forced the colonial power to 'find a chief' of an area large enough to be a viable N.A. As early as 1930, attempts were made to re-draw boundaries in line with traditional culture – in order that the local taxation could be regarded as a community tax. But, as a result, there were numerous authorities, few of them viable, and very few comparable to those of the North.

Initially, the only exceptions made to the N.A. pattern related to those urban centres which housed relatively large expatriate communities. These were given legal autonomy under the Township Ordinance of 1917 in which Sole Authority was vested in a D.O. From their inception, the townships attracted large grants to enable services to be provided up to Western standards, but from the start they represented only small enclaves within larger (African) conurbations. Nevertheless, their existence in the past, and their survival in four of the twelve states up to 1976, effectively checked the evolution of a single urban government in many of the largest cities.[13]

Local Self-Government Prior to Military Rule: 1950–1966

In a paper dealing with the changing pattern of local government, K.J. Davey observes: 'the colonial secretary's despatch of 1947 heralded reforms throughout the 1950's in the British African Colonies, progressively introducing patterns of local government on the British model'[14] Nigeria, territorially, proved an exception to this pattern. What the despatch heralded in was a policy of regional (rather than federal) responsibility for local government and only the Eastern and Western Regions chose to accept the British, or rather the English, pattern of local government.[15] In accepting the English model *in toto* the two regions not only made a clean break with their N.A. past, but also accepted those features of local government distinctive to the English pattern. In particular, it meant that they accepted the principles of *ultra vires*, an elected majority of voluntary unpaid members, and the principle of members possessing executive and administrative duties through the committee system. Above all, it meant they accepted a tier system of different sized authorities – none subordinate to the others. As elsewhere in Africa the imported model failed to flourish and this failure significantly influenced the post-military reforms.

Initially in the Eastern Region the position of the 'chiefs' was almost reversed. Power and prestige was passed from the appointed N.A. to the hands of the elected representatives – totalling 20,000 in this one region alone. In the Western Region the law allowed for only one-sixth of the members to be nominated from the chiefs and the others being elected. This not only reflected the traditional philosophy of the Yoruba – the largest ethnic group in the west – but also the desire of villages and towns, however small, to have an L.A. boundary drawn around a recognized local 'chief' thus ensuring that some official revenue would remain in the locality.[16] The strongest reaction against the role of the D.O. again came in the East. Under the new law all powers of direct control were at first removed; only the advisory functions remained.

Even given the measure of central control re-introduced in both the East and West, that is approval of contracts, audit and inspection systems, a great deal of autonomy was still left in the hands of the elected. L.A.s throughout most of the political period. Yet, the judgement of most commentators was that this power of the L.A.s was stifled[17] The major reasons for the failures were the unwieldy size (either too remote or too small), nepotism, and a chronic shortage of funds.[18] As a direct result of the perceived failures, both Regions progressively re-introduced the instrument of control by Provincial Commissioners, and in 1965 the Western Region used its powers to suspend all Local Authority Councils and replaced them with either a Sole Administrator or a Committee of Management.

Gradual Change in Northern Nigeria[19]

It has been argued that, unlike the South, the Despatch of 1947 did not provide the North with a welcome opportunity for change. In contrast to the southern politicians, those in the North tended to be part of the traditional N.A. system, who often viewed the reforms as a threat to their power and prestige. Therefore, the first regional local government law – the Native Authority Law of 1954 – did not break with the past in name or substance.

By retaining the established system the North was also *ipso facto* rejecting a uniform local government system. In addition to the townships and the regional capital (administered by D.O.s), there were also a variety of administrative structures. At one end of the spectrum there were the more powerful (Moslem) Chiefs-in-Council, with merely advisory councils to assist them. Marginally less powerful, there were the Chiefs-and-Councils where majority votes prevailed. In both these types, the Councils would be internally organized on a 'parliamentary' model with salaried Portfolio/ Ministerial Councillors heading the functional departments. Structurally rather different were the non-Moslem, non-centralized authorities, the smaller partly administered by the D.O., the larger organized on the committee system basis. It was only in the latter that the 1954 law allowed for an elected N.A. Council.[20] In the Emirates the directly elected representatives were initially restricted to the subordinate district and village councils, and legislative and financial power in all N.A.s remained at the central headquarters – a surviving characteristics in all six northern states.[21] Throughout the political period the authority of the traditional ruler remained high, buttressed as it was by the authority of the regional government whose composition was made up mostly from members of the ruling N.A. families.[22] For this reason the N.A. remained the main avenue for administrative and political advancement until, and even just beyond, the creation of the 12 states. Yet, throughout the political period, the power of the central government was still considerable – albeit it had on occasion to be asserted.[23] The Government was able to extent its influence through its Personal Income Tax Law of 1962 which, following the Western and Eastern pattern, ensured that the most elastic forms of income, including P.A.Y.E., would go to Inland Revenue rather than to the N.A. But above all it was the retention in the North of the D.O. which continued to be the most effective means of central control.[24]

Local Government under Military Rule: 1966–74

First, it should be noted that the term 'reform' and even 'reorganization' is somewhat of a misnomer for describing the relatively minor constitutional changes which occurred in the majority of the twelve states. The real changes in central-local power relationships really took place as a result of underlying economic changes rather than any constitutional discussion, although this was not always recognized by the members of the reform committees at the time.[25]

The Civil War was an important factor in determining future change. As a generalization it can be said that the greater the involvement the more radical and institutional changes. Not surprisingly, it was the changes made in the three war-torn Eastern states which most reflected the extreme reaction against the former system. Broadly, the system adopted in these states bore remarkably similar features to the French Integrated Prefectorial System. On the other hand the reformed structures in the three Western states provide examples of the greatest similarity with the former English-based model, only substituting a 'unitary' single-tier system for that of the two/three tiers existing prior to military rule. Finally, the skeleton, if not the whole substance, of the N.A. system managed to survive in the six states of the North. Here the reformed local structures remained pyramidical with a parallel structure of divisional administration, thereby retaining the characteristics of the Unintegrated Prefectorial System.

Another general point that needs to be made concerns the assumptions and values of the members of the reform committees, although it is recognized that this is a very difficult element to quantify. Again, as a generalization, it has been acknowledged that a common value-judgement was generated by the perceived failures of the politically-dominated councils, particularly in the East and West. Efficiency and honesty came to be equated with a professionally-trained, neutral, civil servant administration. The extreme illustration of this aspect is provided by the example of the South-East State, where the reform committee was mainly made up of highly-trained Federal civil servants exiled in Lagos. In their proposals they argued that any form of local government would be irrelevant for the vast rehabilitation programme needed in that state. Yet, interestingly, in the neighbouring Rivers State a highly-politicized local leader was sufficiently respected to influence the reforms, perhaps to the extent of enabling the former L.A./county councils to be retained during the interim period. In the North attempts were made to balance the committees so that the composition included voices from the N.A.s as well as the civil service and universities. As to be expected, the results were often a compromise. For example, in almost all cases where a new tier was introduced, the controlling power was earmarked for the civil servant/D.O. rather than the L.A. A brief statement on three of the states should illustrate this trend.

Reorganization in Eastern Nigeria: East-Central State

The most important factor shaping the reforms in Eastern Nigeria was the civil war experience and its impact upon the architects of the reforms. Unlike the other two states (South-Eastern and Rivers) the immediate post-war planners in East-Central were not drawn exclusively from those who had been in exile. Also, unlike the other two states, it was ethnically homogenous, with common social customs and traditional spiritual beliefs centred on the place of one's birth. Indeed, the war experience apparently strengthened those community feelings which were beginning to be weakened by commercial pressures. For example, a delegate to the 1971 National Conference on Local Government stated that: 'resulting from these civil war experiences, the average businessman appears to be formulating a new policy, even if subconsciously, that no investment is safe which is not sited in the investors's home.' Recognition of the importance of one's place of birth may have been the reason why the East-Central State alone introduced a modified form of proportionate representation to ensure a majority for the indigenes.

In all three Eastern states decentralized authority at the first tier level was vested in the Divisional Administration under the direct control of the Cabinet/Military Governor and utilizing the institution of a prefectorial D.O. In Rivers State L.A.s with some powers survived the interim measures, whilst in East-Central the new laws stipulated that the Divisional Councils were advisory only. The system introduced in the South-East was wholly controlled by the arm of the development-orientated field administration with only a subsidiary advisory and tax-collecting role allocated to the traditional authority.

In the East-Central State the similarity with the French system was even more marked in terms of name, powers, and boundaries of the over 600 second-tier Community Councils each with an average population of only ten thousand. Within the limitations of their competence and resources, these Councils were empowered to deliberate and take decisions over a wide area – subject to divisional approval. A small establishment staff comprising a secretary, treasurer, clerk, typist and messenger was provided and paid for by the state, as were also the fixed allowances of the councillors. The major sources of revenue were the charges for services rendered such as bicycle, native liquor and motor park fees, plus special levies. It was hoped that these measures would generate sufficient revenue to cover the major services necessary in an area where capital was relatively scarce – although matching grants were allowed for. Property rates and assessment procedures were based on the former regional requirements and provided for the major form of revenue in most urban areas. Finally, the shift towards greater administrative centralisation was strengthened by the transfer of functions to the state. For example, the state took over the establishment, equipping and administration of all schools. Also, the assessment and collection of rates was undertaken by civil servants under the Board of Internal Revenue.

In conclusion, the success of the integrated prefectorial system of local administration has depended upon the degree of community level initiative forthcoming to match the requirements. In their early stages the reforms in East-Central State encouraged so great a number of capital projects that, in some cases, it was found necessary to curtail them for lack of recurrent revenue. This last was not a factor that worried Rivers State too much. As the richest of the states (*per capita*) it could afford to bypass the country councils. However, it did provide a major problem area for the much poorer South-Eastern State, which for some time needed the revenue collected via the traditional chiefs.

Reorganization in Western Nigeria: Western State

There are several salient features of Western Nigeria which have been the source of its most pertinent problems. First, it is the most urbanized area of Nigeria. Unfortunately, as mentioned earlier, the 'indirect rule' principle failed to take account of this feature. So that apart from Lagos City, covering the Island of Lagos, most L.A. units failed to provide a high standard of urban amenities. Secondly, the predominance of chiefs within both the L.A. and Government, coupled with the high social status attached to private property, have often posed serious problems for the maintenance of a viable taxation system The former Mid-Western State attempted to solve this problem by putting forward a variety of occupational development levies and Lagos extended a modified form of property-tax throughout the state. Only Western State, where the position was most acute, was slow to put forward a viable taxation scheme. To meet this it subsequently set up a special committee to review the whole of the taxation system.

The western states have in fact a history of insufficient local authority revenue to meet the ever increasing demands made upon them, particularly in the realm of education. It was the first of the regions to introduce free primary education – relying on revenue from its major cash crop, cocoa, always an unstable factor. Also, it was unfortunate that a significant percentage of the region's capital expenditure was centred in building up an industrial centre adjacent to Lagos, which now lies within that state. Therefore the Western State and its successors have been unable to reap the long-term benefits of its investments. Instead, it has probably led to an increase in the export of its manpower. Another inherited problem prior to military rule was the proliferation of L.A. units under the guise of recognition of a local chief. This ensured that more local money and more jobs stayed within the locality, but at the expense of viability. In addition to all of this, charges of corruption were rife.

The Western State, in December 1972, was the last of the twelve states to announce its reform proposals. Perhaps for that reason, it was in a position to analyze the problems in greater depth than the other states. Certainly, it was the only one to include in its reform proposals an alternative *internal management system*. On the other hand the delay and the apparent radical proposals could have been equally due to the government utilizing the advice of the nearby academics, many of whose expertise lay in the field of comparative local government management.

The major innovations proposed in the local government system of Western State were threefold and aimed specifically at dealing with the problems outlined above. First, they adopted what they described as the 'manager' system based on the U.S.A. model. Secondly, it was proposed that at least 40% p.a. of locally-raised revenue must be spent in the area of derivation on a 50% average over a four-year period. It was hoped that this solution alone would satisfy local aspirations and remove real conflicts. Thirdly, the chief was removed from all *ex officio* political posts and given a separate chain of command from that of local government. Finally, a unitary single-tier system, with boundaries drawn wherever possible upon efficiency criteria, replaced the two/three tier system. One of the ideas behind the proposed 'manager' system of local government was that administration would be able to go about its work without undue interference from councillors or committee men. Criticism that the former L.A.s were primarily 'agencies of partisan politics' and that the voluntary Councillors – particularly the chiefs – misused their position was the most common of the attacks made upon the old system, not without good foundation. In the council manager system the chief executive is the Secretary of the Council. His status depends upon the size of his responsibility. For example, Permanent Secretary status was applied to Ibadan City Council but, unlike the U.S.A. model, the 'manager' was *not* to be appointed by the Council, rather by the independent Local Government Service Board who could draw upon seconded senior civil servants. The duties of the chief executive included the recommendations of appointments, promotion and dismissal subject to approval by the Local Government Service Board.

Within the reformed local government system, the function of the Council became *deliberative*. The four major areas of deliberation were: matters of general policy; preparing the annual budgets for approval; reviewing half yearly budgets; and electing the members of the much smaller standing committee. With the abolition of the other committees, the Council also took over the preparation and overseeing of committee functions, thus bringing the internal organization into line with a major American city model Councillors remained voluntary, drawing only allowance, but having to satisfy literary and income qualifications. The councils were assisted by advisory Area Committees, which were locally-based representative units whose main function was to deliberate on matters referred to or initiated by it and to offer suggestions on the general development in its area. It was this last which was to be its most important function. Fifty per cent of its locally collected revenue was to be spent locally.

In conclusion, it might be noted that, on paper, it cannot claim entirely to be the American type 'manager' system, for it has omitted the essential principle, that the 'manager' is initially appointed by the elected/representative council, and, in theory, is their servant. Also, one must always question the efficacy of an imported model. Moreover, the reforms made little mention of the special committee to review the whole of the taxation system Above all, it should be remembered that all three western state governments retained the ultimate power of dissolution, a weapon that was used in the former Mid-Western State, providing the most significant departure from both the U.K. and the U.S.A. model.

Local Government in Northern Nigeria: Kano State

'Da, mu Keyi; Lokacin ya zo; an yi da mu. Yanzu ana yi, ana fuda mana.' The literal translation of the above can be given as: 'Once we did *everything*: When the time came we did it with others. Now, *they* do it, and they *tell* us.' This quotation aptly sums up the changed position of the Emir of Kano and all other emirates, although it should be noted that the emirate system only covered approximately 50% of the region.

Kano State was chosen to illustrate the changes made up to 1974 under military rule, not because it was the most typical, but rather because it was the one state where the emirate system monopolized the L.A. system.[26] A salient feature of Kano State is that it is ethnically homogenous, again making it different from the other former five northern states. The N.A. boundaries continue to follow historical lines rather than those of the ethnic rivalries. The state is divided into four emirate L.A.s, each equal in power according to law. But, from a geographical, financial and population aspect the area was, and is, overwhelmingly, dominated by the Kano Emirate, within which lies the largest urban centre of the North – the capital city of Kano. In 1972, out of a total recurrent L.A. revenue of ₦7.16m for the whole state, over 6m was from Kano Emirate alone. Out of a total population of 5.8m in 1963, 3.6m resided in the Kano L.A. area, which also covers three-quarters of the states's land mass.

Consequently, a major (if undeclared) motivation of the reorganization was concerned with a transfer of functions, powers, and finance from Kano Emirate to the state government. Without this transfer, some of the newly-created ministries would have had relatively less responsibility than its subordinate level of government. This case provided a situation not dissimilar from the other northern emirate – Sokoto in the former North-Western, Bornu in the former North-Eastern, and Zaria and Katsina in North-Central. However, in Kano the changes mark a direct shift of power from the hierarchical Emirate to the new centre of power – the Military Governor's Office.

Another major characteristic of Kano State is its paucity of skilled man-power resources – again a factor shared by the other northern states. Kano school enrolment in 1966 was estimated at approximately 5.8% of primary school-age population, although the target was to increase this to 15% by 1974. Formerly, the N.A.s were the major employment agency for public servants and the emirate tended to attract the best. Salaries attached to traditional posts were generous indeed. Therefore, it is not surprising that a significant percentage of the manpower needed for the state ministries has been provided for by the transfer of the professionally-trained local government staff. In all the former six northern states the reforms marked a watering down of the emirs' position and powers *vis-a-vis* the state bureaucracy. In all cases the representative element in the N.A. council was to be in a majority – albeit appointed during military rule – and the emirs were thereafter required to work through these councils and be guided by majority opinion. Administratively, certain functions were taken over by the state government, for example, that of natural resources in most states. In four of the six former states, provincial administration was abolished – exceptions being North-Central and North-Eastern States, and the portfolio ministerial councillor system was abolished in the two middle-belt states: Benue-Plateau and Kwara, where the committee system was established. But above all, the reform most loudly acclaimed was that the term 'Native Authority' was abolished; all former Native Authorities were henceforth to be 'Local Government Authorities'. Apart from this change, the three other emirates Kano in the state remained as before, that is a 'two-tier pyramidical' structure consisting of the parent L.A. and subordinate District Councils.

More significant change was that a new tier was created within the Kano L.A. by sub-dividing the area into five Area Councils. In each a designated D.O. became the council chairman. The composition of these councils consisted of three district representatives nominated by the Local Government Commissioner plus each district head in the area and heads of the government departments. The council was empowered to employ an Administrative Secretary, who tended to be transferred from the parent L.A. thereby providing for an informal co-ordinating role. Thus, in Kano there now exists a three-tier system, still within a pyramidical framework. *De jure* power is vested in the Area Councils which in theory are subordinate to the L.A. council. In practice, power rests with the appointed chairman who is directly responsible to the Local Government Commissioner. Also, the seconded staff tend to take their instructions directly from the Administrative Secretary, who in turn works closely with the government administrative headquarters.

The other major change in the balance of power is directly related to the changes in the distribution of revenue and transfer of revenue-earning functions from the Kano L.A. to either the state or the Area Councils. The reallocation of revenue-earning services as urban water supply, printing and surveying has hurt the L.A. financially. Kano L.A. must now pay a further 10% of its taxes to the Area Councils. Other functions transferred in Kano include environmental health services, road and drainage, markets and motor parks. This still leaves the L.A. the high cost services of primary education and health. Consequently, the reforms of Kano L.A., along with the reforms of all the L.A.'s in the former North-Central, North-Eastern, and North-Western States left the authorities with a much smaller share of revenue to maintain its remaining services. One immediate affect was that the *per capita* costs of its administration rose considerably.

With the extreme scarcity of skilled manpower resources, the introduction of yet another administrative tier in the short run only exacerbates the problem. Out of a total staff of 20 in the Treasury Department of the Kano L.A., only three remained who were trained to diploma level (1973), whilst the staff of the newly-created Area Councils were almost all professionally untrained, except for the Secretary. Given this situation, the Area Councils have tended to build up relatively large surpluses in capital accounts due to their lack of implementative executive skills, whilst, conversely, the L.A.s have only been able to maintain their capital development by utilizing their fast dwindling reserves.

In conclusion, apart from the problems inherent in any transitional period of shifts in power, the other major outstanding problem relates to the Kano metropolis. In the short run the reorganization will have only added to one of the major causes of its urbanization problems – that is the proliferation of overlapping local government boundaries. For example, the 1917 township remains as a small enclave – with its superior housing, tarred roads, concealed sanitation, and its more modern commercial buildings – separate from all other L.A.s. Apart from the township, the Kano L.A.'s area includes the entire conurbation, but this in turn is dividedinto what today are rather obsolete subordinate council boundaries, including the old-walled city of Kano and two town/district councils which are predominantly urban, but organized on the same principle as the rural councils.

However, one of the newly-created Area Councils is co-terminous with the boundaries of the statutory Kano Metropolitan Development Board. It is here that the long-run solution for providing a 'unitary' urban government may lie. Even now there is some degree of rationalization in so far as the D.O. designated as the 'Administrator' of the Township is the same person designated as the Chairman of the Kano Metropolitan Area Council, although the final degree of reorganization involved would probably necessitate the bypassing of the traditional authority – marking an absolute decline in their power.

Conclusions

In conclusion, a chapter of this length does not give scope for dealing with the details of any but the major aspects of 'reorganization' that has taken place under military rule up to 1974. The fact that one has had to review the changes being made in twelve rather than four local government systems has helped to exacerbate the problem. All one can do is to make a few general statements which will hopefully illuminate the major trends and perhaps hint at the area of future shifts in power. First, and perhaps implicit in the rather limited terms of reference for the reform committees, was the understanding that under civil war conditions changes could only be of a transitional, temporary nature, apart from the unscrambling of regional arrangements. Consequently, there still exist strong regional similarities, although the more detailed study of the three states show the emergence of distinctive state patterns, for example, the 'manager' system in the former Western State. Secondly, a common result of the changes made in the military period has been a watering down of the prestige and powers of local government *vis-a-vis* the 12 state bureaucracies. Almost all state provisions have marked a shift in powers, relative financial resources and manpower from the local authorities to the state ministries. This trend is likely to increase given the vastly increased revenue that the states now receive from the Federal Government as their shre of the oil revenues. The creation of seven more and hence smaller states in 1976 will serve further to increase financial dependence on the Federal Government.

References

1. Prior to 1967 the Federal Republic of Nigeria was composed of the federal capital of Lagos; the Western Region from which was carved the Mid-West Region in 1963; the Eastern Region; and the Northern Region – the largest covering four-fifths of the land area and over half the population. The immediate reaction to the State Creation Decree was the civil war which only came to an end in 1970.
2. For example, by 1965 all councils in the Western Region were suspended.
3. White Paper on the Udoji Public Service Review Commission whose terms of reference included the review of the Nigerian public services including local government administration.
4. See *South-East State Edict No. 12* (1969) which substituted Development Administration for local government.
5. For example, Kano L.A. in Kano State and Sokoto in the North-Western State represented authorities in which over 50% of the population reside and which accounted for over 50% of all resources going to local government.
6. See Franklin L. Blitz (ed.), *The Politics and Administration of Nigerian Government* (London: Sweet & Maxwell, 1965); M.J. Campbell, *Law and Practice of Local Government in Northern Nigeria* (London: Sweet & Maxwell, 1963); Gray L. Cowan, *Local Government in West Africa* (New York: Columbia University Press, 1958); G. Humes and Eileen Martin, *Structure of Local Government – A Comparative Survey of 81 Countries* (The Hague: IULA, 1969); Ronald Wraith, *Local Government in West Africa* (London: Allen and Unwin, 1964).
7. A.H.M. Kirk-Greene (ed.), *The Principles of Native Administration in Nigeria* (London: Oxford University Press, 1965).
8. Possibly the best general source reading on 'indirect rule' is to be found in Michael Crowder's *West Africa Under Colonial Rule* (London, 1968).
9. In 1900 the total number of British staff was said to be eleven, including Lord Lugard. See Sir Charles Orr, *The Making of Northern Nigeria* (London: Frank Cass, 1965). For an interesting discussion of the emirate system in non-emirate areas, see D.C. Dorward, 'The Development of the British Colonial Colonial Administration Among the Tiv, 1900 – 1949', *African Affairs*, 68,273 (1969), pp. 316–33.
10. R.E. Wraith, 'The Four-Dimensional Administration: Deconcentration, Delegation, Devolution and Decentralization', *Quarterly Journal of Administration*, 5,2 (1971).
11. See Michael Crowder, *op. cit.*
12. This region was never as ecologically or ethnically fragmented as

some writers have implied. For the more orthodox view see N.U. Akpan, *Epitaph to Indirect Rule* (London: Cassell, 1956) For a counter-view of the earlier period see Crowder Michael, *The Story of Nigeria* (London: Faber, 1966).

13. In addition to Lagos City Council there are the second-class Townships of Kano; Jos (Benue-Plateau State); Zaria (North-Central State); plus two new Townships created in Kwara State. A sixth Township was proposed for Maiduguri in North-East State.
14. K.J. Davey, 'The Changing Pattern of Local Government,' European Regional Conference, Oxford 1973.
15. See John Ballard, 'The Constitutional Impact of Administrative Structure, 1914–45', Ahmadu Bello University, mimeo, n.d.
16. Chief Awolowo, leader of the Action Group Party, did however stipulate that the chief should be professionally trained. Despite this, Tugbiyele observed – 'Within the last decade almost every third person is a chief of some sort'. *The Council*, 2, 2 (June 1963).
17. See Ursula Hicks, *Development From Below* (Oxford: Clarendon Press, 1961); J.P. Mackintosh, (ed.), *Nigerian Government and Politics* (London: Allen and Unwin, 1966), particularly Chapter 5 by Ronald Wraith; P.J. Harris *Local Government in Southern Nigeria* (Cambridge: Cambridge University Press, 1957).
18. The best source material on local government finance of this period remains, G.Oka Orewa *Local Government Finance in Nigeria* (Ibadan: Oxford University Press, 1966).
19. For a detailed treatment of local government in Northern Nigeria, see Campbell, *op. cit.* C.S. Whittaker, Jnr. *The Politics of Tradition, Continuity and Change in Northern Nigeria 1946–1966* (Princeton: Princeton University Press, 1970).
20. See, for example, B.J. Dudley, *Parties and Politics in Northern Nigeria* (London: Frank Cass, 1968).
21. It was not until 1963 that most N.A.s had elected majorities and then not directly elected.
22. See S.O. Osoba, 'Nigerian "Power Elite"' (mimeo, University of Ife, 1971) who states that from 1952 to 1965 'between 82% and 96% of the Northern House of Representatives and Representatives to the Federal House were different categories of N.A. Officials.
23. In order to assert its authority over the N.A., the Government made the powerful Kano N.A. a test case when it was dissolved after investigating in 1962. That is, N.A.s were granted freedom 'provided always that certain essential conditions are observed'. See Sir Ahmadu Bello, *My Life* (Cambridge: Cambridge University Press, 1962).
24. See Tunji Oyinloye, 'The Changing Role of Administrative Officers' (Zaria: Institute of Administration, n.d.).
25. See Adebayo Adedeji, 'Financing Local Government in Nigeria,' in A. Adedeji and L. Rowland (ed.), *Local Government in Nigeria* (Ife: University of Ife Press, 1972. All six states increased the L.A. contribution to the state from 12½% to between 20% to 25% (1968/9). When the Federal Government represented 45% of their revenue, this percentage had increased to 70% (1972–3).
26. Kano State remains intact following the 1976 state creations. [Editor].

Community Development: An Introduction

Community Development Departments, with agricultural extension services, are amongst the oldest 'development-oriented' administrative structures at the local level. Established after the Second World War by British colonial administrations, they reflected a new policy concern with social welfare and development at the community level, marked by the Colonial Development and Welfare Acts, as one means of directing rising African aspirations towards non-political activities. New Community Development Departments engaged themselves in a number of areas of activity, although emphasis varied according to the social structure, level of development and corresponding needs of the particular region concerned. In Nigeria, community development included literary work (especially in the North), specialized work with women or youth, self-help projects (in the East) and the encouragement of farmers co-operatives (particularly in the West). Thus activity ranged from the tackling of specific tasks or aspects of community welfare to multipurpose programmes aimed at the transformation of the social organization and values of the whole community. Emphasis in the colonial period was initially on social rather than economic development, particularly in the health and educational sectors. The organization of community development in the colonial period was also closely linked to certain ideological premises of the policies of 'indirect rule' and, after the Second World War, of decentralization and local self-government. Emphasis was placed upon the encouragement and co-operation of African leaders and voluntary associations in the evolving systems of local government and administration.

Thus the rhetoric of community development policy was a curious mixture of pre-Industrial Revolution, community ideals of democratic liberalism, and the Protestant and humanist ethics of self-help and improvement. Community development was conceived as a social process enabling individuals, as a group, to develop their abilities to solve collective welfare problems. Stress was placed upon the organization of community projects which would strengthen common commitment and group responsibility and encourage the emergence of leadership and managerial expertise. Finally, and more problematically, the community development approach emphasized that the local community itself should define its own development goals and formulate its own needs, government agencies providing the technical and capital inputs where necessary.

As an approach or a set method, feedback from early community development programmes had an important influence on the merging 'development administration' movement. In contrast to the pre-existing image of 'law and order' and tax collection administration, the involvement of government institutions in community development appeared – at least in theory – to mark a significant change in the scope and style of public administration, approximating to a new set of methods and even a whole new approach to development. The training of community development field workers sought to cast the trainee in a 'mobilization' role. Community development field workers were required to fulfil an intermediary function as general educators who explained to the community government programmes and projects aimed for example at improving levels of literacy, community health, farming methods, etc. At the same time community development workers, as 'outsiders', were expected to find an entry point to the local community related to peoples' perceived or 'felt' needs. In either case, it is also the task of the community development worker to encourage participation in planned projects. As a participatory approach to development, community development is faced with a number of challenges, most notably the inherited style of public administration with its tendencies towards authoritarianism and paternalism, but also those related to the complexities of matching local initiatives with government policies and proprities. An example is the surge in demand for education and community services after Independence, which placed great strains on government where it was expected to provide for the capital and recurrent (maintenance) costs. Although the community development movement had its origins in the terminal colonial period, it nevertheless appealed in certain ways to new national leaders, since its stress on the 'traditional' rural community, 'co-operation', 'self-help' etc . . . fitted well into the emergent 'nation building' ideologies. Thus Community Development Departments remained committed to the inherited rhetoric. Amongst the several activities loosely grouped together under community development – adult literacy, work with specialized groups like youth and women, the promotion of co-operatives etc. – 'self-help' projects remain an important and one of the more successful elements of community development in many parts of Nigeria as well as other Anglophone countries.

With the exception of 'self-help' projects, government-sponsored community development programmes have not always shown a spectacular record of performance. To some extent, the poor performance of some community development programmes may be explained by the nature of their underlying assumptions. The community development 'approach' is in fact more than a mere set of methods: it also contains a number of ideological assumptions about the nature and development of rural society. Like the inherited public enterprise system, many of the underlying policy premises are vague if not contradictory. In the case of community development, the inherited and unquestioned underlying policy premises include a rather vague image of the 'community' as well as a rather limited conceptualization of the'development' process. First, the community development approach takes as its basic unit the 'village' or 'community'. It assumes a homogenous community, with no social differentiation, elite and class formation, where a complete harmony and identity of interests exists. Such an assumption, however, is quite ahistorical since the community ideal is based upon a pre-colonial model of the village before it was destructured by the market and capitalist forces that accompanied colonial rule. Even in pre-colonial situation it might be argued that the assumption of village equality is fallacious. Equality in poverty does not mean the absence of social stratification, which in pre-capitalist societies may be based in other distinctions such as age or sex or position in relation to traditional hierarchies and statuses. It might also be argued that even the 'village' or 'community' rarely exists. The work cell in most parts of rural Africa is the family. The 'village' is a secondary unit which is only relevant where certain types of collective work have to be done or where there is mutual assistance between neighbours. The community development approach tends to exaggerate the performance of temporary co-operative arrangements of this kind.

Secondly, community development programmes tend to be vague about which groups they are addressing themselves to – the whole 'community' or specific sections such as the underprivileged and powerless or the rural elites. Assumed is the existence of some 'common good' or 'general interest', agreed upon under a tree through the 'palaver', 'baraza' or some other fiction of village democracy. These ambiguities about the techniques and methods of the community development approach notwithstanding, the basic idea of local self-government continues to exert a strong influence over the organization of the machinery of government in some parts. In the post-Independence context, a recurrent challenge has been that of integrating local community initiatives, where they exist into the national development effort. One solution has been to base the lowest local government unit at the community action level.

One of the most interesting local government changes was in eastern Nigeria. There, it will be recalled, a new democratic 'Community Council' level was created, endowed with resources and thus in a good position to act as a nucleus for local development energies released by post-war reconstruction. With the exception of dramatic changes of the latter kind where community development has been made the basis for a reorganization of local government and administration, the regular activities of functional Community Development Departments have not been characterized by very remarkable levels of performance. Resources (including finance for matching grants and supportive staff) have been meagre and community initiatives at times out of line with Government plans and priorities.

Some of the most spectacular cases of community development have in fact been of the pure 'self-help' type, organized from within a local community, without reference to any official agency and its resources. Although rare and sometimes shortlived, such instances are instructive in a number of ways. In contrast to community development doctrine, with its stress on local participation and collective decision-making, the initiation and growth of such projects has centred on a small core of activities, often led by a traditional ruler, an enterprising and efficient yet authoritarian figure who mobilized villagers through combination of physical sanctions and the controlling effects of religious institutions. The importance of village communal social organization in such cases also contrasts strongly with the vagueness of community development doctrine in regard to internal village social structure.

10. Local Government and Community Development in East-Central State

Michael Olisa

Rural development, in the sense of introducing and establishing modern infrastructural and social welfare facilities in the rural areas, started in Eastern Nigeria,[1] as in other parts of the country, with the British colonization of Nigeria, supported or supplemented by the other two well-known Western forces of Christianity and European commercial activities. As soon as the demarcation of each area of the country was completed and civil administration established, the earliest community development projects which followed were Christian churches, primary and secondary schools (Native Authority Schools in the Muslim North), and missionary or Native Authority hospitals and dispensaries. Local markets became the centres for the distribution and retailing of foreign manufactured articles which rapidly penetrated all parts of the country. The significant feature of rural development in these earlier periods (roughly between 1900 and the 1930s) was the passive and suspicious attitude of the rural population towards institutions and services which they regarded as strange and alien. Hence churches, dispensaries and local government stations were often set up on locations regarded as 'bad bush' (haunted by evil spirits) by the local communities, because it was only such pieces of land that the rural communities could willingly and collectively dispense with. Markets had often to function around community shrines after which they were also named. Some of these markets became produce buying stations for the several European trading companies which handled primary produce – mainly palm kernels and palm oil produced in these areas. If we regard this early period as the first phase of rural development in the Eastern areas of Nigeria, we would also describe it as one in which the government, the missions, and the trading companies were the moving factors in rural development.

The period from the 1940s to the 1960s could be described as the second phase in the evolution of rural development in Eastern Nigeria. This phase was characterized by increasing acceptance of Western culture and modes of economic livelihood. More and more people from the rural communities became involved in western economic activities in the fledging money economy and dispersed to the urban centres; many village youths joined the Christian churches, attended the mission schools and acquired formal education which fitted them for paid jobs in the missions, local and central government offices, and in the companies. It was this period that saw the emergence of the first generation of an African elite class conversant with the white man's ways and things and anxious to introduce some of these into their own rural communities. This phase also saw the coming to age of ethnic unions which started modestly to keep kinsmen together in a strange and heterogeneous urban environment, and grew later into agencies for popularizing Westernization as a vehicle for mobilizing home communities towards political and economic modernization. The 'improvement' or 'welfare' unions indeed dominated this period in the organization of rural development efforts. Some details of these efforts will be given later.

The rise of nationalism and a nationalist movement added a new twist to the concept and pursuit of rural development during this period. Nationalist sentiments sharpened demands for community development as a right to be expected from the government, and frequent letters to the editors of the local press carried such headings as 'We are Neglected', 'Obofia is neglected', 'More amenities please' in which the writers enumerated the social welfare and other services denied to their areas although the people there dutifully paid their taxes. These demands were carried over to the nationalist governments on the attainment of independence and woven into the whole make-up of national and regional party politics in the country. Promises of social amenities were easily made by politicians in return for election votes and general support, and such services were easily withheld from areas which did not support the reigning political party. There was the well-known story of drums of tar scattered on the roads on the eve of a general election, only to be removed quickly after the elections, particularly in areas where the government party did not win majority votes. The major determinant on which constituencies judged their representatives in the legislatures was the number of social welfare and other benefits which he secured for his community or area during his term of office.

On the part of government, this period, with its tremendous expansion in the scope of rural development demanded by the rural population, posed a problem of great magnitude. Each area wanted more schools, scholarships, roads, maternities, hospitals and so on for itself, but the revenue of the government was limited. The government had therefore to leave rural development in the hands of local people and concentrated more on giving advice, technical support and limited financial assistance to projects embarked upon by local communities. For rural water supply, for example, the then Eastern Region Government supplied engines, pipes and technicians after a certain portion of the estimated cost of the water scheme had been provided by the people. Unlike the early colonial period, therefore, the nationalist period was marked by high community and low government involvement in rural development; in other words the dynamic forces in rural development were rural communities and their ethnic associations, with government participating to a limited extent. In fact some rural development projects completed in this period were not supported at all by government, financially or otherwise.

The new rural development strategies which mark the third phase now emphasise almost fifty-fifty participation by local communities and government and much of the rationale is drawn from experiences of the second phase. There is also a declared intention to involve traditional unofficial structures (kindred, village, ethnic unions, age grades, etc)[2] more actively and more purposefully in rural development effort. Most of this essay will be devoted to this post-Civil War period; but in order to provide a clear background to this present period, it is necessary to look in some detail at the general pattern and organisation of rural development in the period which we have outlined earlier as the second phase.

Rural Development Strategy, 1940–66

The structures engaged in rural development administration in this period fall into two categories, namely the official structures (local government councils, Ministry of Rural Development of the Eastern Region Government, and the Regional Government itself), and the unofficial structures (villages, community improvement associations, age-grade associations, and the ethnic associations). To the official structures, rural development but was one aspect of developing and improving the general infrastructural and social welfare environment of the Region as well as the fulfilment of the government's commitment to social justice for all sections of the community. To the unofficial structures the emphasis was on more specific projects designed to raise the prestige and material welfare of a more restricted (ethnic, kinship, community) group. The difference in views is reflected in the pattern of rural development projects which were regarded as priority during this period. Communities and their unions showed more interest in community primary schools and colleges, town halls, scholarships, water supply, post offices and agencies, markets, hospitals, maternity clinics and dispensaries. The government and its agencies, while not openly hostile or lukewarm towards these areas of rural development, made efforts to stress such areas as rural agricultural projects based on co-operative arrangements, building and maintenance of roads, and adult literacy efforts, all of which did not in the main attract priority attention from the rural communities, even though they held them as desirable and frequently made demands for them from the government.

Community Improvement Unions

By the middle of the 1950s it was difficult if not impossibel to see any community in Eastern Nigeria which had not formed an improvement or progressive union. These unions were first of all formed in the urban centres by natives of the community living and working there; members in each urban centre constituted a branch of the parent body. The headquarters was usually the home town for sentimental reasons; but for practical operational purposes the headquarters moved from township to township with each annual election of officers of the association and the executive committee. In other words, the effective headquarters was the urban centre in which the general secretary or the chairman was resident. Occasionally one would find an association with a permanent secretariat based in one of the urban centres, with paid full-time staff.

Usually community improvement associations and their constitutions laid down accepted regulations with regard to membership (which was automatic for all 'sons of the soil' living and working 'abroad'); duties and privileges attached to membership (such as obligation to pay all levies, to submit to penalties arising from defaulting, and right to assistance from the association on occasions like death, illness or litigation); management of the funds of the association, and so on. The local chairman of each branch of the association assumed a paternal position *vis-a-vis* all natives of the home community living in the urban centre concerned, and there was hardly any boundary between the official and unofficial concerns of the association about its members. As long as there was a crisis or a serious problem, the union was qualified to intervene. Hence union advice, pressure, or support covered such areas as (a) financial support to members in difficulties, either as gifts or as loans; (b) moral or material assistance to members involved in court cases; (c) moral or material support to members faced with problems in their places of work or business; (d) pressure on eligible bachelor members to get suitable wives; (e) helping unemployed members to get jobs or young ones to get apprenticed in trades; (f) corrective measures or pressures on members with notorious characters or other undesirable habits; (g) organizing savings schemes in the form of thrift contributions for members either in common or in groups; (h) advice to members on voting strategy in elections.

In all these areas much responsibility was placed on members whom, in terms of wealth, or social, professional, and governmental positions, were better placed to achieve the goals of the association. Again in performing services for members the association hoped to ensure their solidarity as citizens of the home town and to mobilize them easily for all efforts towards group advancement.

Mention has been made of the range of projects towards which the improvement unions aspired. The following were among the more regular items: town halls; association almanacks with individual and group photographs of selected outstanding kinsmen all over the country; secondary schools; maternities, hospitals or dispensaries; post offices or postal agencies; local roads to ensure access to the home town and movement within it; funds for legal expenses arising from land disputes; scholarships at various levels, but mainly to sponsor promising kinsmen in higher institutions; local markets at home; water supply schemes; organization of periodical 'mass returns' when all 'sons of the soil' working and living abroad had to visit the home village with their families and take part in various public activities.

The choice of projects to be embarked on by the community concerned was usually made at the periodical general meetings of the improvement association and choice was influenced by what was regarded as most pressing or desirable at the time. During the period under review town halls were regarded as the most basic because they provided a symbol of the community spirit as well as convenient facilities for public meetings.

Perhaps the most important aspect of rural development efforts during this period was the organization of the financing of the projects selected by the community. Once a project had been chosen the financial burden was regarded as the general duty of all adults in the community, male or female female, at home or outside. Methods of extracting resources differed from community to community but the more regular ones included a general flat levy on all citizens, graduated or graded levy, voluntary donations, and sale of communal property. When a flat levy was adopted, distinctions were usually made between men and women, people at home and people abroad. The amount imposed on citizens abroad were usually higher than the amount paid by people at home, and those who lived outside often accepted this distinction without any argument, as they often had to support their relations at home because of the latter's lower income.

In the case of graduated levies the citizens of the community concerned were grouped into several categories demarcated by amounts regarded as proper or fitting to their income levels. In one case known to the writer the grades were something of the following order: Grade I (₦40 per person), Grade II (₦30 per person), Grade III (₦20 per person), Grade IV (₦14 per person), Grade V (₦10 per person). The persons looked upon as the community's most successful 'sons of the soil' were normally placed in Grade I; less prominent ones followed the other grades down the line. Most communities dropped graduated levies after some disappointing results; the system often sparked off bitter complaints about the grades to which persons who felt bigger or smaller were assigned, and this casued bitter divisions and poor yields. The administration of the grading system was also tedious and wasteful because many members took a long time to pay up.

Open donation became popular for many communities because it appealed to the competitive streak in people and it also carried a sense of personal prestige for the donor. Some improvement unions took the trouble to publish outstanding donations in the local press, besides making occasions for donations public ones, often held during the 'mass return'.

Sale of a community property as a source of funds for rural development schemes was not as common as the other sources. It was peculiar to communities in Ngwa, Ibibio, and Anang areas where there are large belts of wild palm trees which are harvested in common at specified times of the year. The palm nuts are sold publicly in bulk after they are cut, and the yield put into the development fund. During the forties and fifties several communities in these areas sustained, if only for limited periods, scholarship schemes at various levels of education.

Administration of the funds collected was entrusted to the executive committees of the improvement union of the community concerned and it is in this regard that a remarkable difference existed between the use of community funds and that of official local government councils. Smock[4] dealt at length with this point in his study of the Abrida Improvement Union. Officers of the unions were usually resident in the urban centres and were familiar with modern accounting and banking methods. Mainly because of the strong community spirit surrounding the fund, and partly for fear of public reprobation by their own people, those who handled these funds were scrupulously honest and careful. An official document on the Development Administration Edict of the former South-Eastern State commented as follows on this point: 'People scarcely misappropriate funds which they themselves voluntarily collect and entrust to others for social [development] purposes. They would regard that [misappropriation] as an abomination. But no such feelings existed among those who stole [local] council's money, because they had no real moral involvement.'[5] And in an intensive study of the activities of two prominent unions of the period under review, Audrey Smock also noted that: 'Officers of ethnic unions seemed more honest in handling funds and other responsibilities than Council members were in executing their charges. The same people who at least passively countenanced corruption in local councils were scandalised by hints of irregularities in ethnic union accounts.'[6]

Citizens found guilty of misappropriating community funds were subject to severe social reprisals and could be ostracized eventually, especially if they failed to restore the misappropriated money quickly. Although disputes over community funds hardly went to the courts of law, there were effective alternative measures for punishing culprits as well as recovering stolen or misappropriated funds, even in cases where the culprits could in the courts wriggle out through legal techanicalities.

Accounts of expenditure on development projects as well as progress reports on them were usually given at the annual general meeting of the improvement union, and it was on the basis of these that any further actions could be determined. The financial stress and strain which arose from projects depended on the numerical strength of the community concerned, the general income level of its citizens and the organizational efficiency of the improvement union. If the strains become too much, dissensions arose and the projects could be delayed or, in rare cases, abandoned. Strains of this type which arose over community scholarships caused financial disasters to several individuals sponsored in overseas universities in this period. As in all voluntary efforts a wide gap between aspirations and achievements is bound to occur from time to time.

Local Government Councils

At the beginning of the 1950s the Native Administration system of the early colonial era in Nigeria was, in Eastern Region, replaced with a modern local government system based on the British model. The Eastern Region Local Government Law of 1950 was modest in scope and content, but that of 1953 established a three-tier (Local, District and County Councils) system, with a wide range of functions and powers for the local authorities thereby created.[7] Their functions, which included layout of buildings, erection of schools, promotion of adult education programmes, building of markets and water supply systems, were clearly rural development functions. It did not take long, however, before clear differences emerged between the effectiveness of community improvement associations and the ineffectiveness of local government councils in rural development efforts. The councils proved after a period to be plagued by a number of handicaps such as: (1) their historical background of being a replacement for the N.A. system which was so notorious with the people on account of the greed, corruption, extortion and other excesses of N.A. functionaries; (2) the alien nature and complexity of the system which made it difficult for even the functionaries to understand it clearly; (3) the poor calibre of men attracted by local government politics. The educated elements, apart from the fact that they lived outside their home areas and therefore could not effectively participate, looked down upon positions in local government and adopted apathetic attitudes towards its affairs; (4) the inferior quality of staff employed by local government councils of all grades (in education, experience and performance local government staff compared very poorly with equivalent staff of the Regional Government's service); (5) the prevalence of corruption among local government councillors and staff. This caused general loss of confidence in every policy and every project put forward by local government councils; (6) the limited resources at the disposal of local government authorities at all levels, which was worsened by their low extractive capacity. Smock pointed out clearly that the extractive capacity of the councils was much lower than that of the community improvement unions,[8] where, for instance, citizens would even be reluctant to pay rates levied by local government councils.[9]

One of the general results was that local councils were tolerated as necessary evils imposed by the government. Another was that they were virtually isolated by both the communities and their improvement associations. As Smock illustrated: 'Over many years, the Ariba Community Improvement Union probably collected more resources from dues, donations and special levies than the Owuwa Anyanwu County Council received per capita from its local taxes and rebates'.[10] In terms of performance, these limitations set serious limits to what local councils could attain in the matter of community development. Not only that the projects which they often embarked upon were not those most popular with the communities, but that they were not able to muster sufficient resources to carry them out successfully. Even in the matter of education where they scored some good points, local authority schools were centres of low staff morale and unenthusiastic school population. Councillors were known to demand or extort bribes from teachers in matters like employment, deployment and promotions. Party politics also influenced the development planning of local councils.

The period 1940 – 1967 was extremely fruitful for development efforts initiated by voluntary organizations in the Eastern Region of Nigeria, particularly in the fields of secondary education and medicine. These rural development projects were looked upon as objects of pride and prestige for the communities which acquired them; hence the inauguration of each completed item was marked by much publicity and fanfare. Rural development activities ceased in the eastern states during the Civil War when these areas became the theatre of military operations and tremendous damage was inflicted on their infrastructural and other facilities.

Rural Development Strategies Since the 1970s

With the end of the civil war in 1970, the three eastern states (created out of former Eastern Region in 1967) were faced with the enormous problems of reconstructing economies and rehabilitating communities badly battered by the war. Concurrent with the programmes of state governments for tackling these heavy tasks was the Federal Military Government's Second National Development Plan 1970–74. The latter also emphasised the reconstruction of the war-battered areas and the necessity to integrate rural development into the development programme of the entire nation. In the eastern states, for whom the rehabilitation of the rural communities was more acute and urgent, rural development became something to be seriously and comprehensively planned, guided and encouraged. It was to this end that the machinery of local government in these states, hitherto legalistic and economically unambitious, became drastically modified and more development-oriented. This section of the study will dwell on the systems adopted in the former South-Eastern and East-Central States, and will examine the concept, scope, structure and the administration of each system as well as evaluate the results of the performance from the time of its inception.

Following the policy of instituting a development-oriented local government system, each unit of local government in the two former states under review has been officially designated a development area and officers in charge of those units are charged with responsibility for all development activities.[12] The East-Central State Divisional Administration Edict describes the Divisional Administration as '. . . a system of local administration intended primarily to co-ordinate the activities of the State Government functionaries in the Divisions and the local government in such a way as to ensure proper decentralisation of functions and active participation of the local people in the general development and management of their own affairs under the supervision of the Local Authority'.[13] The Division's development significance was made clearer in the 1972 Budget Speech of the Administrator of the State in which he pointed out that 'under the Divisional Administration each Division is named a Planning and Development Area, with a Development Committee headed by the Resident'. In the Administrator's words: 'The Structure we envisaged will provide the framework and the forum for maximum dialogue and consultation between Government and the people in the task of development'.[14]

The Development Administration Edict of the South-Eastern State describes the aims of community development as follows:

(a) The fundamental aim of community development is the purposeful removal of obstacles to the rational utilisation of such of the natural resources of a community as are capable of exploitation by the common effort of its inhabitants, conditioned by the financial resources at its disposal including such Government assistance, in cash or in kind or both, as the Military Governor, with the approval of the Executive Council, may deem necessary, having regard to the nature, complexity or extent of a community project.

(b) By community action through the Development Administration system the community shall participate directly or indirectly in the several areas of government activity for its economic and social progress and the citizens shall become increasingly aware and associated with the implementation of the policy and understand the working of the established machinery of the Government.[15]

From these official statements, it could be easily inferred that in both states, local government machinery is designed as a lever as well as a framework for rural development. Its expected results include (a) maximum utilization of local natural resources; (b) maximum understanding and co-operation between the communities and the state government; (c) provision of much needed infrastructural and welfare services and facilities.

A good indicator of the scope and expectations of rural development is the range of functions assigned to local government units. A total of forty-eight functions were assigned to the Community Council in East-Central State and these functions were grouped under Public Order (eighteen functions), Public Health (seven), Education (three), Agriculture (five), Roads (five), Trade and Industry (four) and Various Matters (six).[16] In the South-Eastern State the functions numbered forty-seven. These were grouped under Agriculture (two), Animals (two), Buildings and Other Structures (fourteen), Forestry (two), Liquor (one), Markets (four), Public Health (seven), Registration of Persons (two), Roads (thirteen), Public Order (two) and Various Matters (two).

The range of functions prescribed in each case is very wide and would, if executed to any considerable degree, result in termendous improvement in the quality of life of people in rural areas. The edicts establishing local administration in each state did not specifically name several of the most popular items – pipe-borne water, town halls, postal agencies and buildings. This does not mean that such items are not officially recognized or encouraged. It may be that practice made it unnecessary to include such items in the list of official functions because they have over the years been undertaken by the non-official structures in the local administration systems, notably the community improvement and the age-grade associations.

Looking at the two sets of functions (i.e. those of South-Eastern State and East-Central State) as presented in the official documents they not only seem rigid but are hardly different from those functions provided in the previous Local Government Law. The needed flesh was put on the dry bones of the language of an edict on the occasion of seminars organised by each state to expound and discuss the development perceptive of the new systems. It was on the occasion of the East Central State Seminar that the Administrator's new slogan of *Olu-Obodo* ('community work') was put across to the people. In his Budget Speech, which was published before the Seminar, he had stated: 'We must now reject for all time the concept of Government as a foreign institution standing outside the community and whose money, property and goals are not the direct responsibilities and concern of the community. The community is the Government, the Government is the Community. It is no longer correct not to describe the business of Government as 'Olu-Obodo! Government business is truly and properly 'Olu-Obodo'.'[17] Discussions at the seminar centred around the rural development aspects of the Divisional Administration Edict and details were given on the necessity and mechanism of co-operation between the new councils (divisional and community) created by the Edict.

In the South-Eastern State Seminar, the Special Committee which prepared the report of proceedings stated the following: 'The Development Administration System would generate in local people the desired impetus for self-help, community initiative and grass-root democracy. . . The emphasis on the system of single administration recommended is to shift the energies of the people from undue concentration on political activity to constructive development, particularly in the field of economic enterprise which would more quickly lead to the raising of living standards and building a healthy society.'[17] As in the case of the East-Central State Seminar, much time and pains were devoted to explaining the puzzling and rigid-looking aspects of the Development Administration Edict with a view to making it acceptable to both the official and non-official organizations among the communities.

The Structure of Rural Development Machinery

As has been stated earlier, the official instrument establishing the new development-oriented local government system in East-Central State was the Divisional Administration Edict of 1971. The Edict split the entire state initially into 35 (and later into 39) administrative divisions, each with its own Divisional Council and its own Divisional Officer or Local Authority for purposes of law and order. Within each division there are numerous communities varying in number according to the size of the division. Each community has its own community council, membership of which is made up from the number of kindreds in the various major villages in the community.[18] The Njikoka Division is made up of thirty-nine communities and one of these, Enugwu-Ukwu, has a community council of 32 elected/selected members chosen from the kindreds making up Enugwu-Ukwu. Membership of the Divisional Council is on the basis of one member for one community, and this member is often the chairman of the council of the community concerned. Unlike the Community Council, the Divisional Council cannot collect revenue directly from the people. All money collected by the Community Council is paid into the Government Treasury and disbursed according to regulations laid down by the state government.

At the state level the Divisional Administration Department is located within the Cabinet Office to oversee and co-ordinate the divisional administration system. All the divisional officers in the field report to the central department and take their instructions from it. In the divisions itself, the Divisional Officer (or Resident in the case of the urban centres) take precedence over all government field officials representing various units, e.g. the Divisional Agricultural Officer. The Resident or Divisional Officer is the Government on the spot, taking the salute at official ceremonies and taking responsibility for law and order in the Division. The new system is thus a two-tier (community and division) local government system as against the defunct three-tier system which was tried before the Civil War. Each division is officially designated a development area to encourage project initiation and implementation. A Task Force of various professionals under a trained engineer serves three divisions with men and technical equipment, (road graders, earth movers, etc). supplied by the state government. In recent years the Task Forces have not been very much in evidence owing to the fact that some divisions have embarked on raising funds for the purchase of some of the technical equipment. In Idemili Division, for example, levies ranging from ₦1,000 to ₦3,000 have been levied on individual communities according to their size for the purchase of a road grader which will quicken the pace of road building and maintenance in the Division. In the first two years or so following the end of the Civil War, Task Forces were very useful in emergency construction and supply services. Urban centres have their own urban councils, and are under Residents posted from the Divisional Administration at Enugu as sole administrators. Each urban centre is also a development area and is expected to encourage and co-ordinate official and voluntary development projects in the area.

In the former South-Eastern State the official instrument establishing the new local government system, also development-oriented, was the Development Administration Edict of 1971 (revised and enlarged in 1972 as Edict No. 7). The system was also two-tier consisting of County Development Areas that took charge of the urban centres in the state for purposes of development. The overall picture in the South-Eastern State was thus as follows: (1) Urban Development Area (with an Urban Development Council) (2) County Development Area (with a County Development Council) (3) Development Area (with an Area Development Committee.) The Urban Development Area was made up of wards and villages within the urban centre concerned, and membership of the relevant council was on ward and village representation except for the chiefs and government officials who are *ex officio* members. The County Development Area was made up of a number of Development Areas and membership of the County Development Council was based on selection from each village or a combination of villages within the component Development Areas. Chairmen of the Area Development Committees within the County Development Area were *ex officio* members of the Council. The Area Development Committee itself was made up of selection of one person from each village or a combination of villages within the Development Area concerned, plus all councillors of the County Development Council as *ex officio* members. The number of committee members for one Area Development Committee was limited to a maximum of 25, excluding the *ex officio* members.

Like the East-Central State, South-Eastern State created in the Cabinet Office at Calabar a Department of Development Administration for the purpose of supervision, control and co-ordination of field staff and activities relating to rural and urban development. This department was headed by the Co-ordinator of Development Administration, a former Secretary of the old Eastern Region Government, whose appointment clearly indicated the great importance the Government attached to the development administration system of local government. Each field administrative officer in the division was designated a Development Executive in charge of all the Development Councils and Committees within his Division. He reported directly to the co-ordinator in the Cabinet Office on matters relating to development and received directives from him.

Looking at the official structures for rural development in both states, one of the most important, as well as easily recognizable, innovations was the choice of the village in South-Eastern and the kindred unit in East-Central as the minimal unit in local government representation and participation. The South-Eastern Edict specified that the villages constituting a Development Area should have a natural social nexus and occupy contiguous territory.[19] In the case of the East-Central State the kindreds which constitute the communities, and on which representation in the community council is based, had already met those two requirements. In its average size the Community Council area in East-Central State approximates very closely the Development Area in South-Eastern State. But the most important point here is that in the local government schemes of the two states, the basic unit was structured to coincide with the natural or traditional social unit among the people concerned, and representation in the official local government councils was based on those natural units.

What this means in practice is that the size of each community council in East-Central State and each Development Area in the South-Eastern State was determined by the number of kindreds identifiable in the form of villages. Thus in Njikoka Division of East-Central State, Enugwu–Ukwu Community Council had a membership of 32 representing 32 kindreds making up Enugwu-Ukwu Community. In Abak Division of South-Eastern State, Ika Development Area had 49 villages constituting it. Selection or election was applicable in determining who should represent the kindred or the village, thus giving communities opportunity to apply the most locally acceptable or legitimate method of producing a representative.

In East-Central State the constitution of each community into a more or less autonomous development unit harnessed to rural development efforts the Ibo cultural features of achievement orientation, community assertiveness, autonomy consciousness and individuality. Apathy, mutual distrust and traditional animosities which hindered meaningful development efforts in the past seemed to be contained under the new system with its emphasis on a sort of grass-roots, communal democracy. These advantages arose from the removal, under the changed system, of the ambiguities and confusion which plagued the previous three-tier system. In the latter, at district or county council levels, communities of incongruous social and historical connections were arbitrarily lumped together. In the South-Eastern State the provision in the Edict that villages making up a Development Area should have natural social connections was based on the Government's consciousness of the problems implicit in the old system.

No discussion of the structures for the two development-oriented local government systems can be complete if it does not bring into focus the continuing significance of traditional, non-official structures in community development. The most prominent of these non-official structures are the kindreds, age-grade associations and the ubiquitous community improvement welfare unions, littered in hundreds all over the two states since the 1940s. Although neither the East-Central State Divisional Administration Edict nor the South-Eastern State Development Administration Edict mentioned these structures by name, each Edict made adequate provisions for them. Both Edicts (Section 115) stated that Community Councils and Area Development Committees could accept gifts of money from individuals or groups of persons for development or welfare projects, or other purposes aimed at improving the living conditions of the people concerned. The groups of persons refer to the improvement unions which, as has been pointed out earlier in this study, have borne, and still bear, the major burdens in initiating, organizing and implementing community development projects.

The detailed study by Smock[20] of the role and power of community improvement unions stands as the best analysis so far of the development potentials of these organizations. Although Smock based her study on Abriba Improvement Union, her findings easily apply to other such organizations throughout the former Eastern Region. In general the community improvement associations exist side by side with the official local government council of the area and often they work hand in hand in matters of community development.

Improvement unions are broadly of two categories – those formed by individual communities and those formed by a group of communities, e.g. Awka District Union, Bende Divisional Union. At each level the objectives often include the organization and implementation of rural development projects in the areas concerned, i.e. within the community or the division. The organization of the unions is the responsibility of elite sons of the communities who live in the urban centres and generate most of the funds for community development.

During the period 1940–66 these elite 'sons of the soil' showed little or no interest in official local government activities and politics owing to the structural and other weaknesses referred to earlier. Since 1970 their involvement in official local government has become remarkably common and serious. One of the reasons for this change of attitude is the communal homogeneity created by constituting each community – no matter its size – into an identifiable and district community council. Both the relatively uneducated kinsmen at home and the relatively well-educated brethren 'abroad' now see the development of their individual homelands as a common challenge and each completed item of development as an achievement of common pride. No day passes without news items in the press about the public launching of development projects in various communities, and similar publicity is given to completed projects. To heighten the emotional importance attached to these events, state commissioners (and very occasionally the state governors themselves) often feature in the public ceremonies. The media coverage of the rural development activities in one community immediately generates similar activities and publicity requests in other communities and, in the former East-Central State especially, occasionally generate unrealistic projects and targets.

Contemporary elite involvement is looked upon as a key advantage in getting access to the public media, in generating financial and other support from governmental circles. One can also argue that this is partly due to the fact that military rule has excluded party political activities, thus releasing more talents for rural development service. Communities also see the involvement of prominent 'sons of the soil' as a good advertisement. Thus many community and divisional councils as well as improvement unions are chaired by lawyers, doctors, pharmacists, contractors, graduate college teachers and the like.[21] Elite involvement has also, more than the pre-civil war days, brought closer and meaningful co-operation between the community improvement unions and the official councils. With the emphasis now heaviest on development, the official community council has been seen by many communities more and more as an instrument for giving official sanction to decisions taken by the improvement unions on development in the community. The money-raising ability of the community improvement union remains, as the Smocks pointed out, much higher than that of the official community council. Quite often the community improvement union, through its executive committee, takes part in selecting the chairman and other officials of the community and divisional councils. In a case observed by the writer, the nomination of the chairman of the community council was made in a general meeting of the community improvement union, and when the former incumbent objected he was made to withdraw by the collective pressure of the whole community who made it clear that they wanted a lawyer to fill the post. The new councils, for their part, have also in many places accepted the realities of their limitations and have relied heavily on the improvement union in getting through their councils' policies and programmes.

The Weakness of the New Strategy

In spite of all the credits which the new system has won in the two states under consideration, notably the popularization of the concept of a development-oriented local government, there are also serious weaknesses. These can broadly be grouped into financial and administrative.

Taking the financial weaknesses first, the most outstanding problem is the wide gap which often exists between goals and available resources for attaining the goals. Practical experience has now shown that while local sentiments have been met by constituting each community into a separate council, financial viability has been lost in the process. Very few, if any, of the community councils have generated sufficient funds to implement a meaningful proportion of the projects publicly launched. In the first assessment of the new system in South-Eastern State, the Co-ordinator described this situation as follows: ". . . At the end of the fanfare only a couple of hundred naira is raised; none of the high-sounding schemes got off the ground. Human efforts are best encouraged by definite achievements".[22] The last sentence in the quotation points to the fact that quite often the magnitude (in size and money) of the projects planned is terribly out of proportion to the resources, potential and actual, which the community concerned could generate. And yet there is a striking similarity in the assortment of projects that each community plans for itself. Populations of the village, which in two states have been constituted into separate community councils, range from a few hundred persons to tens of thousands. Because of the emotional importance attached to the identity of communities and to the projects embarked upon or completed, the obvious solution of amalgamating a few communities for purposes of effective development has not been adopted. Projects are duplicated in communities separated by only a few miles even though the inhabitants know these projects cannot be supported financially. Another obvious difficulty arising from this phenomenon of community individualism is that the state government's financial assistance is not easily attracted because of the numerous autonomous units which plan and execute community development projects. In order to do something for all, the Government in 1974 made a grant of ₦1500 to every community council in the state as assistance to community development generally. This sum of money could be no more than token assistance; it had more political value (every area is remembered) than development importance.

Management of development funds still presents numerous serious problems in spite of the new arrangements. In many communities collection and management of funds fall into the hands of unscrupulous persons and proper accounts are never given; development projects have been suspended in several communities because of this. In other cases the total costs of projects were underestimated, with the result that more and heavier levies had to be imposed, thus discouraging many members of the communities concerned.

Rigid bureaucratic procedures have been serious obstacles to many communities in the execution of projects, even when sufficient money had been raised. Under both systems – the divisional administrations of the former East-Central State and South-Eastern State – money raised by the communities had to be paid into the Government Treasury and withdrawn for development work under close security of the Local Authority i.e. the Resident or his deputy. Community councils were not allowed to spend more than ₦400 without the approval of the Treasury, and this approval could come only after tedious processes which often frustrated the semi-literate brethren in the urban areas. Recently modifications have been made in the financial procedures, resulting in an increase in the amount that local councils can spend as well as freedom of community improvement unions to bank their development funds and disburse them in consultation with government authorities. More could still be done to allow maximum local initiative in project execution and at the same time protect communities from the exploitation of unscrupulous persons. State government control of funds from local sources appeared to be too close. Community councils could retain only 20% of all amounts collected by them, 10% of the same amount going to the divisional council and the rest to the State Treasury. Similar provisions applied to urban councils, with the result that the executive capacity of the urban councils seems to be severely impaired in terms of maintenance of general infrastructural facilities.

In the case of administrative problems, the most significant one arises from the relationship between the divisional councils and the community councils. The divisional councils have not been given precedence over the community councils, with the result that the former is unable to plan development without the co-operation of the latter. In fact the high degree of autonomy allowed to community councils seems to have reduced the divisional councils to an assembly of delegates with more deliberative powers. And yet, if the divisional council is given more vitality, legally and financially, it can plan and tackle projects like water supply, rural electrification, rural roads, etc. which are cheaper when undertaken on a large scale. Such revitalizing of the division could then elimitate the uneconomic and effective development programmes so common now at the community level. Duplications of projects where amalgamation could be cheaper and quicker could also be minimized, and benefits from economies of scale could be secured by all communities with the division.

Administrative problems also arise in official circles where frictions are frequent between the co-ordinating centre and units in the field, as well as among categories of staff in the field. With the emphasis which the new system has given in each state to development and community initiative, a larger number of senior professional staff has been deployed in the field than in the past. Each divisional headquarters has now on its team the Divisional Officer (who takes precedence over all others), the Magistrate, the Divisional Police Officer, the Divisional Information Officer, the Divisional Education Officer, the Divisional Agricultural Officer, and the Divisional Tax Officer. In practice, serious frictions arose when all officers were requested to report to state headquarters through the Divisional Officer. As a step towards solving the problem, field officers were subsequently asked to report to the Divisional Administration Department at Enugu, but this measure has not altogether eliminated professional jealousy and sense of wounded pride.

At the lower levels, the junior clerks who are the secretaries of the community councils present peculiar problems. By the level of their formal education and experiences, they have not attained sufficient maturity to work with council members who are much older than they. During field investigation conducted on rural development administration in the two former states, the young clerks expressed clear dissatisfaction with their work; one of the senior divisional officers also confirmed this state of affairs.[23] The young clerks often went to urban centres for weeks after receiving their pay and came back again towards the end of the month; they resign at the slightest move to punish them. Lack of interest and experience of the clerk-secretaries have adversely affected the effectiveness of the community councils, especially in the matter of their credibility among rural population.

In both the East-Central State and the South-Eastern State, problems still arise in the matter of proper relationships between the officially-created community councils and the community improvement unions and role of traditional office-holders in the new system. The first problem became much diluted in both states by the increased participation of elite 'sons of the soil' in community council affairs. Although this did not remove altogether the age-long distrust of local councillors, the emphasis on development, and the strict regulation and supervision of councils funds and powers, left little room for old practices.

The role of chiefs in the new set-up seemed to present a more serious problem. The South-Eastern Edict[24] provided that chiefs and clan heads who resided within a Development Area might be selected as councillors and Committeemen. The East-Central State Edict[25] provided that traditional office holders might be selected as *ex officio* members of community councils and could vote only in committee meetings, not in council meetings. Both provisions did not prove popular among the traditional leaders in both states, and whatever feeling of rejection or frustration that arose from these measures was intensified in the East-Central State by the Government's recognition[26] of only three traditional rulers in the whole state.Under the former system of local government, traditional rulers were given sizeable proportion of the total seats in both local and county councils. From the then House of Chiefs, one or two were appointed ministers in the cabinet of the regional government. The chiefs in the state reacted to this in various ways, including public expression of their request for recognition of more chiefs. In a seminar[27] held at the University of Nigeria, Nsukka by the Rural Development Administration Unit in 1974, the chiefs who were invited to the seminar put across vigorously their case for recognition and for being given more meaningful roles in the new system. Attitudes of the chiefs who felt isolated or frustrated differed from area to area, but could be described as unenthusiastic, indifferent and sometimes obstructive. Whether their inclusion in the mainstream of community council activities would produce the opposite situation is still a matter of argument.

In conclusion, it could be stated that the divisional and the development administration systems for rural development are far-reaching innovations which have within the two or three years of their inauguration proved remarkable improvements on the old local government system. Both systems have adopted more rational units of local administration, especially at the community levels, thus giving the new units more legitimacy and acceptance in the rural communities. The new message of development has been enthusiastically accepted by both the urban and rural population of both states in spite of the over-serious problem of unit viability in terms of resource extraction, economy of scale and project execution. It can be easily argued that if enthusiasm in rural development is sustained, it could help eliminate some of the handicaps. Groups of communities could, for instance, initiate, implement and sustain co-operation in large-scale projects. The central issue seems to lie in this trend emerging, and in the state governments increasing the size of financial support for such economically meaningful projects when once assessed and adopted.

References

1. The former Eastern Region was later divided into three states. Until 1976 these were Rivers State, South-Eastern State and East-Central State. This chapter concentrates on the former South-Eastern and East-Central States, although some general references would be applicable to all three as parts of the former Eastern Region.
2. East-Central State, *Divisional Administration Edict, 1971*; South-Eastern State, *Official Document No. 7, 1972.*
3. Direct help in paying bridewealth is not uncommon, but unions have laid down amounts for members, e.g. on their wedding or the naming of their child.
4. Audrey C. Smock, *Ibo Politics* (Cambridge Mass: Harvard University Press, 1971), p. 190.
5. South-Eastern State, *Official Document No. 7,* p. 10.
6. Smock, *op. cit.,* p. 194.
7. These two laws are reproduced in P.J. Harris, *Local Government in Southern Nigeria* (Cambridge: Cambridge University Press, 1967), pp. 141–3.
8. Smock, *op. cit.*, p. 190.
9. East-Central State, *Official Document No. 8. 1973,* p. 11.
10. Smock, *op. cit.,* p. 190.
11. These pieces of land were often the 'bad bushes' which were dreaded and used by the indigenous communities for dumping evil things, e.g. corpses of people who died from diseases considered abominable, dangerous sacrifices and bad fetishes.
12. For example, South-Eastern State, *Official Document No. 7 of 1973,* p. 17.
13. East-Central State, *Divisional Administration Edict (No. 18) of 1971,* p. 6.
14. East-Central State, *Budget Speech 1972,* p. 7.

15. South-Eastern State, *Development Administration Edict, 1972*, p. 14.
16. East-Central State, *Budget Speech of 1972*, p. 11.
17. South-Eastern State, *Official Document No. 7 of 1973*, p. 8.
18. For example see the instrument establishing community councils in Njikoka Division. East-Central State *Extraordinary Gazette No. 54*, December 1971.
19. South-Eastern State, *Development Administration Edict (No. 7) 1972*, p. 5.
20. Smock, *op. cit.*
21. For example in Idemili Division the community councils of Nkpor, Obosi and Ideani are chaired by lawyers and in Nnewi Division a pharmacist is the chairman of Oraifite community council.
22. South-Eastern State, *Official Document No. 7 of 1973*, p. 21.
23. Group meeting at Mgbidi Divisional headquarters with the field staff and community leaders, mostly chairmen of the various community councils. The meeting was an assignment by the writer on behalf of the Rural Development Administration Research Unit of University of Nigeria, Nsukka.
24. South-Eastern State, *Development Administration Edict No. 7 of 1972*, p. 11.
25. East-Central State, *Divisional Administration Edict 1971*, p. 22.
26. The traditional rulers recognised were the chiefs of Onitsha, Arochukwu and Oguta. Government recognition carries with it higher official status than other chiefs, and also an annual stipend from the state government.
27. University of Nigeria. Seminar on Rural Development Administration, September 1974, organized by the Rural Development Administration Research Unit.

11. Communalism and Rapid Economic Development Amongst the Holy Apostles of Western Nigeria

Stanley Barrett

Olowo was founded in 1947 by Yoruba-speaking fishermen, and by 1969 had a population of over 1,200.[1] The village is located at the edge of the Atlantic Ocean in an area called Ilaje, which is part of the Western State of Nigeria. During the wet season most of Ilaje is covered with water, houses are built upon stilts, there are no roads, and the main mode of transportation is canoe. Olowo is separated from the Yoruba mainland by about 50 miles of swamps and rivers, but in spite of its isolated location, harsh environment and brief existence, it has enjoyed unusual economic success. Shortly after the community was founded, a network of boardwalks on stilts was erected to connect every house. Bicycles, motorcycles, and even eventually a car for the *oba* (king)[2] were operated on them. This was a major innovation in Ilaje, for not only were there no bicycles in the other villages, but in order to move from one house to another it was necessary to enter a canoe. As early as 1953 the community had purchased a generator for electricity; even in 1970 only two other Ilaje villages enjoyed this amenity. Within a few years several factories had been established, almost twenty large passenger boats (servicing the rivers and lagoons from Lagos to Cameroon) had been built, as well as seven fully-mechanized ocean-going fishing trawlers – with almost no help from outsiders. As early as 1951, only four years after Olowo was established, it was described as Nigeria's most successful case of village-level development.[3] By 1957 it was said to have the highest standard of living of any village in the country.[4]

One possible cause of Olowo's success was its religious beliefs. The village emerged from a protest movement against the killing of twins in Ilaje that began about 1942 and eventually produced almost fifty theocracies. Olowo people, who became known as the Holy Apostles, formerly were Cherubm and Seraphims, which is a branch of the Aladura independent church movement that is widespread among the Yoruba.[5] Olowo people themselves contend that their economic success was a result of their religious beliefs.

Another possible cause was the village's communal social organization. In 1948, one year after the village was founded, communalism was introduced. All personal possessions such as cash, jewellery, and watches became community property. Apparently even the extra clothing that wealthier members had brought with them was taken from them and distributed among those in need. From that point onwards no money was exchanged among members for goods or services. People worked in large groups on projects selected by the village leaders, and all profits went to a central treasury. In turn, everyone was provided with food, clothing, and housing. Food that could not be produced by the people such as yams, plantain and rice was brought in bulk by a trusted woman known as the community mother. Periodically clothing was distributed, and a small building called the Community Shop stocked minor items such as flash-light batteries and soap, which were provided without payment. The communal system also affected the family. Not only did the wealthy have to relinquish their extra clothing, but men who had been accompanied by two or more wives were allowed to retain only one; the others were distributed among men who had no wife. This policy was necessary because apparently more men than women had joined the community. At two different periods marriage was banned entirely. Even when it existed, husband and wife did not live together, because the village was split into male and female sectors separated by the central boardwalk. Although the rule was not enforced absolutely, children over five years old were not allowed to be raised by their own parents. Even before this age they spent most of the day in the kindergarten apart from their parents. The result of all these policies was to reduce the strength of the family and foster the communal system.[6]

A third possible cause was Olowo's political organization. The village was not a democracy. A small group of men, led by the *oba,* constituted the elite and ruled with an iron hand. Religious and political authority were highly correlated, for those among the elite were the most powerful prophets in the village. The vast majority of members had no voice in their education, occupation, or choice of spouse. These decisions were made by the elite, who also directed economic activities, and took an active interest in social control. Laziness, disobedience and other forms of deviance were severely punished.

How can we measure the influence of these factors on Olowo's economic success? Although Olowo emerged from a religious movement in Ilaje that produced numerous small theocracies, it was the only one to achieve unusual economic success. I undertook a comparative study with one of the other theocracies, which I call Talika, whose population in 1970 was about 900. Located about twelve miles along the coast from Olowo, Talika had been founded by a prophet who had been a charter member of Olowo in 1947 but decided to leave in 1950. His decision was partly based upon his unhappiness with the communal system that had been adopted, and partly because he wanted to be the leader of Olowo. Several members of Olowo followed this man to the new village.[7] Olowo and Talika were similar in terms of religious and political organization. Both have their roots in Cherubim and Seraphim, and emerged from the protest movement against the killing of twins. Members of the two villages claimed that their religious beliefs were identical, which I found to be essentially correct.

Talika, too, was led by an *oba* and a handful of men who were the most powerful prophets. The outstanding difference between the villages was that Talika was organized in terms of private enterprise. People kept the profits from their work, and the extended family, which had not been suppressed, was the basic economic unit.

In this essay I shall focus upon the communal system. Because it was the basic difference between Olowo and Talika, it might appear to be the key factor in Olowo's success. My argument, however, is that while its contribution was important, it was likely no greater than religious beliefs and political organization. This has significant implications for the comparative method. While constants such as religion and political organization cannot by themselves explain why Olowo was successful and Talika was not, they cannot be eliminated, and indeed may be as important or more important than inconstants such as economic organization.

Finally, while communalism, religion, and political organization were the key sociological factors in Olowo's economic success, a number of other factors also were involved, the most important of which was the personality of the *oba.* He was a brilliant, innovative, awe-inspiring man, both loved and feared by his subjects: many of the innovations in Olowo, including the communal system, can be traced directly to him. In 1963 he died. The man who succeeded him was less capable, and during his reign the rapid expansion of the economy ceased. The second *oba* fell ill, and in 1966 was replaced by a younger man who struggled to revitalize the economy, but never succeeded. This was due more to the fact that Olowo was a generation older than to the *oba's* leadership qualities, for the force of the beliefs that had held the Apostles together had begun to diminish.

Economy

The main occupation in Ilaje in the past was fishing – both in the ocean and in the freshwater rivers and lagoons. Only men were allowed to fish in the sea, operating with net from large canoes. Both men and women fished in the inland waters, which were highly regulated. For example, nets could not be used at the time of year when fish were carrying eggs. Inland fishing also was differentiated by sex: certain types of traps were used to catch 'women's fish' and could not be used by men. Fishing rights to specific sectors in the rivers and lagoons belonged to specific lineages. Some men also made a living from cutting timber and tapping palm vine,and women from making mats out of palm raffia, but except in Olowo there has been virtually no industrial growth in Ilaje.

When founded in 1947 Olowo too was dependent upon fishing. At first dug-out canoes were used, but in a short time enough funds were accumulated to allow the purchase of outboard motors and better fishing gear. Then in 1963 the village built the first of its seven fully-mechanized sea-going trawlers. In 1969 a large ice-making machine was imported in order that the trawlers could range further into the sea and remain out longer without fear of the catch spoiling. In 1969 fishing was still the main industry in Olowo, absorbing 37% and 56% of the men and women respectively (see Table 1).[8] Each trawler had two crews, but only when fishing was good did both of them work on a single day. About 40–50 men still fished in large canoes with motors. While their catch could not compare with that from the trawlers, it was similar to the catch obtained by other villages along the coast. There was a tendency for the older and less educated men to work in the canoes. As in traditional Ilaje society, fishing in Olowo was differentiated according to sex: only the men went to sea, while the women dried and marketed the fish.

Another major occupation was the launch passenger service that Olowo established. The first launch was completed in 1955 with the help of men who had been hired from the mainland. After this the community constructed about twenty large launches on its own, which plied westwards throughout the swamps to Lagos and – prior to the Civil War – eastwards as far as the Cameroons.

In addition to the fishing and passenger industries, several factories gradually were established. The first to appear were the weaving, shoe, and tailoring industries. While at the beginning the equipment used was crude, by 1969 all had modern machinery. For example, the weaving department began with home-made hand looms, which were eventually replaced by ten automatic looms. Raw cotton was made into cloth, dyed, and transferred to the tailors. The shoe factory was first located in a small house with only manual equipment. In 1961 a new factory was built, and equipped with up-to-date machinery imported from abroad. The tailoring industry grew from a few manual sewing machines to twelve electric machines in 1959, as well as numerous manual ones. In early 1960 a bakery was established. Unlike the older factories it was equipped with modern machinery at the outset.

In Talika the main occupations were fishing and trading. Over 43% of the men were fishermen, which was slightly higher than the proportion of men in Olowo who did this work.[9] Talika people had no fishing trawlers, although some men had outboard motors. A number of Talika men also were traders, although 27% of them only traded part-time. In Olowo 50% of the women worked in some capacity connected with fishing, while in Talika only 15% did so full-time. The difference was the result of the much greater catch in Olowo, made possible by their seven fully-mechanized trawlers. Another significant difference was that all Olowo people worked on community enterprises, most of which kept them in the village, whereas 40% of Talika men worked at least part-time outside the village. This indicates the restricted opportunities of work in Talika, and suggests that it was a less closed community than Olowo.

The two main sources of income in Olowo were the fishing and transport industries, which according to one of the best educated men in the village produced an annual income of approximately ₦220,000. The same member estimated that the annual income of the remaining industries was only about

₦10,000. Yet these industries contributed by providing products for the village such as clothes, footwear, and bread that would have had to be purchased outside the community at a higher price. They also provided a variety of work for members, and created outlets for leadership aspirations, which may have reduced the temptation of the youth to run away.[10]

Table 1
Occupations in Olowo

	Male		*Female*		*Total*	
	n	%	*n*	%	*n*	%
Fishing	158	36.8	111	56.3	269	46.0
Passenger Boats	54	12.5	22	11.1	76	11.9
Carpentry and Boatbuilding	55	12.8	–	–	55	6.6
Tailoring	17	3.9	11	5.5	28	4.7
Shoemaking	10	2.3	8	4.0	18	3.1
Sawmill	9	2.0	–	–	9	1.0
Bakery	5	1.0	2	1.0	7	1.0
Weaving	5	1.0	5	2.5	10	1.8
Soapmaking*	4	0.9	8	4.0	12	2.0
Laundry	1	0.2	8	4.0	9	2.0
Other **	88	20.5	18	9.1	106	15.0
Unknown***	23	5.3	4	2.0	27	3.6
Total	429	99.2	197	99.5	636	98.7

* The soap factory actually has been abandoned, but in 1970 the myth persisted that the industry would be revived, and hence members insisted that those formally assigned to this industry should be shown.

** Consists mainly of making mats out of palm raffia (women's work), jobs in the technical workshop, schools, and community hotel, and occupations involving only one or two people, such as the medical dispenser and postal agent.

*** Consists of those who had several jobs, which made it hard to classify them.

A high percentage of the total income of the various industries was reinvested in the economy. This was made possible by the strict ascetic life-style led by the Apostles for the first several years. For example, the basic food eaten then was cassava and fish. Clothing was limited to simple working uniforms made out of khaki, and a suit of clothes to be worn when a person was not working. Shoes were considered a luxury, and were rarely worn, and there was rule against having a wristwatch or jewellery of any kind. The self-reliance of the Apostles also contributed to the high percentage of the income that was re-invested in the economy. They caught their own fish, some of which was traded for cassava. They eventually made their own shoes and clothes. They cut the timber for their houses in the surrounding forest, and did their own carpentry work. As a result, the income from selling fish to outsiders and from the passenger boats was not seriously depleted by purchases of consumer goods.

Table 2
Occupations in Talika

	Men			*Women*	
	n	*%*		*n*	*%*
Fishing only	35	43.7	Making mats	18	47.3
Trading only	4	5.0	Trading fish	6	15.7
Fishing and Trading	22	26.7	Making mats and trading fish	6	15.7
Other	19	23.0	Trading (not fish)	3	7.8
Unknown	1	1.0	Other	5	13.0
Total	81	99.4		38	99.5

Origin of Communalism

Before suggesting the manner in which the communal system contributed to Olowo's economic success, I shall try to explain why it was adopted in Olowo. To my knowledge, the only community in West Africa that was organized communally, had no private ownership, and did not use money among members was the Sect of the Second Adam in Ghana.[11] Although little data are available for this community, it apparently did not enjoy unusual economic success. The Sect of the Second Adam existed about fifteen years before Olowo adopted communalism, but it is doubtful that anyone in Olowo knew of its existence. Some collective economic behaviour existed throughout West Africa that might have acted as a model. Ames,[12] for example, describes the co-operative work groups among the Wolof of the

Gambia and Senegal, and Goody[13] documents a similar phenomenon in Ghana. In a comparison of Ghana and Uganda, Brokensha and Erasmus[14] found that self-help work parties existed in pre-colonial times, and that these have been fused with present-day community development projects. In Nigeria communal work projects and contribution clubs are prevalent among the Igbo. The Yoruba themselves are not devoid of collective economic activity; the *esusu* is a contribution club similar to that found among the Igbo, and among both ethnic groups co-operative farms have been established for several years. While these are not necessarily an expression of indigenous communal behaviour, they indicate that such models are not absent.

Schwab[15] has shown that within traditional Yoruba society itself the Yoruba lineage has semi-communal functions. Although lineage members did not normally work on a collective basis, they did help one another at certain stages in the farming cycle, and for large-scale projects such as the construction of a house. Moreover, the lineage was responsible for contributing goods and services during ceremonial occasions such as a marriage or a festival. Within Ilaje itself there was some communal activity. For example, villages co-operate with each other to clear the shallow rivers and canals that lead to larger waterways in the interior and from there to the mainland. Each village is usually assigned a section of the river to dredge.

It is clear, then, that communalism is not alien to West Africa in general, to other parts of Nigeria, or even to Ilaje. The crucial factor, however, concerns the range of communal behaviour. The collective work gangs among the Wolof, the Lo Dagaba, the Igbo, and to a lesser extent among the Ilaje are hardly comparable to the Olowo case, for they amount to a small fraction of economic activities. In Ilaje, for example, one may contribute less than half a dozen days in a year to communal work. In contrast, almost all economic activity in Olowo consists of labour devoted to communal work projects or to the various industries, with the profits being claimed by the treasury. Moreover, phenomena such as the contribution clubs and a few days of communal work do not modify the basic structure of the economy. People continue to be motivated by an economic system that gives priority to a self rather than a collective orientation. What this means, I suggest, is that the decision to establish communalism in Olowo cannot be explained in terms of pre-existing models.

Olowo people themselves stressed that before the village was founded they had no idea they would adopt communalism. Some of them siad it was done in order to copy the model of the early Christians. Yet no other Ilaje theocracy adopted communalism, which suggests that the early Christian model was not crucial to the religious movement in general. Other people said that the communal system was the idea of the first *oba*. While I think this is correct, it invites a significant conclusion: the communal system – and hence the economic growth of Olowo as well, assuming that communalism was a necessary cause - was basically fortuitious. Given the emergence of a village like Olowo in similar circumstances in Ilaje or elsewhere again, the probability of communalism being adopted is negligible, for it was a stab in the dark by a single individual.

Contribution of Communalism

A major contribution of the communal system in Olowo was to make labour and capital available to a central administrator who could direct them to specific economic ends. An enormous amount of work was accomplished within a few years of the founding of the village. The houses were built on stilts, an entire network of broadwalks linked every dwellings, and a canal seven miles long had been dug by 1949 that connected Olowo to the large rivers and lagoons in the interior. Without the supply of labour to the *oba* it is improbable that these feats could have been realized. The communal system also made the projects economically feasible, for the workers were supplied only with food and clothing. If it had been necessary to pay them a regular salary, this alone would probably have ruled out the projects. The profits derived from the labour of several hundred people in the fishing industry – who accepted only basic living necessities – were retained by the community treasury, rather than divided among the workers. As a result capital was soon available for investment in the economic infrastructure.

By making labour and capital available to the *oba,* the communal system allowed *early* innovations to be introduced. Funds were used to buy machinery necessary for improving the fishing industry and expanding the range of industry. For example, nets, boats and outboard motors were purchased, and in 1953 a generator for electricity was bought. This encouraged the mechanization of industries such as shoemaking and tailoring and led to greater production. Because people still did not receive a wage for their work, the returns of the investment were quickly realized.

Organization and Motivation of Work

Any explanation of Olowo's economic success that failed to consider the efficient manner in which the activities of the people were organized and their willingness to work hard would be inadequate. Almost every hour that a person was awake was devoted to work that had been organized by the leaders. People toiled in large gangs at the beginning, but as the economy became more diversified and complex, work gradually was organized in three distinct patterns. The most important was departmental work. Every major industry such as fishing, weaving,and boat-building became a separate department. All adults of both sexes were assigned to a particular department, and even children of primary school age were included. After school was closed at 2 p.m. each child had to report to a specific department. While I am not certain, I think this usually was the department to which the child's guardian (i.e. landlord or landlady) had been assigned, rather than the child's mother or father. This permitted an early apprenticeship and helped to socialize the children into collective working conditions.

A second pattern or work was carried out in large gangs. While this type was dominant when the village was first founded, its importance declined after the departmental structure emerged. However, communal labour continued to occur whenever a job existed that was too big for a particular department, or was not the direct responsibility of a specific department. For example, people were often summoned to help the boat-builders draw the fishing trawlers up on land for repairs, or to cut the long grass that quickly grew around the village. In 1970 communal labour occurred on an average of twice a week in the dry season.

A third pattern of work involved individual labour. For example, before the factories opened in the morning, and after they closed in the evening, people often waded into the sea with nets. The fish that they did not eat were sold in the village market to outsiders or in nearby markets. Some members kept chickens and ducks and attempted to grow oranges and bananas. This was the only type of work in Olowo that was not a collective enterprise addressed to a specific aim and chosen by the village leaders. The profits from all three types of work were claimed by the central treasury.

While in the conclusion I shall suggest that several factors – including the political organization, the personality of the *oba* and the religious base of authority – contributed to Olowo's efficient organization, the communal system was extremely important in this regard. Communalism *per se* does not lead inevitably to good organization, but is a social type conducive to it. If private enterprise had prevailed in Olowo, it is unlikely that the outstanding projects such as the canal would have been completed. The obstacles to organize hundreds of people and to persuade them to co-operate would have been insurmountable. Virtually every other village in Ilaje illustrates this argument.

Not only were Olowo people well organized, but they also worked exceptionally hard, as reflected in the following descriptions of a typical day of communal work and a typical day of a particular member. My example of communal labour is a road-building project. In 1970 there was a plan to replace the board-walks built upon stilts with cement roads. This was achieved by digging into the swampy ground and transferring the earth to the site of the new road, where it was pounded into a smooth surface. On the evening before this particular communal work was done, the town-crier circled the village and announced the project. At dawn of the next day approximately 600 men and women gathered at one edge of the village. From then until dusk they toiled with hardly a break, not even stopping completely to eat. Instead individuals would take a few minutes to drink water or eat the food provided by a group of women who had set up a makeshift kitchen next to the work site. The work force was split into three gangs, each of which was given an equal portion to complete. In spite of the tremendous heat, the pace maintained was furious. The three gangs competed with each other to see who would finish first. On this particular occasion the leader of one gang periodically shouted encouragement. The result was astounding: a couple of hundred people who had been labouring without break for hours would begin to run back and forth carrying huge loads of mud. By the time darkness fell a stretch of road about 150 yards long had materialized from the swamp. To put this in perspective, the nearest village to Olowo is not able to muster the will and co-operation in order to construct a narrow footpath from the main river to its primary school. In the wet season students and teachers must force their canoes as close to the school as possible, then trek through the mud the rest of the way.

My example of a particular member is one of the village's school-teachers. At the time the data were collected, he usually rose at four a.m. and went to the technical school to teach four technicians who were preparing for examinations. At five he returned to his house and bathed. At six he attended a meeting in the palace during which the day's activities were discussed. At eight he began to teach in the secondary school, continuing until it finished at two p m. Then he returned to eat at his house, rested until four (unless there was communal work) and made his way once more to the technical department where he taught the same technicians until six p.m. From six until nine he taught in the evening school. If he had a spare period he may have had time to eat. If not he would take his meal after nine, and try to get to bed by 10 or 11 p.m. While this young man's case was slightly extreme, most other members also worked with great determination. For example, the other teachers in the secondary school carried a full load in both day and evening sessions, took in any communal work that occurred, and contributed what time remained to fishing or to some other economic activity.

Conclusion

Olowo's remarkable economic success was partly a result of the communal system, which led to early innovation and to the efficient organization of village activities. Communalism also was a source of motivation for the Apostles. One reason that they worked so hard was that any collective activity in Olowo was considered to be moral activity. Some Olowo people even told me that communalism was their religion. They said that in spite of the numerous religious organizations such as Anglican, Cherubim and Seraphim, and traditional Ilaje beliefs in the surrounding villages, these villages were without religion. This must be the case, they argued, for the outsiders were not organized along communal lines. The remarks of Olowo people can be interpreted to mean that communalism occupied a central position in the village's value system. It may even be suggested that Olowo's communal system was a greater source of motivation than Talika's private enterprise system: not only did an Olowo person interpret the community's interests as one's own interests, but because a lazy person caused everyone to suffer, the sanctions against such behaviour were severe.[16]

Nevertheless, the main reason that I argue that communalism was not the key factor in Olowo's development is that there were more important sources of motivation, such as religion. Olowo was founded mainly for religious reasons and the basic religious values were salvation and immortality. In 1947 Olowo people believed that their prophets had defeated death. This explains at least partly why they do not take their dead to the traditional burial grounds in Ilaje, and do not have a burial ceremony or a marked burial ground. Indeed, burial is carried out under the cover of darkness, and a member's death is not a legitimate subject of conversation. The power of the prophets is reflected in their capacity to learn God's will through dreams and visions, to communicate with the holy spirit through *ede* or glossolania (sometimes called angel language in the village), and to cure sickness through prayer, or with water that had been blessed.

The basic religious values in Talika also were salvation and immortality, and they too did not have a burial ceremony or marked burial ground. Visions, *ede,* and spiritual healing also were characteristic of their beliefs. The main difference was that only in Olowo was it argued that hard work and economic progress were a measure of faith and hence a means to immortality. This is a crucial difference between the two villages, but the explanation of it is much too complicated to be attempted in the remainder of this essay.[17] All that I shall suggest is that for a number of interrelated factors, the prospects of rapid economic development became realistic in Olowo. At that point most aspects of the social structure and the belief system – including religion – became articulated with the goal of development. This is not to deny that development itself may have been conceived of as a means to achieve religious superiority over other Ilaje theocracies and thus ultimately could be seen as a political phenomenon.[18]

Economic development did not occur haphazardly in Olowo. Instead it was pursued with great deliberation and with single-minded dedication. The centralization of power and authority was crucial in this regard. It partly explains why the *oba* was able to introduce innovations such as communalism and why his subjects were prepared to work so hard. Quite apart from the religious connotation of work, the leaders had the authority to publicly flog lazy people and to refuse them food. Religion is important in this context because it was a base for power and authority. Given the spiritual strength of the prophets, Olowo people were afraid to disobey them. Religion also contributed to social control in general. For example, the third *oba* once told me that the only reason he held church services was to make sure his subjects behaved well; by limiting disorder, religion indirectly contributed to the village's economic success.

While Olowo and Talika were similar in terms of political organization, there was a significant difference in the manner in which authority was exercised. Talika people were free to choose their job, education, and spouse. They also could leave the community at will, which was not allowed in Olowo. In other words the Talika *oba* had much less control over his subjects than his counterpart in Olowo. Whether this was due to personal capacity or interest is difficult to tell, but my judgment is that the greater authoritarian nature of Olowo can be traced to the differences in the personalities of the two leaders. The effects of the Olowo *oba's* personality can be seen on virtually every factor that contributed to Olowo's development. It was he who introduced and institutionalized the communal system. Because of the fear which he inspired in his subjects, he also was instrumental in controlling deviance and persuading his subjects to accept an ascetic life style.[19]

Two other important factors in Olowo's development were the village's technical workshop and the available economic resources. Founded in 1953 by the first *oba,* the workshop was soon equipped with modern machinery. Many Olowo people became expert electricians, welders, plumbers, etc., and were able to install the machinery in the factories, maintain the equipment in good running order, and even perform the sophisticated work involved in the construction of the large passenger launches and the fishing trawlers. Olowo was fortunate in that two potentially lucrative economic enterprises were available for exploitation: the passenger service on launches throughout the swamps and fishing in the ocean. However, Talika and the other villages in Ilaje also had access to these resources. The crucial problem again concerns motivation: why was it that only Olowo was unusually successful in taking advantage of these resources?

In recent years Olowo has been transformed. In 1968 private enterprise was introduced, and by 1972 hardly any communalism remained. At the same time the family became legitimate once more, and husband, wife and offspring began to live in family units. Since Olowo was founded there had always been power and status differentiation, but most people enjoyed the same material advantages. After private enterprise was introduced, the village began to be divided into rich and poor people, with the elite becoming the most wealthy by virtue of their control over resources in the village. By 1972 Olowo had begun to deteriorate physically: for example, the boardwalks were falling apart. By 1974 most of the industries had been abandoned, many members had left for the mainland, and this remarkable village was on the verge of disintegration.

References

1. This chapter is taken from a manuscript called *The Rise and Fall of an African Utopia*. Fieldwork was conducted between June 1969 and July 1970, October and November 1972, and May to July 1974. I am grateful for the following support: The Werner-Gren Foundation and a Canada Council doctoral fellowship during the initial field trip; a Research Advisory Board from the University of Guelph during the second field trip; and a Canada Council Research Fellowship and Research Grant which allowed me to take a leave of absence from the University of Guelph during 1973–4 and to return to the field for further

research.

2. For an analysis of the role of *oba* among the Yoruba, see P.C. Lloyd 'The Traditional Political Systems of the Yoruba'. *Southwestern Journal of Anthropology*, 10 (1954), pp. 366–64, and his 'Sacred Kingship and Government among the Yoruba', *Africa*, 30 (1960), pp. 221–37.
3. E.H. Duckworth, 'A Visit to the Apostles and the Town of Aiyetoro'. *Nigeria Magazine*, 36 (1951).
4. Anon, 'Aiyetoro', *Nigeria Magazine*, 55 (1957).
5. J.D.Y Peel, *Aladura; a Religion Movement among the Yoruba* (Oxford University Press, 1968).
6. The effects of communalism on the family are described in S. Barrett, *Two Villages on Stilts* (New York: Chandler Publishing Co., 1974).
7. The main reason that I chose Talika as a comparative unit instead of one of the other theocracies is that in 1969 it joined Olowo in a political union. This made it legitimate for me to go back and forth between the two villages. Olowo made the adoption of communalism a precondition of the union, which Talika accepted in principle, hoping to become wealthy like Olowo. However, not only was communalism rejected by Talika people, but within three years the union had fallen apart.
8. There were 137 and 156 houses respectively in the male and female sectors. The figures on occupations were derived from a questionnaire administered to all of the residents in the male sector and the residents of 76 of the 156 houses in the female sector (or 49%), consisting of 429 and 197 adult men and women.
9. Talika was also divided into male and female sectors, consisting of 40 large and 121 small houses respectively. The figures on occupations were derived from a systematic sample of 50% of the houses in the male sector, containing 175 people of which 81 were adults; and a combination of a systematic and judgment sample of 17% of the houses of the female sector, containing 96 people of which 38 were adults.
10. Olowo was a closed community and people who were disillusioned were not allowed to leave, but had to escape, the term used by the people themselves. I have data for 46 defectors between 1947 and 1972, which is probably under-estimated. After 1972 the rate of defection accelerated, and I have data for 67 people who departed during 1973 and 1974. Offsetting these defections was the recruitment of outsiders, which amounted to 129 women and one man from 1970 to 1974; 35 of these women as well as the man only remained in Olowo for a few months. I have written about conflict and defection in *The World is at Peace: Stratification, Conflict and Control in an African Utopia.*
11. G. Stoevesendt, 'The Sect of the Second Adam', *Africa*, 7 (1934), pp 479–82.
12. D. Ames 'Wolof Co-operative Work Groups', in W. Bascom and M. Herskovits (eds.), *Continuity and Change in African Cultures* (University of Chicago Press, 1963), pp. 224–37.
13. J. Goody, *The Development Cycle of Domestic Groups* (Cambridge University Press, 1958).

14. D. Brokensha and C. Erasmus, 'African "Peasants" and Community Development', in D. Brokensha and M. Pearshall (eds.), *The Anthropology of Development in Sub-Saharan Africa* (Lexington: The Society for Applied Anthropology, 1969).
15. W. Sowab, 'Kinship and Lineage among the Yoruba', *Africa*, 25 (1955).
16. The Olowo case has important negative implications for bodies of theory that assume a close link between achievement and individualism such as McClelland's 'need to achieve' thesis (1967), which I have discussed in *The Rise and Fall of an African Utopia;* also see D. McClelland *The Achieving Society* (Glencoe: The Free Press, 1967).
17. The religious beliefs of Olowo and Talika are compared in two chapters of *The Rise and Fall of an African Utopia.*
18. The main reason why Olowo people worked so hard was to realize their religious beliefs. Yet for reasons that are beyond the scope of this chapter, I argue that it is not legitimate to evoke Weber's Protestant ethnic argument to explain the manner in which religion contributed to the village's rapid development. Indeed, the religious beliefs of the Apostles had no more capacity to motivate the people than the beliefs in Talika and other Ilaje theocracies. M Weber *The Protestant Ethic and the Spirit of Capitalism*, trans. Talcott Parsons (New York: Charles Scribner, 1958).
19. Before my fieldwork in Olowo I was very much opposed to a reductionist explanation, but eventually realized that I held an over-socialized conception of the actor that lowered the calibre of analysis. I now prefer a model of the actor in which norms are seen as parameters that guide but do not determine behaviour, social relationships are seen as dynamic exchanges, and room is left for the individual to manipulate the social setting.

Agricultural Development Administration: An Introduction

Agricultural extension services are key agencies of development at the local level. First, they are one of the few arms of government whose staff penetrate down to the farm level. Second, they are an important point of access to scarce development resources such as seeds, fertilizers, technical advice and credit. Agricultural Departments are assigned a range of functions, including the implementation of planned agricultural production targets and priorities at the local level, the compilation of statistics, experimentation, trial plots and demonstration, and, of course, extension services and farmer education.

As far as the latter is concerned, there may be two distinct areas of specialization. First, there is the initiation of basic institutional change in 'backward' areas: the introduction of cash crop production into areas which, for various reasons, have remained at a subsistence level. Second, there is the servicing of farmers already 'on the move' – the so-called 'progressive' farmers. In practice, extension work – given *inter alia* the sheer physical problem of contacting thousands of scattered smallholders from diverse backgrounds and with differing levels of advancement – has tended to favour the more 'progressive' farmers. This in turn has accentuated in some areas the growing patterns of inequality in the rural sector based on differential access to scarce development resources allocated through government extension services.

As far as the organization of the extension service is concerned, the Extension Service of the former Western State – Ogun, Oyo and Ondo states since 1976 – may serve as an illustration. There the Extension Service of the Agricultural Ministry comprised a hierarchy of three levels. Below the State ministerial headquarters is (1) the Division, headed by a Divisional Agricultural Officer, (2) the Areas, headed by Agricultural Assistants, and (3) Zones, headed by Field Overseers. A zone is designed to be about 5 miles radius so that each Field Officer has to cover about 75 square miles and be responsible for some 2,500 farming families. As far as staff density is concerned, there are about 900 Field Officers and some 450 Agricultural Assistants. Agricultural extension services like this throughout Africa experience a number of common problems of operational effectiveness.

First, a fundamental constraint lies in the fact that many aspects of agricultural development – including credit, marketing and prices – lie outside the control of extension services. Also, within agricultural extension services themselves, a number of aspects are problematic. Manpower shortages, lack of adequate supportive staff and poor finance, combined with bureaucratic organization, may tie senior staff down to purely administrative matters – attending meetings, supervising staff, writing reports and even accounting – leaving little time for professional work, especially in the field. Outside the office, relations with the field staff may be characterised by over-centralization. Where this is the case, delays in the release of urgently needed funds may result. Finally, lack of adequate transport hampering movement in the field appears to be a common deficiency of many agricultural extension services.

A second problem area is the recruitment of staff. Within the public service, recruiting policies place heavy emphasis on paper qualifications. In the case of extension work, these may not be of prime relevance to the tasks to be performed. It has in fact been noted that the less educated may be able to make the best contact with farmers. Extension services also suffer from a high turnover of staff. Because of the low status of work in the rural areas, the more educated tend to see extension work as temporary until they can find alternative employment more commensurate with their self-images. Furthermore, those attracted to extension work, for whatever reasons, tend to be young primary school leavers. In such cases, the gap in age between themselves and the farmer can be great and they may suffer in their work from certain lack of authority.

A third and related aspect is the performance and productivity of extension workers. Because of the low status of rural work, coupled with poor pay and conditions of service, worker motivation is low. In addition, public service organization does not provide immediate sanctions over staff. Hiring and firing and disciplinary action are carried out through the Public Service Review Commissions.

Finally, the operational effectiveness of agricultural extension work has at times been affected by inappropriate methods. The inherited style has been paternalistic if not authoritarian. Extension workers, particularly the more educated ones, do not always regard the farmer with great respect. The farmer is seen as ignorant, lazy and unwilling to change his methods. Consequently exhortation is the most common approach to farmer education. These tendencies are in turn reinforced by the nature of government bureaucracy itself which stressed compliance with superiors above rather than developing meaningful human relations with the farmers as clients. In addition, training and staff supervision is minimal in many cases.

The working and operational effectiveness of agricultural extension services has been particularly well documented and analyzed. The scope for improvement has been limited in a number of ways. First, the question of inappropriate extension service organization, including such aspects as staff supervision, training and conditions of service, is ultimately tied up with the disposition of those in power towards reform in the public service as a whole. Second, manpower shortages and poor support are but a reflection of the low priority accorded the rural sector in the overall allocation of government controlled resources, the rhetoric of 'helping the farmer' notwithstanding.

Faced with the realities of government policies and the sheer physical task of providing services for millions of scattered smallholders, alternative approaches have sometimes been sought after. One such has been to work through co-operative institutions where they exist, or another method has been to set up strategic agricultural service centres as convenient points of contact with the farmer. The readings which follow document and reflect some of these areas of concerns.

12. The Working of the Divisional Agricultural Extension Services in Western Nigeria

I. Adefolu Akinbode

Introduction

In their attempts to combat the evils of poverty, disease and ignorance, especially among rural populations, many countries of the world have adopted varying approaches to achieve rural development and transformation. One such approach which has been widely used in Nigeria and elsewhere is the Agricultural Extension Service.

Within the past few decades, agriculture has achieved the prospects of an accelerated rate of change as a result of the discovery of new technology. However, these innovations have no value unless they get to the farmers who have need for them. The Agricultural Extension Service, therefore, through its extension workers, constitutes one of the principal sources for diffusing new technology. In Nigeria, the Divisional Extension Officers occupy a key position in the formal channel of communication from the agricultural researchers to the farmers. Through these officers, the Ministry of Agriculture and Natural Resources (MANR) in the Western State[1] of Nigeria was meeting the various expectations and demands for action of the farming families.

The Divisional Extension Officer occupies a prominent position in planning and supervising all agricultural programmes at the divisional level. He supervises the work of the agricultural superintendents, assistant agricultural superintendents, the agricultural assistants, and the village-level workers, such as the field overseers. His own work is overseen by senior officers such as the senior agricultural officer, principal agricultural officer, deputy chief agricultural officer, and the chief agricultural officer.

The problems facing the extension workers in reaching their targets are not easy ones. The extension workers, as adult educators, are attempting to influence the behaviour of a large number of people in life situations that are subject to continual change as a result of economic and social developments. Farming families have diverse interests and vary greatly in cultural background and other socio-economic factors. These factors influence their response to educational stimuli. Because of these problems, and because of the limitation of resources at the disposal of the Agricultural Extension Service, the question has been raised in some quarters as to whether extension should aim to reach all farmers or only a section of them.

The purpose of this essay is, therefore, twofold. First, it attempts to examine the roles of the divisional extension officers of the MANR in the Western State of Nigeria on the basis of the emphasis they gave to certain activities that were included in extension work.[2] With the increasing desire in Nigeria in the last decade to change the nature of extension work from service to education, there is a greater need for a clearer division of labour. This is crucial since personnel without a clear understanding of where they fit into their organization are likely to fail in their responsibilities. Without clearly defined roles, the personnel tend to falter, placing emphasis in the wrong places. Adequate job descriptions and clearly defined role expectations and functions are therefore invaluable tools which the divisional extension officers and other extension workers need. Unfortunately, in the Western State of Nigeria very little precise evidence was available about the job descriptions of any category of extension workers. Second, the essay attempts to determine what the farmers expected of extension officers as well as the kind of farmers actually reached.

The Roles of Divisional Extension Officers[3]

Formally speaking, a Divisional Extension Officer is an extension agent in charge of an agricultural division. If the position is manned by a university graduate with a Bachelor's degree in agriculture, he is given an official title of agricultural officer. However, because of the shortage of personnel with such qualifications in the extension division, he may be a high school graduate who has received two to four years of training in agriculture in the Schools of Agriculture at Akure or Ibadan, plus several years of field experience in extension work. The latter may have the official status of Higher Agricultural Superintendent or Senior Agricultural Superintendent.

For the purposes of identifying the role performance of the divisional extension officers, a list of thirty activities were presented to each of the respondents. The respondents were then asked to check any one of these descriptions that applied to their job situation.[4] On the basis of this ranking, the first thirteen activities identified by the respondents, arranged in descending order, were:

(1) Providing farmers with information on improved farm practices.
(2) Holding group meetings with farmers to discuss farm problems.
(3) Writing and replying to official letters.
(4) Writing various kinds of reports.
(5) Making home and/or farm visits.
(6) Providing farmers with information on sale of farm produce.
(7) Training of agricultural assistants and field overseers.
(8) Collecting background information about the division.
(9) Distribution of planting materials and fertilizers to farmers.
(10) Conducting method-and-result demonstrations on farmers' farms.
(11) Developing a calendar of work.

(12) Discussion of farmers' problems with senior officials.
(13) Evaluating extension programmes.

An examination of the findings revealed that six of the thirteen activities could be classified as administrative/service roles,[5] while the remaining seven could be termed educational. These findings indicate that in Western Nigeria, not many changes have taken place in the nature of extension work within the last decade. The divisional extension officers were carrying almost as many educational functions as administrative/service functions. This is in agreement with the general belief concerning the nature of extension work throughout the country.

Furthermore, the data revealed that some administrative activities (e.g. writing and replying to letters and writing of various kinds of reports) took a great deal of the time of the majority of the respondents in the past year. The main reason for this phenomenon is the dearth of administrative personnel at the divisional level. An additional reason is the inadequacy of experience of the clerical (or administrative) staff that are posted to the divisions. One would expect that if lack of funds makes shortage of clerical staff unavoidable, then those who are hired should be trained through well-planned and comprehensive in-service training programmes to enable them to relieve the professional staff of some of the administrative duties.

The eleven activities that were ranked lowest, arranged in descending order order, were:

(1) 'Slave driving' of subordinate staff.
(2) Conducting demonstrations at the extension work stations.
(3) Providing farmers with information on agricultural credit.
(4) Discussing personal non-farm problems with farmers.
(5) Preparing production forecasts.
(6) Assisting researchers in conducting experiments.
(7) Arranging for tractor hiring to farmers.
(8) Touring with senior officials.
(9) Preparing weather forecasts.
(10) Arranging for land acquisition for government projects.
(11) Attending to contractors in the office.

The majority of these activities (seven out of eleven) were administrative/service functions,[6] and only four of them could be regarded as educational. The divisional officers did not devote much of their time to 'slave driving' the subordinate staff because they did not consider it as part of their functions. This position appears rational.

Concerning the use of extension work stations as demonstration farms, the MANR officials are currently reconsidering whether or not to continue using these stations. Many people are now questioning the extent to which the extension work stations are fulfilling one of their major objectives – that of serving as demonstration farms to neighbouring farmers. All these may be responsible for the relatively low emphasis given to the use of extension work stations by divisional officers. A corollary of the explanation given above is that the divisional extension officers might believe that the best places to demonstrate improved agricultural practices to farmers are the farmers' farms. This assertion is supported by the high ranking given to demonstrations on the farmers' farms.

The respondents did not spend much time on the last six activities listed above (the majority of which are administrative/service functions) for the same reason that they regarded themselves as agents of change rather than administrator/service agents.

As a contrast to the actual performances of Divisional Extension Officers, the study also included an examination of the attitudes of the same officers towards their roles. The twelve activities ranked highest were:

(1) Holding group meetings with farmers.
(2) Securing extension teaching materials for agricultural assistants and field overseers.
(3) Providing farmers with information on the sale of farm produce.
(4) Providing farmers with information on improved farm practices.
(5) Training of agricultural assistants and field overseers.
(6) Evaluating extension programmes.
(7) Preparing production forecasts.
(8) Making home and/or farm visits.
(9) Conducting demonstrations on farms.
(10) Discussing farmers problems with senior officials of the Ministry of Agriculture and Natural Resources.
(11) Collecting background information about the division.
(12) Developing a calendar of work.

Thus the divisional extension officers did not perceive their roles radically different from what they performed. Seven out of the twelve activities ranked highest were educational functions,[7] while the remaining five activities were administrative/service functions.

The twelve activities that were ranked lowest were:

(1) Conducting demonstrations at extension work stations.
(2) Discussing personal non-farm problems with farmers.
(3) Arranging for tractor hiring to farmers.
(4) Attending official meetings with other civil servants.
(5) Providing farmers with information on agricultural credit.
(6) Writing various kinds of reports.
(7) Preparing, checking and signing vouchers.
(8) Attending to office calls by farmers.
(9) Preparing weather forecasts.
(10) Arranging for land acquisition for government projects.
(11) Writing and replying to official letters.
(12) Attending to contractors in the office.

The picture of extension work as presented by the above findings is similar to that shown in the role performance data. Eight out of the twelve activities listed above are administrative/service functions,[8] while the remaining four functions are educational. One of the educational functions (demonstrations at extension work stations) is currently being reconsidered as mentioned earlier. The next two educational functions (non-farm problems and agricultural credit) could be avoided by the agricultural extension agents if other rural development agencies performed their roles. The last educational function which was not regarded as one of the divisional officers' roles (i.e. office calls) was so perceived probably because the officers did not feel that the office was the appropriate place for discussing farm problems. In actual fact, the use of this method is related to the level of sophistication of the farmers and the amount of confidence which the farmers have in the extension officers.

Finally, a close examination of the rankings of role activities studied revealed that there was a lack of perfect agreement in the rankings of eight functions. These included:

(1) Writing and replying to official letters.
(2) Writing various kinds of reports.
(3) Evaluating extension programmes.
(4) Securing extension teaching materials for agricultural assistants and field overseers.
(5) 'Slave driving' of subordinate staff.
(6) Preparing production forecasts.
(7) Arranging for tractor hiring to farmers.
(8) Touring with senior officers.

The divisional extension officers spent a great deal of their time on the first two activities in the past year, but did not feel that they should spend as much time in future. With regard to the last six activities, the position was reversed. This means that the respondents did not do much about them in the past year, but felt that they should do more in future. The explanations for these positions are not difficult to see. The first two activities on which less emphasis was desired in future are purely administrative functions which have taken a significant proportion of the extension agents' time in the past years, and probably hindered the educational roles of the agents. In effect, the divisional extension officers were saying that they wanted to be, first and foremost, educators. Although the next five functions are non-educational, they (except 'slave driving' of subordinate staff) could be regarded as 'accelerators' for effective extension work. This probably explains why the officers felt they should spend more time on them in future. The reactions of the officers about touring with senior officers are not surprising. Tours, if well planned and conducted, could be educating and hence be a useful means of knowing one's area of operation. This is a principle much talked about in extension work.

Beneficiaries of Extension Services

In order to have a total picture of the working of the extension service, the position and views of the farmers as clients and beneficiaries must also be considered. On the basis of the amount of time which the respondents spent with varying classes of farmers in the past year,[9] the relative importance of the divisional extension officers' clientele is shown in Table 1. The data revealed that the classes of farmer who were ranked as having been given a great deal of the officers' time in the past year included full-time farmers, illiterate farmers, farmers who are leaders in their communities, and farmers who are members of co-operative societies and/or unions.

Table 1
Rank Order of Divisional Extension Officers' Clientele

	Main Scores and Rank Orders			
	Clientele	*Rank*	*Perceived Clientele*	*Rank*
Full-time farmers	2.74	1	2.44	1
Illiterate farmers	2.52	2	2.35	3
Farmers who are leaders	2.48	3	2.30	4
Farmers who are members of Co-operative Societies/Unions	2.30	4	2.39	2
Farmers operating more than 10 acres of land	2.26	5	2.22	6
Farmers operating 5 acres of land or less	2.22	6	2.04	9*
Literate farmers	2.13	7	2.22	6
Farmers operating 6 to 10 acres of land	2.13	7	2.13	8
Non-members of Co-operative Societies/Unions	2.09	9	2.00	10
Non-leaders	2.00	10	2.30	4*
Part-time farmers	1.87	11	2.00	10
Land owners	1.70	12	1.91	13
Tenant farmers	1.63	13	1.96	12
Absentee farmers	1.30	14	1.78	14
Share-croppers	1.26	15	1.74	15

* Discrepancies in the rankings of Divisional Extension Officers' clientele relative to the perceived clientele.

These rankings, except that of the illiterate farmers, are not surprising and they are in the expected positions considering the characteristics and the size of the population with which these officers have to work. The full-time farmers are, generally speaking, the not very well-to-do farmers. They depend on their family labour, and produce mainly for home consumption. The divisional extension officers spent the greatest amount of their time with them in the past year because they (the full-time farmers) constitute the majority of the officers' population, and they (the full-time farmers) are always available since farming is their sole occupation.

Farmers who are leaders in their communities were ranked as having received a great deal of the officers' time in the past year, mainly because these are the people who legitimize the officers' programmes. They (the leader-farmers) serve as the middlemen between the officers and their clientele.

Farmers who are members of co-operative societies and/or unions were ranked next as having been given a great deal of attention by the respondents in the past year. This was so because these were the farmers through whom officers arrange village meetings. They are relatively easy to contact since the they constitute an already established group of co-operators. Another reason for ranking the co-operative members high was the fact that the divisional extension officers in the Western State of Nigeria had found this group of farmers helpful and effective in discharging some of their service functions. The distribution of material resources, such as fertilizers, is usually done through this group of farmers. Furthermore, the practice of group farming is a commonplace in the State; and since some of these co-operative farmers are in their initial stage of development, it is no surprise that the divisional extension officers spent a great deal of their time with members of these groups.

The data further showed that the officers devoted much of their time to illiterate farmers. Illiteracy here refers to inability to read or write Yoruba and English. Recent studies in the State revealed that the majority of farmers were illiterate.[10] It therefore becomes clear that if the officers were to reach farmers at all, they could not avoid the illiterate members of their client system. Another way of looking at it is to assume that the respondents shared the feelings of previous researchers who advocated that if there were to be an any preferential treatment, the extension officers should have more contact with those constituents who have the greatest need for educational assistance.

Finally, in contrast to the actual allocation of extension efforts as presented above, the farmers themselves were asked to name the kinds of services they would like from government agencies. The responses of the farmers included the provision of:

(1) Credit and/or loans.
(2) Ready and better market for farm produce.
(3) Planting materials.
(4) Technical advice on crops and fertilisers.

(5) Spraying chemicals, pumps and fertilizers.
(6) Farm machinery.
(7) Storage facilities.
(8) Improved communication facilities, such as roads.
(9) More farm and home visits by extension officers.
(10) More demonstration plots in their communities.

The findings above showed that the farmers wanted more service than educational functions, since only three of the ten roles desired (numbers 4, 9 and 10) were educational functions. These expectations are in agreement with the kind of services which the extension agents used to offer in the past. The FAO report on agricultural development in Nigeria rightly pointed this out when it said: 'In the past . . . the field staff of the Government agricultural services in Nigeria were mainly involved in passing on, and frequently enforcing, Government orders and instructions to the farming community'.[11] However, the farmers' desires are not consistent with what the officers have been doing, nor with what they think they should be doing. This means that there is role conflict. This may explain in part the problems which the extension agents are encountering in making a break-through in their efforts to modernize agriculture. The differences in views between the extension officers and the farmers may make the assimilation of the former into their client culture difficult, and hence the officers remain 'outsiders' or 'marginal men' in the social system. This, in turn, may lead to frustration among the officers and the farmers, and lack of confidence of the latter in the former.

The foregoing implications pose organizational problems which call for urgent attention if extension agents are to make any impact on the life of the farmers. There is the need to motivate private organizations to take over the service functions which are supportive of effective extension work. There is also the need for clearer explanation of the present philosophy of extension work in Nigeria to farm families in an atmosphere of mutual trust, respect and confidence. It is hoped that the change-over can be achieved more easily if the needs mentioned above are satisfied.

It is, however, worthy of note that the three educational roles desired by the farmers are included among those which the officers perceived as their roles. These, if carried out, are likely to have some moderating effects on the conflicts discussed earlier.

Conclusions

It may be noted that one salient feature of the present working of the extension service is the large number of administrative/service activities on which the divisional extension officers spent a great deal of their time in the past year and on which they planned to spend much time in future. In other words, the nature of extension work has not changed a great deal from what it was a decade ago. This situation will persist if we continue to pay lip service to the urgent need of relieving our extension workers of their administrative responsibilities. It should nevertheless be added that officers are conscious of the changing philosophy of extension work in Nigeria, and are making efforts to move with the changes. This is reflected in their responses. More than 50% of the most highly ranked functions in the two role dimensions were educational roles.

It was also observed that among the activities about which officers were ambivalent were a large number of educational functions. Two reasons could be advanced for this situation. It is possible that the divisional extension officers had no true understanding of their educational roles. The second possibility is that the means (material resources) for performing such educational roles might not be available. In fact, the data from another study[12] carried out concurrently with this showed that the most insufficient aspects of the divisional extension officers' work were material resources, including transportation and planting materials. No officer can do extension work effectively if he has no transport, or if the seeds and fertilizers are not available when needed. This calls for a reconsideration of our priorities. To ensure better role performance by the divisional extension officers, the extension service should make available adequate human (technical and clerical) and material (transportation, seeds, fertilizers etc.) resources at the divisional level. These are essential tools for effective extension work.

The data further showed that the divisional extension officers did not spend a great deal of time on selecting and training of local leaders, but expressed the desire to do so in future. This change in emphasis may be attributed to an increase in the understanding of the principles, methods and benefits of training and the use made of local leaders in extension work. The involvement of these leaders will enable the professional workers to multiply themselves and reach more farmers.

There seems to be a greater discrepancy between the roles performed and perceived by the officers on the one hand, and those desired by the farmers on the other, than between the two role dimensions on which the officers were probed. It was clear from the findings that the farmers were still living in the past when extension work was mainly service-oriented, whereas the officers had adopted an educational approach.

Our recommendations, based on the findings of this study are as follows:

(1) That there is a need for clearly-written job descriptions for the divisional extension officers in the western states of Nigeria. This instrument will help to remove, or at least minimize, the type of disagreement observed between the role performance and perception (particularly the educational roles) of the officers.

(2) That there is an urgent need to improve the quality and quantity of both the technical and clerical staff assisting the divisional officers. The clerical staff will help to relieve the officers of their administrative responsibilities, while the technical staff, who form the nerve-end of extension service and make contacts with farm families, will help to educate the farmers about the changing philosophy of extension work.

(3) That there is the need to motivate private organizations (preferably farmers' organizations) to take over the provision of material resources. One way in which the Government can assist in this respect is to make credit facilities available on an interest-free basis. The Government should also provide technical advice on organizational and management problems at the initial stages of such projects.

As regards the second aspect of the study, the beneficiaries of extension services, the question that arises is this: Have the divisional extension officers been working with all classes of farmers in their areas of operation, or have they been offering their services to selected groups of farmers? And in any case, who should they reach? An examination of the first six highly-ranked classes of farmers in Table 1 reveals that at least the officers have been reaching the majority of their target system which is made up of a large proportion of peasant farmers.[13]

Another support for this claim is the high rank given to farmer-members of co-operative societies or unions and the farmers operating five acres of land or less. Co-operative societies have become so popular, particularly in the cash cash-crop growing areas of Western Nigeria, that one rarely finds a farmer who does not belong to one of these societies. Even in the food-crop growing area of Oyo, an investigation in 1969 showed that there were 59 co-operative groups.[14] This is an additional confirmation of the traditional group farming characteristic of the Yoruba which was comprehensively discussed by Ojo.[15] Furthermore, the average size of a farm in Western Nigeria is far less than five acres. In 1963, it was claimed that 78% of the farms were under 2.5 acres.[16] These findings point to the fact that the divisional extension officers have no selected classes of clientele; rather they tried to cover all classes of farmers in their areas of operation.

The question that follows from the foregoing discussion is whether what this study has revealed as the actual situation in respect of the clientele of the Agricultural Extension Officers is the best approach to agricultural development. The choice of an extension officer's target group is an important consideration in rural development. A large majority of the clientele of the divisional extension officers in past years in the Western State of Nigeria included the peasant small-scale farmers. The officers also perceived that these same categories of farmers will continue to be their target system for some time to come. There is probably every justification for this position.

During the colonial period, the government maintained a policy of non-intervention in the country's agricultural pursuit; Europeans were refused participation in agricultural enterprise. 'Rather, government decided to encourage and supervise the cultivation of export crops, by providing local farmers with improved seed varieties and technical advice and as well by establishing demonstration plots in the villages'.[17] Even after independence, the indigenous governments have done very little to change the pattern of agricultural production in Nigeria. Consequently, the peasant farmers remain for some time to come the chief source of our agricultural produce, both for local consumption and exports. It is important, therefore, that we start from where we are by improving our present farmers while at the same time we take cognizance of, and respond to, the changes in the pattern of our agricultural production.

References

This chapter amalgamates material from two articles previously published by the author: 'Roles of the Divisional Extension Officers in the Western State of Nigeria', *Quarterly Journal of Administration,* 6, 1 (1971), and 'The Beneficiaries of Extension Service in Western Nigeria: A Methodological Problem in Rural Development', *Odu,* 8 (1972).

1. The research on which this article is based was carried out before the 1976 division of Western State into Oyo, Ogun and Ondo States. [Ed].
2. In Nigeria, very few studies concerned with the problem of role performance and perception of extension workers have been conducted. In a recent study of the roles of the agricultural assistants in the former Eastern Region of Nigeria, Igbani identified some functions such as the distribution of planting materials, seeds and seedlings, fertilisers etc, to farmers as the major roles of the agricultural assistant. Other activities, such as holding group meetings with farmers to discuss farm problems, conducting demonstrations, and providing farmers with information on improved farm practices were rated highly as having received a great deal of emphasis in the past and should be given more emphasis in the future. I.J. Igbani, 'The role of the Agricultural Assistant as perceived by Agricultural Assistants and the Supervisory-Administrative Staff of the Extension Service in Eastern Nigeria', (Unpublished M.Sc. thesis, Department of Agricultural and Extension Education, University of Wisconsin, Madison, 1967).
3. Records of the Ministry of Agriculture and National Resources, previous research, and observation by the researcher of some of the divisional extension officers at work provided the basis for the role activities included in this study. The initial list which consisted of forty-two activities was pre-tested on two officers of the Ministry of Agriculture and Natural Resources in Ife and Ibadan, and the revised list of thirty activities was finally used in the study. The data for the study were collected from twenty-three extension divisional officers employed by the Ministry of Agriculture and Natural Resources in the Western State of Nigeria, between October, 1969 and January, 1970. Two of the twenty-five agricultural divisions had no officers of their own at the time of the study. The respondents were interviewed personally by the author, using a pre-tested and structured questionnaire. The data collected through the interview schedule were supplemented by participant observation in Akura/Ondo Circle, which is one of the four agricultural circles in the State. The date collected from farmers in Western Nigeria between 1967 and 1968 for two other studies constituted another source of data.
4. Descriptive words (*great deal, some, little* and *none*) were placed on

an interval scale to indicate the amount of time devoted to each of the activities in the past year. Weighted scores (*great deal* = 3, *some* = 2, *little* = 1, and *none* = 0) were assigned to these descriptive words. The highest score attainable was 90 and the least score was zero. Weighted score averages were determined and the role activities were ranked using score averages.

5. Items 3, 4, 6, 9, 11 and 12.
6. Items 1, 5, 6, 7, 9, 10 and 11.
7. Items 1, 4, 5, 6, 8, 9 and 11.
8. Items 3, 4, 6, 7, 9, 10, 11 and 12.
9. From a review of literature, 15 classes of farmers were delineated and included in this study. These vary from full-time or part-time farmers through literate or illiterate farmers to farmers who are leaders or followers in their communities. For the purposes of determining the classes of farmers reached by Divisional Extension Officer, descriptive words (*great deal, some, little* and *none*) were placed on an interval scale to indicate the amount of time devoted to each class of farmer in the past year and the time they would like to devote to them in future. The respondents were asked to check any one of these descriptions that had applied to their situations. Weighted scores (*great deal* = 3, *some* = 2, *little* = 1, and *none* = 0) were assigned to these descriptive words. The highest score attainable was 45, and the least score was zero.
10. Robert C. Clark, and I.A. Akinbode, 'Factors associated with, adoption of three farm practices in the Western State, Nigeria', *Research Bulletin 1*, Faculty of Agriculture, University of Ife Press, 1968, pp. 9–10; and S.K. Taiwo Williams, 'Sources of Information on improved farming practices in Western Nigeria', *Department Research Monograph No. 5* Department of Extension Education and Rural Sociology, University of Ife, 1968, p.7.
11. FAO, *Agricultural Development in Nigeria, 1965–1980* (Rome, 1966), p. 300.
12. Isaac A. Akinbode, 'Roles Performance and Perception of Divisional Extension Officers in the Western State of Nigeria'. *Department Research Monograph No. 7*, Department of Extension Education and Rural Sociology, University of Ife, December 1970.
13. For example, the 1963 census of the then Western Region of Nigeria put about 93% of the 1.5 million farming population as having no other occupation besides farming, i.e. full-time farmers. Also, as mentioned earlier, a large proportion of farmers in Western Nigeria are illiterate. A recent study of farmers in the Western State of Nigeria showed that 60% of the respondents were 'complete' illiterates, while another 15% could be called 'functional' literates. *Population Census of Nigeria, 1963, Western Region Vol. II*, Table 7, p. 148; Williams, *op. cit.*
14. S.A.S. Oyo South Division, Letter Ref. No. OY/73/127 of 24 June 1968.
15. G.J.A. Ojo, 'The Changing Patterns of Traditional Group Farming in Ekiti, North-Eastern Yoruba Country', *Nigerian Geographical Journal* 6, 1 (1966), pp. 31–5.

16. K.H. Parsons, 'The Land Reform Problem in Nigeria', paper prepared for Consortium to the Spring Review Discussion of Land Tenure and Land Reform, Washington USAID, 1970, p. 18
17. Reuben K. Udo, 'British Policy and the Development of Export Crops in Nigeria', *Nigerian Journal of Economic and Social Studies*, 9, 3 (1967), pp. 299–314.

13. New Dimensions in the Administration of Agriculture in Nigeria

S.O. Olayide, E.O. Idusogie, and Dupe Olatunbosun

This chapter addresses itself to the legacy of the colonial administration of agriculture in Nigeria, the problem of perpetuating this unresponsive structure by neo-colonialists, and the role of new dimensions designed to usher in a 'green revolution' in Nigerian agriculture. Since the government has become the 'most powerful entrepreneur and director' in developing countries, there is a requirement for new dimensions in the administration of agriculture. The colonial set-up of agricultural administration is most uncongenial to the pace of a dynamic agriculture.

The following argument is divided into (1) an examination of the present structure of agricultural administration and its limitations; (2) suggested new dimensions in structure with their administrative implications; (3) the needs and the effects of the new dimensions on Nigeria's economic growth; (4) the financial implications of the suggested structure; and (5) the summary and conclusions.

The Present Structure

Federal and State Structures

The present structure for the administration of agriculture in Nigeria is a legacy of the British Colonial Administration. This structure was grafted on to the constitution of the Federal Republic. In the constitution, agriculture was made one of the 'Residual Matters' for which the regions of the first Republic were solely responsible.[1] As a result of this constitutional specification, there has been no federal direction on agriculture. This basic and growth-generating sector of the Nigerian economy was given no separate ministry in the Federal Government. Rather, it was broken into five divisions (Federal Fisheries Service, Agriculture & Natural Resources, Forest Research, Agricultural Research and Veterinary Research), the first two of which later formed the nucleus of the Ministry of Natural Resources and Research, established in 1965.

In each of the former regions (East, Midwest, North, and West), a separate Ministry of Agriculture (with or without Natural Resources) existed. The Ministry was broken down into main divisions/departments and each of these

Chart 1
Organization of Agricultural Services in Nigeria, 1965

Western Region	*Mid-Western Region*	*Eastern Region*	*Northern Region*
M.A.N.R.	M.A.N.R.	Ministry of Agriculture	Ministry of Agriculture
Agricultural Services Division	Agricultural Services Division	Agricultural Division	Produce Inspection Division
Training Division	Research Branch	Agricultural Research and Training Branch	Agricultural Education and Training Branch
Extension Services Division	Extension Services Branch	Animal Production Branch	Field Services Division
Research Division	Special Services Branch	Soil Conservation Service	Irrigation Division[3]
Forestry Department	Forestry Division[2]	Agricultural Extension Service	Hydrology Branch
Animal Health Department	Produce Inspection Division	Agricultural Supporting Services	Construction Branch
Fisheries Department[1]	Pest Control Section	Agricultural Economics and Marketing Branch	Agricultural Research Institute (A.B.U.)
Produce Inspection Department	Hide Improvement Section	Farm Settlements Branch	
Western Nigeria Agricultural Credit Corporation	Veterinary Division	Agricultural Engineering Branch	
Western Nigeria Marketing Board	Midwestern Nigerian Marketing Board	Veterinary Division	
		Produce Inspection Division	
		Forestry Division	
		Fisheries Division	
		Eastern Nigeria Marketing Board	
		Eastern Nigeria Development Corp. (Plantations Division)	

1. Nucleus of a new Ministry of Natural Resources created in 1965.
2. Nucleus of a Ministry of Forest and Natural Resources established in 1965.
3. Nucleus of a new Ministry of Water Resources and Community Development established in 1965.

Source: FAO, *Agricultural Development in Nigeria, 1965-1980* (Rome, 1966), pp.292-7.

was in some cases made up of branches/services. This structure is presented in Chart 1 for each of the four regions. A study of these abstracted structures shows that many agricultural services were not included. A more careful study of the F.A.O. document[2] shows that many of the missing agricultural services (units) were scattered, either by accident or design, in other ministries. There were semi-autonomous institutions such as the Marketing Boards, Agricultural Credit Corporations, and the Development Corporation (Plantation Division) within the ministries of agriculture. From 1965, the Ministry of Natural Resources was created in the Western and Midwestern Regions. The Northern Region already had its own separate Ministry of Animal and Forest Resources and the Ministry of Social Welfare and Co-operatives whilst the Ministry for Local Government undertook such agricultural functions as (Native Authority) agricultural extension, veterinary, forestry, co-operative, marketing, farm supplies, and soil conservation services. This structure was carried over with little modification and merger into the 'States' administration, and is broadly applicable to our States today.

Limitations of the Structure

The first inadequacy of this structural set-up is the existence of semi-autonomous bodies. This works against effective co-ordination and supervision apart from the conflicting attitudes to control the seat of authority, and was the breeding ground for nepotism, political manipulation of board operations, and corrupt practices affecting the performance of the semi-autonomous bodies.

Secondly, there is the inadequacy resulting from the establishment of separate ministries for crops, livestock, forestry, and co-operatives. Each of these ministries (and Divisions as in the case of co-operatives in the East, Midwest and West) is designed to perform highly conflicting functions and hence has conflicting claims for scarce development capital and staff at the disposal of the governments. Training facilities are conflicting in their aims and objectives whilst research results are non-additive as well as serving no useful purposes. This picture presents a structural orientation that is certainly ineffective for the administration and implementation of programmes for the utilization of the renewable natural resources found in the ecological zones of Nigeria.

Thirdly, a structure so conflicting and at cross-purposes, as we now have, is rather unproductive in terms of staff utilization. The bureaucratic control has been known to stifle initiative and individual drive in personnel. The salary structure of the ministries, apart from providing no incentive to hard work, industry and enterprise, is too static to be meaningful. In most cases, the salary structure is manipulated to take no account of basic or additional training or qualifications and it is too stereotyped to admit of flexibility.

Fourthly, the absence of an 'Organization And Methods' Division, empowered to act as the watch-dog of the Government and to make constant or periodic changes so as to ensure improved performance and worthy compliance in operations magnifies the level of inefficiency in our agricultural

Chart 2
Ministry of Agriculture: Suggested Structure

Agricultural Divisions / *Departments or Branches*

Administration	Crop Production	Livestock	Fisheries	Forestry	Agricultural Economics	Wildlife	Agricultural Extension	Soil & Survey	Agricultural Engineering	Co-operative Societies
Training and Manpower	Agronomy	Veterinary	Inland Fisheries	Forest Management	Project Planning & Programming	Wildlife Management	Livestock Extension	Soil Analysis	Farm Tools	Marketing Associations
Information and Public Relations	Plant Quarantine	Animal Husbandry	Ocean Fisheries	Silviculture	Farm Management	Economic Mammalogy	Crop Extension	Soil Survey	Transport	Producer Co-operatives
Agricultural Policy	Seed Multiplication	Avian Science	Pisciculture	Forest Survey	Agricultural Marketing	Zoo Admin	Home Economics	Land Use and Management	Tractor Hiring	Credit Societies
Investigation and Internal Audit	Produce Inspection	Feed Depot	Fish Technology	Forest Technology	Agricultural Finance	Wildlife Conservation	Rural Sociology	Photographic & Cadastral	Equipment Design	Co-operative Supplies
Agricultural Co-ordination	Water Resources	Meat Technology	Supplies	Outdoor Recreation	Agricultural Corporations	Supplies	Extension Information	Soil Research	Agricultural Workshop	Co-operative Services
	Food Science and Technology	Supplies		Forest Research	Agricultural Survey		Extension Supplies			Co-operative Training
	Entomology	Dairy Products		Supplies	Agricultural Statistics		Extension Training			
	Supplies				Agricultural Settlements					
					Forestry Economics					
					Rural Development					

ministries. It seems so strange that our government officials stigmatize peasant farmers as indolent, underemployed and unresponsive to innovations, when their own indoor activities leave much to be desired.

In general, the administration of the various ministries of agriculture has not been very efficient. Very little productive work that has far-reaching effects on the lives of peasant farmers has been undertaken. The extension divisions of our ministries of agriculture have achieved very little measure of success due to inadequate and inefficient staffing policies. The results of the various findings from the research divisions have been too technical and too esoteric to effect any worthwhile change in peasant farmers' output, productivity, cultural practices and general level of living. All these point to the urgent need for the production and implementation of new dimensions in administration of agriculture in Nigeria.

Suggested New Dimensions

Federal Structure

It must be pointed out that it augurs well for the future of Nigeria and its agricultural sector that the Federal Military Government has created a strong Federal Ministry of Agriculture and Natural Resources with its own Federal Commissioner (Minister) and Permanent Secretary. The divisions which were previously in the Federal Ministry of Economic Planning such as Fishery, Agriculture and Natural Resources, Forestry, Agricultural Research, Veterinary Research, and Agricultural Planning have been handed over to this new agricultural ministry. It is envisaged that the Federal Government will, from now on, play a very prominent and leading role in agriculture.

It is strongly felt that the present structure does not go far enough. To remedy this deficiency, we have presented a suggested new dimension in federal structure for the administration of agriculture. This is presented in Chart 2. This comprehensive structure envisages the creation of *eleven* divisions within the ministry. These are administrative, crop production, livestock, fishery, forestry, agricultural economics, wild life, agricultural extension, agricultural engineering, soils and survey, and co-operative societies divisions.

Each of these eleven divisions will be made up of relevant departments (or branches) which are designed to handle specific aspects of the agricultural services of the division. Some of these departments already exist in the old set-up but they are too stereotyped and static to make any useful and significant change on the agricultural landscape of this country. The specific jobs handled by the new departments should be designed to improve the conduct and performance of divisional operations and to have far-reaching and positive effects on the country's agriculture in general.

From the chart, it is also seen that separate supplies departments exist for the divisions of crop production, livestock, fishery, forestry, wild life, and agricultural extension. These, supplies departments are meant to be

Chart 3
Suggested Staff Structure for Agricultural Extension Services

Permanent Secretary

Controller of
Agricultural Services

12 Directors

Department Heads
Chief Agricultural Officer

Principal Agricultural Officer

Senior Agricultural Officer

Assistant Senior Agricultural Officer

Agricultural Officers
Grades I, II, III

Assistant Agricultural Officers

Agricultural Superintendents
Grades I, II

Agricultural Assistants
Grades I, II

Field Officers
Grades I, II, III

productive departments designed to manufacture such supplies as fertilizers, chemicals, vaccines, pesticides, sprayers, extension demonstration equipment, etc. The co-operative supplies department is designed to organize and provide supplies for co-operative stores in order to meet the needs of members of their associations in their various enterprises.

State Structure

It is not expected that most of the states in the Federation could have the financial resources to handle or effectively operate a Ministry of Agriculture based on the new suggested dimensions which have *eleven* divisions and about *seventy* departments. Consequently, we suggest some merging or regrouping of divisions as well as merging of departments so that some will be made up of units. For example, the divisions could be reduced through merging as follows:

1. Administrative Division.
2. Crop Production Division.
3. Livestock Division.
4. Natural Resources Division
   (a) Forestry Branch.
   (b) Fishery Branch.
   (c) Wild Life Branch.
   (d) Soils & Survey Branch.
5. Agricultural Economics Division.
6. Agricultural Extension Division.
7. Agricultural Engineering Division.
8. Co-operative Societies Division.

In a similar fashion, departments within each division could be merged such that about five departments (each with sub-units) will be created for each division. This will reduce the number of departments to about forty for each state Ministry of Agriculture and Natural Resources.

Personnel Structure

The new structure suggested above will be very demanding in terms of trained and efficient staff. The urgent need for better trained and qualified staff to man essential agricultural services has been stressed as the dominating problem facing agricultural modernization and expansion in Nigeria.[3] This problem assumes greater dominance and importance if and when the new suggested dimensions are put into operation. The staff structure is presented in Chart 3.

This chart shows that the Permanent Secretary is at the head of the ministry as is currently the practice. He will be concerned with the overall administration of the ministry. Next to him is the controller of agricultural services who will co-ordinate the activities and operations of the various divisions. At the head of each division is the director. Next to the director are the heads of departments in his division who bear the title of Chief Agricultural Officer. All other cadres of civil servants in each department are as shown in the chart.

The levels of education required for the kind of problem-solving and production jobs that need to be undertaken are of two types. First is a university degree in agriculture. This is required for all cadres of officers right from Agricultural Assistant Grade II to the top of the pyramid – the Permanent Secretary. Second is the diploma in agriculture, diploma in agricultural extension, certificate in agricultural extension and agricultural certificates of the various schools of agriculture. These certificates are required for cadres of staff right from Superintendent Grade I down to Field Officer Grade III. Any staff with the second level of education or training cannot be promoted beyond the level of Agricultural Officer Grade III. Such promotions will depand on the experience and efficiency of the officer as manifest by apparent or significant contributions to the success of operations in his department.

One important incentive to work which has been little employed in our ministries is the salary structure. The gap between the salaries of the top echelons and the lower cadres is far too wide for comfort. Even in the top echelons, the concept of 'group salary scales', which are not subject to any annual increases, is a serious disincentive to work and is the 'Pandora's box' for the creation of sycophants, jealousy among colleagues, and sense of frustration among many officers. In addition, new structures for the promotion of staff have to be devised. Such structures should be based on visible output, level of training and retraining, experience, research, and distinguished performance in rural areas. Unless this is done, it is very likely that the new dimensions suggested in this paper may deteriorate in conduct and performance and gradually gravitate to the level of the old structure which is generally accepted as unconducive to progress.

Possible Effects of Suggested Structure

The comprehensive dimensions in the administration of agriculture which we have attempted to present in this essay will have some salutary effects. Five of these possible effects will be briefly considered in this section.

Structural Effects

The question may be asked: What will this suggested organization be like in terms of size? Such a question has particular pertinence for young people moving out of universities, technical colleges and schools of agriculture, and who will have a lifetime of contact with organizations ahead of them. Obviously, no one can say with any certainty what lies ahead. Nevertheless, the process of predictions does serve a useful purpose. If the trends of today and the inadequate situations for healthy growth are reconciled and projected into the future, it is safe to contend that the size of agricultural ministries in the country will continue to increase. The cultural environments for successful operation will lay increasing stress on the needs of the individual.

Instead of looking like a pyramid, the future administrative organization for a rejuvenated and modernized peasant agriculture will look more like a rectangle. This implies decentralization based largely on the model of federalism as an increasingly useful means of coping with the problem of size.[4]

In this connection, education and training should be problem-solving oriented and much more practical than at present. Apart from making students productive and creative, the new orientation of training and education must enable graduates to acquire managerial capacity and equip them to perform such managerial functions as planning, organizing, actuating and controlling.

Employment Effect

The employment effect of the new dimensions cannot be over-emphasized. In the next two decades, agriculture will continue to be the largest single employer of the adult working population of Nigeria. The question then is: Is there an optimum size to this administrative sturcture and the employment level that could be generated through its services in the rural areas? In economic literature, there is a point of diminishing returns in the size of enterprise. Boulding argues that there is an 'iron law of size' and that 'the third iron law states that all organizations have an optimum size. . . '[5] Even though this so-called law would apply differently in various settings, Boulding insists that is is present. Dimock has also indicated that the optimum size of an organization is reached when 'the chief executive can no longer synthesize the work of his programme and deal with his subordinates personally'.[6]

It must be stressed that in actuality the optimum size of an organization is not as simply ascertained as is suggested by Dimock, neither is it as iron-clad a matter as Boulding suggests. Apart from the fact that we are in the infantile stage in the organizational administration of agriculture in Nigeria, and we are still groping in the dark, there are sound reasons for big business in the future. These reasons include the considerable importance of land and other agricultural resource endowments in Nigeria's economic growth, the increasing emphasis on stability of the economy, the near-primitive stage of our agricultural economy, the near-complete absence of virile and stable organizational framework for modernizing peasant farming, the dearth of infrastructural facilities in the rural areas, the current irrelevance of the loss of individual initiative, and the need for flexibility which a large decentralized or departmentalized administrative organization connotes. In the next twenty years, it is very unlikely that we would have reached the optimum size. And in the event of any industrial miracle, a reorganized, modernized and rejuvenated peasant farming with a commercial orientation and made to contribute more positively to Nigeria's economic growth will have a considerably high employment effect. It is in this connection that the new dimensions will provide ample employment internally as well as externally in the agricultural sector.

Agro-Industry Effect

One significant effect of the new dimensions is that modernized peasant farming will be able to perform one of the useful roles in economic development. This role is the provision of raw materials and manpower for agro-industries. Apart from expanding the food supplies for the growing urban areas, the increase in raw materials for the industrial sector (located both in the urban and rural areas), the release of seasonal (slack) labour supplies to rural-integrated industries as well as to infrastructural service establishments cannot be over-emphasized.

The association between economic growth and the contraction of the agricultural sector has usually been termed the 'law of declining importance of agriculture' by Lewis.[7] It is pertinent to contend that, as of now, this stage of contracting importance of the agricultural sector is not likely to be meaningfully reached until Nigerian agriculture has been completely modernized and commercialized. The modernizing and commercializing process will mean the beginning of the performance of the role that we have attempted to spotlight here.

Development Effect

The modernization and commercialization of peasant agriculture, which the new dimensions set as the overall objective, will have a salutary developmental effect. First, improved peasant farming will enhance farmer's income and his standard of living. Second, it is when farming becomes business-oriented that it can contribute its own quota much more significantly to the development process. The parading of the idea that industry constitutes the growth centres and that agriculture has therefore to be left on its own is a misguided statement of many armchair and theoretical economists, who are welded to the classical and neo-classical historical process of development in Western Europe and the U.S.A. There is nothing to indicate that Nigeria must follow the same or similar historical process of economic development.

Research Effect

The suggested dimension in its problem-solving orientation must rely exclusively on the results of meaningful agricultural research. In this connection, many crucial policy issues and decisions have to be taken and implemented if the research programmes are to have any significant impact. First, policy should be directed to reconciling and co-ordinating the research activities of the various federal research stations *vis-a-vis* those of agricultural faculties and the federal and state ministries of agriculture and natural resources. In other words, agricultural research under the new dimensions should be based on three approaches: the group approach, the graduate programme approach, and the national problem-solving approach.[8] Second, by effecting a balance between emphasis on export/cash crops and food crops in research funding, timing, and additive nature of the research results. It is in this manner that the beneficial effects of developing meaningful and useful research programme can be attained.

Financial Implications of Suggested Structures

The financial requirements of the suggested administrative structure may be considered as very substantial. But when it is realised that the structure has a productive modernizing and problem-solving orientation, the benefits will certainly be greater than the costs. The educational and training requirements for personnel will involve substantial grants to the university faculties of agriculture to the tune of about ₦8,000,000 per annum, realizing, of course, that we have four faculties of agriculture in Nigerian universities. Such grants are to be utilized for expanded research and training facilities. In addition, the Lagos State government should consider very seriously a three-year grant of about ₦7 million for the development of a faculty/college of agriculture in the University of Lagos. Such a faculty will concentrate research and training interests on the development of mangrove swamp and upland arable farming, avian science, landscape farming, horticulture, marine fisheries and pisciculture, food science and technology. Such a faculty should have productive divisions and be closely integrated with the farm settlement at Ikorodu.

Secondly, the increased size of the departments and the consequent increase in personnel in the state and federal ministries of agriculture and natural resources will mean additional financial expenses for the payment of salaries, equipment, allowances etc. This will probably mean a doubling in the recurrent expenditure. This is not likely to be money down the drain since the ministries have to be involved in income-generating investments in production, storage and processing of farm crops.

In general, the detailed costings of the new dimensions have to be based on a costs-benefits approach. This means that a 'budgeting' approach to the operations of the various ministries must be adopted and the 'budget' must be much more detailed and comprehensive than it is at present. In addition, efforts should be made to introduce treasury control processes into the operations of the income-generating units whose net returns should swell the financial resources for the efficient operation of the new dimensions in agricultural administration.

Summary and Conclusion

In this paper we have attempted to present new dimensions which emphasize a structural change in the administration of agriculture and related services in Nigeria. We have also stressed the beneficial effects and the financial implications of the adoption of such a new structure, in general terms. It must be stressed that the success of adoption will depend largely on competent and well-trained staff whose emoluments have incentives bearing on their qualifications and capabilities.

Furthermore, we are of the opinion that, whichever of the old fallacies – classical growth fallacies, infant industry fallacies, and comprehensive industrialization fallacies[9] – are employed by the protagonists of industrialization, it must be emphasized that an increase of one percent in industrial employment will require about eight percent increase in GDP under Nigerian conditions. This shows convincingly that agriculture will continue to be the backbone of this country in the next few decades. This situation points vividly to the need for a rural-integrated enterprise approach to development in Nigeria. It is in this light that we consider a new structure for the administration of agriculture highly invaluable, demanding though it may be in terms of finance and manpower.

References

This is a shortened verions of an essay first published in the *Quarterly Journal of Administration*, 6, 1 (1971).

1. Government of Nigeria, *An Act to Make Provision for the Constitution of the Federal Republic of Nigeria,* No. 20 of 1963
2. FAO, *Agricultural Development in Nigeria, 1965 – 1970* (Rome, 1966), pp. 281–97.
3. Glenn Johnson *et al., Strategies and Recommendations for Nigerian Rural Development, 1969–1985.* CSNRD 33 (July 1969).
4. J.M. Pfiffner and F.P. Sherwood, *Administrative Organization* (Englewood Cliffs, N.J.: Prentice-Hall, 1960), pp. 442–67.
5. Kenneth Boulding, *The Organizational Revolution* (New York: Harper, 1953), p. 78.
6. M.E. Dimock, *Administrative Vitality: The Conflict with Bureaucracy* (New York: Harper, 1959), p. 259.
7. W.A. Lewis, 'Economic Development with Unlimited Supplies of Labour', *Manchester School of Economics and Social Studies,* 22, 2 (1954), p. 173.
8. S.O. Olayide, 'Towards Realistic Economics Research in Nigeria'. Paper presented at the International Seminar on 'Research on Employment and Income Distribution Problems in Developing Countries' held at the Kellog Centre, Michigan State University (East Lansing) on 16–18 December 1970.
9. Dudley Seers, 'The Role of Industry in Development: Some Fallacies', *Journal of Modern African Studies,* 1, 4 (1963), pp. 461–5.

Co-operatives: An Introduction

'Co-operatives' in Africa denote a wide range of organizational forms involved in varying activities. Within the rural sector alone they include – more rarely – producer co-operatives where agricultural production and the ownership of land involves a significant collective element, and – more commonly – marketing co-operatives which leave the individual farmer to get on with production on his own farm while performing servicing functions such as the supply of inputs and credit as well as the marketing of produce.

The Tanzanian 'Ujamaa' village is probably the best African example of a producer co-operative. All land is owned communally, there is no hiring of labour, and there is some form of elected management. Producer co-operatives of this kind are very difficult to organize and success stories are very rare. The problems are obviously immense and require a massive investment of administrative time at the early stages. They include the whole question of resettlement – getting people from different backgrounds to move on to new land and to work under new conditions; they also involve problems of institutionalizing patterns of participation and self-management as well as working out divisions of responsibility and work organization. Marketing co-operatives on the other hand, although they also have their problems, have been more successful. The focus of this section is on the latter type and in particular on the increasing role of government in what were originally semi-autonomous farmers' organizations.

The colonial encouragement of co-operatives in many African territories after the Second World War had a twofold aim. Politically, their encouragement may be viewed as a device to provide a non-political outlet for the energies and increasing expectations of certain sections of the African population, paralleling the development of local government in some parts at this time. Economically, the colonial encouragement of marketing co-operatives in the indigenous smallholder sector was part of the attempt to increase output of key export cash crops.

Thus co-operatives may also be seen as an institution which facilitates administration of government policy in the rural areas. Faced with a very large number of small farmers spread over a wide area and a critical limitation of skilled administrators, governments usually look to self-help among farmers as an aid to agricultural development. Essentially this means that farmers themselves undertake some of the management required in providing the necessities for a modernizing agriculture – for example, supply of improved inputs, better marketing channels, and agricultural extension and credit. Frequently co-operatives are the institution chosen as the vehicle for mobilizing the managerial abilities of farmers in order to promote agricultural development policies.

Because of the various historical nuances and the wide range of organizational forms embraced by the term 'co-operative', the working of some African marketing co-operatives has at times been appraised against early European or Israeli utopian experiments. The principles behind co-operatives were first developed by nineteenth-century industrial workers in England as an alternative to the existing capitalism. Their vision was to replace ownership by the few with group ownership, replace authoritarian decisions with democracy, and to make the amount of business done the basis for distributing profits – that is, to supply the services of the co-operative to members at cost.

Co-operatives tend to be confused with some of these early experiments. The farmers co-operative organizations that exist in Africa today differ in many important respects from the utopian experiments which are often pointed to as a model. First, most co-operatives were organized from above during the colonial period rather than being initiated voluntarily by farmers themselves and prices have always been controlled from outside, especially in the case of export crops. Secondly, co-operatives in Africa were never in any way socialist or anti-capitalist institutions; they were simply directed against the elimination of the exploitative activities of the middleman. Indeed, as we shall come to see later, producer members of co-operatives may be exploited by rich farmers who have become entrenched in co-operative union positions.

The organization of the cash crop sector is in fact more a mixture of collective, co-operative and private enterprise. Co-operatives are more akin to hard-headed business associations of individual producers who have seen benefits in pooling resources and making economies of scale – as for example in the supply of inputs and credit and the organization of marketing. A lot of rhetoric about African co-operatives is misleading where it also links their organization to aspects of pre-capitalist or 'traditional' village life. Marketing co-operatives can in no way be seen in these terms since they do not represent face-to-face groups in the way that traditional working parties did or still do. Marketing co-operatives simply service individual smallholders by providing them with inputs credit and marketing facilities.

After Independence in Africa marketing co-operatives continued to be of concern to central policymakers who saw them as important sources of surplus capital to be skimmed off for re-investment in development programmes, or for private consumption by the elite. Thus the economic efficiency aspects of co-operatives assumed greater importance and there was a de-emphasis on the political aspects. In other words, co-operatives have come to be regarded less as organizations of the farmers, and more as government agencies for extracting as much of the rural surplus as possible. The trend since Independence has then been towards putting co-operatives under government control and supervision.

14. The Administration of Institutional Change at the Village Level: The Experience of Farmers' Co-operatives in Nigeria

Roger King

The Blueprint for Co-operatives in Northern Nigeria[1]

The basis for the co-operative movement in northern Nigeria is similar to that introduced by the British in other parts of the world. The description below is specific to Co-operative Credit and Marketing Societies, which account for the majority of farmers' co-operatives in northern Nigeria. The nature of co-operatives is spelled out in the Co-operative Societies Law, and the subsidiary legislation made under the Co-operative Societies Regulations (Section 58), which came into force in 1956.[2] The individual societies are free to make their own by-laws subject to the approval of the Registrars of Co-operatives, but in fact a high degree of uniformity exists, and the following description of rules guiding co-operative operations includes those from the standard book of by-laws provided by the Co-operative Registrar's office.

The Co-operative Law established a registered co-operative as a 'body corporate' with a life of its own and the ability to enter into contracts and be subject to other legal obligations. To be eligible for registration by the Registrar of Co-operatives who heads each state's Co-operative Division, a co-operative should have at least ten members over the age of eighteen within its area of operation. The area of operation is usually a village and surrounding hamlets. Membership is voluntary and open to all farmers subject to the approval of existing members. A condition of membership is the purchase of a minimum number of shares in the society. No member can purchase more than 20% of the total shares issued. Once a member of a Co-operative Credit and Marketing Society, a farmer can take part in its economic activities. He can deposit savings, receive low interest loans (interest limited to 20% per annum), and sell his produce to the co-operative which resells it at the best possible price. The member also becomes eligible for a share of the profits arising from the societies' activities. A proportion of the profits must be deposited in the societies' 'reserve fund' but the rest is distributed on the basis of business done (bonus) or shares held (dividends).

The major decisions of the co-operative, as described by the regulations, are taken by democratic vote at general meetings. Other decisions are looked after by an elected committee who are obliged to meet at least once a month and are elected at the Annual General Meeting. Day to day affairs are managed by the Secretary who may or may not be paid a salary. The society is subject to an annual audit by the registrar's department. The regulations and by-laws describe in some detail how the society should undertake its activities. The basis for distributing loans is stated, as is the method of organizing the marketing of produce. The by-laws list fourteen types of books and accounts which every society must maintain. There are procedures laid down for resolving most of the disputes which might occur. Frequently, as for example in applying for an extension of the loan repayment period, members are required to follow a written procedure. In addition to the primary societies described above, there is provision for secondary societies, or co-operative unions, providing services to member societies.

The objectives stated in the by-laws also reveal a number of additional underlying aims to the business operation described above. These include encouragement of improved methods of agriculture by supplying expert advice, and improved inputs. Members are, in fact, legally obliged to use loans received only for agricultural purposes. In addition to the emphasis on agricultural development the societies are supposed to encourage 'the spirit and practice of thrift, mutual help and self-help' and 'to promote co-operative spirit among the members, to work for the improvement of local educational and living standards, and to encourage the development of the Co-operative Movement in the Northern Region of Nigeria'.[5] The blueprint is therefore of a well-defined organization which can operate with near independence. Ideally, the economies of scale arising from the group effort should result in loans to farmers at interest rates below those of alternative sources and in increased incomes from lowering the cost of produce marketing. The fulfillment of such a blueprint requires qualities among the members which may initially be in short supply in rural areas. These include an understanding and appreciation of democratic decision-making, the managerial ability to run a credit programme on a bureaucratic basis, the sophistication to deal with urban institutions such as banks, and the ability to build up the trading links essential to efficient marketing. A minimum of literacy among members and the availability of a skilled secretary are essential. Elected officials must embrace an ethic of selfless business honesty which village society has previously given them little opportunity to develop. The government co-operative officials receive a training which emphasises the rules and principles of the blueprint. They then have the unenviable task of approximating the blueprint in societies where few of the qualities essential for its achievement are immediately available.

The Administration of Co-operatives in Practice

The co-operative movement in northern Nigeria has had problems in the past which were not directly attributed to the aims or the administration of co-operative policy. In terms of increase in numbers the greatest period of growth for the co-operative movement was during the 1960s. In 1972 there were 250,000 members in 2,700 registered societies.[6] Some societies were not formed on a genuine basis, but were inspired by politicians who used them for collecting and distributing patronage. There are many stories of money loans being distributed to hastily-formed societies who felt no obligation to repay, or of members repaying in good faith only to find later that there was no record of their repayment. In addition to undermining the concept of a co-operative among farmers, this inference was partly responsible for the accumulation of a ₦2,776,870 debt by 1970.[7] At this point most of the loans to farmers were halted by the newly-formed state governments pending a review of co-operative activities. The withdrawal of government-guaranteed production credit effectively halted co-operative activity societies. In recent years a number of states have cautiously resumed distributing production credit to those co-operative societies which have achieved the best repayment records in the past. It is revitalized societies in Kano State and the former North-Eastern State that form the basis of this section of the chapter.[8] The farmers involved in the six primary Co-operative Credit and Marketing Societies which form the basis of the study were engaged in hoe agriculture and farmed an average of three hectares per family in those villages studied in the North-Eastern State. Most farmers used some chemical fertiliser and a minority used bullock ploughs or government tractor hire services. The main food staples were millet and sorghum; the main cash crop was groundnuts. The average size of the societies was about one hundred members, varying from forty in the smallest to two hundred in the largest.

Co-operative Credit

The co-operative credit operation consists of the annual distribution of pre-season loans and collection of repayments at harvest time. In one of the two states studied, part of the loan was given half-way through the growing season. Towards the end of the dry season, after satisfactory repayment of the previous year's loan, a meeting is called by the government Co-operative Officer to complete the loan applications forms for the next farming year. Usually every member applies for and receives a loan. The information included on the forms varies from state to state, but includes area farmed, crops grown and the previous year's harvest. Government Co-operative Inspectors necessarily assist in this process as very few of the farmers can read or write and sometimes the forms are in unfamiliar English rather than the local Hausa. In the past the estimates of farmed area, expressed in area, have often been widely inaccurate as most farmers have no concept of an acre nor any alternative area measure. The application form is signed with the member's thumb print and verified as accurate by the society's president and treasurer. In one state an additional person must sign as surety, while in the other this regulation has been abandoned on the grounds that enforcement would be difficult and socially unacceptable. Following head office approval a second meeting is called and the credit is distributed to the entire society at a single meeting. The money is handed from government officials direct to individual members in front of the remaining members.

The amount each farmer received was determined differently in the two methods stated above. In one, a formula based on an estimate of agricultural needs per acre was used by the Co-operative Office to determine the size of individual loans. In the other, information on the forms was not used and the members decided between themselves who should get a small, medium or large loan. In both cases the size of loans was limited by the total amount allocated to that society by the local Co-operative Office, which in turn was limited by the total amount allocated to the local co-operative union by the headquarters of the Co-operative Division. Similarly the total credit programme of the Co-operative Division itself is limited by the decision of the State Government. This control over co-operative credit by the government is possible because the co-operatives are dependent on government financing. Contrary to the blueprint the societies have been unable to collect savings, accumulate profits or become creditworthy in their own right. The finance for the loans is from government-guaranteed bank overdrafts and the state governments bear the cost if co-operative members do not repay their loans.

The continuing existence of a co-operative credit society is most directly dependent on its ability to collect repayments from its members. It is here that the institution makes its greatest contribution. The six societies which were studied in detail were among those which historically had good repayment records. The repayment system is for the elected officials of the primary society to collect money from members whenever they can. The Secretary of the society issues receipts, but as nearly all members are illiterate the essential basis for the system is one of memory and trust in the leaders. The ability of a society to enforce repayment and receive the trust of the members seemed to be dependent on the authority of the one or two leaders. This was certainly true for the four most rural societies, where in three cases the authority could be traced to the village head. In the fourth village, the head was young and distrusted (and excluded from the co-operative), and the co-operative president, a respected village elder, was regarded as an alternative leader in the village. The basis for success in the two societies located in small towns was not so clear. Probably these societies, whose members are relatively cosmopolitan, are less dependent on traditional authority. Traders who stood to personally gain by becoming co-operative produce buyers were prominent among the leaders of these societies.

The Government Co-operative office has come to play a much more central role that is suggested by the theoretical blueprint. Rather than supervising co-operative activities through organization, it has come to control many decisions because of the societies' dependency on government financing. In extending its control the Co-operative Division has built direct links between itself and members, and has undertaken much of the administration which the blueprint makes the responsibility of the society. The co-operative union has no life of its own, all its decisions being made by the Co-operative

Office.

In reality the co-operative pre-season loan operation is not very different from a typical government sponsored group credit scheme. The system of decision making outlined in the co-operative blueprint is hardly utilized. Success seems to be mostly dependent on respect for traditional authority, or the forcefullness of a few modern thinking personalities who may be partly motivated by the opportunity the co-operative offers for personal gain.

Co-operative Marketing

An obvious difference between theory and practice in co-operative marketing is again the central role of the Area Co-operative Office in managing the operation. A second equally striking contrast is the lack of linkages between members and the marketing operation at the union level. The only linkages in the marketing operation is in the election of the buyer. The buyer then buys independently and indiscriminately, delivering to the union and receiving personal compensation for his work. The members disregard their legal obligation to sell through the co-operative and receive no bonus or dividends from the marketing operation. Not surprisingly the ordinary member does not see co-operative marketing as one of the benefits of co-operative membership.

The co-operative buyer uses the produce purchasing advances to buy from individuals or traders at the best price he can. He is usually indistinguishable from non-co-operative buyers. Sometimes the co-operative buyer can obtain a better price for the produce he buys by selling it somewhere other than the union. This is illegal, but it is difficult to control in practice. Repayment records for purchasing loans are far better than for production credit, because of the smaller number of people involved.

In reality the effect of the co-operative marketing policy is to increase the money available in the existing marketing system. The average member sells to the sub-agents to whom he habitually sells and does not know whether his produce eventually is resold to the co-operative buyer or not. The elected co-operative buyer is almost certain to already be a buyer, because members recognize that only established buyers have the skills tofill the post effectively. Thus the financing is a way for some existing traders to increase their scale of operation. There may be some indirect advantage for the co-operative in that the co-operative buyer is frequently highly motivated to support other co-operative activities and to ensure the co-operative's continued existence.

Co-operative policy has therefore not replaced the existing marketing practices but has utilized them. As the members themselves do not receive an any direct benefit, the government justification for the policy is found in the general benefit to all farmers. If more money is made available to buy farmers' produce, it is argued, farmers will be more willing to increase their production. Further, the co-operative buyers are elected by farmers which should mean that the more trustworthy buyers are those which receive government support. Co-operative marketing has therefore been financed by government and used to promote its agricultural development policy. In one state this deviation from the idea of a co-operative as a business was taken further when grain purchased by the co-operatives was sold at below market price in an attempt to control urban food prices.

Summary, Conclusions and Implication

At the beginning of this chapter, co-operative policy was described in terms of an attempt to promote institutional change which would mobilize farmers' managerial abilities in the service of agricultural development while developing desirable social attitudes. A blueprint was designed and a Registrar appointed to head the Government Co-operative Division which would administer this change. In practice, however, farmers have not come to run co-operatives according to the blueprint, and an institution different to that envisaged has evolved. Compared to the blueprint, actual co-operative administration involves a much greater degree of government involvement and control, and makes more use of the traditional way of doing things. There are good reasons for both of these trends.

Much of the record keeping has been transferred from the co-operatives to the local Co-operatives Office of the Government. The laws requiring so societies to keep fourteen types of books were unsuitable for village societies which may be dependent on a barely literate, unpaid schoolboy to keep their records. Such records do not in any case improve farmers' faith in an institution when they themselves cannot read.[9] The necessity for the government to keep the records has been reinforced by the co-operatives' dependency on government financial support. When the source of funds essential for any co-operative activity comes from the government, it is reasonable to find the government keeping a watchful eye on transactions.

The fact that the societies have been unable to create their own funds probably reflects a wrong premise that it is simple for co-operators to market produce more efficiently than private traders. In fact co-operative marketing policy has shelved the aim of making profit in favour of an agricultural policy affecting all farmers. In operating this policy the co-operative officials have generally made use of the skills in their agricultural development policies, but not solely for the benefit of members as envisaged in the blueprint.

In the operation of co-operative credit a useful institution has been built among farmers. Although many important decisions have been removed from it, the primary society still has the important functions of vetting loan recipients and recovering loans. The managerial ability to do this is often dependent on using the existing institutions of village authority. The village unit provides the mutual knowledge and trust necessary for success. The primary society has also sometimes given the opportunity for alternative leaders to emerge when traditional authorities are unacceptable.

Many of the formalities of the blueprint are followed, although they have little substantive function. Thus money is nominally channelled through co-operative unions, although its fate is in fact controlled by the government Co-operative Officer. Loan recipients sign application forms stating that they will use the loan for agriculture and will sell their produce to the co-operative, while neither of these provisions are enforced. The farmer sensibly uses his loan and sells his produce to his own best advantage. A new member must still buy shares in the society. As these never yield dividends they are regarded by members, not as an investment, but as a registration fee necessary before government money can be received. The lesson to be drawn from these experiences is the one that development policies and their administration must be sensitive and adapted to local conditions and realities. Any attempt to introduce an institution not fully suited to existing conditions has resulted in something quite different from the original plan. A *modus vivendi* has evolved to accommodate the strength of established institutions and the lack of suitable skills and attitudes to operate an independent co-operative organization. This need not be regarded as failure if the reality is fully acknowledged and seen as the basis for more effective policies. Co-operative officials partially recognise this with their acute awareness of the need for more education among co-operative members. At the same time, perhaps as a result of the training for co-operative officials, deviation from the latter of the co-operative laws is often regarded as a failure. Thus there is a danger that practical policies which make the best use of the existing situation to promote agricultural development and self-help may be deliberately stifled under a facade of co-operative propriety.

What is probably needed, if farmers' managerial abilities are to be mobilized in the service of agricultural development, is encouragement to devise simple, flexible institutions which farmers can operate themselves. This implies an attitude by government administrators which bears in mind the social aims co-operatives were designed to serve, rather than the myriad restrictions of the co-operatives regulations. This does not necessarily mean the blueprint should be abandoned as an eventual objective, only that it is not a practical short-term aim. In the short term policies of institutional change will, while trying to reform the existing structure, have to make some use of existing institutions such as the village community and adapt themselves to skills and attitudes which already exist. In the longer term new skills are gained and new leaders emerge as farmers gain experience of the new institution, a process which can probably be accelerated by intelligent education and propaganda policies.

References

1. Institutions are simply the way things are done in society. By making promotion of co-operatives part of its policies, a government is

indicating that it is not satisfied with the way certain things are being done. For example, government promotion of co-operatives which made loans to farmers and sold their produce would indicate that the government considered the traditional credit and marketing arrangements to be unsatisfactory. It might also indicate that the traditional methods of decision making and the distribution of economic power in rural communities were unacceptable to the government, who wished to replace them with the principles of democracy and shared ownership inherent in co-operatives. Thus co-operative policy is an attempt to promote institutional change which would mobilize farmers' managerial abilities in the service of agricultural development whilst developing desirable social attitudes.

2. *Northern Region Co-operative Societies Regulations Co-operative Societies Law, 1956.* (Kaduna: Government Printer).
3. *Bye-laws of the Co-operative Credit and Marketing Society Limited.* (Kaduna: Government Printer).
4. *Bye-Laws,* p. 1. para. 4(vii)
5. *Bye-Laws,* p. 2. para. 4(ix)
6. Data collected by the author from the Registrar offices of the six northern states between January and March 1973.
7. B.J. Youngjohns, *The Co-operative Movement in Nigeria* (London: Ministry of Overseas Development, 1970), p.2.
8. Three primary co-operative societies and one union in each of the states were studied in detail. All the societies had been registered more than eight years and had received production credit for the last two years at the time of the study (1973–74). The societies had between 25 and 200 members. North-Eastern State was divided into 3 in 1976.
9. It is possible to devise methods whereby illiterate farmers can manage co-operative affairs. Gentil, for example, describes a simple system of recording co-operative groundnut marketing which was successfully used by illiterate farmers in Niger. Gentil, 'The Establishment of a new Co-operative System in Niger', paper prepared for the *Second International Seminar on Change in Agriculture,* Reading, England 9–19 September 1974.

15. The Farmer and the State in Western Nigeria: The Role of Farmers' Organizations and Co-operatives

Christopher Beer

The Co-operatives

The problems confronting farmers' co-operatives in Western Nigeria are acute; nevertheless, collectively, they still form much the strongest institutionalized farmers' group in the state. The problems of inefficiency and of under-capitalization, of corruption and of employee-control, of the over-involvement of government and of mass membership illiteracy are in large measure a consequence of, or at the least are greatly magnified by, general economic underdevelopment. As such, these problems are shared by co-operative movements in many other systems.[1] Attention will primarily be focused in this chapter on certain areas in which reforms might significantly improve the co-operatives' economic and political performance and also thereby, indirectly, the political stability of Western Nigeria.

The situation whereby the co-operatives like the farmers' unions tend to attract the support of wealthier, cash-crop oriented farmers is not likely to change easily; Saul has noted a similar tendency for Tanzanian co-operatives to be captured by what he termed the 'economic activists' (or 'capitalist' farmers) in the villages. Such a division of interests, he claims, does much to explain the 'problem of corruption' in such societies: 'Co-operatives . . . in a transitional society . . . readily fall under the sway of "economic activists" . . . to be seized by that group for its own aggrandizement and manipulated against the interests of their more parochialized kinsmen.'[2] In Western Nigeria, co-operative committees are composed in the main of the larger farmers, and committee members have indeed often used their influential positions primarily to promote private, rather than collective ends (for example in the seeking of loans or chemicals over and above their entitlement as members, or in using their position to operate as produce sub-buyers).

This being said, it is certain that a majority of farmer co-operators, if growers of cocoa, could not be considered 'large' farmers. The influence of smaller, relatively less wealthy farmers in their societies could probably be considerably increased by certain rather self-evident reforms, for example by a greater use of the Yoruba language in the keeping of society reports, records, minutes of meetings and co-operative literature generally. The process whereby meetings conducted in the vernacular are transcribed for record purposes, into a language incomprehensible to a great majority of the membership, derives from the colonial past. In addition, whilst the non-Yoruba speaking Midwest was part of the Western Region the Co-operative Department rightly felt that the use of the majority language in co-operative affairs would be resented by minorities. At the present time, there is no reason why Yoruba cannot be more widely used, and the present 'competence gap' between employees, large farmers and government officials on the one hand, and the generality of peasant farmers on the other thereby lessened. Such a policy would not only increase member-participation but would also facilitate members' control over business and employees.

The dominance of cocoa marketing, and therefore of the cocoa farmer, inside the co-operative movement has been an ever present feature in Western Nigeria. Cocoa brought the Yoruba peasant into the cash economy, into contact with foreign buyers, and caused the first indigenous and spontaneous growth in agrarian co-operative enterprise intended to substitute for capitalist relationships. Until recently all other forms of co-operative activity have tended to be viewed, by co-operative leaders and by government officials, as tertiary.

It was unfortunate, though in the circumstances understandable, that development of the cocoa marketing societies preceded that of thrift and credit. Much the best way for independence, self-reliance and vigilance of membership regarding employees' actions to be built up, would have been to ensure that the movement developed on its own capital. Farmers, it might be hypothesized, would exercise greater care concerning their own money, than over funds which are considered to derive from government.[3] Thus, for example, grants from the Marketing Board during the 1950s, though they can be justified in terms of the percentage of the Board's reserves which had been built up through the endeavours of farmer co-operative members, have been dissipated and have had the unfortunate effect of making co-operative members expectant of further similar government support. When patronage has dried up, as it has tended to do over the past decade, the result has all too often been apathy and a falling away of membership.[4] Though the Co-operative Department and the Co-operative Union of Western Nigeria (CUWN) are at present making strenuous efforts, through the development of thrift societies, to increase the internal accumulation of capital in the movement, other developments, notably the cessation of the Association of Nigerian Co-operative Exporters (ANCE) compulsory deposits scheme, have worked in the other direction.

Much the most significant legacy from the past however, and surely now the most damaging, is the excessive control over societies exercised by the Registrar and his lieutenants. This subject has been treated at some length by other writers.[5] The present Co-operative Law in short needs to be substantially redrafted in order that a more progressive concept of the entire movement/government relationship might be embodied within it. Considerably more power of initiative should be given to policy-making bodies at all levels inside the movement.[6]

At the present time there exist built-in disincentives for the movement to achieve 'take-off' from government, for as long as supervision and inspection is being carried out by the Department, societies are receiving a *de facto* subsidy. If such functions were to be carried out, in so far as they would still be required, by the CUWN, additional costs would be incurred by the movement.[7] The present hidden subsidy, encouraging a maintenance of the government connection, needs to be replaced by a system which would promote the desire and ability to sustain co-operative self-government. Perhaps the most feasible way of achieving this would be to give societies, which by their performance in terms of efficiency, profitability and internal democracy indicate that they are able to operate without Department supervision, a status different in law to societies still needing Department inspection. Such societies would thereafter be supervised by the CUWN, a body which is in turn responsible to them.

One central factor would remain to be solved. The CUWN's chronic financial weakness prevents adequate performance of present functions, not to speak of additional burdens. The union is agitating for an endowment from the Marketing Board to ease its difficulties, though it must be said that a favourable decision is unlikely, given existing conditions of low reserves, declining world prices for cocoa, and, since the peasant riots of 1969, relatively high producer prices. Perhaps such an endowment might be more acceptable if the costs of supervision of a considerable number of societies and unions could thereby be removed from the State government's recurrent expenditure. What is certain is that the present policy of expanding the Co-operative Department, without any thought given to the progressive decontrol of the movement, sweeps the real problems under the proverbial carpet.[8]

A strengthening of the CUWN as the political, educative and propaganda apex of the movement – which must ultimately, any endowment apart, be undertaken largely by the corporatives themselves – is a prerequisite to increased independence.[9] In order that the CUWN might be able to provide necessary supervision at fees which would not prove a disincentive to societies leaving the Department's wing, any new Co-operative Law should emphasize the central role to be played by the union, and should make contributions to it mandatory for all societies (perhaps to be calculated as a percentage of turnover?) In addition, certain positive incentives could be provided to encourage societies to seek independent status, for example preferential treatment with regard to produce advances, or supplies of spraying chemicals.

Finally, attention needs to be directed to the chronic lack of agricultural expertise within the co-operative movement. The type of supervision provided by the Co-operative Department has been narrow in scope and entirely non-agricultural. This emphasis is reflected in the training of co-operative inspectors, who receive no instruction on agricultural matters, even though all but a small proportion of the societies they will supervice are concerned with agriculture.[10] Neither does the CUWN possess any qualified agricultural personnel. While it would not be desirable to duplicate the work of the Ministry of Agriculture and Natural Resources (MANR) extension service, certain basic training of its field staff in agricultural methods would greatly enhance the union's value to farmers' societies.

Moreover the present lack of MANR attention to the co-operatives is harmful; indeed relationships between individual societies and the local extension service could well improve were Co-operative Department staff to withdraw from their present pre-eminent position. Informal consultative links at district and divisional levels should be established between co-operatives, local Co-operative Department and CUWN extension staff, and their MANR counterparts. At the central level, a joint planning committee between the Department, the MANR, the CUWN and the Co-operative Bank might be envisaged. If the dismal experiences of the Farm Settlement programme and the Agricultural Credit programme are not be repeated, the co-operative movement and the Department must be drawn into policy-making when co-operative development is involved. Though this might appear self-evident, it has never been observed in the past.

The Farmers' Union

Whereas the political centre of the co-operatives (the CUWN), as a federal structure, has had great difficulty in persuading affiliates to subscribe and lend support, in the successive regional or state-wide farmers' unions the centre has normally been dominant. One might employ in this context Lipset's categorization of common patterns of organization in trade unions:

> There are two general processes through which organizations are created. One is organization from the top down, where the group which originally starts the association organizes other individuals or branches into a larger structure. In such a situation a formal bureaucratic structure exists from the start, with the new subordinate officials deriving their authority from the summits of the organization.
>
> A large national organization may also come into existence as a federation, either through the successive but autonomous formation of one group after another, or by the comparatively simultaneous formation of a number of unconnected groups which later unite. In both cases a ready-made opposition is built into the organization.[11]

On two occasions in particular, the farmers' union structure has been deliberately altered by government – in 1961 with the creation of the Western Nigerian Farmers' Council, and in 1969 with the MANR build-up of the Western State Farmers Union. Both instances were intended primarily to increase the representativeness of the farmers' lobby. It has been seen that on each occasion the former union leadership was able to re-establish itself. In part this was due to the actions of the Administration, in part to the operation of certain factors which have served to strengthen leadership's control over membership. The overall impression is of a surprising degree of leadership continuity, despite the rise or fall of individual organizations.

Union leaders, like those of the co-operatives, tend to have been drawn from the ranks of the more educated; such men possess not only the tangible benefits of literacy over their fellows, they are also accorded a relatively high status. Farmers have tended to defer to those of their number who are able to deal with government functionaries on an equal footing, and who are presumed to know the accepted ways of transacting business, of keeping records, speaking at meetings or applying for credit. In the farmers' unions there had been a tendency for the wealthier cocoa farmers to exercise leadership functions especially at the local levels. At the centre, leaders have often been at most part-time farmers, and at times possessed a minimal knowledge of farming problems.[12] Here, a 'professional' union leadership has emerged, in the sense that some of these men are primarily dependent on their union positions for their income. At the same time, because legitimate returns in such positions are relatively low and insecure, this leadership has tended towards a dependence on the good-will and patronage of outside political leaders to supplement both income and status. In addition, the large-scale misappropriation of union funds has been commonplace.[13]

The leadership has had all the advantages over the general membership possessed in any association by the 'active minority.' It has, in particular, been careful to retain control over union communications, and has possessed a near monopoly of political skills. The education and skill of union leadership has, more often than not, and more blatantly than in the co-operatives, been used to gain advantages and exercise control over the membership, rather than to forward mass goals. The unhappy experience of the Farmer's Council, and the growing certainty that the WSFU has also been manipulated for leadership ends, leads one reluctantly to echo the view that 'study and education has helped some people to succeed. . . with their knowledge they are better able to exploit ignorance. They are able to cheat more dexterously.'[14]

Due to the presence of influential groups of large cocoa farmers, and educated, often part-time farmers, the farmers' unions have been relatively 'long' on organization but 'short' on interest. Their superior command of organizational resources has in the most successful instances led to government recognition, which has been made the more likely because, in the eyes of MANR civil servants, such groups appear as interest groups should. Nevertheless none of the unions have gained large-scale support, and they have tended to atrophy over time. By way of contrast, those organizations which have derived principally from spontaneous mass outbursts, and which we have termed 'populist', have at their height mobilized the mass support of people who have previously 'suffer(ed) in silence;'[15] they have at the outset been the groups most closely committed to mass peasant goals. Populist movements have been 'long' on interest but 'short' on long-run organization; literacy and organizational and negotiating skills have had to be obtained from outside sources, either through 'brokerage', or through involvement with a wider political movement compatible with their aims.

The formal farmers' unions have at best sought benefits for the larger, educated or improving 'farmers', rather than viewing their role as the achievement of mass objectives for the peasantry as a whole. Thus, for example, the emphasis has been placed upon the seeking of government credit, which can be granted to only a small number of farmers, while campaigns for higher produce prices or better 'feeder' roads have been neglected. Similarly, unions have placed a high priority on the gaining of licences for the marketing of produce. While it is possible to argue that the possession of such a licence might provide 'selective benefits'[16] for the membership as a whole, which would in turn provide incentives for joining, in practice the experience of cocoa-buying operations in the unions supports the view that such selective benefits have been pirated for the leaderships' private ends. The NFU Commercial Society failed largely through a lack of proper inspection and control, and the same has been true of virtually every similar later venture. It appears that only the co-operatives, for all their many inadequacies,[17] have been able to attract a significant number of farmers over a relatively long period, with the promise of high and fair prices, fair weighing and cheap credit.

The actions of the farmers' unions in the period leading up to the 1965 regional elections, and those of the Ibadan WSFU during the *Agbekoya* rebellion when so many prominent union members were strongly identified with the local council establishments and with the 'political class' in general, lend considerable support to arguments which suggest that many 'well-to-do' farmers increasingly find themselves in alliance with a 'new class' of administrators and politicians, inter-penetrating with them as beneficiaries of the existing system.[18] One would desire more information on the levels of wealth of ordinary members (as distinct from leaders) of both the co-operatives and the farmers' unions before drawing firm conclusions, but the hypothesis already stated appears reasonable on present evidence; that wealthier farmers have had a greater propensity to join associational groups integrated into the political system, whilst the poor, intermittently and at times of special hardship, have joined or leant their support to populist agrarian movements.[19]

Finally, and in view of the recent military government's continuing interest in the promotion of group activity among farmers, a note might be added concerning future development of the farmers' unions.

It is certain that major errors were made in the initial planning of the WSFU, resulting in the union falling into the hands of those elements which had made former unions unacceptable, both to the MANR and to a great majority of farmers. Emphasis might in future be placed upon developing strong district and local unions which could interact in a meaningful way with field officials. A centralized union will not, in the foreseeable future, be allowed a significant voice in the determination of central policy, either in the MANR or in the public corporations; one is therefore led to question what functions the central secretariat is supposed to perform, other than manipulation of the affairs and funds of the branches. If, after strong local units have been established, such units voluntarily wish to federate, this would be a different matter. The essential factor is that the union should exist first and primarily in the towns and villages, not in an air-conditioned suite of offices in 'Cocoa House'. In order that such local unions might prove of real value to the farming community the MANR might also consider changes in its own administrative methods, including perhaps a gradual devolution of authority over junior grades of the extension service to those farmers' groups which prove themselves relatively capable. Farmers would then be able to associate more positively with, and themselves adapt, local agrarian development. They would also be given more incentive for continuing and for peaceful association.[20]

Many local unions have existed in the past, and given the proper encouragement many more would emerge. The MANR up to the present, with what has amounted to an obsession with administrative neatness, has done all in its power to encourage such groups to come together into one 'all-embracing' organization. Whatever else history has shown, it has surely indicated the ineffectuality of trying to combine the co-operative movement with a more broadly based representative union. Moreover, aside from the co-operative/non-co-operative division, acute factionalism has been a feature of almost all the regional or state farmers' unions.

The politicians' motives in desiring 'unity' among farmers are fairly easily explained, the civil servants' less so.[21] A multiplicity of independently formed local groups, even competing groups within the same village, might do much for their efficiency, might make leaders more responsive to members' interests, and would certainly increase the total number of organized farmers interacting with government agencies. Without doubt, such groups would be attractive to outside political interests. Centralization nevertheless, has proved to be no instrument for 'insulating' the unions from party politics in the past, and has only placed political decision-making in the hands of an unrepresentative and unresponsive central leadership.

References

This is an excerpt from Christopher Beer, *The Politics of Peasant Groups in Western Nigeria* (Ibadan: University of Ibadan Press, 1976).

1. See, for example, Mahassin Khider and Morag C. Simpson, 'Co-operatives and Agricultural Development in the Sudan,' *Journal of Modern African Studies,* 6, 4 (1968)), pp. 509–18. Also, John S. Saul, 'Marketing Co-operatives in a Developing Country: the Tanzanian Case' (Paper presented to the Conference on the Social Prerequisites for Agricultural Co-operation, Institute of Development Studies, University of Sussex, March–April 1969).
2. *Ibid.*, pp. 14–15.
3. See Khider and Simpson, *op. cit.* , p. 516, when commenting on the

prevalence of fraud in Sudanese co-operatives: 'More depressing, however, was the failure to convince farmers that they were merely robbing themselves in the long run, not just "cheating the Government" – which they generally regarded as a rather commendable practice'.

4. An ILO co-operative expert assigned to report on the Western Nigerian movement has commented to the author that in many instances, for example in the Farm Settlement Scheme, or in the establishment of rural co-operative weaving units after 1961, government has provided all production requisites too readily and too early. When withdrawal has subsequently been attempted settlers and weavers, who by that time have come to regard themselves as government employees, have grown resentful and lethargic. One could also cite the instance of the 1965 operations of the Agricultural Credit Corporation in this respect, when farmers were encouraged by the governing party to believe that the formation of a co-operative was a sure way to receiving a government cheque.
5. Michael Koll, *Crafts and Cooperation in Western Nigeria* (Dusseldorf: Bertelsmann Universitatsverlag, 1971), pp. 68–77; S.O. Adeyeye, 'The Western Nigeria Cooperative Movement, 1935–1964' (M.A. thesis, University of Durham, 1967). pp. 283–84.
6. The opportunity could also be taken to simplify co-operative 'Model ByeLaws' and the Cooperative Regulations, thereby reducing the amount of clerical work and number of books involved in the running of each society. A revised Cooperative Societies Law could also include provision for the tying of the marketing of a members' produce to the issue of loans in marketing societies, and for the surcharging of committee members where it can be shown that through negligence or dishonesty they have involved their societies in losses.
7. Thus, in the only case of functional transfer which has taken place between Department and CUWN, namely the audit of societies' accounts, the move was followed by protests from societies that the CUWN should not charge for a service which the government had provided free. Many societies remain unwilling to pay their audit fees.
8. In 1970 the Department underwent expansion, the most prominent features of which was the creation of a new, fourth 'circle' centred on Oshogbo. New personnel were also recruited to deal with the marketing of cotton, which has now been largely removed from the MANR.
9. See Koll: A closer study of the CUWN would certainly reveal that its achievement run short of its present potential; but its potential is too small for its tasks. It is hypocrisy to allocate tasks to the CUWN which it cannot fulfil, and then to blame it for failure. There are some proud and energetic men in the CUWN; they are competent to teach farmers how the Marketing Board witholds profits from the sale of cocoa by fixing a low purchasing price. But such "cooperative education" would counter government's interests and is prevented. The CUWN is not consulted whenever Government turns one of its 'bold ventures' (such as farm settlements or weaving factories) into 'cooperative societies,' or when the Ministry of Agriculture diverts tractors formerly hired by cooperative farmers to newly founded farm settlements.' Koll, *op. cit.* pp. 74–7.

10. The ambitious one-year syllabus designed for co-operative inspectors at the Cooperative College Ibadan, is composed of bookkeeping and accountancy, auditing, general economics, law and principles of co-operation, duties of inspectors, secretaries and committees, comparative cooperation, economics of co-operation, social psychology and rural sociology, commercial law, principles of communication, statistics, business management. *Cooperative College, Ibadan, Prospectus,* 1968–69 (Ibadan: Government Printer, n.d.) p.4. There is little time for giving guidance on the complex problems involved in handling or storing produce, or supervising agricultural credit. Secondary school economics and histories of Robert Owen and the Rochdale Equitable Pioneers are given great emphasis; practical matters, aside from the keeping of books, all but ignored. The training of inspectors is the main task of the State Government financed College. Little time is given to courses of committee training, designed for members of the movement; rather more courses are run for union managers and society secretaries.
11. Seymour M. Lipset, 'The Political Process in Trade Unions', in *Political Man* (London: Mercury, 1963), p. 378. The federal concept could be applied only to the Nigerian Farmers' Union (NFU) of the main farmers' unions. On the other hand, groups like the Western Nigerian Farmers' Union (WNFU), Western Nigerian Farmers' Council (WNFC), All-Nigerian Farmers'Congress (ANFC), and, though in a different sense the Western State Farmers' Union, have all been organized from the top down.
12. Thus, for example, Ayoade is a retired railway booking clerk, and Odeyemi formerly a reporter on the *Daily Times* and information officer for the Ibadan Secretariat of the NCNC. Neither has impressed the author, their organizational energy apart, with their knowledge of agricultural questions or problems. Other central leaders, Akeredolu-Ale, Chief E.I. Banjo, E.P. Folarin and Chief Samuel Abiodun, have had stronger farming interests, and they have in general been men of some education; Folarin, for instance, attended St Andrews Theological College, Oyo, and took up farming rather than the church only a year before his scheduled ordination. Abiodun also has strong commercial interests.
13. Such characteristics do not appear to be confined to Western Nigerian farmers' unions. See A.L. Stinchcombe: 'Agrarian movements, except in highly advanced societies, tend to enjoy limited intra-class communication, to be poor in politically talented leaders, relatively unable to put together a coherent, disciplined class movement controlled from below. Contributions to the treasury of the movement tend to be small and irregular like peasant incomes. Peasant movements are thus especially prone to penetration by relatively disciplined political interests. Further, such movements tend to be especially liable to corruption since they are relatively unable to provide satisfactory careers for political leaders out of their own resources.' Arthur L. Stinchcombe, 'Agricultural Enterprise and Rural Class Relations,' *American Journal of Sociology*, 67, 2 (September 1961), p, 173.
14. Compare the view of peasant society given by a young teacher in

Montegrano, Italy. E.R. Banfield, *The Moral Basis of the Backward Society* (Glencoe Ill.: Free Press, 1958), p. 92. Lipset has also pointed out that the wider the status gap between leaders and members in any organization, the stronger and more cohesive will be the leadership, authority legitimating itself 'in a familiar self-reinforcing pattern of power and status: union office carries with it power, develops skills, supports a middle-class way of life . . . All of these, together with the position itself, are accorded relatively high status by the rank and file – status which make the entire role and actions of its incumbent legitimate.' Lipset, *op. cit.* pp. 369–70. Perhaps only by means of such arguments can one explain the resilience of farmers' union leadership over time in Western Nigeria, in face of continual evidence as to its shortcomings. The long-term solution, a predominantly literate peasantry, should have been brought nearer by the policy of free primary education adopted by the Action Group administration in the early 1950s. At present, however, it remains largely true that the boy who goes to school is the boy who leaves the farm. Urban unemployment is preferred by the primary school leaver to the frustrations, hard work and lack of status which is the lot of the farmer.

15. M. Olson, *The Logic of Collective Action* (Cambridge, Mass: Harward University Press, 1965), p. 165.
16. *Ibid.*, p. 51.
17. And of course with the aid of considerable government supervision.
18. J.S. Saul, 'Africa', in Ghita Ionescu and Ernest Gellner (eds.), *Populism: Its Measuring and Characteristics,* (London: Weidenfield and Nicholson, 1970), p. 140.
19. Compare Weiner on the Indian experience; having given instances of farmers' groups, led by the better educated rural leaders and the middle-class, he states that the poorer peasant has nevertheless had little access to the local power structure, to the administration, or to policy-makers. The existence of certain peasant organizations has not served to change his unorganized or basically inarticulate status. M. Weiner, *The Politics of Scarcity* (Chicago: Chicago University Press, 1962), pp. 5, 16.
20. See the proposals of Guy Hunter, *Modernizing Peasant Societies* (London: Oxford University Press., 1969), p. 181 and P.G.II. Barter, *Problems of Agricultural Development,* (Geneva: Libraine Droz, 1969). Such strategies have also had considerable success in the case of farmers' associations in Taiwan.
21. The Bateye recommendations derived from the civil service, as did much of the effort to implement them. In 1967, before the appointment of 'Bola Ige as Civilian Commissioner at the MANR, Aribisala had also initiated unsuccessful merger attempts, though there was a view in certain sections of the ministry on this occasion that the creation of a strong centre was not the correct policy.

PART 4
Administrative Reform

16. Current Issues of Administrative Reform in the Nigerian Public Services: The Case of the Udoji Review Commission

Paul Collins

Why Administrative Reform?

The growing concern with administrative reform in Africa since Independence has several clear origins. First, there was the experience of certain early programmes undertaken by the public sector. Two examples may be mentioned here. One is the crash localization programmes demanded in the civil service immediately after Independence. These raised questions about the content of the training programmes. The latter were necessarily dependent on overseas technical assistance and this meant the employment of 'Western' techniques and procedures – for example, in relation to such things as staff inspection, O. & M., schemes of service and standards of performance. Disappointing outcomes tended to be associated with continued reliance on inherited and foreign methods.

The second example is economic planning. The early planning experiences suggested that the public service was not ideally geared in terms of structures and procedures to the new planning roles. For example, training programmes, as mentioned above, tended to be rather orthodox and preoccupied with the internal aspects of public administration rather than the administrative requirements of development plans, programmes and projects. A second and related condition of the current reformist mood is the changing role of the public sector itself, both with respect to the adoption of new functions – such as economic planning – as well as by way of dramatic enlargement in some states. The various forms of state intervention were examined in Part II of the Reader.

A third catalyst of the reformist trend has been the political experimentation taking place elsewhere in the machinery of government and the feeling that the civil service was falling behind in terms of innovation. This was particularly so in states adopting a one-party form of government where traditional civil service neutrality, for example, no longer made any sense. Finally, with respect to the timing of administrative reform, it might be pointed out in the Nigerian context that the advent of military rule and the end of the Civil War has helped much in creating a reformist atmosphere.

Approaches to Administrative Reform

Apart from the inappropriateness of inherited techniques and procedures, common diagnoses of public service ineffectiveness have also included the following ailments. The first is low productivity, which is seen sometimes as the result of the pursuit of private business activities by public servants and sometimes as the result of resource-wasting rivalries between departments. It is also seen as the result of narrow bureaucratic perspectives that place the premium on controlling resource use, particularly public expenditure, rather than on the output or social and economic impact and benefits of expenditure. The second is poor policy-making and decision-making. The third is low executive or implementation capacity. The fourth and last is defective structures, usually overcentralization.

Whilst diagnoses have been fairly common, approaches to reformist action have sometimes been quite different. The first distinctive approach might be called ideological since it seeks to socialize administrators into the norms of public service and the values and goals of the political leadership. Such an approach has been extensively applied in Tanzania, where a national ideology has been well articulated and widely accepted, and where a well-developed private sector is largely absent and as such does not provide the temptation for civil servants to divert their energies away from public duties. The second approach is socio-psychological and concentrates on the motivational aspect of administrative work. Here the stress is upon the design of appropriate incentives – ranging from plain remuneration to developing a sense of pride in achievement in order to increase output. The third is the systems or procedural approach which involves the use of techniques such as Programmes and Performance Budgeting and Management by Objectives. The fourth is the institutional approach, which involves solutions such as the decentralization of responsibility to local authorities or public enterprises, or the creation of new institutions such as the Ombudsman. Particular countries may in fact adopt a mixture of these approaches in their administrative reforms.

The Nigerian Experience

In Nigeria a number of enquiries into the civil service have taken place since the later colonial period. The first was the Gorsuch Commission in 1954–5. Its terms of reference were 'to enquire into the structure and remuneration of the public service with special reference to problems arising from constitutional changes proposed at the conference on the Nigerian constitution. . .' The general finding of the Commission was that the civil service structure was a stratified one, the upper echelons being almost exclusively occupied by Europeans (the 'Senior Service') and the lower echelons by Africans. Its submission was that this pattern of organization was incongruent with the normal organization, which is pyramidal in structure with gradually increasing responsibilities from the bottom to the top. It argued further that the lack of a middle grade was detrimental to the efficiency of the service and that routine jobs meant for this grade were being performed by administrative and professional staff, many of whom were expatriates and very expensive to maintain. The Gorsuch Report recommended the abolition of the junior/senior service distinction in favour of a three-tier structure which included a middle-level grade. A number of other salary/wage revisions and grading teams were appointed thereafter,[1] but the next major review of basic structures did not take place until the Adebo Salaries and Wages Review Commission in 1971–2.

The Adebo Commission was set up principally 'to review the existing wages and salaries at all levels in the public services and in the statutory corporations and state-owned companies'. The Reports of the Commission in fact went beyond these strict terms of reference and considered various aspects of public service organization, including the role of the civil service in a developing country, its departmental and class structure, and the importance of appropriate training.

The 1974 (Udoji) Public Service Review Commission

The Adebo Commission was followed two years later by an extensive public service review – the Udoji Commission Report. The terms of reference of the Commission were:

> The Commission shall, having regard to the need to secure adequate development and optimal utilization of manpower and to increase the efficiency and effectiveness of the Public Services in meeting the challenge of a development-oriented society –
> (a) examine the organisation, structure and management of the Public Services and recommend reforms where desirable;
> (b) investigate and evaluate the methods of recruitment and conditions of employment and staff development programmes of the Public Services and recommend such changes as may be necessary;
> (c) examine all legislation relating to pensions as well as the various superannuation schemes in the Public Services and in the private sector and suggest such changes as may be appropriate with a view to facilitating mobility within the Public Services, and also between those services on the one hand and the private sector on the other, while at the same time providing for the retention in the Public Services of qualified and efficient personnel;
> (d) undertake, with the aid of appropriate grading teams, the regrading of all posts in the Public Services, establish scales of salaries corresponding to such grades, and as a result of a job evaluation of such posts, recommend salary scales to be applicable to each post in the services; and
> (e) enquire into and make recommendations on any other matters which in the opinion of the Commission appear to be relevant to the foregoing and therefore ought in the public interest, to be inquired into'.

In its enquiries and recommendations the Commission covered not just the central civil service departments but also the local authorities, police, judiciary, public enterprises, universities and the teaching service.

Broadly speaking, the findings and recommendations made by the Commission in their Main Report[2] fell into the following three major categories, in order of their specificity and the priority allocated to them in the implementation of the subsequent Government White Paper.

In its Main Report the Udoji Commission saw the central problem in these terms: 'The civil service of a development-oriented society must itself be change-oriented if it is to meet the present and future demands upon it. Any change must include the introduction of modern methods of managing complex organisations like government and the injection of new blood and the removal of obsolescence.'[3] 'The injection of new blood' was indeed a salient theme throughout the Commission's Report. Many of the measures recommended, including standardization of conditions of service, were aimed at facilitating mobility of personnel between sectors, particularly between public and private sectors. The Report continued: 'In view of the expanded and complicated nature of the present demands on the service, every effort should be made to bring into the service, especially at higher levels, suitably qualified and experienced candidates from outside the service'.[4]

Second, the Report proposed a package of modern techniques and procedures which, in tandem with the improved pay and conditions of service, and mobility of manpower between sectors, may improve and enhance civil service decision-making and productivity. They include Management by Objectives (M.B.O.), Project Management, and Programme and Performance Budgeting (P.P.B.). Unfortunately, the Report's presentation of these is rather academic and no real attempt is made to show how they could be made operational under Nigerian conditions. What might be noted here, particularly in relation to later discussions, is that the attempt to introduce techniques of this kind does mark a desire amongst certain sections within the civil service to develop a more efficient and technocratic type of public administration.

The third and most interesting – if vague and least heeded – aspect of the Public Service Review is its attempt to focus attention on a rather neglected dimension of public administration in the less industrialized countries – its relationships with interest groups and the general public. This, in classic parlance, is the problem of impartiality and accountability, and in the Nigerian context, the whole question of an appropriate administrative style.

First there was a round of backdated salary increases and improvement in conditions of service, with the disastrous consequences mentioned below. the increases were preceded by a restructuring of the old grading and classification system, introducing a unified one for all classes in the public services. These aspects of the exercise received great prominence as an attempt to 'harmonise' conditions in the public and private sectors and hence encourage inter-sectoral mobility.

The Government White Paper on the Udoji Report did not by any means accept all the recommendations made therein and described below. The main purpose of this concluding chapter is to explore the salient themes of the Udoji Report in so far as they raise some of the major issues of administrative reform in new states. The fact that the Federal Government did reject many of them does nevertheless raise another important issue on administrative reform – the forms and problems of implementation.[5]

Dimensions of Administrative Reform

Improving Internal Public Service Organization

Many countries since independence have contemplated or actually embarked upon administrative changes aimed at improving internal public service organization. These may not be necessarily considered 'reforms', which suggest rather sweeping innovations affecting all aspects of the public service. *Ad hoc* and piecemeal though these improvements might be, they nevertheless indicate growing dissatisfaction with existing performances.

Recruitment and Selection: One aspect of central civil service organisation to come under scrutiny, perhaps understandably given the political importance of civil service positions in regionally and ethnically competitive states of Africa, has been that of recruitment and selection. In the first years after independence recruitment of staff was a priority task of new regimes committed to the rapid indigenization of their civil services. Thereafter it continued to be a political problem in ethnically and regionally stratified states, where national stability required an even spread of top government positions amongst indigenes of all parts of the country. More recently, civil service recruitment has also been scrutinized as a technical problem of achieving levels of staff quality, as well as quantity and a balanced regional composition.

In the Nigerian context recruitment and selection have been a topic of discussion amongst both civil servants and academics in recent years.[6] The sacking of many top Federal and State civil servants after the July 1975 coup adds a new dimension to the recruitment issue. The old generation of civil servants had been in office for a long time, were still relatively young, and therefore likely to hold back the new generation for some time. But given the historically uneven development of Nigeria and the educational backwardness of the North, the axe has inevitably fallen mainly on southerners, particularly those from the West. Hitherto, northern interests had been protected at the Federal level by an informal arrangement whereby certain Ministerial portfolios (Finance, Mines and Power and the Inspectorate General of Police) were allocated to northerners. It remains to be seen whether there will be any change in the inter-regional composition of the Federal civil servants as a result of the replacement of those dismissed after the 1975 coup.

Classification: The second major area of public service organisation to come under recent scrutiny in Nigeria is the inherited system of classification.[7]

The Nigerian career service is basically a closed and class-based one modelled on the British. The four principal classes – administrative and professional, executive and higher technical, clerical, and sub-clerical – originated in the 1954 Gorsuch Report. In addition to these four basic classes, there are cadres within any particular class, each with its own grades and salary scale.[8]

The Udoji Report is particularly critical of the multiplicity of cadres and salary scales within the existing career service.[9] The system of classification, they argue, breeds tensions between administrators and professionals, and affects overall public service morale and productivity. It also impedes cadre mobility and does not make for the best development and utilization of manpower. This can happen, for example, where under the present system an officer loses some seniority by moving from one cadre to another. In sum, the Udoji Commission argues that the career service is a closed system and does not provide incentives for change, modernization or excellence and can lead to inbreeding and obsolescence.

As an alternative, the Commission recommends a unified grade structure to embrace all posts and provide equal opportunity for every officer to advance to the highest post in the service irrespective of his professional background. Within the proposed unified Ministerial structure, the dual hierarchies are abolished and overall management vested in one person, who replaces the Permanent Secretary and is to be known as the Chief Executive or Director-General. What is proposed is thus the integration of all senior management posts within a Ministry into one pyramid, with divisions and sections organized in accordance with the objectives to be achieved. The Commission argues that 'The proposed unified Ministerial structure is based upon principles of authority and responsibility, i.e. that in every organisation the supreme authority must rest at the top and that there should be a clear line of communication from the supreme authority to every individual in the organisation. The supreme authority bears ultimate responsibility for achieving the objectives of the organisation'.[10]

The proposed reorganization is also linked to recommendations elsewhere in the Report for the introduction of improved management techniques, particularly Management by Objectives. In an attempt to borrow from the practices of the private sector, the Report recommends that under the Chief Executive should be functional managers. At the top level, they argue, every senior officer must be a manager and should be responsible for the achievement of specific objectives with clearly defined resources of men, money and materials at his disposal. Regarding State machineries for recruitment and selection, namely the Heads of the Civil Services, the Ministries of Establishments, and the Public Service Commissions, they recommend a clearer definition of the authority and responsibilities of the major agencies involved. Specifically, they suggest that the Heads of Civil Services might be assisted by two new units for Co-ordination and Research and Policy Analysis respectively, that the Ministries of Establishments be renamed Ministries of Personnel and Public Management, and that the Public Service Commissions be reconstituted to ensure their independence from political influences. They also suggest the advertisement of all posts and the improvement of selection procedures.

Conditions of service: The third major aspect of internal public service organization and management is conditions of service – including promotion, discipline, and remuneration. These have also been much discussed in academic and administrative circles in Nigeria in recent years.[11] The thinking and recommendation of the Udoji Commission on these matters will be discussed later in relation to strategies of administrative reform for increasing civil service productivity.

Administrative Reform and Re-organization

The second and more recent pattern of administrative reform has been characterized by a concern with the overall performance and productivity of public administration in implementing the emergent goals of national social and economic development. Underlying the search for alternative strategies and techniques is often a growing disenchantment with piecemeal improvements in internal public service management. The resultant attempts to reorganize the public services have tended at times to be dramatic.

Areas of reformist concern may be grouped into two. First, administrative procedures – the search for increased productivity and an alternative style. Here the search is for strategies and techniques for re-orienting the behaviour of individual administrators as public servants, managers and decision-makers. As public servants, the need is sometimes expressed for administrators to maintain standards of leadership, integrity and democracy in their relations with clients. Norms of good public service are stressed in the effort to maintain the image of the civil service. The quantitative aspects of public administration have also received attention where the productivity of civil servants has been called into question. Finally, the need for manpower development has received stress, particularly in relation to the equipping of administrators to perform managerial and planning roles. Training has been the most common strategy adopted for the development of skills and the encouragement of innovations on the part of administrators. The use of ideology has been considered in some states in the effort to maintain or raise the quality of service to the public, whilst pay and conditions of service are commonly seen as major barriers to civil service productivity.

The second area of reformist concern has been with structural reorganizations. Some of these have been dramatic, involving the creation of new authority and communications patterns between parts of the machinery of government. In some cases, new organizations have been created – for example, integrated rural development agencies organized on a multi-functional basis. In others, reforms have taken place within a particular functional area – for example, by way of the decentralization of administrative responsibilities to public corporations or local authorities. In Nigeria, since the end of the Civil War, a concern over administrative methods, productivity and style has been expressed on a number of occasions by both practising administrators as well as academic observers.[12] Interestingly, many of the suggestions made have been taken up and developed in the Udoji Report.

Administrative Productivity

Essentially, the Udoji Report puts forward four major ways of increasing civil service productivity:

(1) The first way is through the introduction of modern techniques and improved procedures. Hereunder, the Report calls for 'a new conception of management, providing a more production or results-oriented approach to public service management'.[13]

(2) Second, it recommends corresponding training and manpower development, with emphasis on 'more specialized personnel and . . . scientific knowledge. . .'[14]

(3) Third, the Report puts heavy stress on the motivation side of administrative behaviour. It desires that '. . . the new public service will need to manage its human resources in such a way as to motivate them to achieve defined goals'. The major way recommended is through an improvement in conditions of service.[15]

(4) The fourth way of enhancing productivity is through more effective discipline.

Modern Techniques and Improved Procedures

The Udoji Report presents its 'results-oriented' management in these terms: 'The new style public servant is conversant with the objectives and broad outlines of the Development Plan and knows his role in the achievement of targets that come within his area of responsibility whether large or small. He is results-oriented and as such is not so much interested in minuting a file or writing a memo as in what actually happens on the ground: he wants to see results. He does not merely administer the established order by processing matters that come before him; he manages, that is, he makes things happen, by organising men, money and materials in order to achieve the particular objectives of his Ministry, or organisation, within the targets'.[16] In order to bring about 'results-oriented' management, the Udoji Report recommends the adoption of three specific techniques by Nigerian civil servants: Project Management, Management by Objectives, and Programme and Performance Budgeting.

Project Management: Underlying the Report's stress on improved Project Management is the view also expressed by contributors to this Reader that the compartmentalized organization of the public service is in many ways unsuited to the needs of development planning and administration. For example, at the level of central planning, it was noted that Plan preparation and implementation is often inhibited by the way in which development responsibilities are fragmented amongst several ministries. Also, at the local level, the fragmented administrative framework likewise inhibits any integrated rural development effort. The Report states the problem in this way: 'The basic organisation of government is by Ministries and Departments . . . functional organisations are weak in some respects, particularly in responding to changing and complex situations. They are resistant to change, emphasis separate functional elements at the expense of the whole organisation, tend to be a closed system, discourage collateral relationships and thus inhibit co-ordination.'[17] Unfortunately, the Report argues, the functional organization of ministries encourages a separation of technical skills. This runs counted to the requirements of project management which involves a variety of skills and abilities. Most projects cut across several ministries, thus making it difficult to agree on responsibilities and contributions by participating ministries, and most importantly, fixing accountability.[18] The Report in fact hammers home its point with some vigour. It argues that, '. . . individual departments must not be allowed to pursue their own limited objectives regardless of overall priorities or possible conflicts of interests, grabbing as much of the cake as their political strength, personal influence, and bargaining skill permits. Individual effort and loyalty must be subordinated and directed to achieving the overall goals of the organisation with as much harmony and impact as possible'.[19]

As an alternative to existing arrangements, the Report recommends the adoption of the 'task force' or 'team approach', with a stress on project management.[20] This approach, they state, is a system whereby 'various skills and requirements can be brought together from various Ministries and departments . . . to design and carry out projects. They are temporary groups, existing only until the project is completed. Then the members revert to their normal place within the organization. This design provides more flexibility in solving problems than is typically afforded by the traditional, functional bureaucratic structures. It allows various specialized skills and resources drawn from throughout the service to form a problem-solving team and apply their special abilities to the project'.[21]

Management by Objectives: The second technique recommended by the Commission is Management by Objectives (MBO). This it describes as '. . . the process of identifying goals and objectives, defining managerial responsibility in terms of expected results, and measuring performance and achievement against these goals and objectives. In this approach, the superior and subordinate managers in the organisation identify objectives in the major areas of responsibility in which the men will work. They design an action plan to achieve expected results in these areas and set performance standards for acceptable work. They are then in a position to measure actual results against these projected plans and standards'.[22] As an operational device, the Report's presentation of MBO is less satisfactory. As the authors themselves admit,[23] they give but a sketchy outline of MBO and make no suggestions as to how it might be applied to the particular needs and conditions of the Nigerian public services. The question is in fact hedged by a proposal to set up a Department of Public Management.Such a Department, presumably, would also have to undertake the massive re-training programmes necessary to introduce the new management techniques.

Programme and Performance Budgeting: The final technique recommended is Programme and Performance Budgeting (PPB).[24] According to the Commission, the objective of PPB is to base and use the budget on the results desired rather than the expenditure incurred. In other words, the authors are urging decision-makers in the public sector to think more in terms of what is likely to be achieved by the money spent, rather than just in narrow cost accounting terms. An example of one area of public administration where these perspectives are at times in conflict is central planning. Here, it will be recalled, certain conflicts of interest may arise between finance ministries, on the one hand, traditionally conservative, cautious and restrictionist in policy orientation, and planning agencies on the other, which are essentially expansionist in outlook.

In practice, the problems of adopting a more rational mode of decision-making, in which 'the administrator chooses between the most cost effective of several approaches', are great. Given the scarcity of such factors as time and information, it is likely to be difficult for the administrator to estimate the probable impact of various alternative projects, even if there was the interest in doing so. As the Udoji Commission itself points out, decision-making in reality tends to be based upon 'intuition, influence or political horse-trading'.[25]

With the exception of PPB, the general stress of the Commission on the managerial aspects of the civil servant's role tends to neglect the crucial part he plays in policy-making – the basic activity of government.[26] That is to say, the reliance on PPB as a technique of decision-making rests on a managerial model. This tends to conceal the real nature of public policy preparation, which in the last analysis is a political exercise, involving the assertion of values and priorities.[27]

Supportive Training and Manpower Development

Despite the heavy emphasis of the Report on improved techniques and procedures, relatively less space is devoted to the training and manpower implications of what is proposed. The main suggestion made by the Report is that the priority should be given to management development and supervisory training.[28] Supervisors, it argues, are particularly crucial to the effective adoption of new management techniques, since they are directly involved with work assignment and production, discipline and productivity.

In their specific recommendations, the authors of the Udoji Report drew attention to the ineffectiveness of the existing machinery – the National Manpower Board and the Manpower Secretariat of the Federal Ministry of Economic Development.[29] Deficiencies include lack of manpower planning capacity – for example, to evaluate projects for manpower implications or to do demographic studies to assess manpower resources – lack of information, and lack of institutional links with the education sector for supply and demand data and co-ordination. The Report makes three recommendations for improvement.[30] First, the Manpower Planning Division of the

Ministry of Economic Development should be reconstituted to comprise 5 sections, including ones for Educational and Labour matters. Second, the National Manpower Board should be reconstituted. Third, a national manpower survey should take place.

Improvement of Conditions of Service

At the core of the Udoji Commission's quest to increase civil service productivity is its recommendations for improving conditions of service. Whilst the presentation of new techniques is largely academic, the proposals for changes in grading and pay, for example, are worked out in great detail and have been largely accepted and implemented by the Government. The Report sees poor pay – both in relation to the rising costs of living as well as in relation to the higher salaries of the private sector – as the major barrier to increased productivity.

In considering the existing system of grading, the Report states: 'The present system of grading is based upon the traditional British Civil Service concept of classes, administratives, professional, clerical, etc., in which evaluation criteria focus on the educational attainment of the individual rather than the specific work content of the post'.[31] These features of the inherited grading system, the Commission argues, inhibit the free movement of personnel and cause jealousies within the services. Thus, one of the major objectives of the changes is 'harmonisation' – to bring public service salaries into line with the private sector and to narrow the gap between the highest and lowest salaries in the public sector by raising the minimum level.

In pursuit of these objectives, the Commission proposes a unified grading system for all classes in the public service. The unified system includes 8 major elements; the Senior Management System, the Professional, Technical and General Systems, and systems for the police, public enterprises, universities, teaching services, judiciary and local authorities. The basic premise underlying the proposed salary policy is that 'public servants should be paid on the basis of the worth of the work performed'.[32]

The Udoji Commission also gives separate consideration to pensions and fringe benefits[33] as related aspects of remuneration. With respect to pensions the Report proposes, for example, a standardization of retirement benefits for all public and private sector employees in order to facilitate inter-sectoral mobility. On the question of fringe benefits, the Commission's views are particularly interesting: 'Our Civil Service Task Force found that the cost of providing fringe benefits in the Civil Service is rather high. In a society which is aiming at reducing the disparities of wealth and income, some types of allowances and fringe benefits carry considerable disadvantages. First, they tend to be heavier at the top than the bottom and thus favour the better-off as against the worse off; second, they are less open than the straight salary, they breed suspicion and resentment; thirdly they may be inequitable as between individuals'.[34] In their recommendations, the Commission urge the 'gradual move towards establishing the principle of a clean wage. This would involve abolishing or modifying tax-free allowances, anomalies in housing, children allowances and leave.'[35]

Other aspects of the conditions of service mentioned by the Report include inadequate office accommodation, poor social amenities (particularly the housing and transport for the lower grades),[36] promotion and staff relations. On promotion and performance evaluation, the Report proposes the substitution of new performance criteria for seniority and the adoption of an Annual Performance Evaluation Report.[37] On staff relations, it mentions the problems of trade union organization and calls for more effective staff consultative machinery.[38]

Discipline

Finally, the Udoji Report relates low levels of productivity to poor discipline within the civil service.[39] They observe that many officers find themselves powerless over their staff. Their reason for this is that disciplinary action is is carried out through the Public Service Commissions and hence no direct sanctions exist over employees as they do in private firms. The Report recommends improved regulations for procedure in disciplinary matters might be introduced.

The Civil Service and the Public

The Report, in its (significantly) second chapter entitled 'Cultural and Environmental Factors' examines the economic and social context and the pressures which arise from this in Africa. In the case of 'corruption', for example, the most prevalent manifestation of the economic pressures and social ties of administrators, the Commission submits that elimination is impossible and that it is more realistic to think in terms of measures to minimize the worst effects.[40] In this respect, four lines of approach are suggested for combatting corruption. First, corruption should be publicly exposed whenever it is found. Second, the auditing of accounts and records should be improved. Third, an open system of communications within government might be encouraged whereby incompetence and dishonesty would come to light. Fourth, a free press and free expression of public opinion would be an asset. As regards the improvement of these aspects of civil service performance, two specific recommendations are made. The first is for a 'Code of Ethics' for civil servants.[41] The second is for the establishment of the office of Ombudsman.[42]

At various points elsewhere in the Report, the Commission also raises a number of related issues about the inherited style of Nigeria's public services and the need to replace continuing tendencies towards authoritarianism, paternalism and elitism with qualities of leadership. The Report traces these negative attitudes back to their colonial origins and suggests they continue to be reinforced by the inherited educational system. Hence the de-emphasis in recruitment and remuneration policy on paper qualifications in favour of ability and work done and the increased stress on training for leadership and public relations'[43] as well as on the relations between superiors and subordinates within the civil service.[44] Within the civil service, for example, one of the major arguments levelled against the existing career service is that it is 'closed' and 'class-based' and thus counter-productive in terms of achieving effective patterns of communications within government organizations.

Scattered though they are, these points are crucial. With some rather notable exceptions, military rule in sub-Saharan Africa – at least under normal circumstances and in relation to the general citizenry – has not been particularly brutal or repressive. Probably it has been the public bureaucracy at whose hands the average citizen has suffered the most on a daily basis. A strong sense of public service has not always been a salient feature of Nigerian administration, particularly at the middle and lower levels of those departments which deal directly with the public.

In some ways the broad hints in the Udoji Report at the need for a cultural revolution within the Nigerian public services stands in marked contrast to the rather narrow recommendations eventually made and accepted for enhanced remuneration *per se* as the means of productivity. Put another way, the tendency has been to continue to think in terms of administrative development rather than the needs of development administration. At its crudest, much of the thinking assumes a simple casual relationship between output, or quantity of work done, and levels of remuneration. Less consideration has been given to the quality of work done and to whether existing methods and procedures are compatible with the promotion of social and economic change.

The unsuitability of bureaucratic organization to the tasks of development administration is brought out most clearly at the local level where government officials and the public interest meet closely. There, as the chapters on local government, agricultural development administration, community development and cooperatives show, the need for a cultural revolution in some parts of the public service is acute. The pervasive administrative style of these agencies and organizations remains elistist and paternalistic, if not authoritarian. The current phrase 'bringing government closer to the people' is characteristic of dominant official attitude. With some exceptions, the post-military changes in local government and administration have resulted in a subordination of local government institutions to central government and this marks a clear move away from an idea of local self-government. The *Main Report* (p. 5) simply notes in passing the desirability of grass-roots participation.

Finally, apart from the rather narrow conception of local government, the major administrative structures concerned with local development – Community Development, Agricultural Extension and Co-operatives – are not really considered *per se,* except indirectly under internal central Ministerial organization and methods.

The Aftermath of Udoji: The July 1975 Coup

The July 1975 coup, which brought about a change in top military and civilian positions, was in many ways a product of the aftermath of the Udoji public sector salary increases. What is equally significant is that the early measures of the new regime of the late General Murtala Mohammed have been directed, *inter alia*, to those aspects of public service performance pinpointed by the Udoji Report that the previous Government's White Paper had chosen to ignore.

The first of these measures has been a conscious effort to improve the style of administration. Whilst the hints of the Udoji Report were cautious, the indictment of the previous regime has been most forthright. In the words of the late Head of the Federal Military Government: 'the affairs of a state, hitherto a collective responsibility, became characterised by lack of consultation, indecision, indiscipline and even neglect . . . All over the country there were allegations of graft, misuse of public funds . . . There were complaints of ostentatious living, flagrant abuse of office and deprivation of people's rights and property, perversion of time-honoured procedures and norms . . . nepotism and favouritism, desecrations of traditional institutions and public humiliation of highly respected natural rulers, all of which gave the impression that the States were being run as private estates'.[45] Although these criticisms were mainly levelled against the former State Military Governors, whom General Gowon had promised, but failed, to remove, the change in style is clearly intended as an example to all – as the mass dismissals of top public servants, from Secretaries to Military Governors and Permanent Secretaries downwards, would suggest. The dismissals have been accompanied by a series of exposures of the misuse of public funds. Government contracts have been suspended and a few assets seized. On 1 October 1975, the setting up of a Corrupt Practices Investigations Bureau was announced.

These measures were accompanied by other gestures to a change in style. Official motorcades were discarded, stories circulated about the late Head of State queuing *in cognito* at the Post Office to see for himself the treatment meted out to the average citizen, and the new State Military Governors made surprise early morning calls at the offices of permanent secretaries.

One issue of public service reform which, perhaps understandably, was untackled by the Udoji Report, is the relationship between civil servants and the political/military leadership.[46] The general stress of the Commission on the managerial model conceals the real nature of public policy preparation which in the last analysis is a political exercise involving the assertion of values and priorities. Under the Gowon regime a personalized system of control had evolved over the bureaucratic machine, in which the Head of State tended to deal directly with selected Federal Permanent Secretaries (popularly termed 'superpermsecs'), particularly in Mines and Power, Finance and Economic Development and Reconstruction, by-passing on many important issues the formal machinery – the Federal Executive Council comprising the Federal Commissioners. Thus one of the major criticisms levelled by the new regime against the old has been that certain civil servants had exercised considerable power at Federal and State levels without really being accountable to anyone – either the public or the formal government machinery. As Tersin Turner shows in her chapter, one key area of policy-making in this respect had been the management of state participation in the oil sector. Another was the 'indigenisation' of industry and commerce. Superficially, the July 1975 coup has been construed as a reaction to the oil-barrel politics of the Gowon regime, most notably the massive and unplanned increases in public sector salaries recommended by the Udoji Commission and their effects on a mismanaged economy. At another level, however, the process of administrative 'reform' under military rule in Nigeria has been more than merely a response to the narrow pecuniary devices of the bureaucratic elite. In some respects the diagnoses of the 1975 Public Service Review Commission, piecemeal and sometimes contradictory though they are, indicate a certain response to recent events. What the 1975 Commission Report hints at, and the subsequent coup confirms, is the ascendacy within the civil service of elements favouring a public sector capable of a more effective role *vis-a-vis* foreign and domestic private capitalist interests.[47] Thus the emphasis in the rhetoric has been increasingly on the norms of 'efficiency' and 'public service'. This may be seen as an important step towards the consolidation of a more 'technocratic' (as well as better-paid) state as the organizational basis of a successful national capitalism. Interestingly, after the publication of the Udoji awards, professional and technical grades of the civil service felt compelled to threaten state action over the more favourable increases received by the administrative grades – the core of the 'collaborationist' element in the Gowon regime. In an attempt to dismantle this system, the new regime has ruled that Permanent Secretaries will now only attend Executive Council meetings at the request of their Commissioners, and then only in an advisory capacity, and that State Military Governors, as military officers, would be responsible in the first instance to the Chief of Staff, Supreme Military Headquarters, and would not be represented on Federal Government organs.

Sweeping though these measures appear to be, particularly in contrast to the preceding five years, the challenges remain great. Sacking the old guard and their servants and promoting the younger generation will not necessarily bring about any qualitative change in the conduct of public affairs. The purged civil servants have been retired with 'full benefits' – thus creating a privileged class of pensioners. And it remains to be seen how the proposed Corrupt Practices Investigation Bureau will work. Also, the decision to create 7 more states, whilst ostensibly justified in terms of protecting minority groups, and in a few cases in terms of splitting up physically unviable units (North-Eastern State for example), will, if implemented without caution, create many more administrations and hence multiply points of access to office and contracts throughout the country.

The rhetoric of the new regime has tended to create the impression that the basic problems are technical ones and can be put right by the proper management of the government and the nation's resources. Whilst there may be certain truth in this, the socio-economic fact remains that – gestures towards an improved style notwithstanding – the higher civil service, together in the private sector with the emerging managerial and entrepreneurial elites, have benefitted and continue to benefit inordinately from Nigeria's recent economic boom whilst other groups – most of the workers, peasants and the urban underemployed and unemployed – remain marginal.

In the final analysis, bureaucratic performance and the prospects of administrative reform in the less industrialized countries is rooted in the underlying social conditions and dominant economic institutions. Thus, shortfalls in performance are to be understood more as a reflection of the major contradictions of Nigerian society, particularly the ambiguities over the role of the state, than as a failure of organization bureaucratically defined as in the manner of Udoji. In an inflationary economy and a society characterised by the drive for personal gain where prestige derives from material display, 'public' administration, presently unchecked by a mass movement or even parliamentary institutions, is always vulnerable to informal pressures from foreign firms (mostly multinational corporations and their subsidiaries) and increasingly some indigenous ones, competing for contracts supplies and markets.[48] In the last respect, multinational subsidiaries not only have the earlier mentioned market effect of setting very high salary levels for their African executives (which tend to be followed in the public sector),[49] they also reinforce the skewed pattern of income distribution referred to above by creating tastes and demands for a range of sophisticated semi-luxury goods which, in terms of purchasing power, are within the reach of only the highly paid few.

References

1. For example, there was the Elwood Team which was appointed to identify anomalies in the gradings and other conditions relating to all postings in the civil services. There was also the Mbanefor Commission of 1959 and the Morgan Commission of 1959 and 1963.
2. Federal Republic of Nigeria, *Public Service Review Commission: Main Report* (Lagos: Federal Ministry of Information, 1974).
3. *Main Report,* p. 28, para. 106.
4. *Ibid.,* p. 34, para 129.
5. As regards the forms of implementation, the broad choice is between 'outside' or expert commissions of enquiry, like the Udoji Commission, and internal or permanent civil service reform. In the former case, a major disadvantage is that the indictment may be too sweeping to be accepted *in toto* by any government in power. As with public enterprise since Independence, it is probably better to have some means of continuous review, rather than allowing things to deteriorate to the point where a massive public investigation has to take place. The major disadvantage of internal and permanent civil service reform is

that it may be more inhibited and conservative than any 'outside' evaluation.

6. For example, at the annual conference at the Institute of Administration, Zaria. See for example, O. Oyinloye 'New Perspectives for the Nigerian Civil Services' in M. Tukur (ed.), *Administrative and Political Development: Prospects for Nigeria* (Kaduna: Baraka Press, 1971), p. 151. P. Asiodu, 'The Future of the Federal and State Civil Services in the Context of the Twelve States Structure', in *ibid.*, p. 164; A. Ciroma, 'Executive Organs and Interactions between them: Managing Public Affairs for Results', in M. Tukur (ed.), *In Search of a New Political Community: The Nigerian Case* (Zaria: Institute of Administration, 1972), p. 259.
7. See, for example, Oyinloye, *op. cit.*, pp. 146, 169, 177; Ciroma *op. cit.*, pp. 265, 273, 279.
8. The dual hierarchies of professionals and administrators, for example, were created in the 1950s when Departments were merged into newly newly-created Ministries. Administrators were charged with financial and overall policy control and professionals with technical aspects and execution. The post of Permanent Secretary was also created to advise the new Ministers on policy.
9. *Main Report,* chs. 5 and 15.
10. *Main Report,* para. 120.
11. On promotion see Oyinloye, *op. cit.*, p. 1971, Asiodu *op. cit.*, pp. 135–6; on discipline see Ciroma *op. cit.*, pp. 248–252,'257, 267 and 279; on remuneration see Asiodu *op. cit.*, pp. 139–44, 176; D. Phillips. 'Two important aspects of the Economic Arrangement: Economies in Administration Cost and Financial Institutions', in Tukur, *In Search of a New Political Community.*
12. On methods, for example, it has been recognized that the changing and expanding role of the public sector requires administrators to be equipped to perform new planning and managerial roles. Common diagnoses of manpower development needs in these respects include: Asiodu, *op. cit.*, pp. 133, 138–9, and Oyinloye, *op. cit.*, p. 308. Recommendations for reform have focussed on training – its objectives, content and problems of implementation: Asiodu, *op. cit.*, p. 138, and Oyinloye, *op. cit.*, pp. 152–7, 173–4, 177. On the question of motivating civil servants to work harder, the traditional view relating productivity to levels of remuneration has been well expressed by Asiodu, *op. cit.*, p. 150. On the other hand, discussions of ideology at the 1972 Zaria Conference suggest a growing disenchantment with the manipulation of conditions of service *per se,* in favour of the view that the problem is also embedded in ecological factors – the nature of the wider society of which they are part – and cannot be solved by just improving piecemeal aspects of internal public service management and organization. See, for example, S.O. Osoba, 'Ideology and Planning for National Economic Development, 1946–72', A. Koko, 'National Ideology and Nigerian Integration', I. Tahir, 'Towards a Rational System of Order and National Regeneration', all in Tukur, *In Search of a New Political Community.* Finally, on the question of administrative style, attention has been called to the need to re-orient

the behaviour of civil servants in their interaction with the public: Oyinloye, *op. cit.*, p. 150; the relation of the civil service to local communities: Tahir, *op. cit.*, pp. 121, 224–5, good leadership on the part of civil servants: Dudley, p. 127 in Tukur, *In Search of a New Political Community*, and Koko, *op. cit.*, p. 84, 113 on the need to find ways and means of ensuring responsiveness and accountability.

13. *Main Report*, ch. 3, paras 27–30.
14. *Ibid.*, ch. 4.
15. *Ibid.*, chs. 15–17.
16. *Ibid.*, para. 27.
17. *Ibid.*, p. 8, paras, 31–2.
18. *Ibid.*, p. 9, paras, 37 & 38.
19. *Ibid.*, p, 12, paras. 51 (i).
20. *Ibid.*, p. 8, para. 34.
21. *Ibid.*
22. *Ibid.*, p. 10, para. 40.
23. *Ibid.*, para 46.
24. *Ibid.*, pp. 11–13, paras. 48–54.
25. *Ibid.*, p. 12, para. 51.
26. MBO, for example gives prominence to the achievement of defined goals and allocates to managers the task of identifying them. Thereafter the Commission is vague if not rather unconvincing when it proposes the objectives of the Second National Development Plan as guidelines for public servants in their decision-making!
27. To be fair to the Commission, the overall machinery of government was not strictly within their terms of reference and any meaningful evaluation of the policy-making process would have involved some consideration of the relations between administrators and the political leadership.
28. *Main Report*, p. 5.
29. *Ibid.*, ch. 5.
30. *Ibid.*
31. *Ibid.*, p. 24, para. 93.
32. *Ibid.*, p. 159, para. 658.
33. *Ibid.*, p. 165, para. 701.
34. *Ibid.*, Chapters 16 & 17.
35. *Ibid.*, p. 183, para. 772.
36. *Ibid.*, pp. 187–8, para. 792.
37. *Ibid.*, p. 489, para. 176.
38. *Ibid.*
39. *Ibid.*, pp. 51–3, paras. 188–202.
40. *Ibid.*, p. 47, para. 171.
41. *Ibid.*, p. 3, para. 12.
42. *Ibid.*, p. 6, para. 24.
43. *Ibid.*, pp. 50–1, paras. 181–7.
44. *Ibid.*, pp. 48–9.
45. *Daily Times* (Lagos), 1 August 1975.
46. To be fair to the Commission, the machinery of government was not within its terms of reference and any meaningful evaluation of the policy-making process would have involved scrutinizing the relations

between top civil servants and the military leadership. *Main Report*, p. 5.

47. For a classic statement of this position, see A. Ayida, 'The Nigerian Revolution, 1966–76', proceedings of the Nigerian Economic Society, Ibadan University, 1973. Mr. Ayida was then Permanent Secretary of the Federal Ministry of Finance. Since July 1975, just before the coup, he has been Secretary to the Federal Military Government.
48. Interestingly, one former Military Governor actually suggested that one effect of the Udoji awards might be to curb corruption.
49. The Ndegwa Commission in Kenya marks a similar tendency in that country.

Further Reading

The Context: Underdevelopment and Development

Amin, S. *Neocolonialism in West Africa.* Harmondsworth: Penguin, 1973.
Argwala, A.N. and Singh, S.P. (ed.). *The Economics of Underdevelopment.* London: Oxford University Press, 1958.
Arrighi, G. and Saul, J.*Essays on the Political Economy of Africa.* New York: Monthly Review Press, 1973.
Bernstein, H. (ed.). *Underdevelopment and Development.* Harmondsworth: Penguin, 1973.
Frank, A.G. *Capitalism and Underdevelopment in Latin America.* Harmondsworth: Penguin, 1971.
Green, R. and Seidman, A. *Unity of Poverty: The Economics of Panafricanism.* Harmondsworth: Penguin, 1968.
Hayter, T. *Aid as Imperialism.* Harmondsworth: Penguin, 1971.
Leys, C. *Underdevelopment in Kenya: The Political Economy of Neo-Colonialism.* London: Heinemann, 1975. Chapter 1.
Meier, G.M. *Leading Issues in Development Economics.* New York: Oxford University Press, 1964.
Myint, H. *The Economics of Developing Countries.* London: Hutchinson, 1964.
Myrdal, G. *Asian Drama: An Inquiry into the Poverty of Nations.* London: Allen Lane, 1972.
Robinson, R. (ed.). *Developing the Third World.* Cambridge: Cambridge University Press, 1971.
Seers, D. and Joy, L. (ed.). *Development in a Divided World.* Harmondsworth: Penguin, 1971.
Streeten, P. (ed.). *Frontiers in Development Studies.* New York: Halstead, 1972.
Worsley, P. *The Third World.* London: Weidenfeld and Nicholson, 1964.

Part I: Development Administration: General Works and Perspectives

Adu, A.L. *The Civil Service in Commonwealth Africa.* London: Allen and Unwin, 1969.

Heady, F. *Public Administration: A Comparative Perspective.* Englewood Cliffs: Prentice-Hall, 1964.
Hyden, G., Jackson, R., and Okumu, J. (eds.). *Development Administration: the Kenyan Experience.* Nairobi: Oxford University Press, 1970.
Ilchman, W.F. 'Rising Expectations and the Revolution in Development Administration', *Public Administration Review,* (December 1965).
Ilchman, W.F. 'The Unproductive Study of Productivity', *Comparative Political Studies,* 1, 2 (1968).
Kriesberg, M. *Public Administration in Developing Countries.* Washington: Brookings Institute 1965.
Lapalombara, J. *Bureaucracy and Political Development.* Princeton, N.J.: Princeton University Press, 1963.
Montgomery, J., and Siffen, W. *Approaches to Development: Politics, Administration and Change.* New York: McGraw Hill, 1966.
Riggs, F. *Administration in Developing Countries.* Boston: Houghton Mifflin, 1964.
Riggs, F. *Frontiers in Development Administration.* Durham: Duke University Press, 1970.
Riggs, F. *The Ecology of Public Administration.* New York: Asian Publishing House, 1962.
Schaffer, B.B. 'The Deadlock in Development Administration', in C. Leys (ed.). *Politics and Change in Developing Countries.* Cambridge: Cambridge University Press, 1969.
Schaffer, B.B. *The Administrative Factor: Papers in Organisation, Politics and Development.* London: Frank Cass, 1973.
Schaffer, B.B. (ed.). *Public Administration Research Project: Administrative Training and Development: A Comparative Study of Zambia, Kenya, Pakistan, India and U.K.* New York: Praeger, 1974.
Swerdlow, I. *Introduction to Development Administration.* Syracuse: Syracuse University Press, 1963
Swerdlow, I. *Development Administration: Concept and Problems.* Syracuse: Syracuse University Press, 1967.
Younger, K. *The Public Services in the New States.* London: Oxford University Press, 1960.

Central Planning

Barbour, K.M. (ed.). *Planning for Nigeria.* Ibadan: University of Ibadan Press, 1972.
Clark, P. *Development Planning in East Africa.* Nairobi: East African Publishing House, 1965.
Dean, E.R. *Plan Implementation in Nigeria, 1962–6.* Ibadan: Oxford University Press, 1972.
Enos, J., and Griffen, K. *Development Planning.* London: Addison-Wesley, 1971.
Green, R.H. 'Four African Development Plans: Ghana, Kenya, Nigeria and Tanzania', *Journal of Modern African Studies,* 3, 2 (1965).

Helleiner, G.K. 'Socialism and Economic Development in Tanzania', *Journal of Development Studies,* 8, 2 (1972).
Jackson, R. 'Planning Politics and Administration', in Hyden, Jackson and Okumu, *Development Administration: The Kenyan Experience.*
Kamarck, A.M. *The Economics of African Development,* London: Praeger, 1967.
Kilby, P. *Industrialization in an Open Economy: Nigeria 1945–66.* Cambridge: Cambridge University Press, 1969.
Leys, C. 'The Analysis of Planning', in C. Leys (ed.). *Politics and Change in Developing Countries.* Cambridge: Cambridge University Press, 1969.
Livingstone, I. (ed.). *Economic Policy for Development.* Harmondsworth: Penguin, 1971.
Meier, R.L. *Development Planning.* New York: McGraw-Hill, 1965.
Osoba, S.O. 'Ideology and Planning for National Development, 1946–72', in M. Tukur (ed.). *In Search of New Political Community: The Nigerian Case.* Zaria: Institute of Administration, 1972.
Rweyemamu, J. *Underdevelopment and Industrialisation in Tanzania: a Study of Perverse Capitalist Industrial Development.* Nairobi: Oxford University Press, 1973.
Seers, D. and Faber, M. (ed.). *Crisis in Planning.* London: Chatto and Windus, 1972.
Seidman, A. *An Economic Textbook for Africa.* London: Methuen, 1972. Part V.
Seidman, A. *Comparative Development Strategies in East Africa.* Nairobi: East African Publishing House, 1972.
Seidman, A. *Ghana's Development Experience, 1951-65.* Nairobi: East African Publishing House, forthcoming.
Stolper, W. *Planning Without Facts: Lessons in Resource Allocation from Nigeria's Development.* Cambridge, Mass.: Harvard University Press, 1966.
Tinbergen, J. *Development Planning.* New Haven: Yale University Press, 1964.
Uchumi Editorial Board. *Towards Socialist Planning In Tanzania.* Dar es Salaam: Tanzanian Publishing House, 1972.
Van Arkadie, B. 'Planning in Tanzania' in L. Cliffe and J. Saul (ed.). *Socialism in Tanzania: Politics and Policies.* Vol. II. Nairobi: East African Publishing House, 1973.
Waterson, A. *Development Planning: Lessons of Experience.* Baltimore: Johns Hopkins Press, 1965.

Public Enterprise

Beg, M.A.K. *et al.* (ed.). *Problems of Public Enterprise.* Lahore: NIPA, 1967.
Friedman, W. (ed.). *Public and Private Enterprise in Mixed Economies.* London: Stevens, 1974.
Glentworth. G. 'Public Enterprises in Developing Countries: Some Suggestions on Creation, Organisation and Control', *Journal of Administration Overseas,* 12, 3 (1973).
Greenstreet, D. 'The Government and Manufacturing Sector in Ghana, 1951–66', *Nigerian Journal of Economic and Social Studies,* 15, 3 (1973).

Hanson, A.H. *Public Enterprise and Economic Development.* London: Routledge, 1959.

Holland, S. (ed.). *The State as Entrepreneur.* London: Weidenfeld and Nicolson, 1972.

Loxley, J. and Saul, J. 'Nationalisations, Workers and Parastatals in Tanzania', *Review of African Political Economy,* 2 (1975).

Musolf, L.D. *Mixed Enterprise: A Developmental Perspective.* Lexington: Lexington Books, 1972.

Nwanwene, O. 'Public Corporations and State Owned Companies', *Quarterly Journal of Administration,* 5, 1 (1970).

Ranis, G. (ed.). *Government and Economic Development.* New Haven: Yale University Press, 1971.

Sachs, I. *Patterns of Public Sector in Underdeveloped Countries.* Bombay: Asian Publishing House, 1964.

Shivji, I. 'Capitalism Unlimited: Public Corporations in Partnership with Multinational Corporations'. *The African Review.* 3, 3 (1973).

Teriba, R.O. 'Accountability and public control of public corporations – the experience of Western Nigeria', in D.J. Murray (ed.). *Studies in Nigerian Administration* . London: Hutchinson/Institute of Administration, Ife University, 1970.

Teriba, R.O. 'Some Organisational Problems of Western Nigerian Public Corporations', *Administration,* 2, 1 (1967).

United Nations, Department of Economic and Social Affairs. *Organisation and Administration of Public Enterprises: Selected Papers.* New York, 1968.

Van Arkadie, B. 'The Role of the State Sector in the Context of Economic Dependence', *The Bulletin of the Institute of Development Studies at The University of Sussex,* 3, 4 (1971).

Government and Private Sector

Capital

Amsden, A. *International Firms and Labour in Kenya.* London: Frank Cass, 1971.

Arrighi, G. and Saul J. 'Nationalism and Revolution in Sub-Saharan Africa', In Arrighi and Saul, *Essays on the Political Economy of Africa.*

Bonte, P. 'Multinational Corporations and National Development: MIFERMA and Mauritania', *Review of African Political Economy,* 2 (1975).

Bostock, M. and Harvey, C. *Economic Independence and Zambian Copper.* New York and London: Praeger, 1975.

Campbell, B. 'Neo-Colonialism, Economic Independence and Political Change: Cotton Textile Production in the Ivory Coast', *Review of African Political Economy,* 2 (1975).

Curry, R.L. and Rothchild, D. 'On Economic Bargaining between African Governments and Multinational Countries', *Journal of Modern African Studies,* 12, 7 (1974).

Cooper, C. (ed.). *Science, Technology and Development.* London: Frank Cass, 1973.

Dunning, J. (ed.). *The Multinational Enterprise.* London: Allen and Unwin

1971.
Esseks, J. 'Government and Indigenous Private Enterprise in Ghana', *Journal of Modern African Studies,* 9, 1 (1971).
Faber, M., and Potter, J.G. *Towards Economic Independence: Papers in the Nationalisation of the Copper Industry in Zambia.* Cambridge: Cambridge University Press, 1971.
Genoud, R. *Nationalism and Economic Development in Ghana.* New York: Praeger, 1969.
Green, R.H. 'Political independence and the national economy: an essay in the political economy of decolonisation', in C. Allen and R. W. Johnson (ed.). *African Perspectives: Papers in History, Politics and Economics of Africa Presented to Thomas Hodgkin.* Cambridge: Cambridge University Press, 1970.
Green, R.H. 'The Role of the State as an agent of economic and social development in the LDC's', *Journal of Development Planning,* 6, (1974).
Kidron, M. *Foreign Investments in India.* London: Oxford University Press, 1965.
Kilby, B. (ed.). *Entrepreneurship and Economic Development.* New York: The Free Press, 1971.
Langdon, S. 'Multinational Corporations, Taste Transfer and Underdevelopment: a Case Study from Kenya', *Review of African Political Economy,* 2 (1975).
Leys, C. *Underdevelopment in Kenya: the Political Economy of Neocolonialism.* Chapters 4–6.
Livingstone, I. (ed.). *Economic Policy for Development.* Harmondsworth: Penguin, 1971.
National Christian Council of Kenya. *Who Controls Industry in Kenya?* Nairobi: East African Publishing House, 1968.
Odell, P. *Oil and World Power.* Harmondsworth: Penguin, 1974.
Penrose, E. *The Large Multinational Firms in Developing Countries: the International Petroleum Industry.* Cambridge, Mass.: M.I.T. Press, 1968.
Seidman, A. *Comparative Development Strategies in East Africa.* Chapter VI.
Sutcliffe, B. *Industry and Underdevelopment.* London: Addison-Wesley, 1971.
Tugendhat, C. *The Multinationals.* London: Eyre and Spottiswoode, 1971.
UNIDO. *Training of Economic Administrators for Industrial Development,* Training for Industry Series, No. 1. New York, 1969.
UNIDO. *Planning for Advanced Skills and Technology.* New York, 1969.
Wilber, C. *The Political Economy of Development and Underdevelopment.* New York: Random House, 1973.

Labour

Allen, V.L. *Trade Unions and Government.* London: Longman, 1960.
Bates, R.L. *Unions, Parties and Political Development, a Study of Mine Workers in Zambia.* London and New Haven: Yale University Press, 1971.
Beling, W.A. (ed.). *The Role of Labour in African Nation Building.* New York: Praeger, 1968.
Borg, E.J. and Butler, J. 'Trade Unions', in J.S. Coleman and C.J. Rosberg

(ed.). *Political Parties and National Integration in Tropical Africa.* Berkeley and Los Angeles: University of California Press, 1964.
Bienefeld, F. 'Labour in Tanzania', in L. Cliffe and J. Saul. *Socialism in Tanzania.*
Cohen, R. *Labour and Politics in Nigeria, 1945–71.* London: Heinemann, 1974.
Cohen, R. and Sandbrook, D. (eds.). *Towards an African Working Class.* London: Heinemann, 1976.
Davies, I. *African Trades Unions.* Harmondsworth: Penguin, 1966.
Friedland, W. *Unions and Industrial Relations in Underdeveloped Countries.* Ithaca: New York State School of Industrial and Labour Relations, 1964.
Galenson, W. *Labour in Developing Countries.* Berkeley and Los Angeles: University of California Press, 1963.
Roberts, B.C. *Labour in the Tropical Counties of the Commonwealth.* Durham: Duke University Press, 1964.
Sandbrook, R. 'The State and the Development of Trade Unions', in Hyden, Jackson and Okumu, *Development Administration: The Kenyan Experience.*
Scott, R. *The Development of Trades Unions in Uganda.* Nairobi: East African Publishing House, 1966.
Yesufu, T.M. *An Introduction to Industrial Relations in Nigeria.* Ibadan: Oxford University Press for Nigerian Institute for Social and Economic Research, 1964.

Local Government and Administration

Adedeji, A. and Rowland, L. (ed.). *Local Government Finance in Nigeria: Problems and Prospects.* Ife: University of Ife Press, 1972.
Alderfer, A. *Local Government in Developing Countries.* New York: McGraw-Hill, 1965.
Collins, P. *Decentralisation and Local Administration for Development in Tanzania.* Brighton: Institute of Development Studies, 1976.
Gorvine, A. 'The Utilisation of Local Government for National Development', *Journal of Administration Overseas,* 4, 4 (1965).
Griffen, W. 'Local Authorities, Government Control and Economic Policy', *Comparative Local Government,* 2, 1 (1968).
Hicks, U. *Development From Below.* Oxford: Clarendon Press, 1961.
Hyden, G. 'Local Government Reform in Kenya', *East Africa Journal,* 7, 4 (1970).
Leemans, A.F. *Changing Patterns of Local Government.* The Hague: International Union of Local Authorities, 1970.
Leys, C. *Politicians and Policies: An Essay on Politics in Acholi, Uganda, 1962–5.* Nairobi: East African Publishing House, 1967.
Maddick, M. *Democracy, Decentralisation and Development.* Bombay: Asian Publishing House, 1963.
Murray, D. 'Field Administration', in D. Murray *Studies in Nigerian Administration*

Rado, Emil D. 'Improvement of Local Government and Administration for Development Purposes', *Journal of Administration Overseas,* 1, 3 (1962).
Smith, B.C. *Field Administration: An Aspect of Decentralisation.* London: Routledge, 1967.
Tordoff, W. 'Provincial and District Administration in Zambia', *Journal of Administration Overseas,* 7, 3/4 (1968).
Wraith, R. *Local Administration in West Africa.* London: Allen and Unwin, 1972.

Community Development

Brokensha, D. and Hidge, P. *Community Development: An Interpretation.* Novato: Chandler, 1972.
Collins, P. 'Local Government and Community Development in Tanzania', *Community Development Journal,* 7, 3 (1972).
du Sautoy, P. 'Some Administrative Aspects of Community Development', *Journal of Administration Overseas,* 1, 1 (1962).
du Sautoy, P. 'A Guide for the Administrator to the Principles of Community Development', *Journal of Administration Overseas,* 2, 4 (1963).
Huizer, G. 'Community Development, Land Reform and Political Participation, *American Journal of Sociology,* 28, 2 (1969).
Mbithi, P. 'Harambee Self-Help: The Kenyan Approach', *The African Review,* 2, 1 (1972).
Meister, A. 'Characteristics of Community Development and Rural Animation in Africa', *International Review of Community Development* (Summer 1972).
Mould, P.S. 'Rural Improvement by Communal Labour in the Bombali District of Sierra Leone – a Case Study', *Journal of Administration Overseas,* 5, 1 (1966).
Myrdal, G. *Asian Drama,* Chapter 18.
O'Kelly, E. 'Administrative Problems of Community Development in the Southern Cameroons', *Journal of African Administration,* 12, 1 (1960).
Prosser, A.R.G. 'Community Development and its relation to development planning', *Journal of Administration Overseas,* 8, 3 (1969).
Stavenhagen, R. 'Changing functions of the community in underdeveloped countries', in H. Bernstein. *Underdevelopment and Development.*
Sharman, B.S. 'Local Government and Community Development in the Sudan', *Journal of Administration Overseas,* 8, 1 (1969).
United Nations. *Popular Participation in Development: Emerging Trends in Community Development,* UN. E71 IV 2.273, 1969.
Worsely, P. *Two Blades of Grass: Rural Cooperation in Developing Societies.* Manchester: Manchester University Press, 1971. Chapter I.

Community Development and Co-operatives

Apthorpe, R. (ed.). *Land Settlement and Rural Development in East Africa.* Kampala: Transition Books, 1969.
Belshaw, D. 'Agricultural Extension, Education and Research', in G.K.

Helleiner (ed.). *Agricultural Planning in East Africa.* Nairobi: East African Publishing House, 1968.

Chambers, R. *Settlement Schemes in Tropical Africa: A Study of Organisation and Development.* London: Routledge, 1969.

de Wilde, J. *Experience with Agricultural Development in Tropical Africa.* Baltimore: Johns Hopkins Press, 1969.

Dorner, P. *Land Reform and Economic Development.* Harmondsworth: Penguin, 1972.

Dumont, R. *False Start in Africa.* London: Andre Deutsch, 1966.

Harrison, D. 'Work and Motivation: a study of agricultural extension workers in the Western State of Nigeria', in D.J. Murray. *Studies in Nigerian Administration.*

Helleiner, G.K. *Peasant Agriculture, Government and Economic Growth.* Homewood: Irwin, 1966.

Joy, L. 'Strategy for Agricultural Development', in Seers and Joy. *Development in a Divided World.*

Hill, P. *Studies in Rural Capitalism in West Africa.* Cambridge: Cambridge University Press.

Hunter, G. *Modernising Peasant Societies.* London: Oxford University Press, 1969.

Hunter, G. *The Administration of Agricultural Development: Lessons from India.* London: Oxford University Press, 1970.

Hunter, G. *The New Societies of Tropical Africa.* London: Oxford University Press, 1963.

Lamb, G. *Peasant Politics: Conflict and Development in Murang'a.* London: J. Friedman, 1974.

Lehman, D. (ed.). *Agrarian Reform and Agrarian Reformism.* London: Faber, 1975.

Mellor, J.W. *The Economics of Agricultural Development.* Ithaca: Cornell University Press, 1966.

Ness, G.D. *Bureaucracy and Rural Development in Malaysia.* Cambridge: Cambridge University Press, 1967.

Post, K. 'Peasantisation and Rural Political Movements in West Africa', *European Journal of Sociology,* 13, 2 (1972).

Nigerian Economic Society, *Rural Development in Nigeria.* 1972.

Robinson, R. and Johnson, P. (ed.). *The Rural Base for National Development.* Cambridge: Cambridge University Overseas Studies Committee, 1969.

Shanin, T. (ed.). *Peasants and Peasant Societies.* Harmondsworth: Penguin, 1971.

Schultz, T. *Transforming Traditional Agriculture.* New Haven: Yale University Press, 1964.

Trapman, C. *Change in Administrative Structures: A Case Study of Kenyan Agricultural Development.* London: Overseas Development Institute, 1974.

Tung Ta-Lin. *Agricultural Cooperation in China.* Peking: Foreign Languages Press, 1959.

Watts, R. 'Bureaucracy and Extension', *East Africa Journal,* 6, 8 (1969).

Wharton, C. (ed.). *Subsistence Agriculture and Economic Development* London: Frank Cass, 1970.

Widstrand, C. (ed.). *Cooperatives and Rural Development in East Africa.* Nairobi: East African Publishing House, 1971.

Saul, J. 'Marketing Cooperatives in Tanzania', in P. Worsely. *Two Blades of Grass.*

Administrative Reform

Adedeji, A. 'Formulating Administrative Reform Strategies in Africa', *Quarterly Journal of Administration,* 6, 3 (1972).

Akingbade, J. 'Administrative Reform of the Civil Service: the Nigerian Experience', *Quarterly Journal of Administration,* 6, 3 (1972).

Baker, C. 'Administrative Reform in Malawi', *Quarterly Journal of Administration,* 6, 3 (1972).

Caiden, G. *Administrative Reform.* London: Allen Lane, 1970.

Collins, P. *Decentralisation and Local Administration for Development in Tanzania.* Brighton: IDS, 1976.

Development and Change, 2, 2 (1970–1), special number of administrative reform.

Tukur, M. (ed.). *Administrative and Political Development: Prospects for Nigeria.* Zaria: Institute of Administration, 1970.

Tukur, M. (ed.). *In Search of a New Political Community: the Nigerian Case.* Zaria: Institute of Administration, 1972.